Introduction to Systems Theory

Niklas Luhmann

Edited by Dirk Baecker

Translated by Peter Gilgen

polity

First published in German as *Einführung in die Systemtheorie*
© Carl-Auer-Systeme Verlag, 2002

This English edition © Polity Press, 2013

Reprinted 2013 (twice), 2014 (twice), 2015, 2016, 2017, 2018 (twice), 2020 (three times)
2021, 2022

We are very grateful to The Holcombe Academic Translation Trust for the
provision of a grant to finance the translation of this work.

Polity Press
65 Bridge Street
Cambridge CB2 1UR, UK

Polity Press
350 Main Street
Malden, MA 02148, USA

ISBN-13: 978-0-7456-4571-1
ISBN-13: 978-0-7456-4572-8 (pb)

A catalogue record for this book is available from the British Library.

Typeset in 10 on 11.5 pt Palatino
by Servis Filmsetting Ltd, Stockport, Cheshire
Printed and bound in Great Britain by TJ Books Limited, Padstow, Cornwall,

The publisher has used its best endeavours to ensure that the URLs for external
websites referred to in this book are correct and active at the time of going to
press. However, the publisher has no responsibility for the websites and can
make no guarantee that a site will remain live or that the content is or will
remain appropriate.

For further information on Polity, visit our website: www.politybooks.com

Introduction to Systems Theory

Contents

Translator's Note and Acknowledgments

In the winter semester of 1991–2, Luhmann taught a lecture course entitled *Introduction to Systems Theory*. The present volume is the translated version of these lectures. Transcribed and edited by Dirk Baecker, they were originally published in 2002. By April 2009, Luhmann's *Introduction* was in its fifth edition.

Luhmann presented his lectures without the use of a manuscript. He merely jotted down a few of the key points. The taped version of his *Introduction to Systems Theory* had a discernible oral character, which Dirk Baecker tried to preserve by keeping his editorial interventions to a minimum. The resulting text did not always lend itself to a straightforward translation into English. In order to offer the reader an idiomatic and grammatically sound text it was necessary at times to restructure some of Luhmann's run-on sentences, which did not pose problems in German but would have become close to incomprehensible in English. In addition, a few obscure and elliptical passages required more interpretive interventions on the part of the translator than is customary. Finally, it seemed advisable to add some translator's notes to the text as well as a brief list of further readings for each chapter. This list can be found at the end of the volume. I wish to acknowledge Michael King's invaluable expertise and help in preparing it. I also wish to thank Samantha Zacher, Michael King, and Caroline Richmond for numerous stylistic suggestions that have greatly improved this translation. Of course, I am solely responsible for any remaining errors.

Peter Gilgen

System – Autopoiesis – Form:
An Introduction to Luhmann's
Introduction to Systems Theory

Peter Gilgen

On the opening pages of his lecture course *Introduction to Systems Theory*, Niklas Luhmann states that contemporary sociology finds itself in a "theoretical crisis." It appears to have proceeded for too long under the assumption that its disciplinary contours were established for good by its founders, Marx, Weber, Simmel, and Durkheim. As a consequence, sociology has not sufficiently addressed its own status as a science of the social. Instead, it continues to pile on empirical data and "gathers complexity" with no direction.[1] Sociology has fallen short not only of providing a universal theory of society, but also of justifying its own status as an independent scholarly discipline with its own object of study.

When Luhmann published *Social Systems* in 1984, he presented the book in no uncertain terms as a watershed not only within his own corpus but also in the field of sociology at large. Having stated the need for a general theory of society (as opposed to a mere collection of data and interesting local insights), he laid out the conceptual framework on which such a theory eventually could and, in fact, would have to be based. It was his so-called *autopoietic turn*[2] that enabled him to formulate his own "general theory of social systems" and thus step out of Talcott Parsons's shadow once and for all.[3] It should be said that Luhmann's earlier work can still be read profitably even after this "paradigm change," as he himself self-consciously called it.[4] Thus, the insights into love and intimate communication contained in *Love as Passion*,[5] to cite only one example, can be integrated into the more comprehensive autopoietic edifice of Luhmann's mature theory with the help of some redescriptions and terminological clarifications that serve to reframe his analysis within his more comprehensive theory of autopoietic social systems.[6]

A dense systematic outline of Luhmann's theory, *Social Systems* was a sort of road-map or, as he put it retrospectively, a "systems theoretical introductory chapter" for his lengthy studies of individual social systems that were to follow in the remaining fifteen years of his life (or were, in some instances, prepared for publication posthumously), culminating in the comprehensive theory of society that he presented in *The Society of Society*, the capstone of his theoretical edifice.[7]

Comparing Luhmann's *Introduction to Systems Theory*, a lecture course held in 1991–2, with *Social Systems*, an attentive reader cannot help noticing a significant shift in emphasis. The lectures open with a self-consciously historical account of the beginnings of systems theory and the related search for an adequate definition of *system*. The fourth lecture, in which Luhmann introduces "the differential or difference theoretical approach" and arrives at the definition of "system as difference" is, in his own estimation, the most important part of his course. It is the conceptual centerpiece, the hinge that links the historical narrative of the development of systems thinking (which is also a genealogy of Luhmann's own theory) with the subsequent more systematic unfolding of an array of increasingly complex concepts and problems that are central to his systems theory. The overall effect of this pedagogically astute sequencing is cumulative. By the end of the course, the reader will have experienced a rich web of cross-references that counteracts the necessarily linear presentation of a theory that is recursive and self-reflective through and through.

Compared to the often abstract and apodictic style of argumentation in *Social Systems*, Luhmann's *Introduction* feels more open and experimental. At times, this transcribed text, which Luhmann had not planned to publish, reads like a report from the theorist's workshop. It offers glimpses of the handiwork involved in theory building. The dedicated student of systems theory may be most interested in the distinct theory elements that Luhmann managed to synthesize almost seamlessly in his grand design. Three moments in his theoretical development are especially prominent in these introductory lectures. First, there is a lengthy engagement with Talcott Parsons, whose main legacy is the "continuing emphasis on systems theory"[8] that is in evidence in all of Luhmann's writings. Luhmann never abandoned Parsons's argument that the social domain is a *system* all of its own that cannot be reduced to biological or psychological elements. However, in Luhmann's view, Parsons's system concept needed further refinement. Humberto Maturana and Francisco Varela's biological theory of *autopoiesis* appeared a suitable remedy. In turn, Luhmann had to overcome Maturana and Varela's biological reductionism. Eventually, Luhmann shifted his theoretical emphasis from system as autopoiesis to George Spencer Brown's formal theory of *system as difference*. This, in short, is the story that Luhmann recounts between the lines of his lectures. The following pages, intended as an introduction to an introduction, take the liberty of filling in some of the background. Most importantly, if the argument of the *Introduction to Systems Theory* is put in context and read against *Social Systems*, the different stages of Luhmann's theory construction are put in sharper relief.

System

The first theorist whose work Luhmann discusses at length in his *Introduction* is Talcott Parsons. Luhmann had studied with Parsons at Harvard in 1960–1 during a leave of absence from his job in the Ministry of Culture of Lower Saxony. After his return, he left his administrative post and embarked on a career as a sociologist.[9] In his lectures, Luhmann acknowledges the extent to which Parsons's approach laid the ground for sociological systems theories, including his own. Although the system concept needed further refinement, and Parsons's action theory had to be transformed into a theory of communication in order to serve as a coherent description of the social domain, Luhmann leaves no doubt about his indebtedness to Parsons's conception. He appreciates the latter's sophisticated structural functionalism, which was roundly dismissed in the 1960s as consciously conservative or inadvertently affirmative. For Luhmann, the problem of structural functionalist theories was that they fell short of and even foreclosed genuine systems thinking, precisely because they addressed neither the most fundamental question – namely, how social order is possible – nor the constitutive differences between social, psychic, and biological systems. Rather, the object of study, the social system, was simply taken for granted.

Parsons at least seemed aware of the problem when he pointed out that one had to start somewhere, since sociology was not yet in the position of offering a comprehensive theory of society. His more manageable alternative consisted in investigations of specific system structures that would reveal those functions that contributed to the maintenance of the social system. This limited systematic framework of structural functionalism, the "second-best type of theory," as Parsons called it, could at least provide some guidance for "completely raw empiricism,"[10] but its focus on specific social structures obscured the fundamental problem of finding a valid definition of social systems.

A social system, Parsons wrote, consists in "a plurality of individual actors interacting with each other in a situation which has at least a physical or environmental aspect, actors who are motivated in terms of a tendency to the 'optimization of gratification' and whose relation to their situations, including each other, is defined and mediated in terms of a system of culturally structured and shared symbols." Such a social system is, however, just one of three aspects that structure the more comprehensive system of social action, the other two being "personality systems" and the "cultural system."[11] These three system types are linked by non-reductive "interpenetration." Luhmann adopted this term as well as Parsons's insight that personality systems – or psychic systems – are necessary for the emergence of social systems, and vice versa. For Parsons had recognized "homologies" between the two system types, yet insisted that neither can be reduced to the other. For this reason, psychology could not serve as "the 'foundation' of the theory of social systems."[12] Moreover, the human individual was unsuitable as a basic unit of psychology and sociology, since Parsons's analysis had decomposed the unity of man into distinct social, psychological, and biological parts. On all of this Luhmann agrees, but he cannot accept Parsons's claim that action is "the 'stuff' out of which both personality systems and social systems are built up."[13]

In his eleventh lecture, Luhmann claims that the so-called controversy between systems theory and action theory is really based on a pseudo-problem. In fact, it is not at all Luhmann's intention to eliminate the concept of action from social theory. Rather, he doubts that action is a suitable elementary unit for formulating a coherent theory of social systems. What initially appeared attractive about the concept of action – namely, its rootedness in both the psychic and social domains – created more problems than it solved.

The social domain is constituted *as a sui generis reality* only by means of *communication* as its basic process. Once communication (defined by Luhmann as the unity of utterance, information, and understanding) is set into and kept in motion, "the formation of a bounded social system cannot be avoided."[14] Action, in contrast, does not meet the requirements for functioning as a system-producing type of operation. It presupposes a subject who acts and, unlike communication, cannot generate its own continuance. Furthermore, action is not limited to social contexts but can also occur as a solitary operation. Finally, it is difficult to determine the limits of actions. On the one hand, actions cannot easily be separated from motivations and, on the other, it is not clear which consequences of an action are still part of it. Nonetheless, as Luhmann concedes, "decomposing" the process of communication into actions is a convenient way of reducing its complexity and thereby enabling it to "steer itself."[15]

Autopoiesis

Whether a system is actually capable of steering and directing itself depends, however, on its ability to produce and maintain its own boundary. In their essay "Autopoiesis,"[16] the biologists Humberto Maturana and Francisco Varela conclude that only a system's "unity in some space"[17] allows for a consistent distinction between system and background. In other words, the unity of the system and the distinction between system and environment coincide. Therefore, the origin of an autopoietic system "is cocircumstantial" with the establishment of the operation of distinction of which its autopoiesis consists. One important consequence of this conclusion is that there are no intermediate systems: "either a system is an autopoietic system or it is not."[18] From the viewpoint of a general theory, the concept of autopoiesis thus provides a coherent and sufficiently

rigorous system definition. This was recognized by Luhmann. The criterion of autopoiesis allowed him not only to cut through the inconclusive
debates about the definition of a social system but also to explain the
differentiation of modern society into distinct "value spheres" (to use
Max Weber's term) that can be conceived as operationally closed social
systems.

The difficulty Luhmann faced was that, hitherto, the specificity of
the social had been obscured, precisely because its unit of reference had
always been taken to be the human individual or, as in the case of action
theory, processes that could be described only as intended and executed
by human subjects. Naturally, Luhmann does not deny that social
systems require humans for their existence. However, unlike classical
social and political theory, his does not define social systems as aggre-
gates of individuals. Furthermore, following Parsons's lead, he rejects the
indivisibility of the human individual.

However, Maturana and Varela's "unity in some space" poses a different challenge for social systems theory. That is to say, if social systems
consist entirely of communication (that is, the unity of utterance, information, and understanding, but no anthropomorphic sender and receiver),
as Luhmann claims, then it is hard to see into what kind of "space" they
could inscribe their unity. Yet, if we adhere to the alternative view that
social systems include the materiality of human individuals, it is impossible to conceive of them as autopoietic. Apparently, autopoiesis cannot
be integrated in a theory of the social as a distinct system without some
conceptual adjustments.

Maturana and Varela point out that autopoietic units frequently are
combined into second-order systems. There are different types of organization that occur at this meta-level: organisms, colonies, societies, to name
the most obvious. Yet the question remains as to which of these higher-
order systems are also "first-order autopoietic systems" and display an
autopoietic organization that can sustain their own system boundaries
and system maintenance. Maturana and Varela remind us that, at present,
"we are still ignorant of the molecular processes that would constitute
those metacellulars as autopoietic unities."[19] All we can claim is that
such systems are operationally closed. Thus, in their biological view,
autopoiesis in the strict sense can be ascribed only to the units that constitute first-order autopoietic systems. If the autopoiesis of a particular
system is in question, the investigation will always have to proceed all the
way to this fundamental cellular level, which for Maturana and Varela
constitutes the autopoietic degree zero.

From this perspective, it is not justified to speak of social systems as
autopoietic without giving an explanation of how material autopoiesis is
achieved at the second-order level. Autopoiesis, for Maturana and Varela,
consists of more than the operational closure and boundary maintenance
of a particular system. The concept also has an ontological dimension

that privileges biological processes over mental and social ones. Strictly speaking, the term "autopoiesis" does not apply to emergent psychic or social levels.

Naturally, psychic and social systems supervene on biological systems, without which they could neither come into existence nor continue to exist. Materially, the psychic and the social depend on biological states. Yet, as Parsons reminds us, the social cannot simply be reduced to the biological. In fact, Maturana and Varela also acknowledge that, in social relations between autopoietic biological systems – that is, when such systems enter into reciprocal structural coupling – the involved "co-drifting organisms give rise to a *new phenomenological domain*."[20] However, in their ontological hierarchy, autopoiesis always refers back to the first-order, material-biological level. Supervening layers are autopoietic only to the degree that they manage to integrate this fundamental first-order autopoiesis in their own autopoiesis.

At this juncture, Luhmann and Maturana part ways.[21] For the latter, the biological individual remains the decisive unit. Sensitive to the danger of making individuals expendable, Maturana insists on taking into account "ethical and political implications" in addition to strictly biological considerations when trying to determine whether human societies are in fact "biological systems." Critical of much evolutionary theory, he intends to demonstrate that "[b]iologically the individuals are not dispensable."[22]

Luhmann interprets the relation between social, psychic, and biological systems differently than Maturana. Autopoietic systems are always *biological systems* for Maturana. If there were autopoietic social systems, they would have to be superorganisms – that is, collective biological systems.[23] In contrast, Luhmann recognizes that the social *qua* social relies on biological systems, but is not reducible to the biological level. Similarly, social and psychic systems are tied in a structural coupling and thus depend on each other from an evolutionary perspective, although this does not mean that psychic systems actually enter into social systems. On the contrary, what happens in psychic systems is entirely inaccessible to the social system, and vice versa. What is in your head can neither be observed nor thought by others.

Likewise, the operational levels of biological and psychic systems are inaccessible to each other. Although contemporary cognitive science states that occurrences in the mind correspond to material changes in the brain, this does not mean that the psychic system's own perspective can be reduced to a biological description. As John Searle has pointed out, an eliminative reduction that would show that consciousness is merely an illusion cannot succeed, precisely because in this instance no distinction between appearance and reality can be drawn. In the case of consciousness, "the reality is the appearance. If it consciously seems to me that I am conscious, then I am conscious."[24]

For these reasons, Luhmann strips the concept of *autopoiesis* of its biological origins and redefines it in a way that makes it applicable to different types of self-reflective and self-reproductive systems. His generalized concept of autopoiesis allows him to supplement Parsons's elaborate sociological theory at the point where it is most in need of additional theoretical work: the conception and definition of *system*, especially as applied to the social world. At the same time, Luhmann finds support for his theory of autopoietic systems in Parsons's theoretically informed treatment of the social as irreducible to biological, psychological, and cultural facts.

No doubt, psychic and social systems have "biologic roots."[25] However, as emergent phenomenological domains, psychic and social systems can be observed on their own terms. New findings in evolutionary biology that can help explain the emergence of such phenomena as consciousness and language may provide increasingly more sophisticated and detailed accounts of the linkages between the different system levels – biological, psychic, and social – that constitute human existence. However, as long as comprehensive and generally accepted explanations are not forthcoming, it is prudent for a theory of social systems simply to acknowledge the biological substrate and the co-evolution *qua structural coupling* of psychic and social systems, and focus exclusively on the social phenomenological domain.[26] This is Luhmann's option. He stresses that psychic systems – or, human subjects – are a necessary condition of social systems. Despite its operational autonomy, the self-reproduction of a social system depends on the continuation of life and consciousness. This material dependence lies at the bottom of the seemingly "natural" notion of the autonomous "subject" as the basic unit of human existence. What such thinking does not sufficiently take into consideration is that both the organism and consciousness also depend on their environment for their own autopoiesis, and that society is part of that environment. No human individual would survive long without society. For these reasons, Luhmann reconceives the closure and openness of systems "not as an opposition but as a relationship of conditioning."[27]

Perhaps it should also be said that Luhmann's insistence on placing human beings in the environment of social systems (rather than inside them) should not be taken as a sign of misanthropic or anti-human tendencies on the part of systems theory, as is frequently claimed by its critics. On the contrary, human beings – or rather biological and psychic systems – are better off if their processes are not determined by society. The alternative would be the total social engineering of bodies and psyches, which is not only unrealistic but also undesirable.

In summary, Luhmann relied on Parsons's definition of the social to counter Maturana and Varela's autopoietic materialism and, in turn, adopted their concept of autopoiesis to reformulate Parsons's unsatisfactory system concept. The conception of autopoietic social systems breathes new life into the sociological system concept. Earlier applications of this concept were arbitrary and *ad hoc*. Any type of iterated social interaction seemed to lend itself to a description as a system. The extension of the system in question was hard to determine, since elements did not have to be autopoietically produced but could simply be added under changed circumstances. Autopoiesis, in contrast, provides a clear criterion for system status. It requires, however, that only the actual autopoietic operational level be considered a system. Everything else, regardless of its ontological import for the continued existence of the system, is located in the system's environment.

Form

Biological systems distinguish themselves from their environment by means of spatial material boundaries. Psychic and social systems are not material in the same sense. Their material conditions are part of their environment but do not enter into the autopoiesis of their specific medium, which is meaning.[28] Rather, the distinction between system and environment depends on the system's own observation, which distinguishes self- and hetero-reference. The boundaries of social and psychic systems are therefore not material artifacts but two-sided forms, which is to say, distinctions.[29] Describing systems in this way has the added advantage of obviating misunderstandings of autopoiesis in terms of *mere* self-reference. System constitution and maintenance are processes that refer not only to the system itself but also to the system's environment *as its environment*. George Spencer Brown's elegant calculus of distinctions reminds us at every turn that the process of indicating one side of a distinction always references its other side as well.[30]

Already in the opening chapter of *Social Systems*, Luhmann pointed out that the fundamental difference of systems theory – the difference between system and environment – can be phrased "more abstractly" by going back to Spencer Brown's calculus of distinctions.[31] Luhmann's strong emphasis in his *Introduction to Systems Theory* on *system as difference* or *system as form* should therefore be read not as abandoning the autopoietic turn of *Social Systems*, but as pushing it further to the purely formal level. If *autopoiesis* still contains connotations of organicism (and thus of a certain romantic heritage), the same cannot be said of *form* in Spencer Brown's sense.

In Spencer Brown's calculus, *distinction*, "the original act of severance," is the beginning of everything.[32] Distinction *is* form, and a form, therefore, is always the distinction between the very form and its environment. That is to say, a form has two sides: there is no form without context. Based on this radical conception, the analysis of form may well be pushed, as Luhmann speculates, far beyond systems theory. Perhaps a general theory of forms that could be derived from mathematics would exceed and "relativize even the systems theoretical approach in spite of its universal pretensions and its scientific claims." Luhmann thus draws attention to the unavoidable contingency of systems theory. (Similar gestures abound in the entire lecture series.) It could have been constructed differently, but one cannot help beginning somewhere.

In short, Luhmann derives two decisive insights from Spencer Brown that significantly augment his theory design. First, a system is a two-sided form. This is the most general definition of *system* understood in differential terms. Second, on the basis of Spencer Brown's calculus, it is possible to define a system with the help of just one operator. This is a departure from traditional systems definitions that, as Luhmann is well aware, used a combination of terms. Systems were said to be sums of elements or to consist of elements linked by relations or the interplay of structure and process.[33] In contrast to such combinations of seemingly more basic constitutive elements, Luhmann's operational approach stresses the irreducibility of *system as difference*.

To conclude, if the concept of autopoiesis puts social systems on a sound operational footing, the definition of system as difference lays the ground for a general systems theory that deserves the name. Luhmann combined the concepts of *system*, *autopoiesis*, and *differential form* into a productive dynamic network in which all elements depend on, explain, and support one another. Perhaps this is the reason why he claimed that his theory, "with regard to the content of its conceptual frameworks and statements, wrote itself." However, arranging it in the most suitable way took "much time and deliberation"[34] and, it would seem, several equally valid attempts. In his own writing practice no less than in his theory, Luhmann refused to conceive of systems in terms of wholes and parts and rejected the related preference of identity over difference. After all, a self-identical whole – not unlike *Heaven* in the eponymous song by Talking Heads – is a place where nothing ever happens.

Editor's Preface to the German Edition

The present book is a transcript of the lecture course *Introduction to Systems Theory* conducted by Niklas Luhmann at the University of Bielefeld during the winter semester 1991–2. Luhmann held his lectures extemporaneously, supported only by a brief outline. The present book attempts to preserve, as far as possible, the oral character of the text. For the most part, Luhmann's lectures were presented in a polished, publishable style. Nonetheless, some sentences had to be reformulated.

The largely oral character of the text underscores that this lecture series, as all of Luhmann's lecture courses, was intended as a work in progress. True, there was a book, Luhmann's *Social Systems* of 1984 [trans. 1995], which provided a printed version of the subject matter covered in the course, and Luhmann could have limited himself to offering an explanatory commentary on this earlier work. However, during the six intervening years since the publication of the latter, which he called his first *magnum opus*, Luhmann had already shifted certain emphases, which meant that, at this point in time, he would have formulated the content of his book slightly differently than he had originally written it. Moreover, Luhmann stressed the introductory character of his presentation much more strongly in his lecture series. In other words, he expected that his audience would consist largely of students who were encountering systems theory for the first time. At the same time, he assumed that the students of sociology, to whom his lectures were primarily addressed, would have already come in touch with the fundamentals of sociology.

For Luhmann, presenting an introductory lecture series meant that he had to emphasize much more strongly than he did in *Social Systems* the fact that any theory is a constructive achievement. At numerous junctures, a theory can be traced back to conceptual decisions for which guidance can be derived neither empirically from the subject matter nor deductively from the theory itself. For this reason, Luhmann is very concerned in his lectures with keeping his options open in regard to numerous issues that had been decided in a specific way in his book and even with suggesting possible alternatives. His volume *Social Systems* is his version of a theory of social systems, even though it also contains an invitation to each reader to change the architecture of the theory and experiment with different possibilities. The lecture series puts a considerably stronger emphasis on this invitation. Luhmann himself experiments with his own formulations, and it becomes obvious rather quickly that these experiments aim not only at varying the details but also at the coherence and consistency of the architecture and thus the entirety of his theory.

Luhmann's shifts in emphasis in these introductory lectures distinguish them from the presentation in his earlier book. They are rooted in the subject matter, the method, and the particular situation within which the lecture course took place. In the lectures, the observer is assigned a considerably more prominent role [than in the earlier work]. This has consequences for the theory design that point to a gradual shift of emphasis from Humberto R. Maturana's concept of autopoiesis to George Spencer Brown's calculus of distinctions. Moreover, the increased emphasis on the role of the observer makes it possible to present Luhmann himself as an observer of a theory that is, if nothing else, his own – an observer, no less, who invites other observers, namely his audience, to put themselves into play as observers with their own distinctions.

At the same time, Luhmann is sufficiently sociological so as not to allow his treatment of open questions concerning the design of a theory to lead to an empty play of concepts. His reflections, as well as his continuous efforts at incorporating in them the difference between his and other observational perspectives, are determined by his own situation within which the theoretical work takes place – namely, the lecture hall, the university, sociology as a scholarly discipline, the context of a Western civilization, and the self-endangerment of world society that is, in the most inclusive sense of the word, an *ecological* self-endangerment. In the final analysis, every concept has to be empirically convincing. On this the sociologist insists, even when he has said farewell to the idea that a concept refers to a real existing state of affairs simply because one has coined said concept. Luhmann does not succumb to the "fallacy of misplaced concreteness," as Alfred North Whitehead called it. He does not succumb to the misunderstanding that concrete facts can be derived from abstract concepts, precisely because he shares Immanuel Kant's and Gregory Bateson's conviction that concepts may help in describing and categorizing explanations, although they do not themselves constitute such explanations. This, in fact, is the reason why Luhmann proceeded cautiously when introducing the observer. For the observer is not just another fact that one has to accept. The observer is an explanatory principle whose introduction into science leads to unpredictable consequences, since innumerable other explanatory principles are in need of being brought into alignment with it.

Moreover, the observer is not only a sociological figure (although he may perhaps appear to be most plausible in this function), but also a figure that was introduced at the level of general systems theory by Heinz von Foerster, Humberto Maturana, Francisco Varela, and others. That is to say, this figure also has to be tested at the level of such phenomena as the organism, neuronal systems, consciousness, artificial systems, and perhaps also physical systems, although it is unknown whether the distinction of these phenomenal levels will survive this test. It is therefore not difficult to imagine what has attracted but also complicated (and, in many instances, even made impossible) the interdisciplinary discussion concerning the concepts of second-order cybernetics, self-organization, autopoiesis, and the form of distinction since the 1960s.

I am quite certain that Luhmann never would have entertained the idea of publishing transcripts of one of his lecture courses. Too many parts of the presentation would have seemed too unfinished and uncertain to him. I suppose, however, that he would not have resisted the plan of editing the present transcripts as a workbook. An editor bears a different responsibility for a book than its author. It is Luhmann who is the author of this book. After all, he originally held these lectures, which were then transcribed. It is the editor who must take responsibility for the fact that the present book is a book that Luhmann himself would not have published. The editor assumes this responsibility by pointing out that this book (as a supplement to and in combination with the audiotapes of the lecture series) is better suited than any other to serve as an introduction to the lively work of theory building and thus to avoid the impression of dogmatic closure in the case of this particular theory. In principle, I assume that the reader who would like to know more details about specific passages will consult other publications by Niklas Luhmann, in particular, of course, *Social Systems*.

My work was limited to adjusting the style of the text to standard written German. Anyone who would like to read the text alongside the lectures that were recorded on tape may do so. It will, however, become clear that I occasionally changed the word order and omitted certain filler words that typically occur in oral presentations, such as "naturally," "really," "actually," "anyway," and "above all." All annotations [with the exception of the translator's notes] are mine. I generally limited myself to supplying the bibliographical information for Luhmann's own references. The subject index is confined to the main subjects and can therefore be used as a supplementary table of contents.

I owe a great debt of gratitude to the Audiovisual Center of the University of Bielefeld for securing the tape recordings of the lecture series, as well as to Christel Rech-Simon, who transcribed the lectures and established a draft version of the text.

This volume is dedicated to the memory of Niklas Luhmann's precision and concentration, his personal modesty, and his quiet serenity, which were so clearly in evidence when he presented his lectures.

Dirk Baecker
July, 2002

I

Sociology and Systems Theory

First Lecture

Ladies and gentlemen, the lecture course *Introduction to Systems Theory* that I begin today is being held at a university institute for sociology and is addressed first and foremost to a sociological audience. However, the question that must be addressed right at the start is whether today something like systems theory at the present level of research even exists within the field of sociology. For sociology finds itself in a profound theoretical crisis. This much can be said, I believe, without too many reservations. If one attends events that are dedicated to theoretical questions in sociology or reads the corresponding literature, one notices, time and again, the return to the classics – that is to say, discussions of Max Weber, Karl Marx, Georg Simmel, or Émile Durkheim. Today's sociologists are by no means uncritical towards the classical foundations of their field. There is, however, a prevalent notion concerning the contours of the discipline as determined by this classical beginning. True, there are a number of middle-range theories that extend beyond these beginnings and which arose in the context of empirical research. Strictly speaking, however, there are no theoretical descriptions of the problems that modern society has to face today. This is true, for example, in the case of ecological questions. It is also true in the case of problems concerning individuals. And it is true in the case of the entire array of increasing therapeutic needs and many other things to boot.

Today, the truly fascinating intellectual developments are happening outside the discipline of sociology. That at least is the impression from which I proceed. I would like to begin my lectures by showing in a brief first part what kind of work using systems theoretical orientations has so far been carried out in sociology. I would also like to show how and in which ways this work came up against certain limits, dead ends, and fundamental criticisms of theory and was therefore abandoned.

This part will be followed by a relatively extensive section in which

I will attempt to scrutinize interdisciplinary and transdisciplinary theoretical efforts in order to find out, and demonstrate, what elements they might contain that could be of potential interest for sociology. In the closing reflections, I will attempt to draw some conclusions concerning the starting points of sociological theory construction from these theoretical considerations (be they mathematical, psychological, biological, epistemological, cybernetic, or even derived from other sources).

The lecture course will conclude with relatively abstract theoretical concepts that require additional adjustments in, and by means of, everyday sociological practice so that they can become suitable for research applications. This concluding part concerns concepts such as time, meaning,[1] action, system, double contingency, structure, and so forth.

1 The Functionalism of System Maintenance

I begin with an attempt at sketching sociological systems theory as it was formed in the forties and fifties, especially – one might even say, almost exclusively – in sociology as practiced in the United States. Essentially, two areas must be taken into consideration. The first bears the title *structural functionalism* or *maintenance functionalism*. The second area concerns a specific achievement of Talcott Parsons. Towards the end of the sixties, both of these aspects were subject to considerable ideological criticism of the systems theoretical approach. Already this critique had its theoretical basis more in ideology than in substance. Nonetheless, it proved sufficient to eliminate more or less all further work directed at a sociological systems theory.

Nowadays, when one travels to the United States and, in the course of a discussion among sociologists, pledges allegiance to a systems theoretical approach, one is often met with surprised comments – as if one were at least twenty years behind the development of the discipline. From my perspective, precisely the opposite is the case, since those sociologists who assume that systems theory is dead and done for, for their part, just happen to neglect all the developments in this interdisciplinary field that have taken place in the interim.

Of course, barriers between the disciplines play a role in all this, but they may not necessarily be insurmountable. To begin with, there can be no doubt that, seen from today's perspective, the approaches that were developed in the forties and fifties show considerable weaknesses. I will very briefly sketch what was understood back then by "maintenance orientation" and "maintenance functionalism" or, alternatively, "structural functionalism."

The point of departure was marked by ethnological, socio-anthropological research that worked with certain tribal settings – that is, with tribes that in some way appeared to be isolated or containable as objects of research and which, at the same time, could be recognized and investigated in their particular historical form, their specific size, their dimensions in combination with specific structures, and so on. From this point of departure, there was no obvious path that could have led to a general sociological theory – that is, to the general question of how social order is possible at all, or, to put it differently, what distinguishes a social system or a social order from, for instance, a psychic or biological phenomenon.

In his book *The Social System* of 1951, Talcott Parsons gave a plausible rationale for this restricted focus on an already constituted or given object. He maintained that the sociologist must set his sights on a clearly contoured and limited object in order to be able to get his research underway. At the present stage of development, he continued, it is completely impossible for sociology to envision a sort of Newtonian model of variables that would allow us to fix certain variables while leaving the combinatory relationships undetermined. For in the field of sociology there are no equivalents to laws of nature, not even, Parsons surmised, in a purely statistical sense. What is needed, therefore, is a second-best theory – a theory that takes its departure from certain system structures and attempts to recognize from this perspective which functions serve the maintenance of structural patterns. At the end of the forties and during the fifties this led to questions such as What are the conditions for the persistence [*Bestandsvoraussetzungen*] of a social system? And what are, more specifically, the conditions for the existence of a society? What minimal conditions concerning maintenance and problem-solving must be fulfilled so that a society can exist at all? Naturally, it must exist, if one intends to investigate and study it. But all these inquiries resulted, even in the best of cases, merely in a list or a catalogue of such conditions of existence that could not be grounded any further in theory but were introduced *ad hoc* and, first and foremost, with the hidden and unacknowledged assumption that a social theory had to include the domain of the economy as well as the domain of politics, the domain of the family, the domain of religion, and the domain of fundamental values.

But, in addition to this weakness, which, as it seems, has continued to be unamenable to correction to this day, there was a second problem – namely, that conceptual work was limited through the structural-functionalist approach. It did not make much sense to question any further the function of structure or to analyze such concepts as "persistence" [*Bestand*], "condition of existence," and "variable," or even the entire methodological apparatus. That is to say, that conceptual labor on the theory was limited by the assumption that a certain structured object was already given.

Finally, there was the third objection, that no clear criteria for persistence could be given. It was obvious from the start that such a theory had to include two things: on the one hand, there were the deviations from given norms and structural patterns. The entire range of deviance, of deviant behavior, of criminality, and of dysfunction is part of such a theory and cannot be left aside as something outside the social system. On the other hand, even more serious was the historical question – that is to say, the question concerning the period of time during which the existence of a society remains identical and the amount of structural change that would suffice for a sociologist, or simply an observer, or even a participant of a social system, to presuppose a different social system and thus to assume that a change of identity has taken place.

The concept, and also the phenomenon, of "revolution" illustrates this problem well. Was the European society before the French Revolution different from the one that came after? Or will the society that comes about after the revolution (which Marxists expect to take place at some point in time) be a different society from the one before? Will the dissolution of the capitalist order of the relations of production bring about a different society, as is generally claimed? But how much change must occur before observers can unanimously state that the old society had such and such qualities and that the new society possesses such and such different structures?

This problem concerning the criteria for persistence was also discussed in relation to biology, and there it was obvious that the continuation or end of existence for a living organism was clearly defined by the possibility of death. As long as the organism lives, its continued existence is secured. The living organism reproduces itself with its own means, but death puts an end to this system. From this results a clear limit of identity with rather marginal zones of doubt, when one does not know for certain whether an organism is still alive or already dead.

Sociology lacks such clear-cut criteria. This could mean that the question concerning the identity of a system must be posed and answered within the system itself and not by an external observer. A system must itself bring about a decision as to whether in the course of history the changes of structures have altered it to such a degree that it is no longer the same.

With the help of this modification, we can understand why in the fifties and the early sixties the difference between traditional and modern societies played such an important role. It was assumed that modern society was no longer the same society as the one usually described as "traditional society." Yet at the same time there were also debates concerning modernization. One debated the kind of planning that would be necessary to transform the traditional societies that still could be found on earth into modern societies. And this in turn made unclear where exactly the boundary of the identity of a system is located. The concept of a functionalism premised on persistence or a structural functionalism leads to this question. If the question can be answered only with the help of self-description – that is, the internal thematization of the identity of the system within the same system – then one runs into problems of self-reference that have not been addressed, or even become conscious as a theoretical problem, within this classical framework. All of these issues indicated, if one may say so, certain weaknesses inherent in the first type of sociological systems theory – weaknesses that were definitely discussed and were available in print in the sixties and thus were open to the inspection of readers. However, taken by themselves, these weaknesses did not suffice to reject systems theory in principle as a viable theoretical approach. After all, many fruitful and beneficial insights had been gained: these insights concerned precisely the situation of deviance and dysfunction; they also concerned questions about structural contradictions, value conflicts, and the treatment of value conflicts within the social system; and, finally, they also affected questions concerning the handling of structural change – that is, the change of structures and the limits of such change within different social orders.

It was not viable simply to retire this theory and its successful research results in the normal manner of scientific progress without first offering an appropriate replacement – that is to say, without transposing everything that had been researched within this framework into a new theoretical framework. That, however, did not happen. Therefore, it is my impression that we have lost certain things. By foregoing structural functionalism and the specific focus on the conditions of the possibility and the persistence of specific formations [*Bestandsvoraussetzungen*], we have simply given up certain insights and have so far not yet regained a position that would allow us to integrate these cognitive gains into a different theory proposal. For this reason, the history of sociology must deal not just with its classical texts that, so to speak, founded the discipline, but also with a relatively successful mode of research that was respected among other disciplines and was cultivated especially in America in the forties and fifties.

The reasons why this type of research was given up had ultimately more to do with ideology than with, say, the technical aspects of the theory. As I have mentioned, the weaknesses of the theory were well known, yet the reasons for its rejection had different roots. First and foremost, this rejection rested on the presumption that, starting from these particular theoretical foundations, one would not arrive at a sufficiently radical critique of modern society. The normalization of social conditions after World War II initially made possible a number of positive aspects, which is to say that one believed in the possibilities of improving conditions within the general structure of modern society. In the sixties and seventies, however, it became increasingly obvious that such improvements were to be had only at considerable cost, or even at a price bordering on total impossibility. It was recognized that, in the area of developmental policy and the modernization of developing countries, an increasing number of projects failed. Higher and higher levels of poverty and pauperization became noticeable. With increased urgency, the question arose as to whether some factors in the structure of modern society played a role – one spoke of "capitalism" back then – that made it impossible to arrive at a just order of distribution and a comprehensive mode of progress that would include the entire population of the world. Of course, such restrictions of the positive aspects could also be observed without difficulty within industrial societies themselves. Here as well, class phenomena had been preserved and an equable distribution of wealth was unthinkable. Here as well, it was true, democracy had been established, but it had become a party political democracy that was incapable of transforming all the impulses that were directed at the system into actual politics. Here as well, it was precisely the perspective of sociology that rendered visible the impossibility of implementing sociological knowledge and, especially, critical insights in political practice in spite of all the openness of the political and other application-oriented systems towards research.

There were many different reasons, a good number of which are entirely understandable in retrospect, for the recently developed view that a much more radical critical theory was needed and for the increased attention and interest of intellectuals that this view attracted. From this viewpoint, a more thorough examination of the details, the merits and difficulties, the advantages and disadvantages of a systems theoretical treatment of social questions seemed merely superfluous. *The system* was understood, not without reason, as something rather technical, as an instrument of planning, an instrument of modeling social institutions, an ancillary instrument for planners whose intentions were nothing other than repeating, improving, and rationalizing the ruling conditions.

To summarize and conclude this part of my argument, there were different reasons that put a stop to the development of the functionalism of persistence [*Bestandsfunktionalismus*] or the theory of structural functionalism. On the one hand, there were the immanent weaknesses but, on the other – and this was the dominating strand – there was also the ideological critique, the need for a critical theory of society that corresponded to modern conditions – a need that was, however, eventually met merely by resorting in a relatively crude manner to Marxist modes of thought.

2 Parsons

The assumption that Parsonian theory can easily be subsumed under this structural functionalism is widespread. I myself shared this very conviction in the sixties. It is a fact, however, that Parsons never really accepted this version. In his later period, especially in the sixties, he openly turned away from structural functionalism and distinguished his own theoretical efforts from it. But even this story is correct only to a certain extent. In the late forties, in the period of his work that led up to the book *The*

Social System of 1951, Parsons had in fact contributed to the theoretical justification of structural functionalism, even though he himself had always characterized it as merely the "second-best theory." At Harvard, Parsons had instigated and adopted, in his own work, at least in part, a research program that pursued the question of the conditions of the persistence [*Bestandsvoraussetzungen*] of social systems. Working within the framework of structural-functional thinking, he attempted to integrate problems of deviance, of the limitations of social control, of value contradictions, and so forth, in his theory. Thus he contributed decisively to the advancement of structural functionalism. It is nonetheless a mistake – or so I believe – to subsume Parsons wholeheartedly under this system trend. After all, at the beginning of his scholarly work, marked by the book *The Structure of Social Action* of 1937, as well as later against the background of a development that increasingly dominated sociology in the fifties, Parsons developed his own independent and idiosyncratic version of systems theory.

I would like to illustrate this point with a brief sketch. It is possible to understand the entirety of Parsons's work as a sort of endless commentary on just one proposition, and this proposition reads: "Action is system." I don't know whether this proposition can be found in this precise form in any of Parsons's published works. I know it only as an oral statement,[2] yet it seems to me, and always has seemed, to be the quintessence of the Parsonian message. "Action is system!" In a popular game, theoreticians are asked to express the quintessence of their theory in a single sentence; if Parsons had been asked to do this, he would have had to respond – this is how I understand him – "Action is system." This is noteworthy precisely because the theory of action in post-Parsonian times became fashionable again in versions that reverted back to Max Weber or, alternatively, different figures of *rational choice*, and because, taking its point of departure from these earlier positions, a theory program in contradistinction to systems theory was developed, as if the theory of action and systems theory were different "approaches," as the saying goes, that could not be brought into agreement with each other. The theory of action is said to be oriented more towards the subject, the individual, and therefore more capable of including psychic and even bodily states in sociology. In contrast, systems theory is seen as rather abstract and thus perhaps more capable of depicting macro-structures. In any case, the view expressed by a number of representatives of the theory of action is that action and system are incompatible paradigms. Whoever makes such claims ought to be encouraged to read Parsons. Perhaps this does not provide the ultimate answer to the problem, for it is of course possible to reject the Parsonian theory as unacceptable and to revert back, as a consequence of this rejection, to Max Weber's work and similar foundations. Be that as it may, Parsons at least has seen very clearly – and has attempted to create a theory that reacts to this insight – that action and system cannot be separated, or, to put it differently, that action is possible only as system.

For Parsons, the point of departure for this thesis was first of all a stock-taking of sociological theory – that is to say, the attempt to recognize whether it is possible to find something in common among such diverse classics as Max Weber, Émile Durkheim, Alfred Marshall, and Vilfredo Pareto. In fact, the result was that a commonality could be found in the connections between system formation or overarching ordering structures, on the one hand, and actions as the basal operations, on the other. If such a rough approximation may be permitted, one might say that Parsons derives the action component of his theory from Max Weber's work and the system component from Durkheim's. But, at the same time, he also demonstrates that Weber was forced to include system components in his system, while Durkheim could not avoid questioning the type of material out of which societies are made. There are endless controversies about questions as to whether this interpretation of the classics is not rather idiosyncratic and whether it really does justice to the original authors. These are debatable points, but they are more or less uninteresting and of actual interest only for a history of sociology. What is interesting for us is how and with the aid of what kind of conceptual apparatus and conceptual as well as methodological maneuvers Parsons manages to give the impression – to phrase it very cautiously – that one and the same theory is at stake.

Parsons starts with the assumption that action, the individual act, the "unit act," is an "emergent property" of reality as such. In other words, he assumes that there must be components that have to be combined for actions to become possible. Under such circumstances, the task of the sociological analyst would be to identify these components and to design on this basis an analytic theory of action. Parsons speaks of "analytic realism," by which he means that, insofar as there is any "realism," it is a matter of the emergence of real action. He claims that no conceptual construction is at issue but rather a theory that accounts for the conditions of possibility of action, and which therefore can respond to all those cases in which action *qua action* occurs. Such a theory is "analytic" insofar as it identifies components of emerging actions that are not themselves actions. In a sense, it dissects the phenomenon "action" into individual elements that, as such, cannot be inserted as one type of miniature action among others into the chain of actions or into a system that consists of actions.

The concepts that are used in this analysis vary slightly. In the first place, there is the issue of the difference between ends and means, which goes back to a remark by Max Weber: for a primary understanding of action – not for the later structural analyses and such – it is necessary to distinguish first of all between ends and means. (1) To what purpose does an actor make use of his action?; and (2) What does he intend to achieve by this? – these are two components. In addition, this leads to the question of what kind of normative schema lies at the bottom of the choice of ends and the admission of means. This question was imposed on Parsons by Durkheim – that is to say, through his assumption that society is primarily a moral unit and therefore possible only if a sufficient moral consensus can be achieved. This means, however, that the choice of ends, as well as the constraints concerning the permissible means, is not simply left to the actor. Rather, there are social preconditions, for instance the famous non-contractual premises of contracts. A society is always already integrated either morally or by means of values or normative symbols before anyone can act in it. A society is not possible other than as a system. At least, this is Parsons's point of departure. To put it differently, it is a matter of optimizing not just the means–end relationship but also the conditions of possibility of – and the degrees of freedom in – such arrangements of means and ends that are permitted to the individual or other parts of a social order.

In terms of the sociology of knowledge, the specific problem that enters sociological theory in this manner must – or, at least, may – be seen against the backdrop of the global economic crisis, to which Parsons reacted with his theory. Parsons always emphatically rejected a purely utilitarian foundation of sociology. His question was: What are the values that society uses to restrict the freedom of choice concerning the combination of means and ends?

This leads to a further problem: namely, the question of how precisely the actor is placed in the context of this theory of action. If one starts with the concept of action, one might assume that the actor is the one who acts. No action comes about without an actor. In a certain sense, action is the expression of the intention or will of actors, and to this degree it is subsidiary. In Parsons's theory the situation is reversed. Parsons supposes that action happens once these preconditions have been fulfilled – that is, once means and ends can be distinguished, once there are collectively given values, and once there is an actor available to execute the action. The actor is only one moment in the realization of action. One might say that he occupies his place merely accidentally. For someone else could also execute this particular action – but some sort of readiness for action, some sort of concretization of an action potential, must occur in a society for action to happen. Thus, it is not action that is subordinated to the actor. Rather, the actor is subordinated to the action. Such is the point of departure for the book *The Structure of Social Action* of 1937.

As a sociologist, Parsons at first turned to the theory of social systems in the forties and early fifties and for this reason ended up in close proximity to structural functionalism, from which his theory managed to liberate itself only very slowly and, as I would claim, only by means of reverting to his general assumption "Action is system." The result of this development can be seen in his famous, and infamous, series of cross-classification tables. Parsons assumes that there are four components that must interact

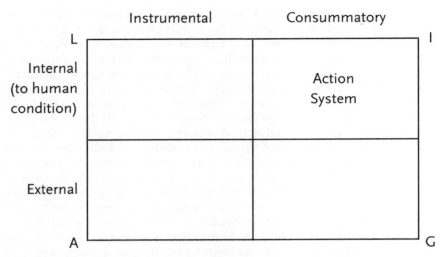

Figure 1 The action system in the "general paradigm of the human condition"[3]
A = adaptation, G = goal attainment, I = integration, L = latent pattern
maintenance

so that an action can take shape. He constructs these four components by means of cross-classification – that is, through the juxtaposition of two different variables. This is his theory technique. One of the series, the horizontal one in the visual representations, distinguishes between "instrumental" and "consummatory." "Instrumental" designates the means in the service of action. "Consummatory" designates the satisfied state that one wants to reach – that is to say, the state when the end has been accomplished. This does not mean merely the representation of an end or a purpose. Rather, "consummatory" designates that which comes about once the end has been reached and a satisfactory situation – one might almost say: the perfection of the system – has come about. Thus the axis "instrumental"/"consummatory" represents the action component of the proposition "Action is system." The other, vertical series distinguishes between "external" and "internal," the external relations of the system and the internal structural realities. This is the systems theoretical side of the paradigm "Action is system."

A cross-classification table based on these four variables contains four boxes, which were named by Parsons. There are no deductive instructions or clear methodological guidelines for this act of naming. Parsons himself wavered when it came to a corresponding instruction. When asked, he admitted openly that it cannot be a matter of a logical deduction or a deductive method. Rather, the naming gains its plausibility from that which must always be understood if it is clear which of the variables have been combined (see figure 1).

The combination of instrumental and external orientation concerns that which Parsons calls "adaptation." The system instrumentalizes, if one may say so, its external relations and attempts to achieve a state that provides a suitable means for creating satisfactory conditions between the system and the environment. In the case of the social system this is, according to Parsons, primarily the function of the economy.

The next case is the combination of external relations and the consummatory realization of values. At stake here is what Parsons calls "goal attainment." It is important to recognize that this is a consummatory state and therefore concerns the attainment of goals and not just some projection of future states. Whereas instrumental orientations represent the future, consummatory orientations are, on the contrary, related to the present. To put it differently, action must achieve satisfactory states or it does not happen. In the domain of social systems this designates the function of politics. Politics, with its quality of "getting things done," as Parsons calls it, must achieve satisfactory states, or it fails *qua* politics.

The next box combines "consummatory" and "internal." At stake is the achievement of satisfactory internal states. Parsons characterizes this as "integration." A system integrates actions, and thereby actors, if it provides them with satisfactory combinatory possibilities. The concept of "integration" remained rather unclear in the theoretical analysis – a fact that has been criticized. For instance, systems integration and social integration, which introduces actors into the system, have been distinguished. That, however, is merely a critique of the *naming* of these boxes. If one considers the theoretical structure instead, it becomes clear that, under the indicated conditions, there must be in any system a present state that has to be realized internally and must be acceptable as the present situation.

Finally, the last combinatory possibility concerns "instrumental" versus "internal." Here, Parsons inserts the rather strange expression "latent pattern maintenance." The thought behind this name is as follows: structures must be constantly at one's disposal, but they are not continuously actualized. One goes to the bank to withdraw money only every once in a while. One does not love incessantly. One does not go to church all the time. And this leads to the question of what occurs in the meantime and how it is guaranteed that structures are available and can be activated and actualized in spite of being merely latent during the intervening periods. Therefore, there is the problem of "latent pattern maintenance" – that is, of the stabilizing of structures even in the case of their not being used. For Parsons, this is characterized by the combination of "internal," for the structures in question are the system's own, and "instrumental," for it is necessary to make sure that such structures will also be available in the future.

The result of these thoughts as represented in Parsons's cross-classification table is the famous "AGIL" schema, a schema that consists of the four functions "adaptation" (A), "goal-attainment" (G), "integration" (I), and "latent pattern maintenance" (L). Parsons insists quite obstinately that there can only be these four functions, that this schema permits a complete representation of the action possibilities of the action system, and that everything in addition to these four functions is merely a mode of articulating them. In the later phases of his work, he even states that the corresponding cross-classification table characterizes the human condition, the position of man in the world as such.

Thus, one might say that the AGIL schema is Parsons's commentary on the principle "Action is system" or his implementation of the theory program that could be introduced by this name. Hence his theory technique is that of the cross-classification table – a technique that is used consciously in order to characterize the closure of a combinatory space. The schema underlying this technique guarantees that nothing is overlooked and that one must instead continually ask what happens in box number 4, or what is the case in box number 2.

For Parsons, this guarantee of completeness appears as evidence in a way of his theory's claim to universality. If everything that is necessary for the emergence of action has been taken into account, then the completeness and, as a consequence, the universality of the theory is guaranteed. In that case, everything that can be said about action must and can be built into this theory. And this project is indeed characteristic for Parsons's mode of thinking. One can observe it at work in the manner in which he manages to accommodate external suggestions in his schema of the four boxes and distribute them among the different functions.

If we take into account this idiosyncrasy, we can see that Parsons is one of the great theory architects, who is capable of trying out a peculiar pattern of construction only then to make the following visible: (1) all that can be achieved by means of this theory pattern; (2) the consequences to which the design of a particular theory leads; and (3) the contrast between this design and other theory patterns, such as, say, a dialectical theory. In this sense, we owe to Parsons the visibility of a certain mode of theory construction. Of course, such visibility always also exposes the theory to opportunities for criticism and to judgments as to how far one can get with it and what cannot be done by means of it. It is a matter, one might say, of the logical space of possibilities. The question that arises, then, is what kind of guarantee there is that all the indicated possibilities are really used and that all the fields that the schema provides are in fact occupied in reality. This question becomes even more urgent once one realizes how the schema is worked out in further detail and the four boxes become sixteen boxes, and so on, depending on how the system is subdivided. For Parsons there is no such question, simply because he assumes that, whenever action happens, all these boxes must be occupied. This is what analytic realism means – that is, realism in the sense that the theory shows that action is not possible in any other way.

Second Lecture

How does Parsons proceed from here? What does he do with these pre-suppositions? First of all, his schema offers the possibility of drawing attention to certain focal points. I already indicated this. In the case of an action or an action complex that concentrates on one of these functions, Parsons speaks of "functional primacy." In such a case a corresponding system emerges, or rather differentiates itself, around an individual function. Thus, in the case of, say, a concentration on the function of "adaptation" in the area of the social actualization of action, an economic system takes shape.

But how can such a system be a "system"? How can "action" occur in such a segregated complex? According to Parsons, this is possible only if, in the area reserved for "adaptation," all four functions are fulfilled in turn. Economic action must perform its own adaptive functions. It must perform its own goal attainment – for instance, it must yield a satisfactory economic profit. It has to be integrated, and it must latently maintain certain patterns – namely, its own structures – which is to say that it must be capable of creating structural patterns that can be continued and passed on. All other functions recur within the individual, fully differentiated, functionally specialized system.

All this leads to the general theorem that the system can be repeated within itself, and that from each box four subordinate boxes, or from each partial system four – and always only four – other systems, may emerge in turn. The question of how far this can be pushed – whether, say, a system that consists of the sixteenth part of the original system can be divided up even further – is a practical question concerning the level of system complexity that can actually be reached and the complexity of the reality within which action occurs. Is it useful? Does it happen? Is there enough material so that these increasingly refined sub-systems can be formed? It is not necessary to pass a final judgment on all of this. Instead, the theory is, one might say, left open and defers to social reality. This means that one must find out whether or not, and in which societies, a special system for the economy or for politics has constituted itself.

Here one sees that Parsons's theory possesses a considerable his-torical and evolutionary openness. It is capable of describing different historical situations by scrutinizing whether certain special systems for specific functions have differentiated themselves – that is, whether there is a money economy or a politics of the territorial state or not. Correspondingly, it may also pose the question as to what degree, say, the economy has differentiated its own suitable sub-systems. From the viewpoint of the theory, one cannot help having, at least at first, the impression that all of this amounts merely to a horrible complexity: four times four times four, *ad libitum*, without any limit that the theory would impose on this development. As far as the matter itself is concerned, however, Parsons can always respond that we must find out empirically whether these opportunities are actualized or not. The real limitation lies in the fact that, under any circumstances, there can be only four functions, which is to say that all evolution must proceed on the given track of a specific differentiation. But it may nonetheless display imbalances along the way: for instance, in the course of such an evolution, the economy may be strongly differentiated and overall integration may be neglected. Such a state of affairs would correspond to Durkheim's problem of solidarity in a society in which the division of labor has reached a high degree. But such imbalances are – this is Durkheim's hope – only temporary and at some point require a corrective supplementary development within the other functional systems. Parsons, too, attempts to exploit these possibilities in reflections that are more noticeably oriented towards history and developmental theory. But such a procedure can succeed only to the degree that it is possible to attach names or other plausible terms to the boxes, so that it is always possible to state which concrete reality is hidden behind a specific combinatory possibility. This, it seems to me, is the true difficulty of Parsons's system since, as already mentioned, this problem cannot be solved deductively but only through an inventive and inventorying imagination, and thus also requires a good measure of theoretical creativity. It is a rewarding task to observe in detail how Parsons proceeded, which of the boxes contain which names, and which newly gained insights, as well as what degree of realism, are due to this mode of operation. This cannot be accomplished within the framework of this brief presentation of the theory. Our thinking through two specific cases will have to suffice.

The first case is the most general version of systems theory – that is, the action system as such. The second case, from which I have already drawn examples, is the case of the social system. By the way, Parsons calls such levels or degrees of detail that occur in his theory "system references." One of his more remarkable insights states that one must always distinguish between system references, which is to say that one must know at which system level of detail within the total complex one's own argument is located and at which level one wants to place certain mechanisms or interchange possibilities, and so forth.

To begin with, we now find ourselves at the level of the general action system, the most general level that was provided in this theory, if we disregard for the moment the much later development of a general theory of the "human condition." So, we are dealing with action as such. But what guarantees the possibility of action as such (see figure 2)?

Here the adaptive function (adaptation) is occupied by something that Parsons calls a "behavioral organism" or "behavioral system." This does not refer to the entire biology of an organism such as its cellular chemistry or all those things we know about hormones, and neither does it refer to the anatomy of the human body or anything comparable. What

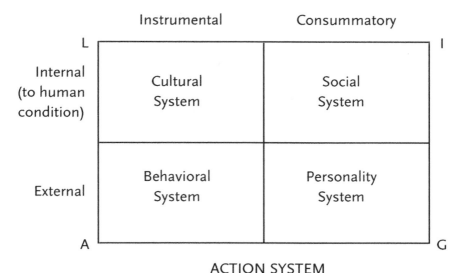

ACTION SYSTEM

Figure 2 The action system
A = adaptation, G = goal attainment, I = integration, L = latent pattern
maintenance

is meant is always just what an organism must do to make behavior possible, which is to say, to bring about the behavioral component of action.
Besides, here it can be seen that the so-called subject, the actor, is dissolved; one of its parts is precisely this "behavioral organism." Why the
"behavioral organism" is placed in this particular box – that is, why it is
said to produce instrumental functions and externally oriented behavior
– as well as the degree of fanciful interpretation involved in such an
ascription remain questions about which one may very well disagree. For
a start, Parsons simply posits this definition. He sees the organism as that
component of action by means of which action adjusts itself to external
conditions or, alternatively, attempts to establish long-term balanced
states with the external ecological conditions. This view is of some interest
precisely if we consider the more recent interest in the relations between
action or society and ecology. For it tells us that the ecology, the environment, affects action only in the sense of exerting an influence on the
behavioral organism – that is, only in the sense of disturbing one aspect of
action – which, to be sure, is precisely not the cultural aspect – or requir-
ing adjustments on this level. Society cannot survive as an action society
if the organism does not provide the opportunity for continuous adjustment to the ecological conditions and is not equipped accordingly. Thus,
to quote a favorite example of Parsons, the organism must be capable of
keeping the blood temperature constant in order to supply the brain with

enough blood, and all this while adjusting to the changing temperature of the environment.

As soon as one asks whether this particular box could not also be occupied by something completely different, doubts arise. But if one instead simply follows the Parsonian directive, one finds a high level of plausibility and gains specific insights, for which one would look in vain elsewhere in sociology. In any case, such insights would not be found in a context that would not also provide other increases of insight – that is, a theoretically integrated context.

The next box, dedicated to "goal attainment," is occupied by "personality." Here subjective functions – in the sense of psychic functions or functions that are based on consciousness – are located. Why here? And why are *they* located here? Apparently, Parsons considers it important to introduce the psychic system as a system that monitors whether actions take place in a "consummatory" fashion – that is, either whether they are satisfactory in the performance of the action itself, in the Aristotelian sense of "praxis," or whether they take delight, if you will, in representing and achieving goals. Once again, this is a rather idiosyncratic view of psychology. The subject is condensed, so to speak, to the function of monitoring the satisfactory states not just of the subject itself but of the entire action system. And it has an external orientation. Why is this so? Perhaps one might say – but this goes beyond what Parsons provides – that the psychic system is capable of continuously mediating between internal references[4] (that is, between self-consciousness or the consciousness of consciousness) and external references (that is, perception). If one is willing to entertain this thought, one will notice that, in contrast to the long European tradition, the actual psychic achievement consists less of thinking and more of perceiving, and that the orientation towards the environment, which is relevant here and which is monitored so that satisfactory values can be maintained, can be located in psychically enabled perception. After all, the "behavioral organism" only has the possibility of monitoring its own states. The nervous system merely serves to observe the organism, or perhaps even only itself. It is completely closed and is adjusted to environmental conditions merely through evolution or evolutionary selection. Yet, under the aspect of pleasure or displeasure, the psychic system can monitor itself in relation to a variable environment – this was, by the way, a topic of Parsons's research in the fifties.

Again, we end up with a curious double effect. On the one hand, the question why exactly this option was selected for this box must be posed. But, on the other hand, one still has the incentive of trying to find out what can be seen by means of this option. I think that, if one decides to thematize psychic systems primarily via perception, or at least thematizes their contribution to action via the possibility of perception – that is, via the psyche's perceived world – one can find a high degree of plausibility in the Parsonian option that determines this particular corner of the entire model.

The next box combines consummatory and internal rules, relations, functions, variables, or whatever. Here, Parsons inserts the "social system." At first glance, this seems once again rather curious. Why does the social system serve the integration of action? And why is integration understood as the production of internal order according to consummatory aspects, which is to say, aspects of the present? Parsons's thought seems to be that the decisive point concerns the coordination of the actions of different organisms and systems of people. What matters, then, is integrating people with their contributions into a network of action that consists of a number of people. The pronounced separation of personal systems and social systems is striking. Under the aspect of their contributions to the emergence of action, both stand side by side. In the context of the internal differentiation of the action system, they are both part of each other's environment. If, in addition, one also considers the "behavioral organism," then it becomes obvious that the visible, perceptible unity of the human being is undone and presented as divided into three components. Everything is seen according to the aspect of what contribution each component makes to the emergence of action. At stake is not an anthropology. The constantly fashionable and constantly recurring question "Where is the human being in sociological theory?" is thereby answered in a precise manner.

Finally, we have the last remaining case, the case of "latent pattern maintenance" at the level of the general action system. In other words, we are dealing here with the coordination of instrumental orientation – that is, the need not to forego or lose the structural patterns during the phase of latency – with internal orientation, which is to say, with an orientation towards the action system itself and not towards the environment. Here, Parsons inserts "culture." As a decision in keeping with his theory, this choice appears rather plausible at first glance. Cultural patterns indeed assure the possibility of reactivating behavioral patterns. For instance, they assure the possibility of reactivating roles or individual action types in temporally remote situations. At the very least, this is one of many possible definitions of culture. Due to this conception of culture, Parsons got himself dragged into a number of controversies, which I cannot discuss in detail here. Their main interest consisted in determining to what degree technical artifacts, such as tools or writing and so forth, could be included in such a conception of culture. In the fields of ethnology, anthropology, and even archaeology, there is a tendency at times to take everything that can be found in excavations as culture, and therefore to underestimate the semantic component of culture or treat it, in turn, merely as a tool, which is to say, as something that finds expression only in language [as opposed to all other cultural artifacts]. For Parsons, this difference is less important. His concept of culture also extends to the reusability of a tool,

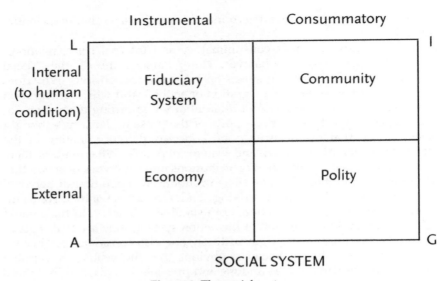

Figure 3 The social system
A = adaptation, G = goal attainment, I = integration, L = latent pattern
maintenance

the reusability of linguistic combinatory possibilities (which refers to the fact that one recalls the words and the grammar), and the reusability of, say, a hammer after it has not been used for weeks. One knows where it can be found and what its purpose is. All this enumerates rather convincingly the presuppositions of an integration of the entire action system. In this context, the possibility of integration ought not to be understood in the sense of the specific function of integration but rather in the sense of system integration via signs.

Parsons's theory program states that these four partial or functional systems must have undergone a primary evolutionary differentiation before further sub-differentiations within the individual functional systems can occur. In order to illustrate this problem, I will at this point merely examine the social system and show how Parsons envisions its sub-differentiation according to the AGIL schema. In fact, this is the most developed part of his theory and, if you will, the earliest, since Parsons, after all, designed his entire system with sociological objectives in mind (see figure 3).

Figure 4 makes clear within which one of the fields we are moving at this point.[5]

I have already indicated that the adaptive sub-system of the social system – or, to put it differently, the adaptive sub-system of the integrating sub-system of the action system – is called "the economy." The differentiation of this complex occurs always when long-term adaptations

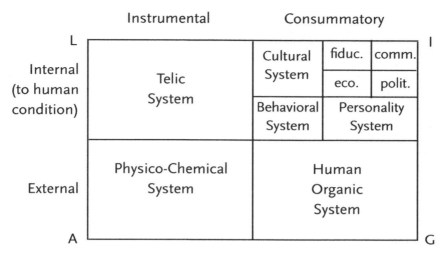

Figure 4 The social system within the action system of "the general paradigm of the human condition"
A = adaptation, G = goal attainment, I = integration, L = latent pattern maintenance

of the action system to environmental situations are at stake – that is, to put it crudely, when capital is created, which is to say, when a monetary mechanism is introduced. This monetary mechanism ensures that one is always capable of reacting to hitherto unforeseen situations in the environment by using capital in order to, say, produce or buy something, to draw resources from the environment or, these days, to remove the refuse. The realism of this conception, it seems to me, consists in the fact that the monetary mechanism plays the decisive role in the differentiation of the system. This means that only the evolutionary achievement "money" (Parsons calls it a symbolically generalized medium of communication) led finally to a state of affairs in which the economy differentiated itself. As a consequence, the conditions of environmental adaptation were improved, which amounted to a guarantee that the persistence of the action system was secured in the long term.

The function of "goal attainment" within the social system is defined by Parsons as politics. This, too, led to controversies that I cannot discuss in detail here, although they are quite interesting in and of themselves. The controversies had to do with Parsons's view of politics, which was in stark contrast, on the one hand, to classical – that is, Aristotelian, Old European, etc. – views, which perceive politics as having the function of making the authentically human a reality, and, on the other hand, to critical theories, which perceive politics merely as a supplement of the economy. For Parsons, politics is an independent system within the social system of the action system. The specificity of politics consists in the securing of states that are consummatory – that is to say, satisfactory in and of themselves in the present. This definition, too, stands in a peculiar contrast to a conception of politics that we take for granted: namely, a view of politics as an instrumental contrivance that attempts to bring about increasingly better outputs – that is, increasingly better social situations. Parsons poses the question as to whether this truly is the meaning of politics. As Parsons formulates it, politics in his specific sense is "collectively binding decision-making."[6] That is to say that politics must be capable of making decisions that create, as I would like to suggest, a collective bond at the moment of decision. Therefore, such decisions are recognized and supported and, for this reason, also provide satisfaction. They rest on trust in the decision-making ability, the correctness of the decisions, and perhaps also the authority of the politician in charge. In this very sense, they are consummatory in spite of the fact – and this is the second component – that it is always a matter of external functions – that is, the relation between system and environment.

Now, whereas the two externally directed functional complexes "adaptation" and "goal attainment" have, as one may say, rather well-known terms and for this very reason got Parsons entangled in controversies with the standard views in economic and political theory, respectively, the two remaining boxes carry innovative and relatively unstable designations. Why these terminological deficiencies occur precisely in these areas is hard to say. Perhaps it has to do with a certain one-sided perspective in modern social sciences or, more generally, the modern theory of society, which always insisted rather strongly on the difference between state and economy or state and society, as one put it in the nineteenth century. In comparison, the distinction of other domains was neglected; thus, science, art, education, the law, and so forth, were not given the same consideration and vigor. Parsons, however, is faced with the necessity of supplementing this dichotomy of politics and economy, state and society, with two further distinct functions – and that is it, for there cannot be more.

The function of integration in the domain of the social system is assumed by that which Parsons calls "community" and occupied by terms such as "communal system" or other emotional, affective expressions. However, this component is not really worked out or strengthened theoretically. It must be conceded that we encounter a peculiar composition here, insofar as we are dealing with a function of integration that occurs within the function of integration. After all, the social system already serves to integrate the action system. And now we have a situation in which the same function is repeated within this function. The reason for this can be seen when we pose the question of how the social system itself can be integrated – that is, how it is that the social system all by itself can motivate actions in the service of purely social functions. This is an important point, especially since people are involved who would rather act in their own name or for their own benefit, or since culture is involved, which strives to operate under its own problems of consistency and its own consequences that result from certain semantic schemata, and therefore does not at all take into account the social consequences of its own operations. The theological quarrels of the Middle Ages may serve as an example. They led to the Reformation and could no longer be socially contained once the printing press was added to this constellation.

Thus, on the one hand, integration in respect to the action system is accomplished within the social system but, on the other hand, the social system must also be able to fulfill integrative functions by itself, which is to say, within the different social components such as the economy, politics, and so forth. This entire area is designated by the expression "social community" (and similar terms).

Finally, there is the fourth case – namely, that "latent pattern maintenance functions" must be performed in turn within the social system. For within the social order the problem of the maintenance of patterns in their latent phases poses itself as well. Parsons calls this area the "fiduciary system," in the sense that he envisions a culture that has its own dynamic and within which change happens – for example, in much longer intervals (or perhaps in much shorter intervals, say, in the case of fashion) than can be reproduced in the social system. As a consequence, the social system relates to culture in ways that are suitable for the reformulation, the internalization, and even the integration [*Einbau*] of culture in social patterns.

At this juncture the question arises whether it makes sense at all to distinguish between culture and social systems. For this is a rather unusual distinction, since it is hardly possible to think of social operations that are directed with precision at purely cultural aspects; at the same time, it is also hardly possible to think of social action that could do entirely without this function of "latent pattern maintenance." Nonetheless, Parsons considers the possibility that something like this distinction happens and that a specialization of social functions and social action areas in the direction of culture is possible in the case of fiduciary functions. He wrote an entire book on the American university from this perspective. This means that there must be social systems that process culture and make it suitable for social functions – regardless of whether such relics of a culture are still culture at all. One of the interesting versions of this conception has it that there are evidently "intellectuals" who take upon themselves the task of representing culture socially.

I will leave it at these two analyses of the action system in general and of the social system in particular. The only thing that matters in the present context is my attempt to present to you the argumentative capacity of such a theory – that is, to present the self-generated difficulties in which it gets entangled, and show how reflecting on and coming to terms with the difficulties that one has created for oneself in the first place may take us in innovative directions – at least if one happens to be a theoretician of such creative power as Parsons was. But, at the same time, this procedure also reveals a certain hermeticism inherent in Parsons's theory conception. Concepts are always defined simply within the schema of the four boxes. The necessity of filling the boxes with plausible content guides the theory decisions. Under such circumstances, it makes less and less sense to consider whether the Parsonian concept of culture is connected, say, with the concept of culture as used in cultural anthropology or with problems of hermeneutics *à la* Gadamer, and so on. Comparisons between theories become increasingly difficult the more prominent a specific theory pattern becomes.

If you have followed my argument thus far, you might now be of the opinion that Parsons's theory is essentially preoccupied with the definition of, filling in, and making plausible these boxes. But that would be completely mistaken. At the very least, such a view would capture merely one aspect of his theory. An essential part of the additional theoretical considerations deals with the relation between these boxes, the relation between the partial systems. All the additional theoretical instruments are aimed at the consequences of functional differentiation. This accounts for the noteworthy style of the theory. It deals with the differentiation of the action system and the consequences of continued differentiation. As such, it very much stands in the tradition of Durkheim's views concerning the division of labor or, in fact, the sociological tradition in general, which has described modern society as a differentiated society.

This is not the place to discuss in detail individual efforts aimed at establishing relationships between partial systems. I will merely mention the essential accounts that have been proposed. A first account consists of the idea of a hierarchy of control. Here, the systems are ordered according to a double hierarchy – top-down and bottom-up, A G I L and L I G A.[7] Culture directs the systems "cybernetically," as Parsons puts it, in that it influences social systems using little energy, and these then influence personal systems, which, in turn, exert their influence on their underlying organism. This requires an increasing amount of energy the farther down in the hierarchy we move, yet the means of control itself is information. From the opposite point of view, what is at stake is the fulfillment of certain conditions – that is to say, that energy possibilities have to be provided for action to occur – for instance, the possibilities of physical movement or sensorimotor abilities, motivational energies on the part of the personal system, communication capacities, if you will, in the domain of the social system and, finally, the grounding necessary for the conveyance and transmission of culture that is so provided. This exemplifies the idea of a hierarchy of control.

Another option – and perhaps this is more important – is the idea of symbolically generalized media of exchange: between the systems there are "interchange relations" (Parsons even speaks of "double interchange relations"), both at a more general and at a more concrete level, and every system possesses its own media to control these relations of exchange. In the economic system, for instance, this is money; in the political system, power; in the social system of the community, influence and authority; and, in the culture system of the social system, "value commitments." There is a very elaborate theory concerning the construction of such media of exchange according to "comparable criteria."[8] I consider this one of the most magnificent efforts to find standards of comparison and thereby to include both identity and difference within a single theoretical framework. Max Weber had posed the problem of rationality in a general manner for action as such and then had gone on to divide it into types for which no further justification was given. In addition to all its other merits, Parsons's theory is an interesting attempt to relate Weber's problem of rationality to his own differentiated system and to realize that, in the economic or the political, the communal or the fiduciary domains, and, in fact, in all systems that form media, completely different criteria of rationality operate.

Finally, there was yet another theoretical effort to create relations that also brought very interesting additional insights with it, and which was conducted under the title "interpenetration."[9] According to this theory, there are relations between systems that are based on their partial overlap, on the insertion of complex achievements of other partial systems into the receiving system. The concept of interpenetration makes it possible to integrate fragments of a theory that had accrued entirely independently of each other. For instance, the interpenetration of the L function and the I function – that is, of "latent pattern maintenance" and "integration," or of culture and the social system – occurs via "institutionalization": culture must be institutionalized, which is to say, socially processed and made usable. The interpenetration of culture and the personal system happens by means of "socialization": people must be socialized through their personal contacts so that they can make their contribution to the action system. And the interpenetration of the personal system and the "behavioral organism" – I find this interesting – occurs via the concept of learning. The body must learn to obey the personal system – that is, it must learn to keep itself upright, to behave properly, to execute exactly those movements that the psychic commands designate, and so on.

These three aspects of inter-system relations – the cybernetic hierarchy of control, the media of communication or exchange, and interpenetration – are poorly integrated among themselves, and it is also rather difficult to integrate them by means of the internal divisions of the systems into four boxes. Parsons put much work into this problem and presented more or less plausible and increasingly complex solutions. This already indicates that, in working out his theory, he increasingly entangled himself in compulsions and restrictions that he had created himself, and that he deviated more and more from the standard use of language. He had to react increasingly to problems of his own making and began to lose touch with the common jargon of sociology. Besides the ideological critique of the theory, which never made contact at the argumentative level and thus never really engaged with the theory, this rather fine-grained self-disciplining of the work that contributes to his theory is, it seems to me, one of its main difficulties and, in fact, *the* primary difficulty that hampered or even substantially reduced the circle of Parsons's disciples, who saw themselves confronted with the requirement of concentrating on individual boxes or special problems of his theory; otherwise they were not in a position to contribute at all.

To be sure, it does not make sense to claim that the Parsonian theory has failed or to say that fundamental mistakes had been built into the theory – mistakes that we could recognize today. But, in a certain sense, this theory was a dead end in the development of a specific sociological systems theory. Neither before nor later was so much sociological knowledge brought together within such a thoroughly structured framework. Yet the hermeticism of the theory indicates that, from this particular position, it is no longer possible to follow, and relate to, the interdisciplinary progress of systems theory in general.

Like no other sociologist of his time, Parsons managed to integrate non-sociological theoretical achievements. This is true for the theory of economics as much as for Freud. It is equally true for the input/output language of systems theory, for certain aspects of linguistics and cybernetics, and so forth. But, in direct correspondence to systems theory's switch to self-reference, Parsonian theory appeared to be no longer capable of being received and transmitted productively. For this reason, it seems to me that, in this case, we are probably witnessing the end phase of one independent development of sociological theory. This gives us all the more reason to begin to examine the interdisciplinary space more closely.

II

General Systems Theory

---

1 The Theory of Open Systems

Third Lecture

I begin this lecture with an attempt to bring together some thoughts about a general systems theory. The word or concept "general systems theory" aims far beyond the actual state of affairs. To be precise, there is no such general systems theory. It is indeed the case that in sociological scholarship there have been, time and again, references to systems theory, as if this concerned something that exists in the singular. But, as soon as one examines the matter more closely and looks beyond sociological scholarship, it becomes difficult to find an object – that is, a theory – that would correspond to this way of speaking. There are several general systems theories. There are attempts to generalize systems theoretical approaches – that is to say, to transcend the limits of a particular discipline. But, generally speaking, even these attempts still betray quite clearly the discipline from which their abstractions in each case originated. In general, there are also considerable obstacles between different disciplines or theory models that attempt to formulate generalizations from their particular vantage points. Perhaps this situation is historically determined. The attempt to formulate a general systems theory originated in the fifties. The corresponding terminology had its beginning in this period. Back then, a society for "general systems research" was founded.[1] A *General Systems Yearbook* was created as the focal point for publications dedicated to this direction in scholarship. And there was this idea that, taking one's departure from different starting points, one could collect and combine different thoughts in order to produce something like a general systems theory. This enterprise was not without success. It is, however, most worthwhile to start by going back to the sources of these considerations and to line up the different points of departure in order to locate in each case the critical focus as well as the problems of such generalizations. We can then also see why a certain threshold of systems theoretical development was never crossed.

In this lecture, it is my intention first of all to reconstruct this development and to mark its limits, so as to arrive at a new approach that allows us to formulate individual perspectives of a sort of second generation – that is, of "second-order cybernetics," a "theory of observing systems," and related conceptions.

Therefore let us start by getting to the points of departure of general systems theory. One line of development can be seen in the metaphor or the models that worked with the concept of an equilibrium or balance. To begin with, this approach had a mathematical foundation insofar as one worked with mathematical functions. But the metaphor itself is also of interest, independent of its mathematical connections, since it belongs, after all, to the oldest sources of systemic thinking. It had already been in use for a long time before the word "system" rose to a certain prominence and, of course, long before one could speak of a "systems theory" in the proper sense. I do not know when exactly this metaphor took root, but by the seventeenth century it was already taken for granted and used in the idea of the "balance of trade." Moreover, by the end of the century it also motivated the idea of an international, specifically a European, balance of power between nations (or political factors). In addition, the metaphor was used in a more general and relatively indeterminate manner.

If one surveys this development in retrospect, one can say that it can be characterized by means of a distinction: namely, the distinction between a stable state and a disturbance. Normally, the emphasis is put on stability. One imagines a balance or equilibrium as something stable that reacts only to disturbances and, in fact, reacts in such a way that either the old balance is re-established or a new state of equilibrium is reached. Thus, the metaphor presupposes a certain mechanics, a certain mode of implementation, and a certain infrastructure, all of which ensure that the equilibrium is maintained. It is this viewpoint that coincides with the dominant idea that theories of equilibrium are theories of stability. However, if one examines the matter more closely – and such hints were already present in the seventeenth century – this assumption becomes questionable. If we take our lead from the image of scales with their two sides in balance, it should be clear immediately that this equilibrium can be disturbed very easily. Just placing a small weight on one of the pans suffices to throw the scales off balance.

This means that the idea of equilibrium can be understood as a theory that marks and locates a system's sensitivity to disturbance: one knows what is to be done if one wants to disturb the equilibrium. From a certain point of view – one that will recur time and again in this lecture course – this theory is a theory of a specific distinction and not so much the theory of a desirable state or of a particular type of objects. The concept of balance or equilibrium contains a theory that is interested in finding out how the relation of disturbance and stability can be turned into order. Perhaps one might even say – although this exceeds what can be found in the literature – that it is interested in finding out how the relation between disturbance and stability can be increased in such a manner that a system, despite being severely affected by disturbance, is still stable. The interesting question for us, in terms of mathematics, is from which mathematical equations we can derive such a relation. Yet, although this moment of disturbance has been noticed time and again in the tradition, and in more recent applications, of equilibrium theories, the emphasis has clearly been on stability. It is as if keeping a system stable amounted to a value all by itself! Furthermore, it is as if the devices that are responsible for establishing a state of equilibrium in fact had a duty to keep the system stable! These observations apply especially to the theory of economics, with its concept of a balance or equilibrium between different economic factors. And it is here, as well, that the first doubts took root as to whether it is appropriate after all to speak of balance or equilibrium as a stable state, particularly if one factors in reality – which is to say, if one does not just look at mathematical functions but tries to imagine how real systems, such as economic and production systems, manage to be stable.

All of this led to the thought that perhaps the opposite was true: namely, that imbalance or disequilibrium might function as a condition of stability. According to this view, an economic system can be stable only if it produces too many goods in order to have something to offer in case a certain market demand arises, or else if it produces, on the contrary, too many buyers and not enough goods so as to have buyers at its disposal who will purchase the goods on offer if the supply is sufficient. János Kornai, a Hungarian economist, developed such anti-equilibrium concepts.[2] It is apparent that the two versions of economic disequilibrium that I have cited represent the Western and Eastern economy, respectively, in terms of the controversy between capitalism and socialism. Either the scarcity of goods has to be maintained while buyers or, rather, demand must be available in abundance, which is the case in the socialist system; or, conversely, there must be a scarcity of buyers and an abundance of goods, which is the case in the capitalist system. Be that as it may, we are dealing here with a version of anti-equilibrium theory that distinguishes itself from classical and neo-classical economic theories by shifting the state of stability from equilibrium to disequilibrium.

In any case, the equilibrium or balance model was at the root of one strand of developments that aimed at a general systems theory. This was no new discovery in the fifties. Rather, it was merely a variant that one could deploy if needed. What was new were two different problem areas that eventually influenced the further development of systems theory much more strongly than equilibrium theory did. The most novel issue arose with a question derived from thermodynamics: namely, how systems can be maintained at all if one must assume that physics, at least the physics of closed systems, tends to produce entropy – which is to say, to dissolve all distinctions and thus bring about a state without distinctions or, to put it in the terms of physics, a state in which no usable energy is left, no energy that could in any way still produce distinctions. If this is a general physical law, how is it at all possible to explain the facts of the physical, chemical, biological, and social world? How is it possible to explain that there is order and that, if one limits one's perspective to a few billion years, it cannot be discerned that such a development towards entropy is indeed in the making? To put it differently, how can negentropy be explained as a deviation from entropy, if it is indeed the case that the laws of physics point to entropy? Asking this question, one acknowledged that the laws of entropy presuppose a closed system, and one imagined, for example, the world as a closed system into which nothing can be introduced from the outside and from whose inside nothing can be removed.

As a model of the world, this model may have validity. But it does not apply to the conditions within the world. What we have here is the model of a closed system. Such systems are not to be found in the world, at least not as far as living systems, psychic and social systems, are concerned, and are therefore of no relevance in the area that is of interest in the present lecture series. For this reason, the notion of a closed system was rejected in the fields of biology and sociology, and in its stead a theory of open systems was developed. These systems were called "open" because they were meant to explain why entropy does not occur in them and why order is created instead. In all cases, openness means that an exchange with the environment takes place. But, depending on what kind of system one has in mind – biological, organic systems or meaning-directed systems [*sinnorientierte Systeme*] – that is, social systems (communication systems) and psychic systems (consciousness) – the conceptualization of this exchange takes on different forms. In the case of biological systems, the consumption of energy and the excretion of useless energy are primarily at issue. In the case of meaning systems [*Sinnsysteme*], it is predominantly the exchange of information. A meaning system obtains information from its environment. One might say that it interprets surprises. In turn, this particular information processing system is integrated into a network of other systems that reacts to it. The basic condition that accounts for negentropy[3] is the same in both instances: namely, the exchange relationship between system and environment. This is what is designated by the term "open system."

At this point in the course, I place special emphasis on this concept, precisely because later we will talk about a counter-theory, the theory of operationally closed systems, which does not, however, revoke the concept of openness but gives it a makeover. In any case, open systems are the answer to the provocation that originated with the law of entropy.

In this context, one should also pay attention to the region of contact between systems theory and the theory of evolution. Ever since Darwin, the theory of evolution saw it as its task to explain structural variety, which in the field of biology is the variety of the species. How can it be explained that the one-time biochemical invention of life led to so many different forms, to worms and birds, mice and men, and so forth? The same could of course be said for social systems. How can it be explained that, once linguistic communication developed, there could already be so many different languages, and further, from a historical perspective, that so many different cultures – developed cultures and less developed cultures – have existed simultaneously? How does the multiplicity of tokens and the variety of types come about on the basis of a relatively simple one-time invention of evolution – namely, the biochemistry of life, on the one hand, and communication, on the other? In all of these cases, one needs a theory of open systems if one wants to venture an explanation. In other words, one needs a theory that describes how environmental stimuli can have an effect on systems that changes their structure. The question is how an event that was merely contingent to begin with and was not planned for or even expected within the system – for instance, a mutation at the cell level or some irritating, disturbing information – can be noticed as such in the system and lead to a structural change – that is, to the selection of new structures and to testing whether these structures can actually be stable or not. This means that the Darwinian distinction between variation, selection in the sense of structural change, and stabilization or restabilization also rests on a theory of open systems. But, over and above the general theory of open systems, Darwinian evolution also accounts for the historical dimension or the dimension of the development of structural complexity that runs counter to those expectations that might be entertained solely on the basis of the law of entropy.

If we presuppose this general theory of open systems, we must acknowledge that secondary, subsidiary theories, and especially a conception of the input/output model, are attached to it. At the level of the general concept of the system, the theory of open systems does not determine what kinds of relations exist between system and environment. Instead, it works with a general idea of the environment and not exactly with the idea that, in the environment, specific conditions and also specific other systems exist that might become especially relevant for a particular system. At this level one ought to distinguish between, on the one hand, the system-environment paradigm – which is to say, the general thesis that systems can prevent entropy only if they exist within an environment and are in contact with this environment – and, on the other hand, system-to-system relations – which is to say, questions concerning a certain dependence on ecological conditions or a certain dependence within a social order on certain other systems (for instance, the dependence of a political system on a functioning economy in relation to both the submission of taxes and the willingness of the population to elect a certain government). In more general terms, we speak of a difference between the system-environment distinction, on the one hand, and the system-to-system relations, on the other. Now, the input/output model concerns the latter. It presupposes that a system can afford a high degree of indifference in relation to its environment and that, by and large, the environment is of no importance to the system. It also presupposes, however, that, under such conditions, specific environmental factors gain all the more importance. Obviously it is not the environment that is in a position to decide which factors are important but rather the system itself. In this sense, a system possesses relative autonomy insofar as it can decide itself (and thereby make this decision dependent on internal conditions and on its own system type) on what it has to rely as its input, and what it passes on to its environment as its output – which is to say, its waste but also its positive results [*Leistung*], its readiness to be of benefit to other systems.

Such input/output models come, roughly, in two different varieties. The first is a rather ideal or mathematical model that is based on the notion that there are certain inputs and that the system performs a transformational function that leads to certain results. This transformational function is structurally determined. It is customary to speak of "machines" in this context, either in the real sense or in the sense of a mathematical function that transforms certain inputs into certain outputs. We are dealing here with a highly technical model, a machine or production model that presupposes, among other things, that one may repeatedly produce the same output with the same input. Such ideas were the reason for the criticism that systems theory is a technical theory and does not do justice to the realities of social life. It is certainly possible to complicate this transformational functional theory [*Transformationsfunktionstheorie*]. Thus one could come up with a system that simultaneously includes several transformational functions or even a system that internally is differentiated into further systems so that the different input/output relations within one system could be linked together. But the basic idea was still the same transparent transformational function that can be recognized by the systems analyst. And this has as its supposition and leads to the prediction, respectively, that, with the same inputs, the same outputs can be produced and that one is dealing with a reliable system.

But the attempt to transpose such models into social reality or to re-enact them at the psychic level – that is to say, to conceive of the psychic system as working with inputs and outputs – ran into difficulties. Thus, for instance in psychology, the behaviorist conception of a stimulus-response model was already in place. It had already put the same idea into action without working with the terminology of input and output. In the field of psychology, it had been recognized by the thirties that a simple transformational function would not do and that one would have to work with an intermediate variable, which in those days was commonly formulated by means of the concept of generalization. A psychic (conscious) system often generalizes its relations to the environment so that different inputs can be grouped under one type and produce the same output; or, conversely, a system may react differently to the same inputs, depending on its own affective state [*Befindlichkeit*]. Such complications make it necessary to dissolve the simple mathematical function and to examine the system more closely.

The same applies to the attempted sociological realizations of input/output models, which even assumed this very same terminology. I have in mind, for instance, David Easton's attempt to transpose the input/output analysis to social systems, particularly the political system, and to formulate a corresponding model that provides for several inputs: on the one hand, there is the official allocation of support, the support of the government by means of general elections; and, on the other hand, we have the input of specific interests by organizations that represent stakeholders, by lobbies, and so forth.[4] Politics is itself viewed as a transformational mechanism, and the output is described by Easton as the "allocation of values" – that is, as the distribution of politically determined advantages or values among the population. The next stage of this circulation is reached when the population in turn reacts to this politics by recalibrating its electoral preferences or interest claims. In this model, it was not possible either to implement quantification or to provide a mathematical formula that would show whether and how politics always acts the same way under the same circumstances.

The reaction to this explanatory gap, this gap in the ability to articulate the internal workings of systems, was a theory of the black box, which was at least in part imported from cybernetics yet found a precise application in these cases. "Black box" means that the inside of a system cannot be recognized because it is too complex and therefore cannot be analyzed either. Only from the regularities of the external relations of the system can the conclusion be drawn that there must be some kind of mechanism that can explain the reliability of the system and the computability and predictability of its outputs if certain inputs are given. The fact that the internal workings are orderly can be derived only from the external regularities of a system. This model still leaves space for specific structural investigations of internal processes. It is therefore no coincidence that the concept of the black box works well with a more or less structuralist systems theory. For example, one could think through what it means, in the input–transformation–output process of politics, that political parties came into being at the end of the nineteenth century, and that subsequently parliament no longer had its moorings in the institutionalized freedom of its representatives making up their minds on their own [*Willensbildung*], as was originally intended, but that instead a sort of advance bundling of political issues by political parties took hold – parties that were themselves competing for electoral approval. It is easy to imagine that this shift instigated developments that led from the classical state, which was based on law and reacted to disturbances, imbalances, and social problems, to what nowadays is called the welfare state – that is, a state that actively changes social conditions and conducts politics by offering or promising such changes.

In the first place, the black-box model is merely a model that provides a frame and does not in principle exclude the possibility of subsequent more detailed analyses. But it does, above all, dissolve the notion of a rigid, machine-like or mathematical coupling of input and output.

It may be quite useful in this context also to consider the legal system, for it is here where the input/output analysis actually appears to work. There is a surprising dearth of efforts to apply this theory to the legal system. The few studies I know of that are important in this sense all date only from the late sixties.[5] To begin with, the thought itself is pretty obvious, because one can easily imagine that the law is in principle an input-oriented program: whenever certain information arrives, certain decisions must be made. On some occasion I actually coined the term "conditional program"[6] for this state of affairs, and this terminology has in the meantime become customary. It is a conditional program in the precise sense that the system always orients itself by means of the input boundary and produces certain decisions as a consequence of certain inputs, regardless of the consequences. Requests that are justified by law are judged positively, and requests that are not justified by law are judged negatively. Complaints are upheld if they are justified according to their legal status, and if they are not then they are not upheld. The legal system would thus, if it functioned in this way in practice, be nothing short of an ideal case for the application of input/output analyses and thus for a machine that, seen from outside, functions in a calculable, predictable manner. But, to be sure, this machine is enormously complicated: because there are many legal rules and so many possible points of entry; because many different possible inputs can be presented, there are very different possible types of complaints through which one can try to obtain legal redress; and also because there are many different possible justifications that can be deployed, and which will indeed be deployed in a mechanical manner whenever such a prospect of redress presents itself.

However, in the course of a more precise analysis, it has become apparent that purposive orientations increasingly enter into the law, which is to say that the law – or, as one might say, a good lawyer – always also reflects on the consequences when it presents a certain legal viewpoint and declares a certain interpretation of the laws to be correct or incorrect. Thus, a good lawyer in our contemporary understanding must always also consider the output boundary. It is this fact that makes the legal system in its model form and also, I believe, in reality rather unpredictable, at least in a certain sense. The consequences of a legal decision are different from case to case. They are conditioned by further empirical terms and thus unpredictable for those who would like to think of the legal system as a machine. Moreover, if one follows legal history and the history of legal doctrine in the twentieth century, one recognizes an increase in the tendencies to transform the law in consideration of interests. The point is not merely to deduce conceptually or legally the result that the law requires in this or that case, but instead always also to take into consideration which interests should be supported in the process and the likelihood of the furtherance of these interests being realized. Alternatively, allowance is made in the individual case for conflicts of interests that were not taken into consideration by the legal norm itself, so as to show how *concrete cases* can be decided in accordance with the law – and that means, with regard to sentiments of justice and fairness [*Gerechtigkeitsempfinden*] on the part of the judge and, presumably, equally on the part of the population at large. This tendency increases to the same degree that we put public law into action in the service of the goals of the welfare state. Today, even the Constitutional Court[7] considers the weighing of different values and interests as one of its tasks and, in the process, interferes to a considerable degree with politics.

I described all of this in some detail to point out what has to be kept in mind when input/output models are transposed into the theory of social systems, and how little information sociological theory stands to gain from general systems theory assisted by the terminology of input, transformation, and output. Perhaps this is one of the reasons why the orientation towards input, transformation, and output lost much of its importance in the seventies. On the one hand it was suspected, and also imputed on ideological grounds, that this theory was a mechanical theory, a purely technical theory. And it must be said that there was this element at the mathematical level or the level of model design. But, on the other hand, there was also the question as to what could be gained concretely if the system boundaries were marked in terms of input and output. In other words, one posed the question of what a system *is*, if it is capable of transforming input into output. What is the basis of this transformation or selection that is performed in order to fit in important, relevant inputs and to produce relevant outputs? What kind of machine would this be? What kind of arrangement of structures and operations would this entail? In terms of the input/output model, this was exactly the question that was assumed to have an answer. But it was never really answered.

At this point, let us pick up the third strand of the development of general systems theory, its third ray of hope [*Hoffnungsträger*], namely cybernetics.[8]

This theory emerged at a relatively recent date. It arose in the forties on the basis of technical considerations regarding the possibility of keeping systems, system states, and system outputs stable under changing environmental conditions. The answer to the question I cited was to be found in the well-known feedback model, which is to say, in the idea that there is some apparatus that measures certain distances – that is, information from the environment – in relation to a desirable system state and, depending on whether this distance translates into satisfactory or unsatisfactory values, turns the mechanisms of the system either on or off. You are familiar with the example of the thermostat. In fact, this example has been adduced in the literature time and again as a "paradigm" in the most basic sense: namely, as an example or prototype. But there were many other problems in the forties that one attempted to solve with corresponding models – not the least of which were in the field of war technologies. Whereas in an earlier period, when one wished to take aim at an airplane, one had to deal with a mechanical device – namely, a ring though which one had to aim at the target, and by means of which one directed guns, and so forth – all this was now automated, and the distance to the target could be measured and directly calculated. As a consequence, the accuracy increased independently of the gunner's eye. This fulfilled one of the tasks at that time. But it was understood immediately that there was a general principle at the root of all this, which also played a role in biology, for instance, where a possible task may be to keep blood temperature or blood-sugar levels constant. Thus, there are appliances that are not continuously at work but function only when certain defects, distances, or differences reach a value that is too high.

Why, then, is this model of such great importance? To begin with, it can be generalized. That is the first point. One of its attractions was that it could be tried out in one new field after another. In the second place, there was the belief that, in this manner, the old teleology – that is, the old theory of purposes – could be reformulated.[9] Within the Old European frame of reference, teleology signified the notion that there are certain purposes that attract causal processes and thus enter themselves into the respective process as its cause in spite of the fact that such purposes are actually future states. Already in early modernity this mode of thinking was abandoned and replaced by the notion of mental states. That is to say, now one conceived of purposes as real and present representations of future states that were themselves determined by past experiences. Moreover, the fact that these representations were present implied that they could mechanically trigger certain motor activities. Taking its lead from the mechanization of teleological causalities, as one might call it, cybernetics managed to explain somewhat better than before how it was possible, or what kind of devices had to be presupposed to exist, if one wanted to keep certain system states stable. There were hopes not only for a comprehensive generalization but also for the reconstruction of a classical way of thinking with the help of modern means that were, shall we say, capable of technical realization. Finally, and this was the reason for the name, notions of steering and control [*Steuerungsvorstellungen*] also played a role. *Cybernetes* is the helmsman of a ship, and it was easy to imagine that, in order to keep a ship on a straight course, one had to correct for the intervening wind and wave conditions. If need be, additional countervailing steering maneuvers had to be performed in order to stay on course. *Cybernetes* is the helmsman, the man at the wheel, and cybernetics is the science of the art of steering and controlling [*Steuerungskunst*] technical, possibly also psychic (conscious), and certainly social systems.

That was the idea. It is noteworthy that what remained of this idea was the notion of steering, social guidance, and so forth. Time and again, this notion thereafter led to the illusion that it was possible to control and guide a system with the help of cybernetic techniques, or perhaps by means that are nowadays conceived of more in terms of the theory of action. But what exactly does "steering" or "guidance" mean in this context? Clearly, it does not mean that the future state of a system can, to use the Old European terminology, be determined in all concrete details, or even in its general outline, so that it would already be possible in the present moment to predict how a system will look in the future. Rather, it is merely a matter of making sure that certain differences do not become too large and, if need be, reducing them. The task is one of reducing deviations from the intended course, deviations from the desired state, deviations from a certain temperature at which one wants to keep a building, and so forth. If it is possible to keep the temperature in a building constant, this does not mean, however, that no burglars will stop by, that the furniture will stay in the house, that the rugs will not be ruined, or that the electricity in the kitchen actually works. In the first place, cybernetics always refers only to specific constants and specific differences. It is necessary to invent a very complicated system of multiple and variable steering mechanisms and even of a steering mechanism for the steering mechanisms – that is, a network of cybernetic circuits – if one intends to approach the position from which one would be able to predict the state in which a system will be in the future.

The transposing of the theory of steering and control from cybernetics to action theory, as it has become customary to call it in today's political science circles, shows, in my opinion, that the problem was underestimated. The evident need for political control and guidance was taken to mean that such guidance must be possible in one way or another. I do not want to deny that the reduction of differences can still be practiced successfully. Thus, if certain diseases are spreading, and we can provide vaccines, it is clear that a vaccination campaign that is promoted by the state and endorsed by the medical establishment will reduce the extent of the epidemic. Corresponding examples can be found for the modern financial control of the economy by means of monetary policies. But, even in these cases, it would be better to stick closely to the original cybernetic meaning of the terms "steering" and "control." This would imply that one always imagines a certain difference that must be reduced – a difference that can precisely not be completely controlled by the system but is subject to external influences and must then be adjusted by the system.

The corresponding discussion has taken place under such headings as "negative cybernetics" and "negative feedback." In the late fifties and sixties, the counter-concept of "positive feedback" was invented and juxtaposed with these notions. Positive feedback means the amplification of deviations.[10] The cybernetic circuit is used to change a certain state that was produced by the system itself in a certain direction that amounts to a deviation from the original state and has a specific tendency. What is at issue is not the reduction of difference but, on the contrary, its increase. This amplification of deviation or positive feedback creates entirely different problems than negative feedback. What is at issue here has nothing to do with the stability of the system and with keeping certain values stable. Instead, it is a matter of changing the system and, more precisely, of change in specific directions. In this context one very soon stumbles upon the question of how far a system can push certain amplifications without endangering itself. In other words, if there are mechanisms of positive deviation amplification, how far can we let them run without finding ourselves in problematic situations? I believe that, in light of certain ecological problems of modern society, this question hardly needs any further comment. It is also possible, however, to address within society the question of how long certain expenditures can be increased in the political program of the welfare state so that increasingly more people's income is used for these purposes. The discussion of positive feedback turns our attention to the question of how far the increase of certain variables can progress if these variables are always merely variables among other variables. For how long can an ever increasing number of people study at university? For how long can an increasing number of people become state employees? For how long can the population continue to grow? And so on. The key question is whether a system has braking mechanisms at its disposal, or whether only catastrophic developments will finally block the positive feedback that was introduced at an earlier point and thus bring to an end the tendency to amplify deviations.

Another, equally important application of the idea of positive feedback can be found in the context of evolutionary theory. Here it is possible to explain by means of the mechanism of deviation amplification how certain small, more or less accidental beginnings can lead to big effects that increasingly determine the structure of a certain system and are, in historical terms, hardly revisable. For instance, what are the reasons for Mexico City to be situated in its relatively unfavorable location? Why do we find this city of about 20 million inhabitants in a place where founding a city is not very expedient on account of the climatic conditions, the traffic situation, and many other issues, including the quality of the soil? Could the reason for this be found in the fact that, when the Aztecs immigrated into this area, they happened upon an uninhabited stretch of land where they decided to settle? Or could it be that the Spaniards encountered an established culture and center of power here, which they could occupy and transform? Is the reason perhaps that the Spanish Empire depended on such centers? And so on.

This theory has no predictive power. It does not explain why Mexico City is located where it is located. Rather, it explains merely how it is possible that certain developments happen by means of a mechanism of self-amplification and cannot be controlled with regard either to their consequences or to their expedience. Compared with the classical theory of evolution, we can discern a skeptical moment in this theory. Thus, it is indeed the case that, recently, one has begun again to speak of "attractors" when one tries to describe how certain system states attract further changes, and it is also the case that starting from a certain system state reinforces this very state and makes it quasi-indispensable. But nowadays "attractors" no longer have the old positive meaning. Rather, they are seen as dangerous factors, or at least as factors that must be kept in mind if there is any possibility at all of controlling the evolution of a system.

I have now come to the end of my description of the generalizing tendencies that were brought together, or were meant to be brought together, in the fifties as a general systems theory. I hope that I have succeeded in showing how full of expectations, how promising, but also how limited these efforts were. What I said refers largely to the fifties and sixties. Extensive criticism of systems theory set in after the kind of results that can and cannot be obtained on this basis became apparent. This criticism also has some ideological roots. It is directed at the assumed connection between, in the first place, system and technology, or system and mechanics, and, in the second place, system and the preferences for stability. I believe that I have made clear that these criticisms are not necessarily justified. Perhaps one could say that they are understandable but not really well founded. But, if one truly wants to judge a certain critique, the best way of going about it is not to observe simply the object of criticism. It is much more advisable to observe the critics, in order to see which kinds of systems actually practice such criticism. With this in mind, however, I have already anticipated developing this issue further in the course of these lectures by introducing the notion of observing the observer.

In sum, I would just like to show that, within this entire development, certain limits or certain unanswered questions became apparent. A case in point is that the question as to what kind of object might be called a "system" went unanswered. We spoke of open systems, and this included transformational mechanisms, the possibility of transforming input into output, and the possibility of keeping certain variables constant or uniformly changeable by means of cybernetic mechanisms. But all this does not say much about what a system actually is or what kind of system can perform all of these functions. And this gap could not really be closed simply by referring to mathematical functions, equations or technical tricks, and technical mechanisms, for instance in the area of cybernetic infrastructures. In particular, these references did not lead to results that a sociologist would expect and welcome: namely, the reformulation of general systems theory in such a manner that it would become sociologically usable in terms of a theory of social systems or even a theory of society. There were, to be sure, important and even lasting insights into the performative modes of systems. But there was no answer forthcoming to the question What kind of system can perform the functions that it actually performs? What is the basis of all this? It is this question that provides the starting point for practically all further developments of systems theory.

Taking this question as my starting point, what I will try to outline in the next few lectures is the attempt made to describe with more precision the meaning of the term "system." I mean this in at least two respects, both of which I will discuss in some detail. The first hinges on the shift from the question concerning the system as an object to the question of how the difference between system and environment comes about, if we locate the system on one side of the difference and the environment on the other. How is it possible to reproduce a difference of this kind, maintain it, and perhaps develop it in an evolutionary fashion by making it possible for its own ever increasing complexity to be available within the system, on just the one side of this difference? The second point concerns the question of how, or on the basis of what kind of operations, the system can reproduce such differences. The answer to this question was provided by the theory of closed systems. At first glance, this may look like a regression to the old theory of closed systems; it is as if one had gone back to the start. But that is not the case. As I will show in more detail, the deciding factor is closure – that is, operational recursiveness, self-reference, and circularity – which has to be seen as the condition of openness. This means that one must ask more precisely how a system refers to itself, which is to say, how it can distinguish itself and its environment in such a manner that its own operations can be connected with the help of this distinction to an increasing number of its own operations.

From one question – namely, What does this open system consist of? – we have thus derived two statements of specific problems. On the one hand, there is the problem of how the difference between system and environment is produced and reproduced. On the other hand, there is the problem of what type of operation can bring this about and how it can be linked internally within a network of operations. How can a type of operation recognize internally that certain operations belong to the system and that others do not? Since the late sixties, this problem has become important in, for instance, immunology, the theory of the immune system.

With the problem of how a system recognizes that an operation belongs to the system and not to the environment, we have already mentioned a further critical point that in a similar manner provided the instigation for further developments: namely, the question of observing or of drawing distinctions. Does one have to assume in general, or at least in the case of certain systems, that systems have operations at their disposal that are capable of observing, assuming that one understands the term "observing" in the general sense of drawing distinctions? Does one have to impute observational capacities to the system, and, if so, which kinds of operations within the system are able to perform these observations? In close connection with these questions, another question arose: namely, whether within a system, by means of whatever processes of differentiation, observers who observe the system can actually develop – that is to say, observers who draw yet another distinction within the system and thereby can distinguish themselves from that which they observe, namely the system. Thus, a nervous system, to cite one example, must be capable of distinguishing itself from the organism it observes. Are there larger systems that internally differentiate their observational performance in order to increase their capacity in relation to their environment? Are there biological, psychological, and sociological examples of such systems? Who or what would be the observer of a social system, if one did not merely mean to say that every individual operation, every action, every communication must know what it is doing – or, in other words, must actualize its cognitive capacity – but, in addition to all this, one tried also to imagine that there are reflective entities and reflecting units that, although they constitute parts of the system, have a higher capacity for reflection than the entire system? These are novel types of questions. I intend to base the following considerations and, furthermore, the evaluation of systems theory in terms of sociological purposes on these kinds of theory concepts.

For the time being, however, it is perhaps useful to consider once again the development in the fifties and sixties and to see how the theory of the observer solved the problem back then. It seems to me that, in those days, the scientist or science itself was tacitly assumed to be an external observer with cognitive capacities – for example, in the form of a subject or as the overarching, scientific research community [*wissenschaftlicher Forschungszusammenhang*] that remains outside the systems it observes. Science was understood as a phenomenon that was located somewhere beyond all systems, a subject at large, as it were, that has to decide which aspects of reality it considers a system and which ones not. This can be seen in the distinction between an "analytic" and a "concrete" system concept that used to be so important. An "analytic" systems theory leaves it to the systems theorist *qua* external observer to decide what he considers to be a system or the environment, which aspects of reality he groups together in a system and which ones he wants to exclude; or, to put it yet another way, how he draws the boundaries of a system. In contrast, a systems theory is "concrete" if it starts with the assumption that system formation happens in reality and that the systems theorist must describe these systems exactly the way they are.

Hidden behind this distinction are different epistemological options.

Any epistemology that derives from a transcendental-theoretical starting point – which is to say, any epistemology that assumes that all knowledge is filtered and determined by the concepts that are at the knower's disposal – almost automatically jumps on the bandwagon of the analytic systems theory option. Anyone who thinks in this manner knows, because he is epistemologically, methodically, and scientifically[11] informed, that everything one sees is determined by the observer's perspective. For this reason, it is likely that he will not believe that things such as systems exist in reality before they have been observed. Instead, he will treat the system concept as the construction of a systems theorist. Yet, this type of epistemological reflection is not customary in normal science. Normally, a scientist assumes that the object of his research does exist, even if he is not conducting research into it. Thus, a political system or an organism or a nervous system exists and also possesses certain qualities that predispose it to being called a system even before any research begins. And these entities will continue to exist well after research on them has ended.

It is difficult to make a decision in favor of one or the other of these two varieties of theories of observation, both of which equally presuppose that the observer is outside the system. Against the analytic theory, one could raise the objection that it cannot simply be up to the analyst to decide which units are subsumed under the system concept. It would not make much sense to say that all red-wine glasses constitute a system and all white-wine glasses constitute another system. For this purpose, concepts of set theory suffice. Presumably it would be no more meaningful to say that all women are a system and all men are another system, or perhaps that all children are a system. Systems theory must offer some limits and criteria that determine under what conditions a reality can be called a system. But, if one asks for such criteria, one runs into the additional difficulty that one justifies them on the grounds of an epistemological intention. One must try to get in touch with reality. At least this is the way it looks if one assumes that the observer is indeed an external being. In the very same way, it is possible to criticize the theory of concrete systems from the perspective that it does not give sufficient justification in respect of the degree to which its own perspective determines the observed phenomenon, which it merely describes as concrete and existing as a given reality. At this level, the disagreement between analytic and concrete systems theories would seem to be undecidable. The key question is whether there is a mistake that is common to both approaches, which is to say, whether there is something in need of correction in both cases.

I would like to explain this need to correct this mistake in regard to two specific points. The first concerns the question of whether one can indeed assume that there is an external observer where one wants to refer to physical, chemical, biological, psychic, or cognitive systems as well as social and other systems. Is it not the case that the observer is always already conditioned as a physical, chemical, biological, etc., being? Could he even exist as an extramundane subject? Or should one rather assume that he partakes of the world that he observes in all essential respects? He must function physically and be alive. He must possess a cognitive apparatus, memory, and so forth. He must participate in science and society. He must communicate and obey, or at least somehow agree with, the peculiar nature of the mass media, the press, the publishers, and so on. All this means that the first question, which is of particular interest to the sociologist, now runs as follows: Is there a difference between object and subject, between the object of observation and the observer, that is not already predetermined due to the operational basis that is common to both sides? Or, in other words, is it not the observer who introduces the difference between the observer and the observed object? Or, in yet another formulation, is it not necessary to ask the question of how the world manages to observe itself and thereby be rent asunder by the difference between the observer and the observed?

Pursuing this line of questioning, we once again encounter the more recent development of systems theory. Specifically, we must consider all the developments in physics after it was recognized that all observations of physical phenomena for physical reasons change these phenomena and that the observer – regardless of whether we are dealing with a human being or an instrument – must function physically in order to be capable of observation. We must also consider the parallel account that biological epistemology would give: namely, that a cognitive apparatus must be available on the basis of living organisms, that life itself already has to produce a sort of cognition of its environment, and that all phenomena that one recognizes as living beings are determined, among other things, by the fact that one is actually alive oneself.

This is one way of criticizing the classical distinction between the analytic and the concrete. This criticism puts this very difference into question with new conceptions concerning a sort of operational persistence that is interrupted only by the somewhat artificial caesura between the observer and the observed – a caesura that must function according to real physical, chemical, communicative, and other conditions.

The second question that follows immediately concerns systems theory directly. It goes like this: How can one conceive of an observation if one does not consider the observer himself as a system? How can one suppose that a kind of cognitive connection, a kind of memory, a kind of limitation on perspectives, a kind of limited interest, and a kind of limited connectivity for further cognitive operations all come about, if one does not conceive of the observer himself as a system? On psychological grounds, for instance, one must face the question of why the subject is not said to be a system or, in a different formulation, how one should conceive of a subject if one does not consider the systematic nature of its operations. The classical transcendental-theoretical answer states that one must distinguish between the *a priori* conditions of experience, which are given and are identical for all subjects, and the empirical enactment of these conditions, which is different for different subjects. But this does not free us from facing the question of how an empirically realized individual object distinguishes itself from its own observations. Moreover, all of this does not help to disperse our doubts as to whether it is even possible to derive deductively the concretely observable from transcendental *a prioris*.

The same certainly applies if science is conceived of as an observer. How is it possible to think of science as capable of observation without itself being a system: namely, a system with a network of communication, a system with certain institutional arrangements, a system with certain value preferences, a system with individual careers, and a system that depends on society? In the present sociological context, there is probably no need to explain this any further. But if this is how it is – that is to say, if the observer is always a system – then all that he ascribes to a system, the entire conceptual apparatus, and, furthermore, the empirical results of his research force him to accept some conclusions about himself. It is impossible for such an observer to proceed strictly analytically, if the condition of being able to proceed in such a manner is that he always has already to be a concrete system himself. The difference between the analytic and the concrete system concepts is ground down, so to speak, or even negated, if this necessity of "autological" conclusions is taken into consideration. "Autological," in this sense, means that whatever is valid for my object is also valid for myself.

[At this point, the tape is interrupted. Apparently, Luhmann begins to outline a research cluster within which the question concerning the observer appeared and a theory of observing systems was developed. Specifically, he speaks of Heinz von Foerster, an engineer and physicist from Vienna, who after World War II emigrated to the US. There, he acted as the director of the Biological Computer Laboratory at the University of Illinois from 1956 to 1972. During these years, almost all the important representatives of this theory were invited to conduct research at the laboratory, which emerged as one of the first centers for the formulation and development of the so-called cognitive sciences that arose at the intersections of biology, neurophysiology, mathematics, philosophy, music, dance, and the other arts.][12]

Another important name is Gotthard Günther. Gotthard Günther is a philosopher. He emigrated from Germany but has had difficulty establishing himself in America. His intellectual background consists of Hegel, dialectics, problems of reflection, and the question of subjectivity. In the American context, he also dedicated himself to the problem of connecting dialectics and an operationally oriented version of cybernetics.[13] Günther's contributions address the question of the kind of logic that is necessary to describe situations, in which several subjects – that is, several cognitive centers – interact. It is relatively easy to imagine how, within such a perspective, the issue of the observation of observers may become relevant.

Humberto Maturana was another occasional contributor.[14] He is interested in a biological theory that tries to focus on the circularity of the reproduction of life as the centerpiece of an epistemological and thus cognitive theory. The key concept here is "autopoiesis," which is to say, the self-reproduction of life by those elements that have in turn been produced in and by the living system. I will return to this conception in detail. For the time being, I am concerned only with describing the zones of contact that stood at the beginning of a further, extremely productive development.

Finally, George Spencer Brown has to be mentioned.[15] As far as I know, he was never a collaborator in this research cluster. Nonetheless, Heinz von Foerster immediately recognized the importance of his decisive book of 1969, *Laws of Form*, and accordingly emphasized it in a review.[16] Without a doubt, Spencer Brown has also had a decisive influence on the process of focusing systems theory on the theory of observing systems. He did this specifically by proposing a mathematical theory, a calculus of form that is based on the concept of distinction.

It is perhaps not immediately obvious how something that would deserve the name of a general systems theory could emerge from the discussion that was characterized primarily by these people and by a single institution. Nonetheless, it is apparent that systems theory, in a manner of speaking, began to react to its own historical situation and thus to that which already existed under the very same name. Systems theory became a sort of self-observing, autopoietic, recursive mechanism. Or, one might even say, it became a system that unfolded an intellectual dynamic all of its own, which, in my opinion, is among the most fascinating phenomena that we are able to witness today in our problematic so-called postmodern situation. I would like to build the further developments of the concept of a general theory on this foundation.

2 System as Difference (Formal Analysis)[17]

Fourth Lecture

I will now tackle what I consider the most important and most abstract part of my lecture series – namely, the introduction of the differential or difference theoretical approach. As we saw, the transition from the theory of closed systems to the theory of open systems drew increased attention to the environment. This change concerned not only the knowledge that there is an environment but also the insight that an open system is based on the relations between system and environment and that these relations are not static but dynamic; they are, as it were, channels that conduct causality. On these grounds alone, it was already obvious that no system can exist without an environment. Such a system would end in entropy or not come about in the first place, since it would revert immediately to a state of equilibrium without difference.

Already Parsons spoke of "boundary maintenance" and thus changed the definition of a system; he shifted from a system definition that relies on an essence, essentials, or other unalterable structures to a definition that depends on the question of how the difference between system and environment can be maintained, possibly even at the same time that structures are being replaced. In this case, the identity of a system requires only persistence without necessitating any minimal or essential elements at the structural level. This change was important precisely because one can no longer account for death when one moves from a biological model to questions of social theory; instead, one must presuppose persistence in the development of extremely varied societies – that is, structural developments that go beyond anything that permits us to typify different societies or categorize them historically. Already here, the reproach of conservatism, which is often leveled against systems theory and aims at the structural level, had become meaningless.

What else could be added to this state of affairs? What has changed compared to the situation that was reached at the end of the 1950s or the beginning of the 1960s? What has been added, in my opinion, is the possibility of a more radical formulation of the system definition. Now one can say: a system *is* the difference between system and environment. You will see that this formulation, which sounds paradoxical and perhaps even is paradoxical, needs some explanations. I thus begin with the claim that a system *is* difference – the difference between system and environment. In this formulation the term "system" occurs twice. This is a peculiarity to which I will return in a roundabout way.

To begin with, my claim is founded on a differential or difference theoretical approach. Theory, insofar as it is intended to be systems theory, begins with a difference, the difference between system and environment; if the theory is intended to be something else, it must be based on a different difference. Therefore, such theory does not begin with a unity, a cosmology, a concept of the world or of being, or anything comparable. Instead, it begins with a difference. For at least one hundred years or so, precursors of such a procedure have existed. I will enumerate some of them in order to show that such considerations did not originate only in the 1970s and 1980s but had already been prepared, one might say, by a number of earlier attempts at working with conceptions of difference in a more radical fashion than previously. For instance, in the Greek language, a notion of difference, of distinctions, of *diapherein*, existed already. The sphere of this notion, however, was limited. In this sense difference was one thing among others. Theology as well as ontology worked with a concept of being. But, around 1900, such unitary concepts started to become questionable.

One of the precursors was Ferdinand de Saussure, a linguist, whose lectures were published only much later. In them, he presents the thesis that language is the difference between different words or, if one would like to formulate the theory in terms of sentence structures, different propositions; language is thus not given, as imagined in classical semiology or semiotics (regardless of the preference one might have for either the French or the Anglo-American name), simply as the difference between words and things.[18] Language functions because, *qua* language, it can distinguish between the word "professor" and the word "student," for instance. It does not matter whether there are actual differences between the two specimens thus designated. When using language, we are bound to distinguish between professor and student. Whether there are also age differences, differences in attire, differences regarding the courage to display unconventional behavior, and so forth, is a different matter altogether. Language is able to draw these distinctions in the first place. And it is this difference between words that keeps language going and controls what can be said next. Whether these differences exist in reality may well remain an open question. Of course, we would not even begin to speak if we did not assume that something existed that could be designated in this manner. However, it is the difference within language that is decisive for the course of a particular linguistic action, of a linguistic process, or, we could also say, of a communication. This difference is detached from the problem of reference – that is to say, from that whereof one wants to speak.

The problem of reference was worked out with increasing clarity in a lengthy, specifically French development. It was recognized with increasing clarity that the designated object could not be known as that which is meant by language or be at one's disposal without language. Therefore, it could be neglected in the theory of language. Theories of sign use and of language that had structuralist affinities resulted from this insight.

At the same time, similar considerations emerged within the field of sociology. Once again this development took place in France, namely, in Gabriel Tarde's work. Tarde is no longer very well known, either in France or in Germany. However, from at least one point of view he is important. He conceived of a theory of imitation, a theory of the spread and consolidation of sociality by means of imitation that also did not begin with unity but with difference. If one imitates somebody else, this somebody else must exist in the first place. One cannot continuously imitate oneself, although some people seem to succeed even in this project, especially in the field of art. But, in that case, one has oneself as that "somebody else," as another who painted a picture that one found so beautiful that one now wants to create something similar once again. In any case, a difference is presupposed – a difference that was expanded into a fundamental social theory in Tarde's book *Les Lois de l'imitation* of 1890.[19]

Today, one can find a similar project in René Girard's work,[20] although I do not know whether Girard refers explicitly to Tarde. In his case, too, it is a matter of a beginning conceived as a conflict of imitation. One enters into a conflict with another whom one wants to imitate. In a certain sense, copying somebody is a friendly gesture; a first thought might be that one imitates somebody whom one admires. However, if the goods of the world are scarce, particularly if there are only few desirable women, and one imitates the person whose wishes and desires – whose *désir* – have a specific aim, one becomes a competitor of the imitated person. The result is a conflict. René Girard's theory discusses the conditions that are required in order to transform such conflicts into social order. One of his examples is the sacrifice of a scapegoat. I will not deal with this question at length; I wanted merely to invoke some examples in order to point out one tradition that poses difference as the beginning and turns the problem of further developments resulting from this initial difference into the basic problem of explaining social order.

Nowadays, information theory is also often conceived of in terms of a theory of difference. This tendency can be traced back to Gregory Bateson's classic formulation that information is "a difference that makes a difference."[21] Information is information only if it is not just an existing difference; it is information only if it instigates a change of state in the system. This is the case whenever the perception (or any other mode of input one might have in mind) of a difference creates a difference in the system. Something was not known; then information arrives – namely, that these, and none other, are the facts of the matter. Now one has knowledge and, as a consequence, one cannot help orientating one's subsequent operations by means of this knowledge. A difference that makes a difference! In this case as well, the question of how a theory arrives at its first difference remains unanswered. One begins with a difference and, interestingly, ends with a difference. Information processing in its entirety takes place between an initial difference and a difference that emerges during, and as a consequence of, the process. The difference that has thus come about can in turn be a difference that sets in motion further information. The process does not follow a course just from an indeterminate to a determinate unity, if we may paraphrase Hegel in this manner, but from a difference to a difference.

At this level, the differential approach is already textbook material. There are reports about the state of philosophy in France and similar topics that presuppose these insights or rehearse them once again.[22] This knowledge is not secret, and it can also be found under the brand name "difference theory" in the literature. In addition, I could adduce many further examples.

Instead, I would like to turn to the form of such differential thinking that I consider the most radical and which is available in a work written by George Spencer Brown. To begin with, it might be worth mentioning that it is often difficult to find his book *Laws of Form* in the libraries, because librarians often do not know that "Spencer" is part of his last

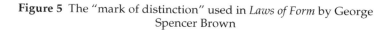

Figure 5 The "mark of distinction" used in *Laws of Form* by George
Spencer Brown

name and therefore shelve Spencer Brown among the many Browns
with the first name "Spencer." Then of course a search under "Sp" turns
out to be in vain. Only after Spencer Brown noticed this difficulty and
began to write his name with a hyphen was the problem resolved, at least
for some of his books. But his name is George Spencer Brown, written
as two separate words, and should be listed under "Spencer" in any
bibliography.

Spencer Brown's text is the presentation of a calculus. He states
explicitly that he is not writing a logic, presumably because he associ-
ates propositions that are capable of fulfilling truth conditions with logic.
His is an operational calculus: that is, a calculus that presupposes time
in the transformation of the signs that are used – or, as I will discuss in a
moment, of Spencer Brown's "mark." The content concerns an issue that
is not of the foremost interest for us, namely, the attempt to combine the
bivalent schema of Boolean algebra with arithmetic and to use only a
single "mark" in the process. This mark represents a distinction. To this
purpose, Spencer Brown introduces a specific symbol (figure 5):

Many of the annotations, preliminary remarks, and afterthoughts in
this book are written in almost standard English and are easy to read.
However, the essence of Spencer Brown's statement lies in the order
of his steps. Step by step, marks are linked with other marks, and their
combinations become increasingly complex. It helps me (I am not sure
that others feel the same way) to imagine that there is first of all a white
sheet of paper; then the marks are put down on the sheet and thereby
gain a peculiar independence: one mark and another one, the second one
copied in part from the first, and so forth. [In this context, Spencer Brown
distinguishes two "laws":]

1 The "law of calling": If I repeat the same distinction (the same mark)
 several times, then the value of the repeated distinctions taken together
 is equal to the value of one single distinction. The "law of calling" can
 be formalized as in figure 6:
2 The "law of crossing": A mark can be crossed within the boundary it
 marks and thus, as it were, be negated. This means that a second distinction can be applied to the first one in such a manner that the original
 distinction is "cancelled." The "law of crossing" can be formalized as in
 figure 7:

Figure 6 The "law of calling"

Figure 7 The "law of crossing"

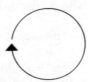

Figure 8 Louis Kauffman's bent arrow

I will now introduce a parallel conception that presents something similar but uses a different mark: namely, an arrow. This mark was created by the mathematician Louis Kauffman and has the advantage that it is better able to depict self-reference (which is of particular concern to me). We have only to bend the arrow, so to speak, and turn it into a circle so that it points to itself (figure 8).[23]

At the beginning we have nothing but the arrow, and Spencer Brown would say: "Let's draw another arrow! Let's copy this arrow from the first one!" Louis Kauffman would answer: "Before anything else, the arrow must point to itself." Both Spencer Brown and Kauffman built a peculiarity into their respective statements. In the following, we will have to deal with this peculiarity, namely, the fact that these marks consist of two parts. Spencer Brown's mark consists of a vertical line that separates two sides and a horizontal line that points to one side and not the other, and could thus be called an indicator or pointer. The mark is consciously thought of as *one* sign, but it consists of *two* components. However, if we start out in this manner, a question arises: Who could designate one but not the other component without already having a sign for this particular purpose at his disposal? Thus, we must first of all simply accept the mark as a unified mark.

Only in the further development of the calculus can it become apparent that it was not as simple as the beginning might have thought – if indeed the beginning could think at all, something that is very much in question.

Figure 9 One arrow: body and pointer

Kauffman's notation has the advantage that it makes clear that the entire thought process begins with self-reference. There is, as is stated in rather enigmatic formulations, no difference between self-reference and difference. Or, to put it differently, in a language that I will be able to introduce only at a later point in my argument: there is no difference between self-reference and observation. For he who observes something must distinguish himself from that which he observes. This fact is accounted for in the circular mark, and everything else – even mathematical infinity, the direction of a process, or anything else – is represented as an unfolding of self-reference. Here, too, the mark (the mark *in the singular*) has *two* parts: a "body," as Kauffman says – namely, the long line that is positioned in space – and a "pointer" that indicates the direction (figure 9):

We begin with a distinction. However, since the result of the distinction must function as a unity, the distinction can be neither designated nor named. It is simply there.

In logic, in mathematics – whatever one wants to call it – in Spencer Brown's calculus, this fact assumes the form of an injunction: "Draw a distinction!" Draw a distinction, otherwise nothing will happen at all. If you are not ready to distinguish, nothing at all is going to take place. There are interesting theological aspects that pertain to this point. However, I will not work them out in this space.[24] Nonetheless, I would like to point out that advanced theology (for instance, the theology of Nicholas of Cusa) contains the proposition that God has no need for distinguishing. Evidently, creation is nothing but the injunction "Draw a distinction!" Heaven and earth are thereby distinguished, then man, and finally Eve. Creation is thus the imposition of a mode of distinguishing, if God himself is beyond all distinction. Interesting connections with our present topic could be made, but they are of no importance for an analysis of Spencer Brown's theory. For he is on earth and stands on the ground – at least on the white sheet of paper – and from there he proceeds, interlocking his operational calculus of marks in the direction of greater complexity.

To speak with more precision and return to the two aspects of the one mark, Spencer Brown remarks that a distinction is always needed simply for the purpose of indicating one side and not the other. (What are called "distinction" and "indication" in his terminology, I translate into the German terms "*Unterscheidung*" and "*Bezeichnung*.") What purpose could drawing a distinction serve other than to indicate one thing rather than another? Every distinction is a boundary, the marking of a difference. As a result, we have two sides; however, they are subject to the condition that both of them cannot be used simultaneously. If they were, the distinction would be meaningless. Thus, if we intended to distinguish men and women, we would have to ask, "Is it a man or a woman?" And if we answered, "It is a microphone," then our distinction would be unnecessary. In case we would like to mix the terms (nothing speaks against it), we would need a new term – for instance, "hermaphrodite" – which in turn would have to be distinguished from other things.

In principle, a distinction contains two components: namely, the distinction proper, marked by the vertical line, and the indication, marked by the horizontal line. It is striking that a distinction contains both a distinction and an indication and thus distinguishes between distinction and indication. If a distinction is supposed to become operational as a unity, it always already presupposes a distinction within the distinction. How this fact is to be interpreted is not entirely clear, at least not in the discussions of Spencer Brown with which I am familiar. I understand Spencer Brown's calculus in the following way (although I am not entirely sure about it). The distinction is extracted, so to speak, from the distinction. And in the end it is made explicit that a distinction had always already been present in the distinction. A unity is put into operation; in the instance of the beginning, it cannot yet be analyzed. Only later, when possibilities of observation are introduced into the calculus – that is, when self-referential figures can be used – does it become apparent that a hidden paradox had already been present at the beginning. This paradox is the distinction contained in the distinction.

This brief description of Spencer Brown's conception is sufficient for my purposes. I will not deal explicitly with the actual calculus. I have never tested it in a technical sense. Experts allegedly claim that it is correct and that it is much more elegant than the original mathematical calculus. But they also claim that something gets lost in the process.[25] For our purposes, the important idea is to use only a single operator. I will return to this point. My interest and the specific interest advanced in this lecture concern applications to systems theory. You may already have suspected that the difference between system and environment can be understood as a distinction. A systems theoretician reacts first of all to the injunction "Draw a distinction!" This distinction is not just any distinction but the distinction between system and environment. The theoretician must use the pointer or indication in such a way that it indicates the system and not the environment. The environment remains outside. The system is on one side, the environment on the other.

In order to clarify this point for further use, I would like to refer once more to Spencer Brown. When the boundary between the two sides of a distinction is marked, he also names this boundary "form." That is the reason for his expression "laws of form." A "form" has two sides. It is not just a beautiful shape or object that can be presented free of all context. Instead, it is a thing with two sides. If one wants to present a context-free object, then one is dealing with an object in an "unmarked space": for example, a mark, perhaps a circle or something else, on a white sheet of paper or something determinable in the world, where other things exist as well, which, however, are not being determined in this instance. In principle, "form" is a matter of two sides: in our case, system and environment.

This is a very general conception. The analysis of form could be pushed far beyond systems theory. I could perhaps say that one could even "redraw" semiology and semiotics with the help of its tools. To this end, one would state that on the one side of the "form" there is a sign – that which one needs to signify something – and on the other side there is the signified. Thus one would arrive at the tripartite figure that plays such an important role for Peirce and others.[26] To speak more precisely, the sign is the difference between signifier and signified. The French expressions Saussure uses are *signifiant* and *signifié*. Something signifies something else. In German we have a tendency to call the signifier [*das Bezeichnende*] that is used for signification the sign [*das Zeichen*]. But by means of a formal analysis we recognize that the sign is a form with two sides and that, in using it as a sign, we must always move to and operate from the inner side of the form – that is, the side of the signifier. Thus, language is used on the assumption that words signify something we do not know very clearly.

I suspect that we could develop a very general theory that would transcend even systems theory on the basis of this very general concept of form that we can detach from its specifically mathematical use in Spencer Brown. We would be dealing with a theory of two-sided forms that can be used only in a one-sided way. I allude to this possibility merely because it could potentially relativize even the systems theoretical approach in spite of its universal pretensions and its scientific claims that are currently being especially well developed (which simply means that there is much literature regarding systems theory). It also could instigate reflection on the possibility of an even more comprehensive general theory of forms and whether such a theory could then be applied to the concept of number, to mathematics, semiotics, systems theory, the medium/form difference between loose and tight couplings, and other issues. However, I will leave it at this.

The consequence of this notion of "form" for systems theory is that the "system" can be called a "form" under the condition that the concept of form must always apply to the difference between system and environment. I have recapitulated this point several times because it may not be entirely intuitive, and one must simply keep it in mind. We will only be able to judge this presupposition after we have seen what can be done by means of it. Against the background of the tradition of open systems and differential approaches of all kinds, we notice that we might have here within our reach a synthesis that could make it possible to include in a single theory knowledge derived from widely disparate sources.

Thus the *first* point we enter under the heading "applications to systems theory" is: a system is a form with two sides.

A *second* suggestion that can also be derived from Spencer Brown concerns the question of whether it makes sense to define a system like Spencer Brown's calculus merely by a single operator and a single mode of operation. If you look at common descriptions and definitions of systems, you will notice that they do not work in this way. Usually, systems are described through a plurality of terms. For example: systems are relations between elements; or: a system is the relation of structure and process, a unit that directs itself structurally in and through its own processes. Here you have unit, boundary, process, structure, element, relation – a whole bunch of terms – and, if you ask what the unity of all these terms is, you end up with the word "and." A system, then, is an "andness." Unity is provided by the "and" but not by any one element, structure, or relation.

The question is whether it is possible to transcend this "and-state" in the description of the object "system." I believe that it is possible if one pursues a principled operational approach. In other words, we must come to terms with the notion that it is actually a type of operation that produces the system, provided that there is time. A mere one-time event does not suffice. If an operation of a certain type has started and is, as I like to say, capable of connectivity – that is, if further operations of the same type ensue from it – a system develops. For, whenever an operation is connected to another, this happens selectively. Nothing else happens; the unmarked space or the environment remains outside. The system creates itself as a chain of operations. The difference between system and environment arises merely because an operation produces a subsequent operation of the same type.

How should one imagine this process? First of all, I believe that the biology of living beings can be described well in this way, especially in light of the information we glean from recent biochemical theories that tell us that life is a biochemical invention that happened only once. It is a circular structure or, to speak with Maturana,[27] an autopoiesis, a circular self-production. At some point in time, such a circular mode of operation was set in motion for reasons that can no longer be known with any precision and which one can state as a living being only if one is already alive. For evolutionary reasons this process multiplied, and then there were worms, snakes, human beings, and all forms that are possible on the basis of an orientational type that, in principle, always has the same chemical composition. From the viewpoint of operation, the unity of life is guaranteed in the strict sense. The necessary presupposition is that the effect of the operation contributes to the creation of a system. Life must live on. Life must be connected to, and followed by, life instead of dying immediately after birth. Additional inventions, such as bisexuality, the central nervous system, and so forth, presuppose such a mode of operation. Among other things, this means – and I will return to this point – that the concept of autopoiesis itself explains next to nothing, except this beginning with self-reference: an operation that possesses connectivity.

The previous thoughts can be applied to social systems if we succeed in identifying an operation that meets the following conditions: it must be one *single* operation; it must always be the same; and it must possess connectivity. It is this operation that either ceases or continues as the same operation. I think that we do not have many potential operations to choose from. In actual fact, communication is the only type of operation that meets these conditions. A social system emerges when communication develops from communication. There is no need to discuss the problem of the first communication, for the question "What was the first communication?" is already a question within a communicating system. In the beginning, the system always thinks outwards from its center. Once it has become complex enough, it can ask the question as to how it all began. There may then be different answers. However, they do not disturb the continuation of the communication. On the contrary, they may even quicken it. Thus, the question concerning the beginning or origin is of no particular interest to us; or, to put it differently, it interests us merely as one question among many.

What is interesting about the model I have presented is that it manages with a single type of operation. Yet much ought to be said now about how the notion of "communication" is to be understood. In other words, which concept of "communication" are we using here? At this juncture of my argument, I want to say only this much: communication can be conceived as the *synthesis* of information, utterance, and understanding. That is to say, that communication happens when information that has been uttered is understood.[28] "Communication" is the structural equivalent of biochemical statements by means of proteins and other chemical substances. It is of primary importance that there is a prospect of identifying an operator that makes possible all social systems, no matter how complex societies, interactions, or organizations might become in the course of evolution. From the viewpoint of an operational theoretical approach, everything exists because of the same basic occurrence, the same type of event: namely, communication.

Naturally, this usage of *communication* is intentional. Provided that we advance far enough in this lecture course, I will say something more about action theory at a later point in time. In relation to Parsons, we have already discussed this issue extensively. It is my opinion that the concept of action, in contrast to the concept of communication, does not meet the necessary requirements for functioning as a system-producing type of operation. For, on the one hand, the concept of action presupposes an agent to whom the action can be ascribed; on the other hand, the concept of action cannot easily be tailored specifically for sociality. Action occurs even when nobody is watching, when nobody else is there, when the agent does not expect that somebody else will react to her action – for instance, when somebody brushes her teeth while by herself. It is done merely because everybody knows that it ought to be done. True, one was told by somebody to do it and somebody put the toothbrush there for this purpose. However, in principle, action can be conceived of as a solitary, individual operation that has no social resonance. In the case of communication, this is not possible. Communication happens only if somebody understands it at least roughly or perhaps even misunderstands it; in any case, somebody must understand enough so that communication can continue. Language use alone cannot assure this possibility. It lies beyond the mere use of language. Somebody must be there who can be reached and who is capable of hearing or reading.

Let me summarize these two points once again. The first statement concerns the analysis of form: a system is a difference. The second statement says that a system needs only one single operation, one single type of operation, in order to reproduce the difference between system and environment if the system is to continue to exist (this "if" is of course not unimportant). In the case of the social system, we have identified communication as this type of operation. Communication is connected to communication.

A *third* point also relies on Spencer Brown and pertains to the concept of "re-entry" – that is, the re-entering of the form into the form or of the distinction into the distinguished. Initially, when I introduced Spencer Brown, I did not say anything explicit on this topic. You will recall that already the initial injunction "Draw a distinction!" is an injunction that concerns an operation which consists of two components, the distinction itself and the indication of one side, the pointer that tells you where you are and from where you might continue. Distinction is already provided for in the distinction. Using Kauffman's terminology, one might say that distinction is already copied into the distinction. In the course of developing his calculus, Spencer Brown eventually arrives at the point where he makes this premise explicit. He presents the re-entry of the form into the form or the distinction into the distinction as a theoretical figure that eludes calculus and therefore can no longer be treated in the form of arithmetic or algebra. However, in the sense that certain mathematical problems can be solved only by means of this figure, it belongs, as it were, to the cornerstones of the entire system. This leads Spencer Brown into a theory of imaginary numbers.

I suspect that we may have some difficulty imagining this re-entry, this entering of the form into the form, at the abstract level that is required. Spencer Brown draws circles in his book, but in the process he always takes the white sheet of paper for granted. However, as soon as we begin to deal with a theory of social systems and can take the regular apparatus of communication (which can also be communication about communication) for granted, the problem loses its difficulty and acquires a certain persuasive power. Therefore, one may ask oneself what purpose our theoretical exploit serves, especially as we merely acquire knowledge that we have known all along. I will return to the question of purpose. It is connected to the concept of paradox. But, for the time being, I will merely explicate what I mean.

What I mean is that a system can distinguish itself from its environment. Its operation *qua* operation produces the difference. This is why I use the term "difference" in this context. One operation connects with another; then a third one is added, a fourth and a fifth one. Then all that has hitherto been said becomes the topic of the next operation and is added to the series, and so forth. All this happens in the system. At the same time, something else, or nothing at all, happens outside the system. The outside world has only limited importance for the consequences of communication. If a system has to decide or to speak with greater caution, create couplings between one communication and another, then it must be able to discern, observe, and establish what is compatible with it and what is not. A system that intends to control its own conditions of connectivity must have at its disposal a type of operation that, for the time being, we may call "self-observation." I will return to the problem of the observer. (The problem is that the concepts are circular. I always have to presuppose something that I will explicate only later. This is necessarily the case for any system design of this type. For the moment, I would encourage you simply to accept observer and observation as terms that are yet to be explicated.) A system has to be capable of controlling its own conditions of connectivity. This is the case at least if you are thinking of systems that reproduce themselves via communication. We can distinguish communication from all that is not communication, particularly in the case of linguistic communication but also in the case of a standardized repertoire of signs. When I say "we," I do not mean individuals with their specific psychic structure, although it may be true for them as well. However, it is also possible that an individual is absent-minded at that very moment and may therefore not notice that communication is happening.

It is crucial that communication itself draws the distinction between communication and non-communication. Thus it is for instance possible to react with linguistic means to the fact that speaking has taken place and that one normally does not have to reckon with a denial of this fact. It is possible to get lost in interpretative difficulties or to look for excuses by explicating what was really meant. However, communication possesses the recursive certainty that it is based on communication; that it can and even has to restrict what can be said in the future (the same holds true of writing); and that, as a consequence, it can observe the difference between system and environment and thus separate self-reference from hetero-reference. This already becomes obvious when we look at the structure of communication. Communication happens only when something – specifically, a piece of information – is passed on by means of an utterance. Information and utterance already indicate the bipartite structure of communication. In addition, communication has to be understood. To begin with, we can say: there is speaking about something. A topic is being dealt with. This topic can even be the speaker himself. He can turn himself into the topic of his speaking and say, "I wanted to say something completely different." Or he can turn his own emotional state into a piece of information: "I don't feel like it anymore, I'll stop." As a matter of principle, there is always this bipartite structure of utterance and information. And communication can continue on the one or on the other side of this divide. Either the question "Why did you pass on something? Why did you say something?" or the question "Did you perhaps lie?" is turned into the topic of the subsequent communication. Thus, one proceeds either from the utterance or from the information, and then communicates about that which has been said.

Here we have an indication that the difference between hetero-reference *qua* information and self-reference *qua* utterance is always already included in the operation itself. This inclusion is yet another illustration of the general topic of re-entry: the system re-enters into itself or copies itself into itself. Communication remains an internal operation. It never exits the system, for the next connection is once again provided for and has to take place in the system. Self-reference (reference to that which takes place in the system) and hetero-reference (reference to the intended internal or external, past or present states of the system) must therefore be distinguished: one is the utterance, the other the information.

I believe that one can make plausible in this manner (even if it would be possible to offer a much more extensive and detailed treatment) that a social system that works with the operator "communication" always already includes re-entry and could not function otherwise. An internal reference or self-reference and an external or hetero-reference are processed more or less simultaneously. In other words, the system can switch from one side to the other at any moment – but only by means of internal operations. This explains the difference between the environment of a system from the standpoint of the observer and the environment as defined by the system itself, as it oscillates between self-reference and hetero-reference or as it chooses specific emphases in one or the other direction for a certain amount of time, but always under the condition that they may and can be revised and changed. This also means that one deals with a different environment depending on whether one has in mind an environment as defined by a system – that is, the hetero-reference of a particular system – or whether one assumes the existence of an external observer whose environment includes the system as well as its environment. It is entirely possible that the external observer can see many more and quite different things that are not necessarily accessible to the system itself. We might add that, in biology, Jakob von Uexküll showed an early awareness of the fact that the environment of an animal is not that which we would describe as its surroundings or *milieu*.[29] We can see more (or perhaps fewer) and other things than the ones an animal can perceive and process. Hence, two concepts of environment must be distinguished.

So far I have limited my commentaries to social systems. However, I would like to add an excursus (anticipating a later part of this course) in order to present the thesis that psychic systems, too, work by means of the coupling of self- and hetero-reference, and that this can be shown not with the help of much additional knowledge, but merely with a clear presentation using the terminology of two-sided forms, including such terms as "internal side," "external side," "re-entry," and so forth. Evidently, these theoretical figures or concepts suit psychic as well as social systems.

In psychology, and even more so in the philosophy of consciousness, these topics were treated for a long time from the viewpoint of reflection. There is a psychology of self-awareness; it poses questions concerning the production of identity and the consciousness of identity. The social-psychological literature produced by the likes of George Herbert Mead has familiarized us with such inquiries.[30] However, the tradition of the philosophy of reflection is much older and has perhaps also been more articulate on many counts.

Here I would just like to address for a brief moment Edmund Husserl's transcendental phenomenology, which is perhaps the most striking example of this philosophical tradition. Husserl arrived at the insight that the operations of consciousness can take place only if they are concerned with phenomena – that is, if they *intend* a phenomenon, no matter what the environment may be (this is an entirely different question).[31] From the viewpoint internal to consciousness, consciousness is concerned with phenomena and, at the same time, with itself. The terminology shifts slightly. Thus, "noema" designates the phenomenon one has in mind or imagines. "Noesis" is the name of the reflexively accessible thought process or process of consciousness itself, or, to put it differently, of the reflexivity of consciousness and the phenomenality of the world with which consciousness is concerned. "Intention" or "intentionality" as the occurrence of the coupling between the two sides is yet another feature. Every intention allows for the possibility of further exploration of the phenomena or of considering the following questions: "Why am I currently thinking about this? Why am I preoccupied with this? What is my consciousness actually doing? After all, there are more urgent tasks; for instance, I am hungry right now or I would like to smoke a cigarette,

yet I am preoccupied right now with phenomena." It is via such reflections that I arrive at other phenomena – a cigarette, say, or a sandwich.
This coupling is strict. Consciousness would never be able to lose itself
entirely in its environment to the point that it could no longer return to
itself. Similarly, it could not constantly be concerned merely with the
reflection "I think what I think what I think." At some point, the need for
phenomena becomes manifest.

For these reasons, this philosophy is called "transcendental phenomenology." It is "transcendental" insofar as it claims that this state of
affairs applies to all consciousness systems (or, in other words, to every
subject) and thus characterizes subjectivity as such, independent of the
empirical multiplicity of differentiated phenomena. After all, there are
many human beings, and each one of them is thinking about something
different at any moment. The transcendental structure is not necessarily
secured by *a prioris* but by this coupling of the reflexivity of consciousness
with "having" phenomena [*Phänomenehaben*]. I take this to be a precise
theory – that is, a theory that corresponds precisely to the one that would
result if we decided to represent consciousness by means of systems
theory, including, for instance, Spencer Brown's terminology. In that case,
too, we would arrive at the following questions: How does the difference
between system and environment re-enter the system? Does this actually
happen at all? In what way does the system depend for its operations on
re-entry? Could it operate without re-entry? (Evidently not.) And, finally,
wherein does the peculiar operational form of the system lie? For Husserl,
the operational form lies in intentionality, by means of which the problem
is solved from one moment to the next. In addition, this starting point
accounts for Husserl's distinct awareness of the importance of time. Every
operation relies on retention (that is, a side glance on everything that has
just happened) and on protention (the anticipation of everything that will
come about during the next couple of occurrences in consciousness). On
this basis, consciousness develops anticipations that are inspired by experience and theory, as well as a long-term memory. In principle, however,
it operates in the center of time, as it were, along an axis that traverses
the distinction between self- and hetero-reference. The result is a rather
complicated theory design.

When faced with such a theory design, we recognize how flat by comparison are the theories that nowadays are pursued under the heading
of "social phenomenology." As a matter of fact, all they express is that
"there is something." In a manner of speaking, all that is offered under
the name of the empirical is having-been [*Dagewesensein*]. One saw it and
now one describes it. All of a sudden, phenomenology serves to justify a
descriptive stance towards objects: "These are phenomena, and, since we
are conscious of them, we may assume that they must exist somewhere.
The precision of our description insures our method against possible
doubts regarding the phenomena. After all, others could go and look for

themselves." This attitude is almost certainly related to the transfer of Husserlian phenomenology to the United States. However, it was already discernible in Alfred Schütz's attempts at creating a unified theory out of both Max Weber's structure of motives and Husserl's phenomenology.[32] It would be possible to show in greater detail how this simplification arose.

If we return to a systems theoretical theory of consciousness, we will see better which fundamental theoretical decisions are at the root of phenomenology. In Husserl's mode of thinking, these fundamental decisions were still very much present. Nowadays, however, they are ignored as being simply present or given, or as of no further interest.

Having noticed that there are two cases in which the operational coupling of external and self-reference works, of course the questions arise as to why there should be only these two, and whether there are in fact further cases. Could we, for instance, discover something like self- and hetero-reference in biology, or at the very least in neurology and neurophysiology? I would prefer not to commit myself to an answer to this question. Such an answer would require precise knowledge of the field. However, at this moment in time I suppose that the difference between the brain and consciousness, or between the central nervous system and the phenomenally present consciousness, lies in the fact that consciousness introduces the difference between self- and hetero-reference. In consciousness, we imagine that all we perceive is somewhere outside, whereas the purely neurophysiological operations do not provide any such clues. They are entirely closed off and internal. Insofar as it is coupled with self-reference, consciousness is also internal, and it knows that it is. And that is a good thing, too, for it would be terrible if someone could enter someone else's consciousness and inject a few thoughts or a few perceptions of his own into it. Consciousness, too, is a closed system. But its peculiarity seems to lie – if we choose a very formal mode of description – in the transition from the purely operational closure of the electrophysical language of the neurophysiological apparatus to the difference between self-reference and hetero-reference. Only this central difference constitutes consciousness, of course on the basis of neurophysiological correlates. I do not intend to claim that consciousness is no longer in need of a brain. However, it is of great interest to ask whether we are dealing not just with a new level of reflection, as is often said – a learning of learning or a coupling of coupling – but with the introduction of a critical difference.

If the operational management of self- and hetero-reference is indeed the mark of a certain sphere of reality, it would be possible to formulate a program that would aim at establishing a link with the concept of meaning. Here, I can only hint at such a connection.[33] For the moment, the only thing of importance is that there are a number of clues indicating that the phenomenal presentation of the world or the informative relations of communication contain patterns or structures; we perceive these patterns as meaning. They are at the disposal of consciousness as well as communication. But in each case the operational base is quite different and the patterns will be marked by discrepancies that we will not be able to clarify without further efforts so long as we rely on world descriptions of the linguistic kind. We try to solidify the difference between the system of consciousness and social systems with regard to their respective operational base; at the same time, we try to maintain that there are agreements all the same – namely, the decisive guiding difference of hetero/self and all the meaning structures that emerge from it. But here is not yet the place to expand on these issues.

There is, however, a *fourth* point that shall occupy us at least for a short while. I have already alluded to it. Spencer Brown's theory design contains a well-hidden paradox. It is constituted by re-entry itself or – if we refer to the beginning of the calculus, the first injunction "Draw a distinction!" – by the fact that the distinction must be and is drawn merely in order to distinguish one side. Thus, every distinction contains two components: indication and distinction. The distinction contains itself, but apparently in a very specific form – namely, as the distinction between distinction and indication, and not merely some juxtaposition such as, say, of large and small, or anything else that could be conceived of as a distinction.

Accordingly, the re-entry of the form into the form – or of the distinction into the distinction, or of the difference between system and environment into the system – should be understood as referring to the same thing twice. The distinction re-enters the distinguished. This constitutes re-entry. Is the distinction now the same distinction it was before? Is that which existed before still there? Or does the first distinction disappear and thus become the second one? The answer is that we might well suspect that we are dealing with a paradox here, and that means that the distinction that re-enters itself is the same and, at the same time, not the same. And this is the whole trick of the theory: suspended between two markers, both of them paradoxical, a purely logical operational space is created. As is typical of paradoxes, this one, too, can be dissolved. In fact, a paradoxical formulation does not make much sense if one does not also possess a transformative formula, a formula that can dissolve the paradox. I think that such a solution can be accomplished with relative ease in the present case. It depends on the distinction that is drawn by an observer who is capable of distinguishing whether what is meant is his own distinction between system and environment (which could be another system or, if the observer is involved in reflection, an earlier state of his own system) or whether he is speaking of the distinction that is made within the observed system itself. The observer can make his appearance in two ways: as an external observer who sees that another system is observing itself, or as a self-observer, which is to say somebody who observes himself, refers to himself, and states something about himself.

With the help of this distinction between external and internal observation, the paradox can be solved or, as logicians sometimes say, "unfolded"[34] – that is to say, it is taken as relating to different identities and variable perspectives. Logically, this method is questionable and disreputable. But the logicians keep using it themselves, so we do not have to expect any reproach from that corner. Typically, the logicians distinguish between different levels. As soon as a paradox occurs, they move to another level in order to dissolve the paradox. To be sure, under such circumstances, one must not ask the question Wherein does the unity of the difference between the two levels consist? One dissolves a paradox by postulating two levels – a meta-level and a lower level, or the external observer and the self-observer – and by making this move more or less plausible. One can achieve this gain in plausibility or fruitfulness by pointing to the phenomena that are made visible through this strategy of solving the paradox and to the efficiency of a theory construction that distinguishes between internal and external observation.

For sociological analyses, especially at the level of the theory of society, it is important that one keeps in mind this entire genealogy, including the concept of form, re-entry, the paradox of re-entry, and the dissolution of the paradox through the distinction between observers. But now it is our turn, so to speak. We are external observers. Of course we know that we exist socially, that we live in a particular era, earn salaries, have expectations for our retirement, and so on – or even that we read books in which others have already written about most of the things we had wanted to write about ourselves. Of course we lead a social existence, but as sociologists we can contemplate society as if from the outside. Regardless of the fact that we ourselves communicate in order to teach these things to other people, we can say that we observe society and see that society presents itself as a self-describing system. This system has two sides. On the one hand, society contains hetero-references. It does not speak just about itself but under normal circumstances also about something that is not communication but the topic of communication. Leaving the logical genealogy aside, I dealt with this question in a little book on ecological communication.[35] In it, I proceeded from the assumption that ecological communication is just communication about ecological questions and that the sociological description of a communicating system reduces the irritation over ecological problems to a communicative phenomenon. "Dead fish are floating in the Rhine." Once upon a time, that could have been a folksong; but nowadays it is alarming news. What is produced by means of this alarm is more obvious. We have certain connective expectations that are available for prospective manipulative purposes. Nonetheless, we are dealing first and foremost with a matter of communication. Whatever happens in society is communication. For this reason, we in our role as sociologists must be able to distinguish between, on the one hand, that about which people talk, write, print, and broadcast and, on the other hand, that which is actually the case, so that we can see that certain topics could also have been chosen differently.

I do not – heaven forbid! – mean to suggest that the choice of topic is arbitrary and that everything could just as well have been done differently. Neither do I mean to say that the preoccupations of contemporary society are mere coincidences, fads thought up by journalists. No, far from it. But naturally we must look at the reasons that lead our society to refer to such states of affairs within a system of communication and to process such topics in a preferential manner, as it were. Along this path, one also gains access to specific questions. One finds out whether only the popular press speaks about them; whether they are only a topic of instruction in schools or of discussion in youth groups; how the economy reacts to them; in other words, which of the three enumerated systems communicates about these topics and what the consequences of such communication are. These are the sociologically interesting facts about the topic at hand – not the fact that the fish are dying.

This double perspective would also allow us to deal with the ideological quality of self-description in a society. Why did societies in the nineteenth and twentieth centuries describe themselves as "capitalist"? Why did they describe themselves in the second half of the eighteenth century as "patriotic"? Why are certain schematic models of society/community and individual/collective preferred at certain times, only to be neglected at other times? Why do notions like "modernity" and "post-modernity" arise? Why is the schema of tradition/modernity used for the representation of society? In our role as sociologists, we can assume the attitude of external observers, who we can never be in reality, and ask how it happens that systems prefer a certain self-description. With this, we return to the sociological tradition of ideology critique or even to the sociology of knowledge or Reinhart Koselleck's version of historical-social semantics.[36] But now we have more theoretical confidence in this position than was possible at a time when a free-floating intelligence in Karl Mannheim's sense[37] was presupposed, or, for that matter, when the mode of self-observation for a capitalist society was described, in keeping with Adam Smith and David Ricardo, by means of market laws, profit rates, and similar phenomena, and nobody noticed that the argument was tied to the position of the capitalist while everything else was neglected. The same restrictions apply in the case of work that relied on Freudian complexes and all sorts of other concepts that gained prominence at one time or another.

We would instead begin with the sociology of self-describing systems, of the systems that couple self- and hetero-reference. They do this in a selective fashion, referring to structures that have been around for some time and to the historical state of society in this very moment with its specific issues. Thus, we can occupy a somewhat more distanced position due to the figure of re-entry. In my next lecture, I will speak about operational closure. This follows more or less automatically from the issues I dealt with today. If there is an operator, it functions only within a system, and thus one arrives at the thesis of the operational closure of this system.

3 Operational Closure

Fifth Lecture

In our last class, we spoke of the difference principle or the differential approach of systems theory. The thesis was that a system is not a unity but rather a difference, and, as a consequence, we have to face the difficulty of conceiving the unity of a difference. If something is said to be distinguished and, at the same time, not to be distinguished, and if thus these two things are said to be the same thing, one encounters a paradox. Once again, I would like to begin with the question of how one might handle paradoxes if one notices them. For there are many paradoxes that one does not notice. To give an example: a few months ago, I stayed in small apartment hotel in Brisbane directly on the Brisbane River. A telephone was hanging on the wall of this apartment. Lifting the receiver, one discovered a small piece of paper on the phone that said "If defective, call ..." followed by a number. This can be translated as "If you cannot act, then act." What should one do with such a paradox? It can be dissolved if one distinguishes between defective and non-defective telephones, copies the number, finds another phone, and calls said number. One deals with paradoxes by finding a distinction that suits them and fixes identities (such as: this telephone, other telephones) and in this way at least remains capable of action.

In systems theory it is not so easy. First of all, one would say that there is the distinction between system and environment. This distinction is the difference that constitutes a system. But the question that immediately arises is: Who draws this distinction? The answer to this question leads us to the topic of this lecture – namely, the topic of operational closure. The distinction between system and environment is produced by the system itself. This does not exclude the possibility that a different observer observes this distinction, which is to say, observes that a system exists in an environment. From the viewpoint of the thesis of operational closure, the important issue consists in the fact that the system draws its own boundaries by means of its own operations, that it thereby distinguishes itself from its environment, and that only then and in this manner can it be observed as a system. This always happens in a very specific way, not just in any way, but in a way that we can determine more precisely with the concepts of operation and the operational – which is to say, by means of the manner in which the system produces itself through system-specific operations.

A living being, for instance, creates this difference simply by living and continuing to live as long as it can. A social system creates the difference between system and environment through the occurrence of communication – that is, by establishing relations between independent living beings – and by the fact that this communication follows its own specific logic of connectivity, the continuation of communication, its own memory, and so forth. In George Spencer Brown's terminology one might say that the system always operates on the inside of the form – that is, in itself, and not on the outside. But this operation on the inside – that is, in the system as opposed to the environment – presupposes that there is in fact an outside, an environment. If one avoids such extravagant formulations, the entire matter appears as rather trivial, for it is probably immediately intuitive that a system cannot operate in its environment and that its operations thus always take place within the system. If systems operations did actually take place in the environment, the distinction between system and environment would be undermined.

All this becomes less trivial and even surprising if one thinks a bit further and considers the consequences of the fact that a system cannot use its own operations to get in touch with the environment. And this is precisely the point made by the thesis of operational closure. Operations are from beginning to end (or, in other words, if seen as events) always possible only inside a system, and they cannot be used to make an intervention in the environment. For, in that case, when a border is crossed, they would have to become something other than system operations. This insight made an impression, first of all, in epistemology. Choosing a radical formulation, one might say that knowledge is possible only because there are no operational relations between system and environment. You may think about this for a long time! Knowledge is possible not only *in spite of,* but also *because of,* the fact that the system is operationally closed. With its cognitive operations, it cannot intervene in the environment but must always search within the system for a connection, a deduction, a further insight, or recourse to the system memory.

The thesis states that systems are operationally closed. They rely entirely on internal operations. Now, this formulation could give rise to the suspicion that all of this is merely a return to the old thesis of closed systems and thus to the problem of entropy. But this is not the case. For within the theory of operational closure one must now distinguish between operation and causality. When we describe a system, operations must be described very specifically. Either we are looking at the biochemical structure that enables a cell to live; or we are dealing with language use, the communicative sequence of operations; or, finally, we focus on the operations of consciousness that rely on actual attentiveness and are distinguished from the biochemistry of life as well as from communication. Operations must be characterized in a way that also determines the type of system we are talking about in each case. In our case this includes the types of living, conscious, and social systems. At least at first sight, this has nothing to do with causality. According to this version of systems theory, causality is a matter that concerns the observer.

Causality is a judgment, the observation of an observer, a coupling of causes and effects, depending on how the observer formulates his interests and in what way the observer considers effects or causes to be important or unimportant. Causality is a selective proposition: one is interested in certain causes because one is uncertain about the effects. Or else one would like to achieve certain effects, and therefore one poses the question backwards from this endpoint and looks for the causes that make them possible. Formally speaking, causality is a schema of world observation. It would be possible to look for a further cause of every cause, and from every effect one could move on to yet another effect, perhaps even a side effect or an unintentional effect. But of course such a procedure has its limits. We are not capable of analyzing the entire world in such causal terms. Such a procedure would explode the information capacity of any observing system. For this reason, causality is always selective and can therefore always be assigned to an observer with specific interests, specific structures, and specific capacities for information processing. This is true simply because of the infinitude of all further causalities that are involved.

This is also true because there are modes of assigning causality that are rather unusual – for instance, the causality of negative facts: "Yesterday evening my car door on the driver's side did not open. If this happens again, I will have to bring my car to the workshop. Then the door must be repaired, or they will have to put the steering wheel on the other side." A negative fact thus becomes the cause of a certain way of acting. The door did *not* open. The assignment of structures constitutes a comparable case of an unusual assignment of causality – for instance, when capitalist society is said to be the cause for certain effects because of certain structures linked to the conversion of labor into monetary terms. Thus, there is not just the infinity of cause and effect. There are also the causalities of omission and of structure, at least for systems that are capable of taking them into consideration.

Once again, we must observe the observer if we want to know which kind of causality is ascribed in a certain case and which effects and causes are brought into an attributive connection. An enormous amount of research exists on this topic.[38] The results of this research on attribution force us to take the concept of causality as relative to specific observers or habits of attribution. This is the flip side, as it were, of the necessary distinction between the operation that constitutes and reproduces a system, on the one hand, and causal claims, on the other. Moreover, it goes without saying that observers who employ causal schemata must in turn function as systems. Thus, for instance, they must live or be conscious or communicate depending on the requirements concerning a causal analysis of the system in relation to its environment. It is this distinction between causality and operation that prevents us from falling back onto the old theory of closed systems, for those systems were conceived as causally closed.

A further step consists in the possibility of distinguishing between meaning systems and technical systems from this vantage point. For a long time, systems theory had to deal with the suspicion of being a sort of technical theory, a theory of engineers and technicians, and even of technologically oriented planners who wanted to secure specific causal connections. It is possible from the vantage point of operational closure to distinguish between technical or causal closure, on the one hand, and meaning-related [*sinnhafter*] openness, on the other. The question of meaning-related openness concerns topics with which I will deal later. For the time being, I would like to say only that the difference between system and environment is at the system's disposal. I have already spoken of re-entry. The system cannot refer to the environment operationally, but it can do so at the level of meaning [*sinnmäßig*]. It can refer to the environment by means of the meaning [*Sinn*] of its operations without, however, using its operations to create causal effects in the environment – effects that are possible only if the environment welcomes them and provides the corresponding causalities. We are dealing here with the distinction between the technical and the meaningful [*sinnhaft*]. In essence, technical systems are causally closed. They react to environmental irritations only under specific conditions. We may think here of machines that run only when the electricity is on or when the necessary influx of energy is regulated in a certain way, and which can be controlled only by means of specific handles or interventions that affect the running of the machine. The advantages of such technical or causal closure lie first and foremost in the possibility of recognizing errors. In the domain of operational closure this is not possible without further ado. If the system continues to operate, it continues. Whether something is erroneous or not depends, once again, on an observer and his standards regarding valuable achievements or survival chances or any other criteria. In technical systems, the problem is much more precisely defined. The machine simply stops running, and that indicates that an error has occurred. No doubt, one can find the error if one is capable of controlling the technical structure of the machine.

Moreover, in the case of such technically closed systems it is possible to plan ahead with regard to the necessary resources. One has an approximate idea of how much energy is needed, how one can accelerate or slow down the process, how much oil must be added, and how much time is needed to manufacture a certain product or bring about a certain movement. In the discussion of technical closure – a question that has become widely debated – it has become apparent that we have reached a technological limit for technically closed systems. The name for this is "high technology" or "high-risk technology."[39] What is meant by this, in the nuclear industry, for instance, is the existence of large chemical production technologies or technologies that include radioactivity. Here, the problem when a machine breaks down is not merely that the performance itself is insufficient. It is also that many other things happen. Containment, as one says in English – that is, keeping the problems inside – is not always successful. The machine may explode, and it can cause immense damage so that a second technology is necessary, which in turn cannot always be subject to technical closure. Whenever technical closure does not succeed, which is to say, whenever the security technology cannot itself achieve security strictly on technical grounds but instead needs psychic or social performance, the price to pay is typically the unreliability of operationally closed systems. First of all, these systems function only by reproducing themselves in one way or another. And often they prove unpredictable for an observer. Investigations of accidents in the nuclear industry, as well as the catastrophe of the *Challenger* space shuttle, have shown us the role that psychic logic and informal organization play. Although the error was noticed, no reaction followed, simply because hitherto everything had always gone well. The first time that the error was noticed, it either went unheeded or was noticed too late for anything to be done. The next time, one knows that the error denotes nothing untoward is going on, since nothing happened the first time around. The organization then gets into the habit of sticking to the timetable, since that appears to be more important than correcting every single error. The logic of this type of social organization sooner or later leads to a point where something will eventually go wrong. Such problems are relevant today; they explode the difference between systems that operate and re-create themselves by way of meaning, on the one hand, and technical, causal closure, on the other. Increasingly, we have to deal with the collapse of this distinction.

It is possible to formulate this insight in the terminology that was proposed by Heinz von Foerster and which may well become important for social analysis. Von Foerster distinguishes between trivial and non-trivial machines.[40] In this context, "machines" should be understood in the cybernetic sense; they include mathematical forms, computational rules, rules of transformation, and similar entities. In this context, the term "machine" is not limited to mechanical or electronic actualizations. At issue are machines in a very general sense. Trivial machines are characterized by the fact that the input is transformed into output according to a specific rule, so that, whenever information or energy quanta are fed into the machine, the machine operates and produces a certain result. If one feeds it with a different input, it operates again and produces a different result, provided it has several functions at its disposal. For instance, if one feeds the number "1" into the machine, it goes "tak, tak, tak" and "A" comes out as the result. And if one feeds the number "2" into the machine, it goes "tak, tak, tak" and "B" comes out as the result. If one then again feeds "1" into the machine, once again one receives "A" as the result. But if, in fact, one were to receive "B" instead, one could not help the feeling that this is already a non-trivial machine or, alternatively, that something is broken. Presumably, one would put one's first bet on repair, since hitherto the machine has been functioning as a trivial machine.

In contrast, non-trivial machines always interpose their own state and pose questions in between – questions such as: "Who am I?" "What have I just done?" "In what kind of mood am I?" "How strong is my interest at this point?" and so on – and only then do they produce their output. A self-referential loop is built in. In the older terminology, one expressed this by saying that the machine uses its own output as its input. It orients and steers itself by means of what it just did, and it contains a controlling apparatus that keeps constant what ought to happen. The general consequence of this concept of the non-trivial machine is that the machine must be considered as incalculable and unpredictable, or, more precisely, that it is predictable only for someone who would know precisely what state the machine is in on each occasion that it has questioned itself.

This distinction makes clear, first and foremost, that conscious systems are non-trivial machines. On the other hand, we can see clearly that, in the field of sociology, a strong wish prevails that social systems ought to be constructed as trivial machines. If you imagine a court in which a judge applies the law, he is taken to function like a trivial machine. Whenever a specific input is fed into the machine, a certain distinction is the result. Thus, if the preconditions of, say, a divorce are fulfilled, then the marriage in question will be dissolved. It would not be tolerated if the court decided that it had already dissolved so many marriages that for once it would simply reject an application for divorce. That is to say, it would not be acceptable if the court, whether out of boredom or some other strange mood that resulted from its own activity, suddenly reacted differently than what would be expected outside. The same case can be made for the educational system. I met with a lot of resistance when I tried to explain to some teachers that they attempt to educate their pupils like trivial machines in that the students have to give the right answers to specific questions. If the answer is wrong, it is wrong. If the answer is right, it is right. If it is wrong, the machine contains an error, and if it is right, then everything is working well. In such a system, it is simply not acknowledged that a student might, for instance, question the question in question; or look for a creative way out, such as looking at a mathematical formula from an aesthetic viewpoint and thus reading it like concrete poetry according to the distribution of letters (or numbers) on the page;

or do something that could be explained only if that student's momentary emotional state was known.

One can see that trivial machines function reliably and that in daily life we depend to a high degree on taking for granted that others function reliably. This is so even if it does not correspond with our humanistic notions of society or the conditions for respecting other people. This distinction is analytically important, because we must reconsider, time and again, whether we really can do without the non-trivial. To what degree can we make something trivial, and to what degree can we make it non-trivial? Alternatively, we could ask to what degree our ability to understand, for example in the field of art appreciation, depends on repetition. We must already know 90 percent of the aesthetic stimuli in order to be surprised by the remaining 10 percent. A lot of things must function exactly as they have functioned all along so that we can see something that contrasts with this routine, something that is innovative and can be explained only if the work is analyzed in more detail.

These are the main points I would like to make on the topic of operational closure. Already the position of this topic in the architecture of this lecture course indicates that this is, in fact, the decisive distinction we need to make. Besides the differential approach, this is the switch that indicates that systems theory is now moving on a different track and will come, at particular junctures, to unusual conclusions – especially the conclusion that the system cannot get in touch with the environment through its own operations. If one thinks this through in general, one will, at particular junctures, arrive at results that are sometimes difficult to understand and definitely do not coincide with the usual conceptions of society or those of individuals. From this vantage point, I wrote a small book on ecological communication, and, although I tried to keep it as easy as possible, it became a difficult text. This happened because it is implausible and even disappointing if one claims that talking is the only thing that can be done about environmental problems and, moreover, does not change anything.[41] Yet if we do not begin to talk, then nothing will happen either. Thus, in light of numerous environmental problems, the operational closure of a communication system presents itself as if nothing at all could happen – which is to say, as if operational closure amounted to the complete isolation of a system. But this is not the case. I will return to this issue in the section on structural coupling. There are structural couplings that, one might say, bundle, accumulate, and channel causalities. Thereby, they coordinate or integrate system and environment without in any way affecting the thesis of operational closure. Indeed, it is precisely because systems are operationally closed that they can be influenced through structural couplings, at least in the long run.

But for the time being, I have to postpone this topic since I still have another section to deal with that is especially important in the current discussion, namely, the issue of self-organization and autopoiesis. It is part of my objective to look at this topic, too, from the perspective of operational closure. Taking my lead from my experiences in many discussions of self-organization and autopoiesis, I have reached the conclusion that the thesis of operational closure is the starting point from which one ought to explain these two concepts, and not the other way around. And I maintain this in spite of the history of the theory that developed in the opposite direction in the course of the scientific genesis of this entire discussion; for operational closure was in fact discovered through a detour via autopoiesis, and not vice versa.

4 Self-Organization, Autopoiesis

First of all, let us examine these two concepts. These are two different concepts that I consciously distinguish. Both are based on the theorem of operational closure, which is to say that both of them have as their foundation not only a differential but also a principally operational system concept. Time and again it must be said that this means that the system has only its own operations at its disposal. In the system, there is nothing but the system's own operations. These operations serve two distinct purposes. On the one hand, they are needed for the formation of the system's structures. The structures of an operationally closed system must be through the system's very own operations. In other words, there is rtation of structures! This is what is meant by "self-organization." he other hand, the system has only its own operations at its disposal in order to determine its historical state, which is to say, its present, s the only point of departure for everything that is to follow. As he system is concerned, the present is determined by the system's erations. What I have just said is the point of departure that I must o account when I try to reflect on what I can say subsequently. er I am thinking about just now, whatever happens in my consciousness at this very moment, whatever I perceive – all this is the point of departure for an understanding of subsequent perceptions. I know that I am in this room at this particular spot, and, if I jumped around erratically, I would have to consider the possibility that I must have taken some kind of drug and therefore am no longer capable of actualizing the normal continuity of perception that supports the interpretation of surprising events. We are dealing here with two issues: the first one concerns "self-organization," in the sense that a particular structure is produced by the system's own operations, and the second concerns "autopoiesis," in the sense that the system state that serves as the point of departure for many further operations is determined by the operations of the very same system.

I would like to begin my discussion with some remarks on self-organization. Perhaps it is best, first of all, to provide some clarity about the fact that, within the confines of an operational theory, structures are effective only in the moment when the system operates. Here we see once again the distance between this theory and classical conceptions, for this point contradicts the idea that structures are what last while processes and operations fade away. In this theory, structures are relevant only in the present. They can only be used, one might say, as long as the system operates. And everything that happened or will happen at some point belongs either to the past or to the future but is not present in the here and now. Every temporally overarching description of structures (for example, everything that can be seen, if one observes that we conduct this lecture course always at the same hour in the same room, although perhaps not always with exactly the same people present but at least with the same lecturer), all of this together, is a structure that in turn requires an observer. And for the observer the same is true. He, too, can observe all this only when he is observing, which is to say, when he is actively operating. Regardless of whether one contemplates the system in operation or relates the operation to the observation of other operations, everything stands in relation to the topic of simultaneity, the present, and actuality. The system must be in operation to make use of structures.

Once this is clear, one also recognizes that the description in question is, once again, the description of an observer (regardless of whether one wants to find out what a psychological structure is; or how one characterizes individuals and how one could describe them or their habits; or, if social systems are at issue, how one describes, say, a university). One identifies the structures – but this is done only when a system that is in a position to do this actually does it. This implies that descriptive characterizations of structures are relative to the operating system. And this means that, accordingly, even the projections into the past – that is, the recourse to the past – and equally the anticipation of the future must be adjusted to this theory. The structure is in each case effective only at the present moment, and whatever past data are used are linked to those future projections that are summoned up. The coupling of something that is usually called "memory" and something else that is usually called "expectation" or "projection" (which would also include purposes or ends, if we are thinking of actions) happens in the present and only in the present.

The memory is not the stored past. What is past is past and can never again become the here and now. Rather, the memory is a sort of consistency test for which it is typically not necessary to recall when something specific was or was not learned. Speaking German at this moment, I do not have to know when I learned this language, or how it happened at all, or when I used or read certain words such as "autopoiesis" for the first time. What is decisive, and what one wants to achieve in the future in the context of expectations, anticipations, ends, and such, is present recall, the present test of the applicability, one might say, of structures. In this sense, this approach is entirely pragmatic. There is a connection between, on the one hand, the theory of memory and, on the other, a pragmatic orientation towards the future. This connection is always rather tight. One might perhaps say that memory is nothing but a continuous consistency test of different information, always in light of certain expectations – be it that one is aiming at certain achievements, be it that one is afraid of something, or be it that one simply sees something coming and would like to react to it. We are not dealing here with a theory of memory that relies in any way on the notion of storage. And neurophysiology seems to confirm this theory.[42] After all, in the nervous system, there are no actual nerve cells where the past can be found to be stored. What one finds instead is cross-referencing, the testing of different established habits on specific occasions at certain points in time.

From this perspective, it would seem advisable to take the concept of expectation as the basis for a definition of structures. Structures, then, are expectations in relation to the connectivity of operations. These operations can consist of mere experience or of action. And expectations should be understood in a sense that is not necessarily subjective at all. There is a critique of this concept of expectation that accuses it of the subjectivization of the idea of structure. But the tradition of this concept of expectation is much older and does not necessarily apply only to psychic structures. The concept of expectation was introduced in psychology in the thirties in order to complicate the rigid input/output relations and stimulus–response models that were prevalent. Thus, it became possible to imagine that stimulus and response do not stand in a fixed relation to each other but instead are controlled by the expectations of the system. A stimulus can only be identified if one has certain expectations. In a way, one is surveying the terrain, where one perceives something and receives stimuli, in light of expectations that come to the fore in specific situations or else emerge habitually. The notion of "generalized expectations" (George Herbert Mead), among others, is derived from this view. In the first place, this indicates a break with the older behaviorist psychology. Secondly, this view was subsequently adopted by social theory – in the precise sense that roles were seen as bundled expectations and communication was understood as communicating expectations, regardless of the actual private thoughts of the persons involved. Expectations thus formulate a certain aspect that may be presented either psychically or in social communication as the future aspect of meaning.

For such a theory that defines the concept of structure by means of expectations, the subject–object distinction is meaningless. Some time ago, there was a discussion with Johannes Berger in Bielefeld, in which he criticized the concept of expectation as subjective and therefore in principle useless for sociologists, since sociologists are more interested in objective social structures.[43] If you have taken courses in structural analysis, you probably also had the impression that, in dealing with structures, one is dealing with objective facts that can be buttressed with a statistical or a Marxist or any other type of account without needing to relativize what individual people think in each case. But the design of the present systems theory makes it apparent that I want to try to escape this subject–object distinction and to replace it with the distinction of, on the one hand, the operation and, on the other hand, the observation of this operation, whether it is performed by the system itself or by another system. This distinction is performatively drawn whenever an operation is performed.

Under such conditions, the concept of expectation no longer contains any subjective component. Instead, the concept of expectation poses the question of how structures can achieve the reduction of complexity without, as it were, limiting the entire system to just one capacity. How ought one to conceive of a system that has at its disposal a rich array of structures, for instance via language, without being limited by the selection of this or that sentence, which is to say, without immediately losing this structural variety again? On the contrary, in many instances structures are built without the need to determine the situation in which these structures are used. The concept of structure must include an explanation as to why the system does not shrink when it continuously has to make decisions, continuously has to perform this or that connectivity operation. It must explain why it does not shrink but may even, depending on the circumstances, grow and gain in complexity, although it is constantly forced to reduce complexity. The more possibilities a system has – once again you may look at language as the extraordinary example that makes this clear – the more selective is every single sentence, and the less stereotypical is the speech. One can see this, for instance, if different social classes are compared – say, the stereotypical form of lower-class language, especially in England, and the elaborate form of upper-class language. An elaborate language finds the right word in every situation and often has the ability to express itself more to the point when its structure is extremely elaborated and complicated than when only a restricted vocabulary is at its disposal. This difference must be captured by means of the concept of structure. The actual achievement consists precisely in connecting high structural complexity with the ability to operate. This also shows why the transition from trivial to non-trivial machines is important. For trivial machines have only those operations at their disposal that have been determined by the program and the input. In contrast, structurally complex systems can bring into play this lesson of adapting to situations on their own and can thereby take into consideration their own thoughts, if you will, or their own communicative habits. As a consequence, these systems have a much greater repertoire of action possibilities. The problem is precisely of how to explain this difference. The concept of structure is important in this context and not so much the question of how to choose between subjectivity and objectivity.

My last point concerns the question Why does one speak of self-organization? A system can operate only with structures that it has built itself. It cannot import structures. This, too, needs to be explained. If you look at research concerning language acquisition, it is almost incomprehensible how a child can acquire language as quickly as it does. Some of you probably know that Noam Chomsky tried to solve the problem by postulating natural deep structures that are innate but can never be discovered empirically.[44] Modern communication research would probably rather say that we learn language in the process of communication itself when speakers lay claim to us, if you like. Such speakers simply assume that their audience will understand even when they know that they do not yet understand. The habit of separating certain noises as language and of repeating certain meanings comes about as a sort of exercise. At least this would not contradict the thesis that structure can be built only inside a system.

If one subscribes to a different concept, one would have to imagine that someone who is learning to speak is educated in a certain sequence. The way such learners have to speak is prescribed, but they do not begin to speak by themselves. Under this assumption, one would be hard pressed to register the variety of different modes of linguistic development. Research on dyslexia and writing and reading errors has shown that, in a school class, the tendency to make mistakes is very unevenly distributed. For this reason, there cannot be uniform didactics of learning how to read and learning how to write because the tendency to make mistakes differs from child to child. One child reacts more to the sound of language, another prefers to shorten words and leaves out letters. The upshot of these findings is that the individuality of the process of learning a language and subsequently of learning how to read and write is very high – much higher, in fact, than is commonly assumed. In order to take this factor into account, it is inevitable, I believe, to reorient the learning process towards self-organization. This is not to say that an observer could no longer determine whether the words a child has learned are the same as those that can be found in the *Duden*[45] or as other people use them. However, this fact cannot be explained by means of an importation of structures, but only by structural coupling, to use a concept about which I will speak in the next section.

At the level of abstraction of a general theory, we still know very little about how structural development actually happens. In any case, I imagine that it certainly does not proceed in the same way as the production of a thing for which one knows the necessary components and simply puts them together. The specificity of structural formation seems to consist in the fact that one must, first of all, repeat – which is to say that one must recognize one situation as the repetition of another. If everything were always completely new, one would never be able to learn anything. Of course, everything *is* always completely new. Every one of you looks different today than in our last meeting, sits on a different seat, has a different way of looking, sleeps differently or writes differently; if you examine a situation very concretely, it will always be incomparable. Yet, there are these difficult phenomena to describe. For instance, one recognizes faces again and again. If you wanted to know what causes you to recognize somebody, or if you had to describe the person that you recognize, you would have considerably more difficulty in solving these problems than in the process of recognition itself! Consider the identikit pictures of suspects [*Phantombilder*] in the newspapers that are constructed with much effort from the descriptions of eyewitnesses and the help of computers. This process is complicated, whereas recognition under normal circumstances happens swiftly. In order to be able to repeat something at all – and this is again a circular argument – we have to be able to recognize something, which is to say that we have to be able to do two things. First, we must be able to make an identification, which means, in classical terms, that we must recognize essential traits or indications of particular identities. In the second place, we must generalize in such a manner that we can reuse this identity in spite of situational differences and often considerable variations from the original situation. Thus, we are dealing first of all with a limitation or condensation of something. At the same time, and for that very reason, we are also dealing with a generalization, precisely in the sense that we can recognize the same people in entirely different situations and after many years, or that in language we can use the same words again although we use them in different sentences, or on another day, or in a different mood, or in the morning instead of the evening, and so forth.

This theory seems to confirm that the continuous testing of identification and generalization, or, to put it even more paradoxically, of specification and generalization, can only be an achievement of the system itself that can be brought about solely in a psychic system or in a communication system. If this communication system did not work, we would never be able to learn a language. The communication system puts words and also standardized gestures at our disposal that can be repeated and used in other contexts, albeit with very different effects, since a word has very different meaning references depending in which sentence it is spoken. It is this ambivalence, or this paradox of specification and generalization, which to me seems to be the reason that this entire development can take place only inside a system. In the alternative case, one would have to imagine that here the production of something, like the production of things, can be learned by means of recipes and, of course, instructions.

In wrapping up this part of my argument, let me refer to Maturana, who spoke of "structurally determined systems." The expression has in a certain sense entered the literature.[46] However, if we take the expression literally, it describes only half of the state of affairs in question. The operations of a system presuppose structures, otherwise there would be only a limited repertoire of operations with fixed structures. The richer the structural choices [*Strukturvolumen*], the greater the variety of operations and the better the system recognizes itself as the determinant of its own state and its own operations. But, on the other hand, the exact opposite is also true. The structures can only be built through the system's own operations. It is a circular process: structures can be built only through the system's own operations because the system's own structures in turn determine its operations. This is obvious in the case of the biochemical cell structure, for the operations simultaneously contribute to the build-up of the programs – in this case, the enzymes – in accordance with which the cell regenerates structures as well as operations. The same is the case in social systems, if we think of language. Language [*Sprache*] is possible only through the operation of speaking [*Sprechen*]. A language would be quickly forgotten, or would never be learned in the first place, if one never had the chance to speak and never had the opportunity to communicate. But, in turn, language is the condition of possibility for speaking. This circular relation presupposes as its framing or as its condition of possibility the identity of certain systems in which this circle is put into operation or transformed into sequences, so that time, as it were, dissolves the circle. Only if this system is described as abstracted from time does it appear circular. In reality, there are operations with minimal structural expenditure that build up more complex structures, which in turn make possible more differentiated operations.

This, by the way, is also the point of contact where evolutionary theoretical considerations enter the picture, which I have excluded in the present lecture. For it would be the task of evolutionary theory to explain how it is possible that, on the basis of one-time inventions (such as the biochemistry of life or meaningful communication, which is to say, the meaningful or sense-producing exchange of signs), highly complex systems or a large variety of species can arise. The task is, to put it differently, to explain how structural richness is generated in spite of the fact that, in each case, it is a matter of only *one* type of operation and that the whole thing is of a circular design. The structures depend on the operations because the operations depend on the structures. The whole thing has the bad smell of paradox only because the paradox is a formulation that is abstracted from time. In contrast, reality takes time and is able to develop only in this way.

The second part of this section concerns the so-called autopoiesis. The point of departure for our considerations is that whatever was said about structures is also true for the operations themselves. I have already let this point tacitly be part of my argument, simply because I was unable to present in any other way the concept of structures and operations that are connected with each other in a circular network. Conversely, the theory of autopoiesis – I will return to the meaning of this term in a moment – is also a condition for the possibility of representing structures in the manner that I just stated. According to Maturana's definition, autopoiesis means that a system can generate its own operations only by means of the network of its own operations.[47] And the network of its own operations is generated, in turn, by these operations. In a certain sense, this formulation says too much, and for this very reason I have tried to pull it apart. On the one hand, we are dealing here with the thesis of operational closure. The system generates itself. Not only does it produce its own structures, like certain computers that are able to develop programs for themselves, but it is also autonomous at the level of operations. It cannot import any operations from its environment. If we take it seriously *as thought*, no foreign thought can enter into my head. And no chemical process can become communicative. If I pour ink over my paper, it becomes illegible, but no new text is produced. Such operational closure is merely another way of formulating the statement that an autopoietic system by means of the network of its own operations generates the operations that it needs in order to generate operations. Maturana in his Chilean-American English speaks of "components." This concept is unclear – but at the same time also covers a lot of territory – because he leaves open whether the term "components" designates the operations or the structures. This distinction may be less important for a biologist, because biology does not deal exclusively with merely event-like operations but with chemical states and with the change of chemical states in the cell. For this reason the concept of an element can, in this case, still be understood in terms of a state, even if it is a state of short temporal duration. In the fields of the theory of consciousness and the theory of communication, however, the event-like nature of basic elements that cannot be divided any further imposes itself. A sentence is a sentence. It is spoken when it is spoken and does not endure after the fact, nor was it there before the fact. A thought or a perception when I see something has actuality in this very moment, but it no longer has it afterwards and nor did it have it earlier. These examples make apparent the event-like nature [*das Ereignishafte*] of these operations. I have a feeling that this leads to a sharper division between structures and operations and to the renunciation of the concept of the "component." However, this remark is intended merely as a sort of reading instruction for Maturana's texts. In principle, I do not see a decisive difference between his theory and mine.

But why "autopoiesis"? Maturana told me how he came up with this expression. Originally, he had been working with circular structures – namely, with the circular reproduction of the cell. The word "circular" is an imported word that does not cause any further problems, but for Maturana it was not precise enough. And then, as it happened, a philosopher gave him a lesson in Aristotle at some dinner party or some other social event. The philosopher explained to him the difference between *"práxis"* and *"poiésis." "Práxis"* is an action that *qua* action has meaning in itself. Aristotle has in mind the ethos of city life, virtue, excellence, *"areté"* – all of which are important not because of their success, resulting in the creation of a good *polis*, but because they are meaningful *as such*. Other examples would include swimming, which one does not do because one wants to get to a particular place, or smoking, or chatting, or rational debate in the universities, which are also actions that are satisfactory in and of themselves without anything concrete following from them. In *"práxis"* self-reference is already included in the concept. And *"poiésis"* was explained to Maturana as something that produces something else outside itself – namely, a work. In *"poiésis"* one does something, one acts – not because this action is pleasurable or virtuous but because one intends to produce something. Subsequently, Maturana found a bridge between the two concepts. He spoke of *"autopoiesis,"* a poiesis that is its own work – and he spoke quite consciously of "work" in this context. In comparison, *"autopráxis"* would be a meaningless expression, for it would merely repeat that which is already meant by the term *"práxis."* No, what is at issue is the system that is its own work. The operation is the condition for the production of operations.

It is also interesting that the concept of *"poiésis"* – that is, of making and producing – like the concept of "production," but even more clearly, never includes complete control over all causes. It is always possible to control only a particular area of causality. For example, if you want to boil an egg then you assume that you need a stove unit, or that you have to ignite a fire in one way or another, but you do not imagine that you could change the air pressure or modify the composition of the egg in such a way that it would boil all by itself. I do not know whether this is technically possible, but there are in fact a whole bunch of possible causes that are usually presupposed in the process of production, and which could actually be varied in order to develop new methods of production. The concept of "production" means, among other things, that one is not dealing with what is called in classical terms *"creatio,"* or the creation of everything that is necessary. That is to say, one is instead dealing with a generation that takes place in the context of conditions that are already given and can therefore be presupposed. This point is not unimportant, particularly since it has been claimed time and again that human beings, for instance, are the indispensable condition of communication. Other examples could be given: blood circulation, the moderate temperature or the normal electromagnetism of the earth, the fact that bone fractures can heal again – all these and further environmental conditions of communication. The concept of operational closure denies this as little as does the concept of autopoiesis. Such a denial would have no place in systems theory anyway, since the difference between the system and the environment is its point of departure.

At issue, then, is *"poiésis"* in the Greek or strict traditional sense of production, the making of a work, in combination with *"auto,"* which is to say that the system is its own work. It is not just a self-explanatory *práxis.* That the thesis concerning autopoiesis has been simultaneously over- and underestimated and that there is a wealth of criticism that does not pertain to the actual issue are, in a sense, effects of the uncommonness of the expression or of the noteworthiness of this word that had been unknown before. On the one hand, there is the criticism that we are dealing here with biological terminology that ought not to be applied to other fields. This objection is understandable, since in the field of biology the infrastructure, if you will, or the chemistry of the autopoiesis is clear. Normal biologists[48] therefore ask what else they gain, in addition to what they already know, if they now also start referring to it as "autopoiesis." The biochemistry of the cell is well known. Why then the term "autopoiesis"? The concept made it easier to find answers for the questions "What is operational closure?" and "Wherein lies the difference between production and causality?" Nonetheless, it is a coincidence that it is exactly biologists and neurobiologists, who in a sense work in an area that is already prepared for them, who have invented this concept. Maturana invented it, Varela adapted it. This does not mean, however, that the use of this concept in other fields constitutes an analogy in the strict technical sense. For either an analogy is based on the ontological claim that the world has an essential structure that produces similarities everywhere because it was preordained in this way in the moment of creation; or alternatively, the analogy is based on the argument that, because something is the case at the level of life, it must also be the same at the psychological and social level. However, this argument is not necessary. If the concept is defined in sufficiently abstract terms, it becomes obvious that it can also be applied in other instances if one can suitably make a case.

I have had relatively long discussions with Maturana on this point. He always told me that, if one speaks of the autopoiesis of communication, one has to show it. That is to say, one has to show that the concept really works in the domain of communication, so that it is possible to state that an individual communicative act can come about only in the network of communication. It cannot be conceived as a one-time event. And it also cannot be conceived as produced externally, in a communication-free context, as it were – say, as a chemical artifact that then has a communicative effect. On the contrary, it must always be produced by and through communication. I believe that this claim does not create much difficulty. It is relatively easy to see – especially if one considers the linguistic tradition of Saussure, for instance, and all that came of it – that communication occurs via its own differences and has nothing to do with chemical or physical phenomena.

The only opposition to this viewpoint can be found in Maturana, when he refuses to designate communication systems as social systems. There is a strong emotional moment that is on his side. He does not want to leave out the human being. Furthermore, he does not have the necessary agility in sociological and linguistic matters that would make it possible for him to see how one could eventually bring the human being back in. He does not want to waive the claim that the expression "social systems" means concrete human beings that form groups and such. This is the only difference.

In the sociological literature that rejects the application of this concept to a theory of social systems, there is the view that we are dealing here with a biological metaphor comparable to the organism metaphor that has been applied to social systems in an uncontrolled fashion and quite possibly with conservative intentions. This is a point where sociologists are rather sensitive. However, I think that this discussion will end sooner or later. After all, it already shows a certain carelessness when someone claims that something is a metaphor. If we return to Aristotle's *Politics* and to other traditional texts, we can say that all concepts are metaphors. Everything has come about in some metaphorical fashion and has become independent of such origins only through the technical use of language on the basis of the procedures of condensation, identification, and the increase of its possible applications. If one has in mind this wide sense of "metaphorical," then there are no objections to a metaphor. Yet this, too, would then have to be generalized, and one would have to grant that the concept of "process," for instance, is also metaphorical. It migrated into sociology from philosophy, into philosophy from jurisprudence, and into jurisprudence from chemistry, or vice versa. I cannot map this process precisely. In the final analysis, everything is metaphorical.

Another angle of this discussion is more important. I believe that the concept of autopoiesis and the theory of autopoietic systems are simultaneously under- and overestimated on account of this concept. On the one hand, the radicality of this approach is underestimated. This radicality is due to the thesis of operational closure. The thesis of operational closure implies a radical change of epistemology and of the presupposed ontology as well. If one accepts this and links it to the concept of autopoiesis – which is to say, if one treats this concept as a formulation of the thesis of operational closure – then it becomes obvious that it is linked with a rupture of the epistemology of the ontological tradition. This epistemology assumed that something enters into the cognizing system from the environment and that the environment is represented, imitated, or simulated within the cognizing system. In this context, it is almost impossible to overestimate the radicality of the novel autopoietic approach.

On the other hand, the explanatory power of this concept is rather weak. This must be stressed especially in a sociological context. Strictly speaking, nothing can be explained by means of autopoiesis. This concept allows for another point of departure for concrete analyses, for further hypotheses, or for a more complex application of additional concepts. But even in biology it is the case that the difference between worms, humans, birds, and fish, as a result of the one-time invention of biochemistry, cannot be explained by means of autopoiesis. The same is true for communication. Communication is a state of affairs that runs continuously, an operation that continuously reproduces itself. It is not just a one-time event or a sign – like a sign that is given by an animal, to which all other animals react and run about wildly, and at some point a new orientation and imitation comes about. Once this state of affairs has been overcome, communication presupposes via separate signals or signs the recourse to past sign uses and the anticipation of connective possibilities. It was only when this level had been secured that society was constituted. But it still could be a society of Hottentots, Zapotecs, Americans or any other culture. The result can vary in time, and its structural development cannot be derived from the concept of autopoiesis. All this is to say that autopoiesis is not of truly high explanatory value. This creates difficulty for a sociologist who is methodologically prudent. To recognize theses without important explanatory power that do not lend themselves to the formulation of hypotheses and are without the capacity to deploy a whole empirical apparatus – to recognize such theses as nonetheless foundational – runs up against the usual doctrine of science. This becomes apparent if one keeps in mind that theories are supposed to be instructions for empirical research and thus are supposed to provide structural prognoses. From this viewpoint, the theory of autopoiesis is a meta-theory, an approach that, in its own way, once again answers to "What?" questions, such as "What is life?" or "What is consciousness?" or ""What is the social?" (that is to say, "What is a social system independent of the specific formation in which it occurs empirically?"). The concept of autopoiesis answers such "What?" questions – this, too, is a thought of Maturana.

At the end of a long course on the evolution of life, a student approached Maturana and told him that he understood everything that had been said but wondered what precisely had transpired in the process. At first, Maturana had no suitable answer. Under normal circumstances, a biologist does not ask the question as to what life is. And, in sociology, the question "What is the social?" is likewise no question to which the discipline devotes much attention. And, in psychology, one usually does not pose the question as to what the soul or consciousness is either, at least not in this form. In general, "What?" questions are shunned. But the concept of autopoiesis aims precisely at such questions.

One is dealing here with the refoundation, if you like, of a theory. But this also means that any further work requires many more concepts than simply the term "autopoiesis." This concept gives little information concerning concrete work. Systems theory has to enrich itself on a more general level in order to be able to work with this concept and in order to make decisions and distinguish specific phenomena. Concerning this developmental juncture, the topic of structural coupling will become important in my next lecture. For it is by means of different structural couplings that Maturana attempts to explain something that he calls "structural drift." The structural development of a system or a system type depends on the structural couplings with its environment that the system has to undergo.

Let me add two further points that concern the current discussion of the concept of autopoiesis. I find it important that one should preserve the "hardness" of the concept – that is to say, that one should claim either that a system is autopoietic or that it is not autopoietic. It cannot be a little autopoietic. For the reference to *"autos"* makes clear that the operations of the system are either produced in the system or, alternatively, are already given in important respects through the environment – for instance, by a program, according to which a computer works. Here, an either/or distinction applies. As far as life is concerned, this is fairly obvious. Either one is alive or one is dead. It is only a matter of seconds during which doctors can doubt whether one is still alive or already dead. A woman is either pregnant or she is not pregnant, but she cannot be a little pregnant. This is Maturana's very own example, *ipsissima verba*. This means that the concept of autopoiesis is not a concept that allows for gradation, and this, in turn, means that the evolution of complex systems cannot be explained in terms of autopoiesis. If one tries to do so anyway, one arrives at theories that claim that a system slowly becomes more autopoietic. Originally, it is said, the system is still entirely dependent on its environment and gains some autonomy only slowly. At first, the system structures become a little less (or more or less) dependent on the environment. And then, it is claimed, the system's operations also become increasingly autopoietic. This tendency can indeed be found in the literature. Gunther Teubner (Florence) has made a corresponding suggestion in order to be able to integrate considerations of evolutionary theory into the theory of autopoietic systems.[49] In the meantime, I have also encountered microeconomic literature that in a certain way gradates the autopoiesis or autonomy of business companies and arrives at a concept such as "relative autonomy."[50] A system is said to be relatively autonomous. It is said to be independent of its environment in some respects but dependent on it in others. But, in the strict sense of the word "autopoiesis," nothing is said about dependence or independence in relation to the environment. For the questions in what ways a system depends on its environment and how the environment affects the system are causal questions. And such questions must be addressed to an observer of the system.

Moreover, it is not possible to assume a zero-sum principle in these matters, according to which a system's independence from its environment increases to the same degree as its dependence on it decreases. Numerous experiences indicate that very complex systems that are highly autonomous (if one may relativize this word) increase equally their independence and their specific dependencies. In modern society, the economic system, the legal system, and the political system possess a high degree of independence but also an equally high degree of dependence on their respective environments. If the economy is not booming, political difficulties ensue. And when politics is not able to provide certain securities – say, via the legal system – or if politics intervenes too massively, this becomes a problem in the economy. Returning to the thesis of operational closure, we cannot help but distinguish between causal in/dependence, on the one hand, and self-generated operations, on the other.

I am not even entirely sure whether this distinction is ultimately convincing. Especially in European culture, we have a strong conception that tends to compute everything in terms of causality. Thus, we tend to understand expressions such as "an operation generates an operation" or "production" always in causal terms. This makes it difficult to discuss operational closure as completely distinct from causal theories. We always slide back to our conception that the thesis of operational closure constitutes a specialized thesis about the internal causality of a system. And to a certain degree this is in fact the case. It is possible to compute operational closure in terms of causality. But, in principle, one ought to understand the situation as follows: the condition of connectivity is not a sufficient condition to bring about the next state. Precisely this issue is addressed by the conception of structural coupling, with which I will begin my next lecture.

5 Structural Coupling

Sixth Lecture

Today, I begin with the section on structural coupling. To this purpose, I return once more to those considerations concerning the distinction between operations and causality as well as those concerning operationally closed systems. The strong stress on operational closure in the discussion of autopoiesis left open the question of how the relations with the environment are regulated – or, to put it differently, which forms and conceptual resources are at our disposal to describe the relation between system and environment. This problematic is thrown into even sharper relief if we proceed from the assumption that the relation between system and environment is something that does not simply exist, but rather that it is connected to the system concept itself. For the system concept is a difference concept. It is, as I said before, a form with two sides. On one side of this form one finds the system, and on the other side the environment. If we combine these two conceptual strategies, we may ask how the system is connected with the environment and to what degree of conceptual precision systems theory can actually represent this dependence.

I think that the demands on the precision of the presentation and also the differentiation of the conceptual instruments have been growing and that therefore classical concepts no longer suffice. This is true, on the one hand, in the case of evolutionary theory, where two tendencies towards explaining the relation between system and environment are apparent. One is the possibility of declaring that this relation is contingent in the

domain of variation impulses [*Variationsanstöße*]. That is to say, that the
concept of contingency is deployed in such a way that it could be proposed
that systems are able to develop in an environment that contingently acts
as an impetus for system changes – for example, a certain mutation that
has come about for chemical reasons is originally not matched to the sur-
vivability of the system but, in those cases where it proves to be effective
in this way, it can be retained and continued. The other possibility is that
one works with the theory of the "natural selection" of forms that survive
without having been planned or prefigured in the system itself. Instead
such forms are the result of the ecological contexts of living organisms.
These concepts are relatively weak conceptually, and they are coordinated with the insight that there can be no prognoses regarding evolution
and thus that there are no causal laws that prescribe to system and environment the direction of evolution. On the contrary, we are dealing here
with statistical issues.

The idea of "order from noise," of environmental noise that can
be transformed into order in the system, functions in a rather similar
manner.[51] Here, as well, one does not say *how* this transformation takes
place. Instead, one states only *that* a system has the capability of transforming mere noise into order inside the system. This is different from the
explanation offered by evolutionary theory. Here, it refers to the self – the
idea being that information is the system's own product. We will return
to this point. But precisely in what way noise is transformed into information is not made very clear – other than the claim that a system is capable
of effecting this transformation.

I would like to push this point at least one step further with the help of
the concept of structural coupling, which was introduced by Maturana.[52]
However, I will fiddle around a bit with this concept and not use it in
precisely the form that Maturana appears to have in mind. We have to ask
in this case also whether the proposed concept suffices to fill the gap with
regard to causal relations between system and environment. Maturana
assumes that two claims can be made concerning a system. On the one
hand, a system is autopoietically organized. For us the term "organization" is not usable, since we as sociologists have a different conception of
organization. Perhaps it is sufficient to state that autopoietic reproduction
is a quality of the system. It either takes place or does not take place and
has a rather wide overall range of possibilities for structural development, a range that is not predetermined by the concept of autopoiesis. On
the other hand, it can be said that a system possesses specific structures.
Depending on the type of living being, these structures differ. They are
different for mammals and for birds, different for fish and worms, different for bacteria and mice. There is a variety of structures, and the thesis is
that different structural developments are possible as long as autopoiesis
functions. As soon as it stops functioning, life ceases, and with it any
chance of developing or using structures ceases as well.

In relation to this distinction, Maturana introduces the concept of structural coupling. The distinction allows us to say that autopoiesis must function in any case since there would otherwise be no system. At the same time, it also indicates that the coupling between system and environment concerns only structures and, as the case may be, everything in the environment that is relevant to these structures. Thus, on earth gravity is coordinated with the musculature of a living being that has to move in order to survive. We can observe a reduction of life chances through the need for movement in correspondingly complex organisms. And we also observe the creation of possibilities for movement, which always emerge in coordination with the conditions of life on earth. This is a case of structural coupling. This concept is adjusted to the autopoiesis of the system, which is to say that the structural coupling does not interfere with the system's autopoiesis. Occasionally, Maturana states that structural coupling is "orthogonal" to autopoiesis. That is to say, that there is no causal transfer that could be called a kind of causal law between the domain of structural coupling and autopoiesis. There is the destruction of the system by the environment, but the environment does not actively contribute to the maintenance of the system. This is precisely the point of the concept "autopoiesis." The causalities that occur between system and environment are located exclusively in the domain of structural coupling.

What we read about in Maturana, then, is the compatibility of all structural couplings with the autonomy and autopoiesis of the system. Among other things, this means that this conceptual framework has no place for the claim that something is more or less autonomous, more or less autopoietic. Structural coupling can take all possible shapes, as long as it is compatible with the system's autopoiesis. The emphasis is on compatibility.

We must work a little longer on this concept of structural coupling. In particular, we must pay more attention to the fact that such a coupling is, as can be derived from the concept of form, a two-sided form. This form does not refer to the entire environment, since not everything that exists is structurally coupled with the system. Rather, couplings are highly selective. Something is included and something else is excluded. What is excluded may very well affect the system causally, but only negatively. In contrast, in the domain of structural coupling, possibilities are stored that can be used by the system and be transformed into information. From this point of view, one could say that structural coupling has, on the one hand, an exclusion effect – in this domain the system is indifferent – and, on the other hand, it brings about the canalization of causalities that can be used by the system. In all of this, the specific quality of the concept is preserved – namely, that structural coupling is always compatible with autopoiesis. For this very reason, there are possibilities of exerting influence on the system as long as its autopoiesis is not destroyed. This point could perhaps be reformulated along the following lines: the division of the environment into that which is included and that which is excluded, as an effect of structural coupling, tends to reduce the relevant relations between system and environment and cut them down to a narrow area of influence, and only under such conditions can the system process irritations and causalities. Only when not everything affects the system simultaneously, and when, instead, highly selective patterns are at the system's disposal, can the system react to irritations and "perturbations" (Maturana) – that is, understand them as information and adjust its structures accordingly or use its operations accordingly in order to transform its structures.

The reduction of complexity, the exclusion of a mass of events in the environment from the possibility of affecting the system, is the condition for the system's ability to do something with as few irritations as such reduction permits. Or, to put the matter in the most abstract terms, the reduction of complexity is the condition of the increase in complexity.

Two examples can be adduced here. The first one concerns the way in which the brain is structurally coupled with the external environment via eye and ear. It thus possesses a very narrow bandwidth of sensibilities that reduces what can be seen, limits the spectrum of colors, and equally reduces what can be heard. It is only because things are this way that the system is not overburdened with external influences, and only because things are this way that learning can take place and complex structures can be built inside the brain. We thus observe a narrow bandwidth of external contacts in connection with an enormous development of structural capacities in the brain and an enormous capacity to exploit the few irritations that the system receives. And, once again, we see that this is compatible with an autopoietic structure or operational closure. Everything depends on the system not establishing direct contact with the environment and instead being stimulated merely photo-mechanically or acoustically by means of light or sound waves and subsequently producing information from this input by means of the system's own apparatus. This information does not exist in the environment but has its environmental correlates that, however, only an observer can see.

In the field of brain research all this is of course well known and is nothing new.[53] But one might arrive at similar thoughts in sociology if one asks oneself how consciousness and communication – two different autopoietic systems – are coupled. In this context, one must take into account that consciousness and communication occur only if there is structural coupling. It is impossible to imagine that a consciousness would have emerged in the process of evolution if there had been no communication. It is equally impossible to imagine communication if there is no consciousness. Thus, there must have been some sort of coordination that, in referring to different forms of autopoiesis, led to an increase in complexity in the realm of possible content of consciousness, on the one hand, and in the realm of social communication, on the other. It seems to me that language has served as the coupling mechanism. This is to say that, from an evolutionary viewpoint, the emergence of consciousness (in the sense of continuous attention to identifiable perceptions, noises, etc.), on the one hand, and the emergence of continuous communication (not just in the sense of giving a sign occasionally), on the other, must be connected with language. According to this thesis, there must have been a simultaneous emergence of structural coupling and autopoiesis in the realm of consciousness, on the one hand, and of social communication in the realm of society, on the other. In the beginning, this co-emergence presumably had a relatively low complexity and the co-emergent systems had a rather limited reach and differentiation, yet their more recent states, with which we are familiar, have been marked by an enormous complexity that we also find in language itself.

In this context, structural coupling means that language excludes a lot in order to include very little, and that it can become complex only for this reason. If we begin with spoken language, we see that noises are excluded except for those few highly articulated noises that can function as language. Even small variations, slight shifts, or the replacement of one sound by another make communication impossible and irritate consciousness. In such cases, it must search for the potential meaning because it no longer understands. In the oral and acoustic range, we are dealing with highly selective patterns. And the same is true for writing. Only very few standardized symbols are suitable for writing, and everything else that can be seen is simply out of the question. Structural coupling is a highly selective form that uses relatively simple patterns. For instance, there are only very few letters in the highly developed alphabetical phonetic writing system. And, in language itself, there are only a few standardized pitches and acoustical signs. But it is precisely because these signs or sounds are so reduced that they make possible highly complex combinations which, in turn, have an effect on conscious and communicative processes.

From all this we can derive that society is coupled with its environment only via consciousness and that, for this reason, there are no physical, chemical, or purely biological effects that influence social communication. Everything must pass through the tiny needle's eye of communication. In spite of all the interest in the individual and society, this point is not really treated in sociological literature, precisely because it is too obvious. Reduction is the condition of building up high complexity within the social system. If chemical phenomena as such had meaning without the contribution of human beings, if chemistry could affect communication directly, then presumably all control within the system of communication would be lost, including the addresses and the memory dependence of communication.

This narrow bandwidth of effective possibilities in combination with the enormous gains in increase, accumulation, and probability, on the one hand, and the exclusion of all other facts in the world except for those that have a destructive effect, on the other, is designated by the concept of structural coupling. Destruction is always possible. From this fact we can derive that, when evolution builds, and is in need of, structural couplings with more and more preconditions in order to adjust the systems with their autopoiesis to the environment, it simultaneously increases its own potential for destruction. Today, society depends on many environmental preconditions, which, however, can have only a destructive effect. The narrow range of communication that is influenced by consciousness is the only area in which society can help itself. It is obvious that this entire analysis describes today's ecological situation well.

In both cases, the relation between the brain and the physico-chemical environment and the relation between consciousness and communication, it is noticeable that the autopoietic system is constantly affected via structural coupling. It is not just a matter of sporadic effects that occur occasionally. Rather, the structural couplings make sure that consciousness, or the social system of communication, or the brain is constantly supplied with irritations.

What exactly does it mean, then, that there is a compatibility of structural coupling and autopoiesis? Is it possible to formulate this in more precise terms? First of all, it must be said over and over again that the environment does not bring about the structural determination of the system. Structural couplings do not determine the state of the system. One might say that they only supply irritations for the system. Alternatively, Maturana speaks of the "perturbation" of the system. I prefer the terms "irritation" or "stimulus," or also, if seen from the system's perspective, "resonance capability" [*Resonanzfähigkeit*]. The resonance of the system is activated through structural coupling. If one uses the term "disturbance," one must be clear about the fact that one is no longer dealing with a theory of equilibrium. Theories of equilibrium or balance had also included the concept of disturbance. In fact, the entire model had been formulated in two directions in terms of disturbances. On the one hand, there was the easiness or probability of a disturbance. If you think of scales, it takes very little force, just a few added grams on one side, to disturb the balance. We have already spoken of these ideas that emerged in the seventeenth century and concerned the artificiality of the balance of trade or the international balance of power. A few additional soldiers for the French, and already the Prussians had to increase their numbers to maintain the balance. But, on the other hand, one always imagined that the equilibrium has a sort of infrastructure or apparatus at its disposal that serves its self-maintenance. As a consequence, a disturbance leads to the reconstitution of the equilibrium, be it by manipulating prices, by means of rearmament, or whatever the object of a specific model of balance may be. However, one was also always aware of the fact that these possibilities have a limit at which one must deal with the loss of balance or its destruction. If one assumed dynamic equilibriums, one of the ways one could go a step further was to say that the system could find another equilibrium. For instance, one developed a new type of coalition within the European balance of power, or it was said that the balance of trade could be achieved in a new and different manner. It is not necessary to maintain the balance by returning to a prior state. Rather, it can develop dynamically, for instance, in keeping with certain ideas of progress or in the sense of functional equivalents. In principle, however, the meaning of this model, which, to be sure, is really a metaphor, was to earmark equilibrium as a condition of stability and to describe a system in terms of its equilibrium as a stable system. Or, if you remember the opening lecture of this lecture series, one might say that, in such a model, the maintenance of the system structure is tied to the concept of equilibrium.

Today, this linkage has become questionable in several respects. On the one hand, in natural science the prevalent idea is that it is precisely imbalances which can be stable, and in economics a system is said to be stable if either too many goods are on offer and there are too few buyers or, vice versa, if there are too many buyers and not enough goods. A precise calibration, however, would be too labile to gain any type of stability. Thus, the socialist system keeps the goods scarce and the capitalist system, the buyers. In either case, there is an imbalance that is, however, stable. This tendency puts the old model in doubt. If, on the other hand, one proceeds from the ideas of autopoiesis, operational closure, and structural coupling, the balance model becomes questionable simply because one would have to regard imbalances and balances as functional equivalents, since both serve to maintain stability.

As a consequence, concepts such as disturbance, irritation, stimulus, and perturbation now have a different meaning. Now, the question is how a disturbance can be conceptualized internally within the system if one does without the equilibrium model. Presumably the best way would be to think of the system as possessing certain structures and thus also a certain range of possibilities for its own operations. This range is very limited, since the definition of what qualifies as *poiesis* at all is severely restricted. In addition, this range is limited by the constraints concerning what can be processed within a pre-existing structural pattern and thus without any far-reaching and incalculable structural changes. In this way of thinking, disturbances are always measured against the structures, or in the domain of meaningful [*sinnhafter*] occurrences against possible operations, or also expectations that have proven their worth in the system and thus provide information from that angle. A disturbance, a piece of information, or an irritation provides the system with a relevant choice from a range of possibilities. Such an occurrence can initiate search or identification processes. Perhaps when there is the smell of smoke, it is not clear at first sight whether there is a fire or whether the potatoes have merely burnt on the stove. Nevertheless, certain smells offer only limited possibilities of interpretation. One does not assume that the gas tank has leaked when there is a smell of burning – or perhaps actually one does. In any case, the range of interpretive possibilities corresponds to the speed and the information-processing capacity of the system.

"Disturbance" therefore means the initiation of information process-ing that can be handled operationally in the system. For instance, in consciousness such disturbances are handled by reflection or by focusing attention on the location where the disturbance occurred, or where in communication they are handled communicatively. One returns to the question and thematizes the disturbance. One warns others and thereby translates what can be formulated verbally in the system into a system process, although it does not appear as a *word* in the environment. Such system processes do not guarantee any results, but they offer possibilities for getting the system in motion and keeping it in motion. The concept of disturbance is thus detached from the equilibrium model and adapted in order to describe something that could better be called an information-processing process [*Informationsverarbeitungsprozess*]. Although I am not well informed in this field, I suspect that nowadays a similar transition from equilibrium models to information-processing models is taking place in economics. The common denominator of these processes of theory transformation is the question of how a system reacts to what it perceives as a disturbance, although in the environment this same occur-rence is of course not a disturbance. Does the system react by re-creating the balance, or by finding another equilibrium, or by instigating modes of information processing that correspond to the capacities of the system?

Not the least consequence of this last possibility is that the concept of information itself must be adjusted to this new interpretation. Ever since the fifties, the concept of information has proliferated in a way that has affected its conceptual clarity. For instance, there was a way of talking about genetic information that, by using this term, treated structures as informative. Thus, in the language use of biologists, genetic codes contain information, although as a matter of fact they consist of structures and not of events. Moreover, the semantic side of the concept and thus the question from what resource information can actually be selected remained unclear. If one kept these two aspects in mind and attempted to express them in the form of the concept of information, this would mean, first of all, that information is always an event and therefore is precisely not something that exists continuously. The University of Bielefeld, for example, is not information. Even if you come here every day, you do not always activate new information that would follow the pattern, "Oh, it is still here!" and then tomorrow you would be astonished again that the university is still here. The University of Bielefeld is a structure that has no informational value. Of course, it has meaning [*Sinn*] – after all, you have a specific idea why you come here – but it does not provide new information. This is to say that one must distinguish between meaning or even relative structural invariants and the surprise effect of a piece of information. In the second place, it is necessary to construct the concept of information once again like the concept of form, which is to say that one must look at it as a two-sided concept. On the one hand, there is surprise, but, on the other, the surprise comes about only because one had expected something and because one limits the range of possibilities within which a certain piece of information states this and cannot state that. If an acquaintance comes by in his new car, there is a specific range of possibilities concerning what type of car it may be. If he says that he will come by in a new car, one will not expect a deck chair.

Information always presupposes that one delimits one possibility as opposed to other possibilities and that, within a range of possibilities, one or the other is presented as information. Information is a selection from a range of possibilities.[54] If the selection is repeated, it no longer contains any information. If one continues to say the same thing over and over again, the meaning remains unchanged but the information disappears entirely, or is reduced to the fact that someone apparently perceives it as meaningful to keep saying the same thing over and over again. It is this fact that surprises because, under normal circumstances, one expects that every sentence has a different sentence and not an identical one as its successor. It is comparable to a record that has a scratch and as a result keeps repeating itself. But in this case one has available, after all, the interpretation that there is a scratch, a flaw, as opposed to regarding it as the normal functioning of the record.

A further double-sidedness is added to this concept of information. Gregory Bateson's frequently quoted formulation states that information is "a difference that makes a difference." Bateson simply states this as a matter of fact.[55] We are presented with this statement as a given, but without any reflection on its conditions. In the context of our lecture series, however, we can see that the concept oscillates between two differences, which is to say that it does not make any mention of the existence of a unity. At issue is a "difference" that changes the system's state and that stands in opposition to everything else that would be possible. We are therefore dealing with two differences. The first is the actual difference, the second concerns the distinction between the system's state before the occurrence of this difference and its state after it has taken note of it.

All of this taken together leads to the conclusion that information can occur only inside systems. Every system produces its information. This is true for a number of reasons that are connected with this specific constellation of concepts. To begin with, the range of possibilities [*Möglichkeitsraum*] that a system can imagine or about which one can actually speak is limited and *in the capacity of possibility* exists only in the system itself. In the environment, this possibility in the form of this particular arrangement does not exist.[56] The system must be capable of creating expectations in order to see possibilities, and it must have types or schemata at its disposal in order to categorize something. This is the system's achievement that can differ greatly from one system to the next. The entire process of selection is a system-internal process and not something that in any way exists in the environment. Furthermore, the temporal structure depends in each case on the system. It is quite possible that something has been around for a long time on the outside, as another observer could ascertain, but a particular system learns of this only at a particular point in time. The exact point in time is determined by the system's own mode of operation. It therefore does not make sense to say that there is a wealth of information in the environment and that only the transmission of this information into a system depends on the system itself. Rather, the system takes recourse to its own states and the irritations that it experiences in order to turn them into information and to process this information. Among other things, this also means that information does not consist of solid bodies or constant elements that could be transferred from the environment into the system.

If you keep this in mind and you look at the literature on this topic, you will see that regular language use is pretty undifferentiated in this respect. Even in, and, in fact, precisely in, the communication sciences, all sorts of statements concerning the transmission of information and such can be found. If one reads that the mass media – the newspapers and the TV news – transfer or broadcast information, this presupposes an unclear concept of information. To put it differently, one presupposes an observer who is able to recognize that a certain text, after it has been read, will be known by a consciousness system, or that a certain text, after it has been distributed by a news agency, will make its appearance in the papers. But in each case the actual information consists of the fact that it happens in this way.[57] The context within which a selection takes place is in each case specific. Only an observer, with the help of crude simplifications, can establish specific identities. If one would like to know what identities the observer has established, one has to observe the observer.

Perhaps I should give another example to explain this once again. One of the most dramatic occurrences of the past twenty or thirty years was the collapse of the socialist economy, which was apparently not capable of transforming economic information into politics. In reality, the planning centers were not informed about the economic occurrences – whatever we may mean by "economy" in this context. On the contrary, they were only able to see whether their own plans were fulfilled or not, and all actors who were involved in the planning process in turn could see that the center saw whether its plans were being fulfilled or not. At stake was a political schema that evaluated situations by means of "oughts" that were more or less fulfilled. The entire system was keyed to such evaluations. The information could be produced by giving either truthful reports or false statements and fictional data. Both of these options kept the entire information processing going, and there was no other information than this political information that was allowed to circulate in the economy. Within certain limits one might even say that the economy and politics were not separated as far as the respective information processing was concerned, since only this political or governmental information was accepted in the economy.

As a matter of fact, market economies do not operate all that differently. I suspect that here, too, information that we treat as economic information may be produced merely for political purposes. True, much of this information may have a basis in the realities of certain companies' or banks' dispositions, but, at the same time, the aggregation of the numbers of the unemployed, the exchange rate of a currency, and many other such data are produced only for political purposes. Thus, politics works with data that are admittedly summaries of economic data but are assigned their informational value for politics only in a political manner, while, at the level where companies operate, entirely different pieces of information play the crucial role. What matters in companies is the bottom line, the orders received, the prices, the activities of competitors, the increase or decrease in demand, and, by extension, the possibilities for production. This world of information is specific to the economic system. It is very much in question whether anybody in this system ever orients himself by means of unemployment statistics. In the economy, market data count as information. The company reads this information with the help of its own accounting office and thus, once again, deals with information it has produced itself, and which may coincide with other, external information provided merely for an observer. The informational content is thus produced and created in the system.

For the moment, this may suffice on the concept of information, which in a certain way occupies the position that the more demanding concepts of equilibrium occupied earlier. However, possibilities of predicting how the system will behave, which the concept of information offers, are more limited. After all, in accordance with the idea of autopoiesis, this would be the system's own task.

I want to return once again to the concept of structural coupling, and, by referring to two examples, I would like to show, or rather pose the question, whether we actually have gained something by it and, if so, what we have gained. The first example is evolution, the second socialization.

The primary task of evolutionary theory is to explain why there is a wide variety of living species, which is to say, of structures within which the autopoiesis of life is regulated. How does this variety arise that always required some sort of theological explanation or argument from design in the older theories because it was unimaginable that such things came about without a corresponding intention? Evolutionary theory deviates from such theological or design explanations. But, in the process, it incurs the problem of explaining how such a variety of species arose. Taking autopoiesis as the starting point in this area means that autopoiesis itself does not yet provide for or determine what species are even possible. As I said when I introduced the concept, autopoiesis is a principle that does not have much explanatory value. Life is a one-time invention that does not contain that which will become of it, not even in the form of a germ. There are many possibilities that did not stand the test, that have been forgotten, and that have become extinct. But, on the other hand, there is also the rich variety of existing living forms. Autopoiesis does not consist of a sort of originary principle that differentiates itself. Such a claim would coincide with the old mythological doctrine of germinal power that is latent and at some point in time will begin to develop. This view reflects the original sense of "development," according to which everything was meshed together once upon a time and subsequently unfolded.

In contrast, autopoiesis explains evolution only with regard to the conditions of the compatibility of structures. For this reason, one needs both of the concepts that Maturana distinguishes – namely, autopoietic organization and structure. For only in this manner is it possible to explain how evolution can test which structures are compatible with autopoiesis and which are not. The emphasis of this theory is on the compatibility of autopoiesis and structural development. At stake is the description of a possibility. Seen in retrospect, autopoiesis, or the invention of a mode of operation that is suitable for autopoiesis, is a proposal that can be maintained only because it can assume many different forms. If one were to conceive of autopoietic systems as surviving merely by means of one type of structure, then their chances of survival would be considerably lower because, in that case, due to structural coupling, the probability of destruction would be much higher. Evolution can survive such destruction because there are always other possibilities to develop the autopoiesis of life via structures in the direction of higher complexity.

This also means, by the way, that one cannot say that structural complexity arises because it is beneficial for survival and that complex systems have better chances of survival than less complex ones. Already at the empirical level, this is incorrect. Complexity ought to be seen as an epiphenomenal development of autopoiesis, as an epigenetic deformation, as it were, of life. The miracle consists in the fact that it still keeps going, even if the gain in complexity constantly requires new structural couplings in order to balance the system with the environment. For instance, there are life forms that move and thus have certain advantages, since they can search for their own food. But, as a consequence, there are also certain dependencies on the environment that non-moving life forms do not have. Or, to give another example, life forms with a central nervous system are in need of constant blood temperatures and all sorts of additional presuppositions. The dependence on the environment increases and complexity increases. In the terms of Darwinian evolutionary theory, the criterion for such increases would be better adaptation to the environment. However, the concept of autopoiesis permits us to state only that such systems function and that the biochemistry of life is apparently so rich in possible forms that they continue to function even though they are becoming more complicated, and the relations between systems and their environments are becoming more complex to the point where increasing numbers of relatively improbable structural couplings are required for their maintenance.

The same could be said concerning the evolution of cultures or societies, if one must use the plural in the latter case. In these cases as well, an enormous variety of systems is compatible with communication. After communication had finally been invented, or, better, after it arose not only as a sporadic attunement of living systems but also as a continuous arrangement, this communication must have effectively functioned as an evolutionary potential. In view of this more permanent establishment of communication, people sitting together and not communicating may be regarded as a disturbance. Here one may be reminded of Paul Watzlawick's famous dictum that *"one cannot not communicate."*[58] Perhaps a train compartment is the exception, but there one has a special permit not to communicate. The fact that communication functions as an evolutionary potential means that it functions as an adjustment to the perceptive achievements of those who are present or, alternatively, as an adjustment to the creativity and intuition of those who express themselves in writing. Although communication always remains communication, and although autopoiesis is always autopoiesis, there are widely different structures of everything that can be said and which can potentially be understood. The domain of understandable messages and, in the final analysis, of that which meets with acceptance, and thus the willingness on the part of others to connect to it, can develop an enormous variety and improbability via all sorts of additional cultural arrangements of communication. Thus, language provides forms for positive as well as negative statements. Language makes it possible that everything that can be said can also be expressed negatively, without therefore losing the possibility of being understood. One cannot be sufficiently amazed by this, since normally negativity tends to have a destructive effect. If negation happened in the domain of life itself, one would expect destruction or something similar. But, in language, negation depends only on the fact that the meaning of the message can be understood. Communication also functions when one says, "I don't believe this!" or "I would not like this!" or "I don't want this!" or if one gives a negative instruction, such as, "Don't do this!" The positive and the negative can be understood equally well. In either case, communication or autopoiesis functions. But culture and society then have the problem of how to deal with negations that contain a potential for conflict precisely when they are understood, and therefore require corresponding mechanisms for conflict resolution.

Cultural developments can create extremely improbable modes of communication and, subsequently, of behavior that do not astonish us, merely because we have already become accustomed to them. Think, for example, of the astonishing fact that you sit here and listen to a lecture whose incomprehensibility can be justified only by theoretical specialization. Why are you doing this? Why does communication function in this case? Why are not all of you running away? There are other examples as well. Why are you given something to eat merely because you make a payment? Why is someone willing to suffer your moods merely because he loves you? For all this there must be patterns that function communicatively but were not provided for by the mere fact or invention of communication. How, then, can such a development of variety be explained, unless one assumes that the operational mode that creates such systems is compatible with many different structural patterns? Language, for instance, is still understood regardless of whether something is negated or something extremely improbable is stated. Moreover, irritability, which is to say, the structural coupling with states of consciousness, also increases in this process. In a society, for example, the sensitivity to the opinions of others increases so that one avoids direct confrontation, looks for argumentative detours, lies, sees through apparently phony positions with a certain understanding, and manages to treat all this communicatively. These phenomena are structural couplings between consciousness and communication that were developed belatedly, as it were, in the course of evolution in order to reach a higher level of complexity.

All this happens if one takes autopoiesis as the point of departure. It is not presupposed in the corresponding mode of operation, and one also does not have to assume that there is an essential "nature" of life or of communication that possesses its own developmental urge and tends to aim all by itself at perfection, multiplicity, variety, and complexity. As observers, we merely observe that this is possible. For this reason, we can no longer accept a theory of progress. We can no longer formulate a belief in its own superiority for the modern, differentiated world or society in opposition to primitive forms. The theory offers no basis for such a claim that would come close to the justifications that were still present, within limits, in the old theory of nature. The only thing that is left is astonishment over the fact that things still function in the way they do and that there is still autopoiesis under conditions of high complexity.

Evolution was our first example. Socialization will serve as the second example. An exact parallel can be recognized here, although I would not want to say that an evolutionary theory could be applied without changes to the developments of consciousness. First of all, one must assume that consciousness is its own autopoietic system, which is to say that it can process attention with the help of the distinctions between that which is mere consciousness and that in it which refers to an object. In other words, we distinguish whether consciousness is treated in terms of self-reference or hetero-reference. If this hint suffices for the moment, the next question is how communicative facts, and thus society and the potential of consciousness, are coordinated. Sociological tradition claims that this happens via the transmission of specific structural patterns from generation to generation. Culture is said to store role expectations, idiomatic phrases, definitions of situations, value patterns, etc. Because these patterns are therefore constantly at one's disposal, the next generation [*Nachwuchs*] adopts them, and they remain the same as they were for other generations. As in all cases of transmission, here, too, we must pose the question of how this identity comes about. How can your idea of a university be the same as mine if I in my relation with the university have to produce completely different behavior than what is expected from you? How can one speak of sameness if no observer is involved who could list certain traits of the university and fix identities of the basis of such a highly selective account?

This is where the doubt arises as to whether social theory can be understood at all in terms of the transmission model. This doubt is not diminished if one conceives of a reciprocal relation – which is to say, if one imagines that the agent of socialization, the teacher or educator, the one who understands himself as the model for correct behavior and demonstrates such behavior, is himself also a learner in the socialization process. What he learns is to take into consideration the limits of the learning capacity of the learner. This reciprocal relation also postulates a transmission process.

If one begins with autopoiesis, socialization would have to be self-socialization. One only shapes oneself in such a way that one lives up to the demands of social intercourse, fulfills specific preconditions, or triggers certain reactions, possibly even negative ones. I believe that it is possible only in this way, and not with the transmission thesis, to explain the enormous variety of individuals. If we assume that consciousness is a sort of blank, and abstract from the fact that it possesses at best a minimal biological preprogramming, be it Chomsky's innate language competency or biologically rooted instincts, then consciousness is extremely plastic. If, in contrast, one considers culture and its offerings as relatively uniform, it becomes necessary to explain how the high degree of individuality that we observe has come about. The theory of autopoiesis appears to offer the better point of departure for this task. It points out that every system develops its own structures. On the basis of these primary structures (such as its own preferences, or its own words that can be used or not used, or its own sentences that can be repeated), it can build up its very own structures by letting itself be irritated by its structures and thereby becoming capable of limited reactions, and finally of making its own way that is not predetermined by any cultural prescriptions.

After all, there is no cultural program for individuality. Of course, there is the program that says that one ought to be an individual and to realize one's own potential. But the formula of being as unique as possible, of being different from all others, of dressing differently, and so on, merely results in the copying of a trivial and banal program and so precisely in not being an individual. This point was already discussed, from a religious perspective, in the nineteenth century. Then, it was pointed out that individuality was a gift of God and given concomitantly with the soul. All individualistic euphoria on the part of the worldly philosophers was seen as basically a collective mania which prescribed that one had to be an individual and make a real effort through self-education [*Bildung*] or some other means in order really to become one. This discussion already demonstrated how vain it is to become an individual through socialization if one presupposes that socialization operates via the transmission of patterns. In contrast, if one begins with autopoiesis, one can understand the structuring of one's consciousness, one's memory, and one's preferences better as the result of an individual system history that has to do, not least of all, with the cultural options that actualize conformity or deviance. If all of this was merely a matter of transmission and everything else had to be described as a defect, it would be impossible to explain how individuality emerges. For, in that case, depending on the reach of a specific cultural differentiation, there would be only a multiplicity of copies. But if every individual, every consciousness that is in the process of socialization, is given the chance to conform or to deviate, to say either "yes" or "no," and to think independently and search for individuality in deviation, one presumably will end up with a much better theory of the genesis of personality traits on the basis of the corresponding history of tactical adjustment, successful deviation, secret deviation, the acceptance of norms that one cannot fully agree with, or the internalization of norms that one agrees with at first only if coerced but later accepts more or less also internally because of the requirement of acting in a way that is consistent with one's own behavior. These different paths that are at an individual's disposal and are compatible with autopoiesis provide a better starting point for a theory of socialization than the transmission model.

With these analyses I conclude my reflections on structural coupling. I have made the attempt to present to you an arrangement of concepts that, I assume, provides more explanatory power than the relatively simple systems theories of an older tradition, such as equilibrium theories or theories that worked with causal models. What is decisive is the idea of an autopoiesis that is enormously robust and capable of absorbing very different structures, and which is practically indestructible. Communication is an extraordinarily robust operation: one can always say yet another thing if one gets into trouble. The structural drift of such a robust mode of operation is practically unpredictable, and for that very reason it results in enormous variety. I hardly see a possibility to explain this in traditional terms.

Now, however, comes a caesura. Hitherto, I have always only spoken of operations under the assumption (which will continue to be valid) that, if one intends to understand systems of the type that produce themselves, one must begin with operations and not with elements that cannot be further reduced. Now, however, I have an important announcement that will be relevant especially for the next lecture. Now, the observer appears. Now, everything will be different. The entire theory design will change, away from the somewhat simplistic ontological language that I have used ever since I have been saying that there are operations that one must take into consideration. Now, we pose the question of who actually says this. Of course I can say, "I tell you, I am the observer, I am the speaker, and this is my way of expressing myself. If you want to grasp what I say, you must, first of all, see that it is I who am speaking, regardless of what this may mean for others." If one introduces an observer, a speaker, or simply one to whom one attributes a statement, one relativizes ontology. In fact, one must always also have an observer in mind if one wants to say what is the case. One must therefore always observe an observer, name an observer, and designate a system reference if one makes statements about the world.

As soon as this theoretical threshold has been crossed, there is no more pure and simple way of doing things. From now on, no world exists without observations. Instead, the one who states that the world exists is the one who says that this is so. It is necessary to know, then, that a theory, a system, a science, a mode of communication, a consciousness, or whatever else could do so, claims that the world has such and such qualities. In comparison with the tradition, if you allow me for a moment to step onto philosophical terrain, ontology is no longer the assumption of a reality that is shared, and of which it can be assumed that everyone sees the same facts, as long as he or she gives the matter enough thought. Instead, ontology becomes itself a schema of observation – namely, a schema of observation on the basis of difference. Something is or is not the case. The difference thus concerns existence and non-existence. It is possible to describe the ontological tradition as the discovery of this distinction. Whether or not philosophers accept this, we will henceforth always be dealing with a world description that filters the presentation of facts, including purposes, action potentials, and so forth, by indicating a reference to an observer. One always faces the questions of who says a particular thing, and who does something, and from which system perspective the world is seen in a particular way (and no other).

You will recall that, already in my earlier lectures, I had difficulty in leaving the observer out of my considerations. For instance, when dealing with the topic of causality I was forced to say, because I saw no other way, that causality is a schema of observation. One observer considers this constellation of cause and effect as important; another has a different conception of what is relevant, a different temporal horizon, and different tendencies to see causality at work instead of something else. In fact, if we wanted to know what is the case, we were unable to do so without any relativization in regard to an observer or without any instruction to observe the observer. In the section on "observation," I would merely like to radicalize this position. If one introduces an observer, then nothing can be said that is independent of the observer. "Everything that is said, is said by an observer," says Maturana.[59] I do not intend to adopt Maturana's conception wholeheartedly. (I will address the theory of observation in greater detail in my next lecture.) For the time being, the only thing that is important is to make clear that such a theory presupposes another ontology or another metaphysics, a more complexly constructed metaphysics, and that this is connected – I am not quite sure how I can put this – with the radicality of the concept of autopoiesis. One can see this already in Maturana. But he limits himself to the case of life and to the problem of the coordination of living beings. If one abstracts from this and formulates the theory of autopoiesis in general terms, one encounters certain conceptual problems due to the reference to an observer. In the next lecture, we will address these problems.

The only thing that is important for the time being is that you see that a fissure runs through systems theory in its entirety. The division concerns the following two views. One may remain at the level of first-order observation, as we now must say, and describe facts and objects as existing in such terms as "there are" operations, "there is" socialization, "there is" consciousness, "there is" life, and so forth. One posits these states of affairs as if they were self-explanatory and as if there were no other possibility of drawing distinctions or focusing on themes. The world is presented as if it was just there in the compact way in which it is described. The alternative variation is that one may choose states that everything acquires, as it were, a modality of being in relation to a reference, an observer, an observing system, or an observing operation. I have good reason (which at this moment I cannot present in detail) for the assumption that the observation of the observers – that is to say, the shift from a consciousness of reality to a description of descriptions, or the perception of what others say or do not say – has become the advanced mode of perceiving the world in modern society. This is true in all functional domains, in science no less than in the economy, in art as much as in politics. One gains information about facts only in regard to what others say about them. One can also be another; it is not necessary that one accept the same things as true. But, if one wanted to take a critical perspective in this regard, one would have to observe oneself and reflect on the reasons why one does not share a particular opinion, or ignores a certain fashion, or considers a mode of politics bad, in spite of the fact that others think that it is good. To put it quite vaguely for the moment, the concept of the observer formulates a certain modernity and, in comparison to the tradition, a loss of reality. It is no longer necessary to know how the world is, as long as we know how it is observed and as long as we find orientation at the level of second-order observation. If somebody shows up and claims that he is in the know and attempts to instruct us, we can always ask – and it is undeniable that we have this tendency – who he is and where he is coming from. "Anybody, even somebody from the post office, could just come and make claims." Somebody states what he means, and we should accept this as fact? We prefer to come to our own conclusions and find our orientation in the legitimizing systems of science, the economy, politics, or the mass media – systems of which we are not independent, but which, in their turn, only observe observations. I have merely said this in order to arouse your curiosity for the next lecture, in which we will deal with the observer in more detail.

6 Observing

Seventh Lecture

In my last lecture, I indicated that now the observer will become the topic of our inquiry. Only an observer can talk about an observer. Thus, we are already in the middle of a circle that will lead us into the danger of having to say again everything that we have said hitherto, but this time with an indication of who has observed or said this. The concept possesses a genuine radicalism that has never been sufficiently acknowledged in the literature. There are formulations that point in this direction. But you would probably have great difficulty in finding sufficient information on this topic under the keyword "observer." For this reason, I will take my time in this section and will save some time when we get to the "re-entry." This latter concept will be dealt with briefly at the end of the current lecture.

I believe that, first of all, one ought to begin with the distinction between observing and the observer. Observing is viewed as an operation and the observer as a system that forms whenever such operations are not just individual events but become linked as part of a sequence that can be distinguished from the environment. In this way, we are using concepts that have already occurred, and this is not entirely without significance. In order to describe the observer, we use a terminology which we have already got used to – or so I hope. We describe an operation that occurs only in the mode of an event in a certain moment, and we use a term for that which comes about when this operation is linked and leads to a difference between system and environment. With the concepts of operation and system we are moving on a familiar level. The observer does not exist somewhere high above reality. He does not hover above things and does not look down from above in order to observe what is going on. Nor is he a subject (I will come back to this comparison) outside the world of objects. Instead, he is in the middle of it all, "*mittenmang*," as one might say if one were familiar with the northern regions of Germany.

What is at stake are operations – in a double sense. On the one hand,

the observer observes operations, but, in order to do so, he must be able
to operate himself. If he is not observing then he is simply not observing.
And if he is observing then he has to observe. In this sense, he is inside the
world that he attempts to observe or to describe in one or the other way.
It is an insight that was derived from computer development, especially
the von Neumann machines,[60] that, to put it in the old-fashioned way,
the operation that uses or perhaps even develops a program with which
it can monitor the system takes place inside the system. There is only this
one level. But there are also the complications that are introduced by the
observer.

On the one hand, the observer observes operations. On the other
hand, he is himself an operation. He cannot occur otherwise than as an
operation. He is a formation [*Gebilde*] that forms [*bildet*] itself through the
linking of operations. With this distinction between operation and observation comes another distinction that quite possibly lies even beyond
systems theory and is even more abstract and perhaps has the prospect
one day of becoming the fundamental theory of an interdisciplinary
science. Within this frame, the distinction between system and environment would be one way of observing, besides which there are other ones
– for instance, the distinctions between the sign and the signified, between
form and medium, and many others that correspond to expectations that
become visible in the relevant moments. Seen in this way, the distinction
between operation and observation is more radical than systems theory.
But systems theory has a way of reintegrating this distinction when it
accepts an operational approach, which is to say, when it includes the
concept of the operational closure of autopoiesis and describes how it
happens that an observation is produced by a system that in turn is produced by the observation. It is this circular network that marks one of the
peculiarities of today's discussion. This peculiarity can be combined with
classical philosophical concepts only with difficulty and is an indication
of the peculiar radicalism and independence of the perspective we have
chosen. We have to be clear about the fact that, at this point, we are entering terrain that hitherto has usually been covered by philosophy, even if
the concepts that we use and their inspirations were not gained from the
interpretation of classical philosophical texts.

What, then, is the specificity of the operation "observation"? I would
like to suggest that we address this question with Spencer Brown's terminology and state that observing is the handling of a distinction in order to
indicate one side and not the other. Referring to Spencer Brown, I do not
have in mind an explicit reference to the calculus of form in his book *Laws
of Form* but merely the conceptual resources with which he works at the
beginning and end of this calculus. How it happens that the observer suddenly appears in a late developmental phase of Spencer Brown's calculus,
although he has been presupposed already from the start, is a question
that would have to be posed inside the calculus itself. No doubt, Spencer

Brown himself saw this and actually posed precisely this question in a later book that concerned one of his own love affairs, *Only Two Can Play This Game.*[61] Here, he has another calculus in sight and appears himself as the person who created the first calculus but who did not get very far with it in matters of love. Love is not an arithmetic or algebraic operation. One sees, then, that Spencer Brown knew that he was presenting merely a limited model for which he had to presuppose at least the white paper on which he could write the marks and also himself, although there was no possibility that he himself could have appeared in the calculus, except perhaps at the very end, where he says that the observer himself is just a mark in the space within which the calculus takes place. But I believe that, for the time being, we can neglect this, as long as we keep in mind the definition that nothing can be observed without a distinction, and that this distinction must be used asymmetrically. It must be able to indicate one side and not the other. This is the case although the indication presupposes the distinction. That is to say, one always carries along the fact that there is another side that is not indicated at the moment and has no operational significance, and on which one is not at the present moment, from which one does not begin or take one's departure, and from which one cannot launch repetitions. Quite possibly, one might reach this other side by a "crossing" of the border. But at the moment when something is done, in the actual present, the other side is of course present as such but is not used. This is a very peculiar inclusion of asymmetry in a form that is, at the same time, symmetrical and which cannot do without the two sides. And it also cannot do without the unity of both sides, which is to say, without *one* distinction. But all this can happen on just one and not the other side. If one were to use both sides, the distinction itself would be sabotaged and no difference would exist anymore.

If you recall that Kant introduced his transcendental theory via the necessity of an asymmetry when he said that the conditions of empirical cognition could not themselves be empirical conditions, then you will see that there seems to be a necessity to interpret a theory as a relation of symmetry and asymmetry. In our case, this happens in a peculiar way via the observer, who uses one side and merely carries or pulls along the other side.

In the terminology that Heinz von Foerster likes to use, one might say that the distinction is the "blind spot" of the observing.[62] One must concentrate on one side only. For instance, we are in a university right now and nowhere else, but this difference between the university and everything else (really, everything else!) currently does not play a role. We cannot reflect on this difference once again when we are getting adjusted to being in the university now, in this lecture hall, attending this particular lecture, and dealing with this professor. The problem can be expressed in the following way: the unity of the distinction has been made invisible. If one wanted to make it visible, one would arrive at a paradox, namely, the unity of a difference. Quoting the title of a talk by Ranulph Glanville, one would have to say: "The same is different."[63] And then one is stuck. One can observe precisely this, and oscillate back and forth between "same" and "different," but one does not get any further, except perhaps by daring to make a dangerous but, as it were, creative jump by offering a substitute distinction.

Such considerations by no means exclude the reflection on, or designation of, distinctions. However, in order to make such a designation one must use another distinction. Of course, it is possible to speak about a distinction. After all, that is what I am doing at the moment. But, in order to do so, I have to be able to distinguish these distinctions from other distinctions or from something that is not a distinction. This problem played a role in theology. In principle, nothing is exempted from being observed. It is possible to observe distinctions. For instance, one may speak of the distinction between good and bad. One may ask oneself when making a moral distinction is appropriate and when not. If you purchase something in the course of a regular business transaction, you will not use the distinction as to whether the purchase is good or bad or whether the seller is good or bad. What you will want to know is how much something costs or perhaps what is the matter with the goods. That is to say, that you will use different distinctions, and if somebody comes and says, "I don't buy anything from bad people, and here we are clearly dealing with a capitalist lady, for she has a calculator and nothing but money in her cash register," one has the feeling that one has ended up with the wrong set of categories and must use different distinctions in order to be able to operate as usual and, in fact, to act at all. If, however, you use a different distinction, such as "personal/impersonal" or "moral/business-like" (or any other), then this distinction is invisible *for you*. You cannot ask in turn what the unity of the distinction between "business-like" and "moral" is.

When handling a distinction, you always have a blind spot or something invisible behind your back. You cannot observe yourself as the one who handles the distinction. Rather you must make yourself invisible if you want to observe. Or, to put it differently, you must in fact be able to draw a distinction between the observer and the observed, which is to say that you must know that you are observing something that is not yourself, but you cannot reflect on this distinction in turn. True, the world is in principle accessible to observations and does not preordain essential forms for the choice of distinctions. There are no correct distinctions that must be applied in certain cases because nature or the essence of the cosmos has predetermined it in such a way, or because creation has put things in such an order that one cannot help doing things in this particular way. But there is the necessity of always working with a blind spot or the invisibility of the unity of a distinction, because you cannot observe at all without a distinction, regardless of which distinction it is, and because you cannot reflect on the unity of the distinction for this very reason.

In all observing, therefore, something invisible is produced at the same time. The observer must make himself invisible as the element of the distinction between the observer and the observed. For this reason, there are only shifts between that which one sees and that which one does not see, but there is no comprehensive enlightening or scientific elucidation of the world as the totality of things or forms or essences that could be worked through piece by piece, not even if the task is seen as infinite. (I will return to this point again in a different context.) In contrast, in the classical theory, the prevalent notion was that one was collecting more and more knowledge and not that at any given point one must obscure something else if one intends to designate something in particular.

Let me now make some clarifications. So far, we have characterized merely the operation "observing" and described the observer as the result of the enchainment of such operations or such a recursive network in the sense adduced in the discussion of autopoiesis. Now, a few issues must be clarified in order to illustrate the context of the use of this concept of the observer.

First of all, I must point out an issue that time and again causes difficulty. One can say it a hundred times, but it is always in vain. The observer is not automatically a psychic system; he is not automatically a consciousness. The observer is defined in the entirely formal terms of distinction and indication. A communication can also perform these acts. One speaks about something specific and thematizes what one is speaking about. Thus, one uses a distinction; one speaks about *this* and nothing else. Such distinctions can also be specific: we now speak about the observer and not about something else. Therefore, the communication system, too, has at least the ability to observe. This leads to terrible confusions in language if one has psychic and social systems in mind simultaneously. Think of a school class. The teacher observes the pupils. That is common. The pupils observe the teacher. They have to. The teacher also observes that the pupils observe him. But now we have the additional case that the interaction observes the pupils and on occasion even the teacher. Admittedly, this latter case is rare, but it happens. The teacher may become the topic of discussion in class. The social system observes psychic systems; psychic systems observe psychic systems; psychic systems can observe social systems. Think of a question such as "Why is this question posed just now? Why does he always ask the questions that I cannot answer?" What happens in this case can be thematized psychologically or communicatively. As a matter of principle, one must indicate the system reference. If one speaks unthinkingly of an observer, then everybody automatically thinks of a psychic system, consciousness. But this is not what is meant if we consider the definition and the intended complexity and abstractness of the conceptual instruments that we have examined.

For the moment, I would like to leave open the question as to whether one can go beyond psychic and social systems and also claim that, for instance, living cells, brains, immune systems, and hormone systems observe. That an immune system is capable of discrimination is obvious. That a brain can discriminate, and process certain stimuli while not processing others, is equally obvious. In brain research, and generally in biology (and I am not talking about ethology, the investigation of animal behavior, which is a separate problem), one must, in light of phenomena such as cells, immune systems, and brains, ask whether it is possible to state that, say, brains actually observe when discriminating their input or that an immune system observes when distinguishing between different states of the body. The brain, too, merely observes bodily states, but in regard to their informational value, as biologists put it. I would like to leave this question open. If one were to give an answer, one would have to have a biochemical equivalent for the other side of the distinction. In this matter, we always and quite automatically also carry along the idea of a negation, according to which we do not mean everything else but only *this*. In language we actually formulate this as a negation. But what would be the biochemical or living equivalent for this other side that is *not* being used in the case of a brain, an immune system, or an individual cell?

I merely mention this problem since there is already a lot of discussion going on, in which, among other things, the question is posed as to whether the concept of the observer can in fact be transferred to the field of biology, from which, in Maturana's work, it arose in the first place, at least in a certain sense. Maturana ties the concept of the observer to language competency but then goes on to pursue a biological theory of language as the coordination of the coordination of interactions between organisms.[64] This is a rather peculiar fixation which circumvents the problem that I posed. But, for the purposes of a sociological lecture course, the complication that is thereby brought in suffices – namely, that the observer can also be observed as a social system. A social communication system is also an observer. This is the first point.

The relationship of the concept of the observer to the concept of the subject and the subject/object schema is difficult to determine. As in any distinction, we first are confronted with the following questions: Who is the observer who uses the distinction? To what purpose does one draw a distinction between subject and object? And when does this happen? We encountered the same questions in the case of the distinction between system and environment. The observer is the final figure but, as such, creates, in turn, a need for an explanation. This explanation can only be achieved with the help of more concrete terminologies, which is to say, specific distinctions. Thus one might say that at some point we disregard the distinction between system and environment and instead focus on distinctions between subjects and objects. In relation to the subject tradition, it seems to me, we then have to deal with continuities as well as discontinuities. One has a certain freedom to decide whether or not one would like to continue with the term "subject." Should the observer be called a subject? Is this a meaningful expansion of the classical concept, keeping in mind Kantian or Fichtean terminologies or the entire philosophical discussion that follows from them? Or would it be better if we drew a distinction and abandoned this terminology? I believe that, for such questions, there is no correct answer. We have only the possibility of stating clearly what we mean. For instance, I continue working with the concept of democracy, for the obvious reason of its general social acceptance, even if its actual meaning is different from being a matter of government by the people. In short, sometimes I decide in favor of continuity and at other times in favor of discontinuity.

As far as the concept of the subject is concerned, the moment of discontinuity seems stronger to me if one aims at working out the individual characteristics of the observer figure. What continues is the concept of self-reference. Consciousness (or thinking, the *nous*, reason) was always able to have a relation with itself. The *"noesis noeseos,"* thinking about thinking [*Denken des Denkens*] is an ancient, Aristotelian formula. The subject, too, was always a subject that knew that it was a subject or a consciousness that knew that it was a consciousness, which is to say that it has always had a capacity for reflection. In this sense, one can indeed say that we are talking about self-referential systems. Although we may bring in more material than merely consciousness, we are still dealing with the central figure of self-reference. Of course, it speaks against such an expanded approach that one easily loses sight of the fact that social systems are subjects, too. This lecture class is its own subject. The usual philosophers of the subject would be a bit disturbed by such a statement. Society, too, is a subject. Under the traditional perspective, one would be reminded of a collective spirit or something similarly terrible, which is to say, one would try to work with analogies of consciousness and run into the familiar problems in the process. From a pragmatic viewpoint, the expansion from psychic systems to social systems, from consciousness to communication, would rather suggest that we ought to do without the term "subject."

I believe, however, that there is a further, more important, consideration. We say that the observer uses a two-sided form. Let us consider situations in which the world is cut into two parts by such a two-sided form – that is, situations when there are only these two sides of the world and no third thing. This is the case in systems theory, for which only system and environment exist. True, there are different systems, and, seen from their viewpoint, the remainder is in each case the environment. Regardless, there are always only systems. The world is divided, cut, split, or torn asunder into system and environment, and the observer is himself also a system that observes other systems by means of the distinction between system and environment. Under these conditions, one finally must ask the question of where the observer is actually located. Is he placed in the system that he observes or in the environment? For the theory of the subject, it is extraordinarily difficult to argue in terms of the theory of difference, for it assumes in principle that self-reference lies at the bottom of everything. It assumes that there is, as it were, a point from which everything can be thematized from an objective viewpoint. I have never really worked through the traditional texts with this point in mind, but I suspect that it would be rather strange to ask the question as to where the subject exists – in the system or in the environment. For a systems theoretician it is easy to make this distinction. If we are dealing with self-observation, then the observer is the system that observes. He is in the system. He is either the system itself, or a reflective part or specifically developed moment of reflection inside the system. Or, in the opposite case, he is in the environment. We therefore have the corresponding distinction of self-observation and hetero-observation. A system can be observed from a viewpoint in the environment, as long as this environment can provide and organize the necessary capacities. In the alternative case, a system is a self-observing system.

Making this decision is of central importance for sociologists. For we have the choice either of perceiving ourselves as external observers or of being internal observers. Talking about the economy or politics without intending to earn money or acting politically in the process are examples of the former. But, when we create theories of society, we cannot avoid being internal observers. Insofar as we intend to communicate, we are already taking part in society. When social criticism thematizes society, it must also, in consequence, thematize itself as an operation inside society. The theory of internal observation satisfies a certain sociological need for orientation, for which we do not require a third, external position. We can perhaps imagine that there would be a switching, a back-and-forth oscillation, between internal and external observation. For instance, if we formulate a sociology of theology or of education, we are dealing with objects that conduct the self-observation of the systems of religion and education, respectively. In this case, then, we are positioned on the outside. But, if we want to understand the self-observation of a system, we must also be able to assume the position that a theologian assumes when he attempts, in the name of God, to recommend faith in God, or the position a pedagogue assumes when he argues, for obvious reasons, that in the final analysis education produces good rather than bad outcomes, and that one therefore ought to have the courage to have trust in education. In such cases, sociology can oscillate back and forth and attempt to describe the self-observation of the system from outside. The question of how successful such a procedure is poses a problem about which we, in my circle, do actually have a bit of experience at our disposal.[65] Nonetheless, it remains a difficult task, since theologians, pedagogues, and also legal scholars always think that one is trying to meddle in their field and do it better. But the distinction between self-observation and hetero-observation shows that this does not have to be the case. If, for instance, we describe the history of theology in the manner of the sociology of knowledge, it is neither our goal nor our claim to explain how faith in God arises.

Thus, the distinction between self-observation and hetero-observation plays a significant role in particular for sociologists. It is difficult to find a place for the subject in this distinction. In terms of the classical figure of the subject, it would not be permissible to bother the subject with the need to decide whether it is located in or outside the system that it describes. An extramundane subject carries a host of problems with it. Does the transcendental subject exist outside the world? Is this the logical conclusion of transcendental theory? After all, it insists on not being an empirical theory but instead relies on the facts of consciousness that are said not to be empirical facts and therefore are not supposed to exist in differentiated versions in five or six billion heads. On the contrary, these facts are abstracted from certain necessities that impose themselves on us when we think about the conditions of our thinking and experience. For these reasons, one might obviously assume that the transcendental subject in question must exist outside the world. But, if this is the case, one runs into difficulty with the concept of the observer, especially if one agrees with the decision that the observer must operate and indicate something. For it is hard to imagine how one could indicate something outside the world while one uses the distinction between the world and the outside of the world to this purpose and then is forced to specify this indication further.

Such questions have been addressed in theology, for instance, in the discussion of the concept of God. If God as the creator of the world is to be conceived as outside the world, he is distinct from the world. But how can he indicate himself, how can he create a relation to himself, if he must perform the distinction that would make this possible? The theologians have the possibility of stating that, *for him*, everything is different. It is said that he has intuition, which is to say that he can indicate without a distinction. He is said to be able to have direct access to the individual, even if this individual is he himself, without thereby excluding or not intending anything else. Nicholas of Cusa used formulations that state that there is no difference between God and world. God does not distinguish, not even between himself and the world. And this unity is observable only for him in a manner for which we have no empathetic understanding, since we are bound to and by distinctions. This may be acceptable as theology. But if one follows the trend of humanist theory since the time of, approximately, Fichte and thinks of the subject as an individual, then it becomes extremely difficult to imagine how exactly a subject could go about such things. If the subject is one of us, or is even like myself, then I could not say how I could think about myself, if I had no body and were not even here in this place, and not somewhere else.

I would like to add a brief remark that does not fit exactly into this lecture. However, it addresses the question of why the concept of the subject has had such importance. I am still asked quite aggressively where the subject finds its place in my theory. I believe that the persuasive power of the concept of the subject is linked to the fact that the theory of the subject was formulated in a historical situation in which a theory of society was not yet possible. Modern society had only just become visible in its vague contours. One knew that one was no longer living in the traditional society of the nobility. Many things had been restated in terms of a temporal relation, according to which one was no longer what one had been, but also not yet what one could be. According to this view of the future, it was claimed that one was heading for a future of constitutionalism, human rights, democracy, and, to remain within the political sphere, increasing welfare, as long as one would let the market operate freely. Needless to say, this mode of talking is still repeated today. This future perspective was unaware of possible costs and also did not see any limits. For these reasons, it became increasingly doubtful. In this situation, no theory of society was possible, except perhaps a sort of theory that would rely on such crude distinctions as the one between tradition and modernity, or slave-holder societies and rural societies of the nobility, on the one hand, and emancipation in tandem with the self-becoming of the subject, on the other. In this situation it was possible to neglect the fact that, from the perspective of the subject, there is no explanation for intersubjectivity. What is the *"inter"* of subjects? Or what exactly is another subject if I am a subject? If the concept of the subject means to say that reflection is at the bottom of itself and everything else (*subiectum*) then it is difficult to understand how another subject can enter the scene. Perhaps one can say, then, that this other does things exactly the same way but, seen from my perspective, I still have primacy in such a mode of speaking. I am the subject that sees others also as subjects with the help of analogy or empathy or, as Adam Smith has it, sympathy, even if I do not know exactly how these others do things.

There is no satisfactory theory of intersubjectivity. Husserl's radical attempt in the *Cartesian Meditations* to think through this problem has led to this negative conclusion.[66] And sociology concluded from this that it ought to proceed empirically, by simply stating that there is subjectivity. For nobody would want to claim that he is the only subject, that all others are not subjects, and that there is nothing going on between subjects. These points were then confirmed by linguistic and related theories. I assume that you probably know all this. But there is no theoretical justification for this step into the phenomenology of intersubjectivity. One spoke of "the social," but how the social as its own reality, in Durkheim's sense, could be coupled with the theory of the subject was never made entirely clear. What is remarkable in this scenario from the perspective of the sociology of knowledge is that a theory of the subject is persuasive in a situation in which one was not capable at all of describing society, because one did not yet have any theory of modern society at one's disposal that would have included all the limitations that we see today with regard to ecology, risk, and technological problems. Instead, the theory that was available at that time was based more or less on the balancing of individual claims via contracts or distributional politics. In this situation, the conceptual implications of the theory of the subject fell into oblivion.

But, at the end of the twentieth century, we are in a situation in which we can no longer proceed in this way. Instead, we now ought to grasp the genuine dynamics of the social as such. And this is independent of the question of what thoughts and conscious experiences human beings in the sense of concrete individuals may actually have. One might also say that the solution lies in a radical decoupling of the concept of the subject and the concept of the individual. If individuals are taken seriously in an empirical sense, and if everyone takes himself and others that he knows seriously in this sense, it is no longer possible to maintain the conception of the subject. This is my aside, a belated justification of my reasons for no longer continuing with this terminology. What is at issue is thus not that there are no human beings or, if there are human beings, that one ought not to take this fact all too seriously. So much for some of the explanations of the theoretical status of the observer as opposed to the prevalence of considerations regarding consciousness, on the one hand, and theories of the subject, on the other.

Another point concerns the question of second-order observing or second-order observation. This means that one observes an observer. According to the requirements of this concept, this does not mean that one watches some random people but that one pays attention to how they observe. The pedagogy of the eighteenth century, for instance, fulfills the requirements of this concept when its attention is drawn to the fact that children see the world in a different way than adults. Children are not just small adults who live in the same world as we do. They have different ideas, different reaction times when they are frightened, different fears, different ways of estimating distances, different interests according to which something is boring or not, and many other different traits. They have their own schema of observation according to which one must observe if one wishes to enter a child's world and see from that perspective what makes sense pedagogically and what does not. Frequently discussed historical studies in this style have been made popular especially by Philippe Ariès.[67] We merely formulate this in a new language when speaking of the discovery of the second-order observer. Pedagogues no longer see children as objects that ought to be (re)formed but as observers whose perspective one must assume in order to educate them.

It seems to me that the theory of second-order observation, of the observation of observers, solves many problems of the discourse on intersubjectivity but with a peculiar inflection that was not part of the terminology of subjectivity. Thus, a second-order observation is also simultaneously a first-order observation. One has to observe an observer. One has to take something seriously and has to observe a state of affairs, find a point of orientation, and designate something in concrete terms. It is not just a matter of a logic of abstract forms. Second-order observation is observation of an observer with a view to that which he cannot see. (I will return to this point.) One has to specify an object from whose perspective one sees the world or in relation to which one wants to re-create how it (or she or he) sees the world. To put it in more precise terms, one must pose the question "With what distinctions does an observer whom I observe work?" I distinguish this observer from other observers, but he or she quite possibly draws entirely different distinctions. For instance, he might act morally, or he might distinguish near and far away, personal and impersonal, and many other things. There are many possibilities. I must therefore pose the question of how I explain to myself (*yes, to myself!*) that he or she draws distinctions in this and no other way.

What is peculiar in this case is that we are dealing here with a massive reduction of complexity. We let the world fall by the wayside, as it were. Or, to put it differently, we move it into the category "everything else" or "all other observers" and concentrate on one observer. From that perspective we then regain the world, as it were, when we become interested in the distinctions with which the observed observer works, and in how he divides up the world, and in what he considers important (or not) in which situations. In this manner, an immense increase in complexity comes about through the reduction of complexity, for now we must be able to handle distinctions simultaneously. There is, on the one hand, our own distinction that justifies observing this and no other observer. And then there is, on the other hand, the distinction that is used by the observed observer. Thus, we are dealing with a world in which everything that can be observed has all of a sudden become contingent, depending on the chosen distinction. Therefore, whatever can be observed in a sense becomes artificial, relative, historical, and pluralist. Whichever term you may prefer, it all comes down to the same thing. From this viewpoint, it is then possible to reconstruct the entire world in the mode of contingency or of other possibilities of being observed.

The world becomes a medium that in a sense lets all two-sided forms, all distinctions, and all observers be what they are when they are observed. This is the first point. Second-order observation is also first-order observation, but a type of first-order observation that specializes in gaining complexity while dispensing with ultimate ontological certainty regarding the data, essential forms, or world contents in question.

The second point concerns the fact that, with the help of second-order observation, one gains the ability of observing what other observers *cannot* observe. Being interested in seeing what others do not see is a fascinating and, it seems to me, specifically European or "modern" achievement that actually reaches back all the way to the Middle Ages. Since about the time when central perspective was invented in the late Middle Ages by Filippo

Brunelleschi and others, attempts were made to reconstruct how others see, only in order then to be able to create one's own optical illusions that corresponded to what back then seemed to be the "natural law" of true seeing. It was entirely clear that in this process the perspective itself would not be seen. If space is not distorted under the influence of, say, LSD or its derivatives, and we are not looking at Vieira da Silva's paintings,[68] in which several spaces open up in different directions, and if we thus have a regular notion of space, we do not see how the unity of the space of our seeing is organized.

The terminology derived from perspective is always also a terminology that ought to carry with it the thought that the perspective is not seen by the one who sees by means of it. From this fact one can derive certain consequences, for instance, in the case of painting. In a space that is painted from the viewpoint of central perspective, it is possible to represent how certain people, due to their specific position in space, cannot see certain things. Something takes place behind their backs. I recall a painting – I believe that it is a Vermeer – in which a woman brings a letter to her husband at his desk. He does not turn around. The letter, in a manner of speaking, comes to him as being carried in from elsewhere. He does not see. But, on the basis of his familiarity with his wife and child, his house and situation, he just knows that a letter is being brought to him. What is painted here is the act of seeing that there is no necessity for looking at something. In painting this can be done quite well as soon as it is possible to work with the spatial imagination, which is to say, as soon as one can establish a central perspective that excludes the possibility of having the same person appear twice in the same image. This was of course still possible in the Middle Ages, when persons appeared in all situations in which they were relevant. But now there is only one space and, for this reason, it is possible to provide for the painting of not-seeing. However, because of its linkage to space, such a procedure does not lead very far. Ever since the seventeenth century or so (I have difficulty in determining when exactly this development began; perhaps it began with Don Quixote), there has also been another possibility, namely, that of describing in a narration that certain people simply cannot see certain things. Don Quixote has read chivalric romances. For this reason, his view of reality has been clouded. This is made apparent with the help of parallel figures, so that even a reader who has not yet become accustomed to this technique can recognize that certain things are not being seen. It is now possible that motives appear that have their basis in not seeing reality for what it is. In the novel of the eighteenth century, this plays a role regarding the questions of sexual interest and the marital interests of women. These interests must neither become conscious nor can they be openly admitted. I will leave it at that.

The developments that are truly of interest for our purposes can be found in social theory, especially in Marx and Freud. There are those theories that have a sort of therapeutic intention and try, as it were, to use therapy to make the blind spot disappear. For instance, the capitalists cannot see that they create their own demise. The entire economic theory is constructed in such a way that, *as a theory of natural economic relations*, it is not suitable to trigger social reflection on the consequences of one's own actions. Thus, the capitalists work towards their own demise, and one runs into the problem of whether one should help this process along a bit or whether it may be better simply to wait until the time has come. In Freudian theory, you have the same pattern at the level of a theory of consciousness. The unconscious is precisely an *un*conscious that marks the blind spot of consciousness and can become conscious only to the one who deals with the person in question. The upshot of the different notions of therapy is that one must, in the first place, bring to consciousness all that has caused a blockage in me. As a consequence, I will be able to deal with the world more freely. Today, the development of this notion of therapy aims more at stating that everyone has his or her own construction of reality. And the therapists are also in the business of constructing but, admittedly, with a bit more experience and professional assuredness. Nonetheless, in this case as well, the therapists' construction is intended merely as a diagnostic and therapeutic attempt. That is to say, in this case, too, the diagnosis is just an attempt that does not reflect about itself sufficiently but merely derives from its results whether something has worked or not. Apparently, there are connections between the generalization of the therapeutic stance towards the world, on the one hand, and the thematization of seeing and not-seeing, on the other.

The theme of seeing and not-seeing actually appears in Heinz von Foerster's book *Observing Systems* (parts of which are available in German translation).[69] There, this theme is addressed from the viewpoint that one does not only not see what one does not see. That is obvious. For, at this moment, we do not see, for instance, how the Christmas decorations are lighting up all over the city, and we know that we do not see this. Instead, Foerster claims that, in addition to all this, one also does not see that one does not see what one does not see. This is the decisive point. One sees what one sees and is so fascinated by it that one is not able also to see at the same time one's own not-seeing of all other things as the condition of one's seeing. I would be tempted to call this "the transcendental condition of seeing." By the way, the eye that cannot see itself seeing is an old metaphor, and in Fichte one can also find its reversal. There, the eye sees itself seeing and, as a consequence, the inside of the subject becomes illuminated.

I do not know non-European cultures sufficiently to make broad claims. But I ask myself whether this second-order observation and the interest for all that others cannot see is not a European peculiarity. The interest in "culture" that begins at about the same time, namely around 1800, also exemplifies the interest in seeing what others do not see. This concept of culture came about rather suddenly, and recently it has experienced a revival like so many other things. Caught in a certain cultural tradition, one cannot see certain things, which we (and one automatically assumes "we Europeans"), however, can see after all. If you consult the entire literature, including the secondary literature, on orientalism, ethnography, ethno-science, and so on, you cannot help having the impression that, slowly but surely, we have begun to see through this interest. We Europeans conduct this second-order observation with interest, in order to see what others do not see. But we now also recognize that this interest is merely a very specific interest and does not prefigure the future order of the world according to which everybody would only have to do things in this way and then everything would be fine and dandy.

A further point in the context of considering second-order observation concerns the question whether something like a permanent shift of the blind spot is even imaginable. We do know that we have a blind spot, but then let us just use a different distinction! The blind spot circulates, as it were, behind our backs. We merely have to be clever enough to know what we can observe behind our backs by means of which distinctions and under which conditions of blindness. To put it differently, if we constantly observe observations in regard to what these observations see and cannot see, the question is whether it is not possible that we are positioning ourselves at a rather peculiar functional level, at which we are satisfied with merely adding the index "observed *by*" in each case. Thus we might add, for instance, "observed *by* modern society," or "observed *by* Gorbachev," or "observed *by* modern physics." It is my impression that a typical attitude of modernity becomes apparent if we describe the state of affairs that I have just outlined as a circulating of the blind spot and thus as establishing recursive autopoiesis at the level of second-order observation.

I would like to adduce two arguments that support this view. In the first place, it seems to me that all modern functional systems locate their central efficiency, which is to say not so much their everyday operations as their characteristic operational conditions, at the level of second-order observation. I have already mentioned pedagogy. The pedagogue must observe how he is being observed. For the children, the necessity of observing whether they were being observed or not had been there all along, simply out of fear. But now, the pedagogues, the central figures in this business, must also hold back their attitudes and see, first of all, how they are being observed and how the world is observed. The same is true in politics. Politics must dance on the screen of public opinion. In spite of all the polls, no politician knows for sure what people really think. At best, one knows what some people claim to think, which then is used as the basis of statistical calculations. It is unimaginable that politics or the individual politician could know or just take into consideration what happens in individual heads. Public opinion, which is the result of communication that is available for further communication, provides a replacement. Under these circumstances, politics essentially consists of arranging the manner in which one is being observed by public opinion. Of course, one wants to arrange things in such a way that one is observed as being better than the competition. To this purpose, one must see how one is seen and how others are seen, and all this at the level of the everyday business – that is, from one moment to the next. Thus, to give an example, important summits ought not to take place so far out in provincial areas that the evening news cannot report about their results in time. One must be faster and address the topics a few hours earlier than the others. But the truly political lies in the reflection of second-order observation.

In the economic system, one uses prices to observe demand and the moves of the competition as well. One asks, "Can they offer their goods for less or not?" or "For how long will they be able to go on like this?" or "Is it still possible to create demand at this price level?" At this level, one constantly adjusts sales figures, scales, and investment costs. The artist also creates his form in a way that makes it possible that the artwork can be observed by means of this form. Ever since the nineteenth century, in fact since Hegel, as I believe, this situation has been expressed in the following terms. It is said that art can only be appreciated if one pays attention to the means that are used in order to create effects. We can reformulate this and say that art integrates distinctions in the artwork as directives that indicate how the artwork is to be observed. Under such circumstances, socio-political intentions or the similarity with nature are not necessarily relevant any longer.

All these claims stand in need of further commentary. The question behind it all is whether we have located the functioning of functional systems at this level of second-order observation and thereby have almost inevitably also included an awareness of the contingency of it all, which is to say, whether we always reflect on the involved artificiality, change-ability, and dependence on certain distinctions and let that be sufficient. This presupposes that we have at the same time a high degree of irritabil-ity and recuperative or corrective abilities in our system. Of course, there are always disturbances. Something unexpected comes through. One must be able to handle it without involving the perceptual level of second-order observation. In politics, there are surprising, unexpected events that require a concrete reaction. The regular functioning at the level of second-order observation is assured only if there is also a swift mode of reaction to disturbances available. One must have the ability to redirect money flows. One must be able to change laws. One must be able to drop certain political views and formulate new ones. In the field of science, it must be possible to bring out new publications and declare that the old ones have been superseded.

This analysis concerned the level of functional systems. Actually, I could imagine, though I still hesitate to state it, that there is a general medium of the modern intelligentsia that refers precisely to such an analysis. In Parsons's theory, you find the medium "intelligence" in one of his boxes.[70] Although this medium is not defined in sufficient detail, it is not difficult to imagine the modern intellectual in our society as a specific phenomenon outside the functional systems. The intellectual would be located outside the research operations that are scientifically grounded, the testing of hypotheses and data collection, and the techno-logical development. Thus, the intellectual could be seen as a phenom-enon that cannot be absorbed by the functional systems and instead has the ability not just to produce better research results, but actually to talk about things in a general manner. We may recall Karl Mannheim's "free-floating intelligentsia," which for him, however, is merely a metaphor. What is at stake here is the generalization of second-order observation. This might also explain why intellectuals talk mainly about other intel-lectuals, which is to say, why Habermas describes how Derrida describes Nietzsche or how Hegel describes Kant, and why others, in turn, describe how Habermas and Parsons describe Weber, whereas Parsons's critics describe how Parsons wrongly described Weber. All of this takes place at the level of discourse as a description of descriptions, as an observation of observations. Realities enter into this autopoietic network of the intel-lectuals only as shocks. Thus, the collapse of the socialist systems was a shock for the intellectuals, at least for many of them. But postmodern theory had already beforehand created a mode of averting or intercept-ing this shock. It was said that all of this could have been predicted, that only the failure of a theory was implicated, and that the social continued to have ethical relevance. The decisive question, however, is whether, in the absence of a theory that refers to reality, this medium of the modern intelligence can actually do anything else but conduct its second-order discourse and merely avert actual shocks with the nimbleness that is characteristic of intellectuals by reformulating or relativizing the relevant realities or by offering new ideas. At present, the "sublime" is on offer. [August Wilhelm] Schlegel already said that it was a good purgative. But currently it is "in." One knows who started the trend, and one can be for or against it. What is lacking at this level is a sociological contribution that would reflect on the figure of observation and thus could treat the medium of the intelligence within the framework of a theory, on the one hand, and also describe the problem of this detachment from reality and the corresponding means of averting it, on the other. I am not entirely sure whether sociologists already know that it is not their business to touch on things in such a light-hearted and silver-tongued manner or whether they are merely incapable of doing it because they have no theory of modern society at their disposal.

Let me finally make some remarks on another version of the same problem. In the literature on this topic, there are some formulations that pose the question of how the world can observe itself. That is, if you permit, a godless question. How *can* the world observe itself? In Spencer Brown and Heinz von Foerster's writings, we find the idea that the world has to create physicists in order to observe itself.[71] The world creates physicists and, consequently, there is an observer in the world who observes the world not just as an object, but as something that is constructed only in the process of observation. Modern physics has its own experiences with the deformation of reality by instruments of observation. Just think of quantum mechanics, to allude to something that is familiar. Of course, we know that the observer does not just see whatever he imagines. But, at the same time, he sees only that which is produced as an effect by his instruments. As it happens, just a few days ago, I found a passage in August Wilhelm Schlegel's doctrine of art in the first volume of the *Lectures on Literature and the Fine Arts* of 1801, where things still looked entirely different. There we read, "If one imagines nature in its entirety as a self-conscious being, what would one think of imposing on it the demand of studying itself by means of experimental physics?"[72] Schlegel speaks of "blind groping." That is useless. True, in some way the subject is no longer the actual measure. One is no longer dealing with an applied Fichtean theory, but one also does not get anywhere with the proposed kind of experimental physics. Nature observes itself. It seems to me that developments in physics during the twentieth century have legitimized the question of how the self-observation of the world can be implemented in the world if distinctions are used to this purpose that actually divide the world. After all, what is at stake is not a mere partial distinction, such as "Arminia Bielefeld and other soccer teams," for which the world is everything else that, as one might say, provides the context of this distinction. Rather, the question is how the world can be divided up into a side that is marked and one that is not, a side that is indicated and one that is not. It could well be that modern theoretical linguistics, on the one hand, and physics, on the other, have motivated us to pay more attention to this question of how the world observes itself.

A number of suggestions for solutions to this problem, posed in the manner just outlined, have been made, for instance, by biological epistemology. Maturana conceives of the observer as in principle based in life and states that the observation of life has to function biologically, since the observer is a living being that possesses language. If the observer does not live, he cannot observe. He is dead and cannot see anything. Yet, in contrast to physics, it is much harder to know in this case what kind of limitations for that which is being observed result from the observer's own equipment. In a sense, what we have here is a copy of the problem in physics. But finding more precise formulations does not seem to play the same role in this case. We can say that a living being must possess a brain. And we can say that this brain has certain data-processing limits, that it must process data simultaneously, and, to this purpose, it has specific capacities, and that for this reason nothing can occur that cannot occur. However, in a certain sense this is doubtful. We have writing and literature, and all sorts of things can be found in it, things that can be (re-) read and thereby realized also biologically, if you will. This includes possibilities for increasing complexity that cannot be captured very well in biological terms. On this issue, one might, for instance, ask what a biologist might mean when he says that an observer must be a living being and is limited thereby.

The sociologists have their own parallel problem, which they formulate in terms of self-fulfilling or self-defeating prophecies. This is to say that prognoses that are introduced into society by way of communication lead to a society that knows itself as it is depicted in the prognoses and therefore must react to this fact. This problem, as worked out by Robert Merton and others, has been treated in the literature almost exclusively as a methodological problem.[73] How is it possible to arrive at the objective knowledge of reality if one knows that stating one's prognosis changes reality? How is this possible if one knows, for example, that a Keynesian economic policy, once it has been formulated and implemented, creates the anticipation of such policy and thereby the expectation of inflation? Yet, independent of this methodological version of the problem, we are faced here, as it seems, with the fundamental epistemological problem of how a society can process cognitions of itself in the form of communication. What is the meaning of objectivity under such conditions? What is in question, then, is not how the problem can be pre-empted by means of suitable methodological precautions, but rather how we live in, and with, this type of circular network.

A talk on management problems that Heinz von Foerster presented in St Gall varies the question.[74] The manager, the planner, is part of the system that he manages. One knows, of course, that he does the planning and in due time organizes a defense in the relevant documents. One puts down the corresponding annotations and prepares for the fact that one is being "planned." And, as soon as the first signs appear that confirm this, one knows ahead of time how one can deal with this situation. And second-order observation is equally applicable in the case of companies or pedagogy. To be a leader is possible only for someone who is capable of manipulating how he is being observed. How this adds up later in the tally of reality or the final balance of the company is a different question altogether. If we assume that what is at stake is essentially the aptitude for managing how one is observed, and that authority has no source outside the company but is instead constituted by the current of communication inside the company, then we arrive at a much more complex theory of leadership, planning, and even risk management. In the last case, the same issues are relevant. Who is visible as the one who took this or that risk? Who is the one who can derive authority precisely from that fact that he is able to say that he is the only one who will have to resign in case of failure?

7 Re-entry

If we bring the preceding considerations into a general form, the topic of re-entry imposes itself once again. The observer re-enters into the observed. The observer is part of what he observes and sees himself in the paradoxical situation of that which he observes. He can observe a company, a society, or a sub-field of physics, as long as he reintroduces the distinction of observer and observed into the object of his observation. If one would like to derive an epistemology from this, one is not facing merely a methodological problem. Rather, in the final analysis, one must face the paradox of re-entry. Is the distinction that was introduced still the same distinction or not? All this would also mean that any type of epistemological constructivism or any epistemological instruction has to deal with a paradox that can be overcome only if one introduces a distinction. On the basis of such a distinction one might say that one distinguishes the physical instruments from the actual observation, or distinguishes the communication through which plans are announced from the system as it existed before and as it continues to exist after. In this manner, one gets back to the level of the observation of phenomena by means of distinctions. But, as a matter of fact, the introduction of this figure of the observer is nothing short of a metaphysical revolution (if, when using this term, we have in mind everything that goes beyond physics). This revolution is linked to the ultimate problem [*Letztproblem*] of the paradox and the operational necessity to replace paradoxes by distinctions that can be posited in this or that manner and are therefore contingent. However, they let us recognize what can and cannot be done with them. So much for the observer.

8 Complexity

Eighth Lecture

In today's lecture, I would like to bring the section on "general systems theory" to its conclusion. This means that I still have to address two further sub-sections – namely, the concept and the problem of complexity, on the one hand, and the question of how we are to understand rationality within this systems theoretical arrangement, on the other. It is not by accident that these two topics are grouped together. However, their connection does not become apparent in conceptual terms. In the early forms of systems theory, in the first attempts to formulate a general systems theory in the fifties and sixties, complexity had been the central problem. It was seen as an obstacle for successful planning and thus, in a certain sense, the problem of rationality *par excellence*. I will return to the conceptual questions in a moment. The point of departure for this entire discussion was the assumption of a complexity differential between system and environment. In other words, this starting point was already posited by the attempt to work with the difference between system and environment. And, in this process, it was assumed throughout – and I do not think that anyone would contradict my account – that the environment is always more complex than the system. For this reason, one was dealing with a complexity differential,[75] which led to the question of how a system can deal with a more complex environment. The problem is repeated inside systems if one has planners who plan a system but are not themselves the system, but merely a division, department, or sub-organization of the system, and therefore have the remainder of the system as their environment.

The initial assumption was that no system that distinguishes itself from an environment would have at its disposal the "requisite variety," as W. Ross Ashby called it, that would be necessary to create a sort of matching, a sort of point-by-point correspondence between system and environment.[76] The system does not have the capacity to connect a state of its own to everything that happens in the environment and to juxtapose one of its own operations to every environmental occurrence, in order either to enhance or to curtail what is happening. Instead, the system has to bundle and even ignore occurrences, and it must deploy indifference or create special arrangements for the management of complexity. In the systems theoretical discussion, this led to the formulation that a system has to reduce complexity in relation to the environment, on the one hand, and in relation to itself, on the other, if it intends to create planning organizations or agencies of rationality inside itself. In terms of the history of science, this problem can be traced back all the way to the functionalist psychology of the thirties. It was then that the limitations of the input/output model or the stimulus/response model, as it was called back then, were recognized. It was recognized that it was not possible to work with a simple one-to-one correlation of stimuli and responses. One saw that something lies between the two poles that brings about the transformation and which cannot be reduced to a mathematical function.

This was worked out in functionalist psychology, in the school of Egon Brunswik. The expression "reduction of complexity" first occurred, as far as I can see, in a book that was published in 1956, *A Study of Thinking* by Jerome Bruner et al.,[77] although it is possible that there are older sources. Similar suggestions were made already earlier. The literary critic Kenneth Burke wrote a chapter on "scope and reduction" as the operations of an action system that creates texts or performs dramas.[78] But the actual term "reduction of complexity" is taken from *A Study of Thinking*. In principle, we are dealing here with generalizations in a double sense. On the one hand, the system can bundle its environment, which is to say, it can summarize different events and things under the same name, see them as the same identical and invariant form, and relate them to its own reaction patterns that are activated whenever such identities occur. One can also imagine that the system has an identical reaction pattern at its disposal that can be applied to very different states in the environment. On the other hand, very different reactions can deal with one and the same state of affairs in the environment depending on the state in which the system finds itself. This concept of generalization as a matter of principle disrupts the one-to-one coordination by means of bundling, as it may be presupposed either in the environment or the system.

As I have already mentioned, Talcott Parsons adopted this manner of talking about the management and reduction of complexity that relies on the term "generalization." The second form of generalization could be summarized under the perspective of step-theories. You have already encountered such theories. For one, they have been formulated in relation to the concept of crisis, which says that there are states of exception in which things that otherwise are not normal and would not be practiced become permissible and even necessary. In crises, unusual things can be done. One may change structures that at other times are not changed. If the concept of crisis were taken seriously – instead of its being perceived as the permanent fate of humankind – it would have a step-structure that is applied to specific situations. This means that, in certain situations, unusual actions would be permissible – for instance, in order to reorganize a company or an economic system, or to resolve the confusion in the legal system by means of a unified law so that it is possible again to know what one can expect.

This is one version of the step-problem. Another, more formal version can be found in the work of W. Ross Ashby, an early cyberneticist whom I have already mentioned. Ashby distinguishes step-functions and calls a system that has such functions at its disposal ultrastable.[79] What he means by this is that, normally, environmental disturbances are dealt with locally. They do not push the entire system towards change. Instead, there are specific devices or arrangements that are affected. If you have a stomach ache, it is the stomach that hurts and not, at the same time, your feet. Pain does not radiate in such a way that it is everywhere. A system can get into economic trouble, but this does not necessarily mean that it is in political trouble. Scientific theories do not have to be changed because inflation is increasing. Instead one maintains the theories in order to describe inflation. This limited capacity for change was an exciting discovery, and it was formulated in an exciting way back in those days, precisely because one had defined systems as arrangements in which everything was connected with everything else. Complete interdependence had been the criterion for the concept of the system. But now, it suddenly became apparent that complete interdependence was actually not as beneficial as one had thought it to be, and that it was not really the form of perfection of a system but, on the contrary, an extremely improbable state. Under the conditions of complete interdependence, every disturbance would require that the entire system be balanced anew. And this balancing would take so much time that, in the meantime, the next disturbance would already have occurred and the system would never achieve a stable state.

In contrast, the idea of step-functions means the interruption of interdependence. In another terminology that adds nothing new, however, one might say that it means "loose coupling."[80] Loosely coupled systems are more stable than tightly coupled ones. "Tight coupling" is a very improbable arrangement. It is not to be found in nature. Organisms are built on the basis of loose coupling, and so are social organizations. We can bear the fact that people in the different offices change. This does not mean that the salaries must change or that the programs must be reformulated. Or, if they are changed, then we are already dealing with specific adjustments. The more a system tends to tight coupling, the more risk it incurs and the more endangered it is. Let me remark in passing that this is a thought that plays a role in the case of problems created by high technology.[81] If technical systems are so tightly coupled that the event of a disturbance makes the entire system explode and creates comprehensive damage, then this is a type of unnatural arrangement. The dangers of such an arrangement are familiar from systems theory. It would be necessary to build a security fence, an encapsulation, or a containment around it that would have to be based on loose coupling. That is to say, those who intervene in the case of a disturbance ought not to be completely disturbed themselves by this disturbance. Instead, they have to keep their cool and methodically do one thing after another. If something fails, they must move to the next step. But they ought not to loose their cool and go crazy!

Under the perspective of the problem of complexity, arrangements are examined that show how high complexity can develop, be it in natural evolution, be it in the planning of organizations, and how the system nevertheless continues to function. If we make the transition to distinction theory now, we can say that Herbert Simon's concept of "bounded rationality" also belongs to this context.[82] For this, too, is a sort of step-problem. Rational calculation is possible only if there are certain interruptions of interdependence or if a frame, a specific set of conditions, guarantees beforehand that one will find a useful solution within this frame in any event. Whether this solution is the very best or not is of no importance, as long as the decision premises guarantee sufficiently secured system maintenance and operation. This theory was formulated in light of the experience that the old economic theory counted on a perfectly competitive market, which is to say, a market that fully determines the prices and leaves little choice to the entrepreneurs' discretion, and thus bases its calculations on a situation that does not exist in reality. Organizations do not make one-man decisions. They have to make sure that the conditions of usefulness for the decisions made are created in the organizations themselves. This leads to a more complexity-conscious theory of the relation between market conditions or macro-economics, on the one hand, and organizational conditions or micro-economics, on the other. I touch on this only in a cursory manner. Some of you may know what I am talking about, and for the others my remarks may serve as a reminder to consult once again the literature that deals with the similarities of such modes of problem-solving with the help of generalization or a sort of step-function.

This would in fact also be true of Parsons's structural functionalism. Parsons also said that he could not imagine that a social order could function as a Newtonian model of variables in which every variable is linked with every other. At least for scientific purposes one would have to reduce complexity (this expression was not yet available back then, but this is what he meant) and assume structures according to which a certain system operates, by which it is identified, and for which the conditions of change can no longer be calculated by this theory.

The tendency to limit the problem to the question of the arrangements that a system has at its disposal to react to the high complexity, either of the system itself or of the environment, did not affect the concept of complexity. For this reason, it may actually be quite important to realize that the literature when working with the concept of complexity at all is using a term that, from a conceptual perspective, has not been well worked out. You rarely find that this concept is defined in this literature or that consequences are drawn from the definition, if there is one. The discussion of the concept of complexity is more likely to occur in a more formal type of literature, or at least in a literature that has little in common with the one that I have just discussed. Classically speaking, the concept of complexity is defined with the help of two other concepts – namely, "element" and "relation."[83] This definition constitutes a reaction to the problem that an increase in the number of elements leads to a disproportional increase of geometric progression in relations between them. The more elements you have, the more each individual element is overstrained by connectivity requirements. If one keeps in mind that connectivity requirements or contextualizations of an element determine its quality, then it becomes obvious that the increase of connectivity requirements must come to a limit depending on which kind of system is under review. This is true for cells as much as for communications. If one looks at individual human beings, then it is also true for the number of possible contacts with others that a human being can have in a certain amount of time. In other words, this insight is valid formally and relatively independent of the question as to what exactly the elements are and what their relations consist of.

The consequence of this is that, from a certain size upwards, each element can no longer be connected with every other, and that relations can now be created only selectively. For instance, the connections might be arranged in the form of a circle in which each element is dealing with two neighbors. Perhaps the direction of the information flow is predetermined, so that each element receives information only from one neighbor and passes it on to the other. But it can never communicate across the circle. Or think of a hierarchical form in which we have a top element and many base elements that can communicate only with elements at the next level up or perhaps merely horizontally with the elements at the same level. A secretary of state cannot directly call the registry of another government department in top-down fashion. That would be very unusual, and it is generally not well tolerated. Instead, there is a network of exclusions and inclusions of potential communications in place. Correspondingly, we find attempts in the literature to test whether star-shaped or hierarchical or circular models are superior in practice with respect to their information-processing capacity and the capacity for innovation (as well as other related issues). Network analyses in this formal sense are research programs that were conducted in the fifties.[84] The task consisted of testing selection patterns and selectivity in comparison to the now impossible condition that everything is connected with everything.

Therefore, if we want to provide a conceptual distinction or form for the concept of complexity, we can say that the problem of complexity is the problem of the threshold beyond which each element can no longer be connected with every other. Simple complexity, if you allow me this paradoxical formulation, still permits the linkage of everything with everything. But complex complexity marks the case when selection patterns have become necessary and progressively become more demanding, which is to say, more selective, more contingent, or richer in information, and thus demand that a particular choice and nothing else must be realized. My mode of formulating already indicates that we can no longer work with the distinction between "simple" and "complex." In this theory, there is no concept of the simple. At best, we have a concept of complexity that still permits the connection of everything with everything and then a concept of complexity that no longer permits this.

The medieval tradition worked with the opposition of simple and complex, in part because it was assumed that only complex states of affairs, since they were composites, could decay, while simple things, since they are not composed of other things, cannot. On this basis a world paradigm took shape in which momentary, passing, and threatened states were described with the help of complexity, and something simple, it was presupposed, could be erased or created only by divine intervention. The soul in particular is a good example for this. The soul is simple and not complex, and it is for this reason that one has the prospect that it might survive after death, since it cannot be destroyed. What sort of decomposition (ashes to ashes, dust to dust) could it undergo if it is not composed of parts in the first place? Similarly, one assumed that certain basal elements like fire or water were simple structures, and that a divine intervention would be necessary to annihilate them. *Annihilatio* was the counter-concept of decay and destruction. This has much to do with a world order that includes sufficient guarantees, sufficient impossibilities, and sufficient necessities in a way that permits, as it were, playing around with the remainder. In such a world order, it is also possible to explain that, in the course of history and among different peoples, one may well find things done in one or another way, but at the bottom of it all there is order nonetheless, and it all takes place within the confines that are determined by the plan of nature or the plan of creation.

This sort of language, which uses "complex" as one side of a distinction and "simple" as its other side, is no longer applicable to the modern understanding of complexity. There is no opposite or counter-concept to the concept of complexity. This has the effect of a theoretical signal, since we have only very few concepts for which there is no opposite. Meaning [*Sinn*] would be one example. For the negation of meaning still has meaning. Another example would be "world." It seems, then, that complexity belongs to the conceptual field and semantics of world descriptions in which one has no opposite concepts but instead has to work with internal distinctions, for instance with "Yes/No" or "selective-complex/non-selective-complex." This also indicates the importance of this problem, which, however, has barely been reflected on in the relevant theories.

I will now return one more time to the statement concerning element and relation in order to show, first of all, that the corresponding image is rather static. The elements are understood as being there and so are the relations. It is possible that a relation exists between A and B. And that is all. Initially, time is not taken into consideration at all. True, the whole can disappear again, but, with the help of the concept of relation, the coupling of one element with another is imagined first of all as abstracted from time. But now one can, in a further step, build time into this model. And this is precisely what happened in the discussion. One can say, then, that the elements can change their relations. As soon as elements can be coupled selectively, they can also be decoupled and coupled in different ways. With this view, one constructs a further dimension within the description of complexity. A system is able to realize different patterns in sequence. Elsewhere, I have called this the "temporalization of complexity."[85] Different complexities follow each other in sequence. Something may be very simple. Yet, in the next moment, the same system may find itself in a situation in which it displays a much higher degree of complexity, which is to say that, sequentially, it uses more relations between more elements.

Just putting the problem in these terms already makes clear that communication systems deal with complexity in sequence. The words and grammar of a language are not real connections of the possible elements of sentences. Rather, the sentences choose their elements, their statements, the words they use – precisely because, as one knows, already the next sentence will use a different combination. For this reason, we must take temporalization into account from the start in dealing with social systems – that is, systems that use communication. But, in the classical discussion, the question of temporal difference is addressed merely as one dimension among others. Different dimensions are distinguished concerning the concept of complexity – the number of elements, the number of admissible relations, sometimes even the different quality of the elements – and the temporal difference in putting the elements in relation with each other. In fact, I am not even certain that the different quality of the elements can be conceived independently of the relations. On this basis, one arrives at a multidimensional concept of complexity, and one also encounters the difficulty of not being able to distinguish whether one system is actually more complex than another. For it is entirely possible that one system is more complex in one dimension and another system in another. That is to say, one system might enable more relations or have more elements, while another might have more diverse elements or allow for a faster change of relation building. This problem was addressed in the literature and led to the question as to whether it is still possible to speak in a meaningful way about more or less complexity. But this discussion never affected, as far as I can see, the thesis that the environment is more complex than the system. That is taken to be so obvious that one does not even have to measure it. One knows it from the start. Especially if one has at one's disposal the microscopic dimensions of the modern natural sciences and can intervene even in the atoms and determine their patterns, one sees immediately that there is an astronomical number of event dimensions that no system could, as it were, repeat inside itself. For this reason, no matching in relation to the complexity of the world is possible. How one chooses to describe this state does not matter at all.

However, under these circumstances one could at least speculate whether, for instance, a brain is more complex than a society. Most people would probably say, especially if they judge without the benefit of theoretical preparedness, that a society is more complex. After all, a society is made up of a whole lot of people. But if the question is broken down into elements and relations, if one counts the number of brain cells and looks at their networking capacities, the question may very much become whether a brain is not more complex than a society. Society would be hopelessly overtaxed if it attempted to translate brain states into communication. The theory of operational closure, finally, expresses that such translation is neither necessary nor possible. After all, society could not develop if it had to deal with the impossible task [*Zumutung*] of turning brain states into communication. Such a statement can safely be made independently of a comparison based on measurements and thus of a measure that could tell us that the brain is indeed more complex than society. For we have so many brains that the problem would anyway never occur in the form "one human being/one society." In the context of the traditional conception of complexity, this problem of measuring is at least discussed. One

must recognize certain limits to precision that apply when one speaks
about issues of complexity.

A further issue that has always fascinated me concerns the question
of what happens when two complex systems get involved with each
other, when they are coupled or enter into interaction, and do not have
the ability to duplicate the complexity of the other system in their own
system, which is to say that they do not have the "requisite variety" at
their disposal that is needed to represent another system inside their own
system. According to a thesis by Donald MacKay, a Scottish cyberneticist
and information theoretician, freedom emerges under such conditions.[86]
Even if complex systems were machines and thus completely determined,
every system would nevertheless have to assume that the other system
can be influenced, which is to say that it reacts to signals. And this reaction
does not happen in a way that could be determined and calculated in the
system itself but rather in a way that is unpredictable. For this reason, the
information has to be sweetened, as it were. One must offer stimulations
which (one believes or knows by experience) can captivate other systems.
One assumes, then, that these systems cooperate voluntarily on the basis
of their own preferences or, if one wants to exclude this possibility, do not
cooperate. Thus, one assumes that they can decide and are not systems
that are completely determined merely to do what they do anyway. The
interesting hypothesis in all this is that freedom emerges from determination through the duplication of systems. There has to be more than one
system, and these multiple systems must be inferior to their environment
in terms of complexity, which is to say that they cannot possess requisite
variety. They must interact and simulate freedom in order to bring themselves into a relation with another system. If this happens on both sides,
then freedom *qua simulation* becomes a reality.

I have no idea what you think of this. It is, in any case, something that
is worth thinking about and which in some ways serves to break up the
old discussion of whether the world is determined or not. Once again, we
are dealing here with a distinction that can be phrased as a paradox. The
world is indeterminate *because* it is determined – not centrally, to be sure,
but merely locally.

Here, I would like to add some further considerations that go beyond
the current discussion but are also intended to explain why it is less
common to talk about complexity today than it was in the fifties and
sixties. Perhaps this has simply to do with the fact that the hopes for
finding a way to manage complexity conceptually, or, in other words, for
dealing with complexity analytically, did not become reality. When variables are combined, one can nowadays handle a high number of them,
but not any number you choose. Normally, it is assumed that a complete
description of systems requires too many variables for a theory to handle.
At this level, there has not been much success. However, recently I spoke
with someone from the Prognos company in Basel (Switzerland) who

claimed that, over the past ten years or so, huge progress had been made concerning the handling of variables in prognostic models. I cannot be the judge of this. In any case, it represents only one line of development. It is a different question whether it is possible for sociologists to investigate step-function arrangements or generalizations in relation to the problem of the reduction of complexity, even if one is unable to calculate with measurable precision how complexity is handled. A third question is whether, in using the concept of operation, we are not already committed to a terminology that undermines the fundamental distinction of the concept "complexity" – namely, the distinction between element and relation. What happens in this conceptual framework if we now say that the element is the relation or that the element is the operation that connects to other operations and cannot exist if it does not make any connections? Does it still make sense to speak of complexity in this case? Or do we have to reformulate the entire terminology? I pose these questions without being able to answer them. At the very least one can see that, in our alternative framework, we are instead confronted with the problem of operational closure. This is a difficulty I have discussed at length and which causes considerable problems. Has the new problem of operational closure replaced the old theoretical problem of complexity? We may recall that the old problem of complexity always was a problem of system and environment, a problem of reducing the complexity of the system in relation to the environment. Is it possible, then, that with the help of a new theory we can formulate the problem of system and environment differently – namely, as a problem of operational closure? If so, it is still difficult to say what this would mean exactly and where it would lead us. For the time being, I would merely like to point out that we are about to find a new language in the course of an actual paradigm shift, and that this new language no longer permits the continuation of the old concept of complexity, precisely because we now treat the distinction between system and environment as a unity. At the same time, it is difficult to ignore what has become of the problem of complexity. (If we intended to ignore it, we would need much more research that would aim at solving it.) Has the problem of complexity gone away, then, simply because we can no longer formulate it? Or has it simply been given a new name?

It is important to see that the primary focus on operation has to do with the elementary structure of complexity. This is related to a second problem, namely, the problem of introducing the observer into a complex system. This is still possible within the classical theory of complexity. It is possible to say that, within a complex system, there is an observer with his own complexity who sees his own relation to the system in terms of a system–environment relation. For him, the system to which he belongs is the inner environment of his own system. For instance, we can think of this observer as a company that operates in the market and which calculates in its own accounting office how it can maximize its profit or maintain its profitability and market share. These and many other possible criteria possess reflective superiority in relation to the market as such. The market is incapable of reflection. It is not a system. The company may not be superior to its competition. That remains to be seen. But we must ask how we can deal with a system that contains a part that has better reflective capacities than the entire system.

Similar considerations occur in Gotthard Günther's logic. Here, the sub-system in question is a subject in a larger system, in a collective. But the subject is reflectively superior.[87] At this very level, this point can be applied to theories of planning. A planner formulates a model of the system. He simplifies the system in a way that is not customary in the system itself. Quite possibly, he is more refined, more calculating, more theoretical, or more rational. The problem consists in the fact that this planner or this reflective relay is being observed. And what happens in a system that differentiates a part as reflectively superior and then observes it? Would this observer have to project, as it were, into the observed reflective capacity the reflection on the fact that it is being observed? Furthermore, would he also have to project into it the reflection that the system is no longer the same as soon as it is being planned, and that instead people (as part of the system) now prepare for being part of a plan, watch out, and take precautions? You know this from budget negotiations, or at least from what can be read about them in the newspapers. A system that differentiates parts that have a planning, observing, descriptive, and reflective function, respectively, and are superior in these capacities, becomes hyper-complex, in the precise sense that this state of affairs is in turn also reflected. One could reserve the term "hyper-complexity" for such a state of affairs, but in the systems theoretical literature the general tendency is simply to state that a system can produce a number of different descriptions of itself.[88] There might be one model for planning, another model for the behavior of those who know the plans but are not doing the planning themselves, and a model of participation that is intended to maximize participation. But all of this is of course utter nonsense. The situation becomes only more confused if everyone (or every sub-system) attempts to apply his own reflective capacity in the "hot center" of decision-making. Still, this is the level of descriptions of descriptions that one has to take into account in contemporary organizational theory.

What, then, happens in a system if the system is described as complex inside the system, or if it is observed from inside the system that the system observes how it is being planned? These are some questions that have been voiced. One has asked whether, under such conditions, there still can be stable states; up to what limits this hyper-complexity can be taken into consideration; and to what degree this possibility depends on standardization. One example of such standardization can be seen in budget negotiations when the previous budget is used as a starting point and demands for increases are made even if one knows that they cannot be fulfilled. Such processes are standardized in such a way that the standardization can provide orientation and enable a game in which one plays with marked cards (or false claims). Every player knows that they are marked, and at some point the time will have come when the game or the negotiation must end because a budget must be passed. It is possible that the reflective capacity can be greatly increased in an extremely standardized process. But then the standardization itself becomes a problem. It may become an attractive option to intervene precisely where others rely on the prevalent standardization. In such cases, we would be dealing with fraud that is raised to a higher power, or with the phenomenon of the free-rider position. In both cases, someone is taking advantage and using opportunities that arise from the fact that others play by the rules.

These considerations mark the current level of the discussion of this topic. The concept of operation, on the one hand, and the function of the second-order observer and second-order observation, on the other, offer us a terminology that is not yet a theory and certainly not a comprehensive solution to the general problem. Nevertheless, it is a terminology that allows us to get beyond the old discussion and observe what really happens when organizations, families, or therapies are planned on the basis of this terminology.

9 The Idea of Rationality

In a way, this entire discussion culminates in the topic of rationality. It has become increasingly difficult to imagine something like order, rationality, or calculability under these conditions, which are, to be sure, entirely real. In the first place, no terminological connection can be made in this transition to rationality. Rationality cannot be formulated with the help of complexity, although, eventually, I will try something exactly along those lines. In the general systems theoretical discussion, the concept of rationality, unlike most others, actually has a historic touch, a sort of historic conditionality about which one must gain clarity, to begin with.

To speak of this historic conditionality means to speak of the European conditionality of rationality. One may ask whether the history and semantics of rationality ran a different course in Europe than in the rest of the world and whether this circumstance requires a sociological explanation. We are moving here in the vicinity of Max Weber.[89] However, we must also ask whether the concept of rationality as used by Weber suffices to formulate the problem in a satisfactory way. From a historical perspective, the first thing that needs to be stated is that the Old European tradition until the seventeenth century relied on what I would call a "continuum of rationality." In terms of action, this means that both actions themselves and the conditions under which action is possible are natural. The actor realizes his own nature by acting under conditions that are themselves natural. For thinking, the assumption of a continuum of rationality means that true knowledge corresponds to the correctness that is actually contained in its object. The object makes an impression by being what it is, and thinking is correct if it correctly represents the essence, form, and specificity of the object. Truth and falsity are based on a received impression. Aristotle speaks of *"pathemata"* – an untranslatable term. In this context, language and also, as a matter of fact, writing are acknowledged as minor activity components. Because of language and writing, one is not quite as passively exposed to such impressions as are, for instance, animals.

Regardless, we are dealing here essentially with the depiction of the (external) world. The world, nature, and later creation all are conceived in such a way that, on both sides of a cognitive or action relation, similarity is guaranteed beforehand. This also justifies arguments from analogy. The *analogia entis*, or analogy of being, means that, from the start, nature or creation guarantees that similarities are possible, as are mistakes in perceiving them. It is possible to act wrongly or unsuccessfully. And it is possible to make mistakes when thinking. But the analogy of being assures that one can find one's footing again and can be cosmically on the right track in one's thinking and acting.

For reasons that may be of sociological interest, this view appears to have become increasingly questionable in the sixteenth century. Doubtless, the reasons for this can be found in the religious wars. People can no longer agree on the truth and therefore begin to attack it. It is possible that the printing press was also implicated in this process. Unlike in earlier times, one now had, all of a sudden, books that expressed very different views lying side by side on the same table, and this was not an exception but the rule. Now, one could order a book that expressed another view and put it right next to the first book. This could be done easily if one used a library. For these reasons, it is quite normal that the inconsistency of knowledge became a topic of discussion. If such discussions are experienced on a regular basis, one might wonder what consequences one is supposed to draw from them. Moreover, independently from this, one may ask whether there is a true religion or only numerous religious confessions that interpret an unknown fundamental truth that is common to all of them in different ways. As usual, the renewed interest in skepticism in the sixteenth century was prepared by the revival and discussion of ancient skepticism and by a more pragmatic stance. We may think of Montaigne in this context. In his Frankfurt lectures, Stephen E. Toulmin spoke of this period as a time that was willing to accept high uncertainty in a "humane" way and tried to react with such a conception as "tolerance," but was eventually drowned out by the new rationalism of the seventeenth century.[90] One may have some doubts about this, but the attempt to deal with the new challenges with the help of skepticism, tolerance, and an attitude that concedes to everyone their own convictions is quite clear.

However, the solution that became dominant in the seventeenth century, especially through Descartes's influence, is quite different. It consists of splitting up the continuum of rationality. On the one hand, we have the mental, reason, or *mens*. On the other hand, we have extended, materially dense space that has no rationality. The continuum of rationality, if you will, is split up into a rational and a non-rational side. What is rational thus moves to just one side of the distinction. In earlier periods, this was not the case. In those days, rationality existed on both sides, although in different ways. One could have the impression that the seventeenth century was the exception, that the Cartesian model did not work, and that the eighteenth century returned to a unified understanding of reason. After all, in our historical keeping of accounts, it is often stressed that the eighteenth century was the century of the Enlightenment and that attempts were made to give a new order to society with the help of reason. Of course, there is no use in denying that such attempts were made. It seems to me, however, that the conceptions that stood in opposition to rationality never really went away. In the eighteenth century, there was not only Newton but also the Baron Münchhausen. There was not only reason but also history. There was a pronounced flair for paradoxes, albeit mostly in the light-hearted, literary vein. There was not only the sovereignty of the rational order of society in the field of politics, but also the sovereignty of love that claimed its own dominion and resisted all attempts at intervention in questions of love out of scientific, political, or family loyalties. There was pleasure, and the concept of *"plaisir"* named something that could not be justified in rational terms. And the self-legitimation of the individual happened via pleasure. Enjoyment, interest, and pleasure are terms that do not permit telling somebody else that *this* is enjoyable, that *this* gives pleasure, or that *this* is somebody else's interest. Everyone must know these things for himself. If you say that something does not interest you, you have the last word. This terminology works quite differently than the terminology of reason. It tends to isolate reason as a special domain within which decisions can be made and insights can be formulated on the basis of criteria.

In America there is a tradition of political liberalism to which much attention has been paid recently. This liberalism also has its starting point in the individual, in human rights, and in the irrevocable and irreplaceable integrity of the individual. This reference to individuality does not lead to moral license for any type of behavior but merely unhinges the old views of order.[91] One is an individual, regardless of the family into which one is born, regardless of one's social position, regardless of the patron–client relations that one has to use in order to satisfy one's interests, and regardless of the religious sect of which one is a member. The concept "individual" formulates the dissolution of the old orders. It is generalized with the help of expressions such as "freedom" or "equality." All individuals are equal, and all individuals are free. Problems that result from this, for instance the problems of creating a political order, have to be solved on this basis – that is, on the basis of freedom and equality. There is a new morality concerning the fulfillment of contracts, tolerance, and commercial rationalism that is related to this situation. I merely mention this in order to relativize, ever so slightly, the notion that modernity is marked by the concept of rational enlightenment and is attached to this tradition with which it stands or falls.

This is especially true of the nineteenth century. When looking at the nineteenth century, I, for one, notice that it works not just in the domain of rationality, but quite generally with numerous distinctions, on whose unity one does not reflect. Thus, there is the distinction between state and society. "Society" is understood as representing more the economical side of things, the satisfaction of individual needs and the corresponding efforts. The "state" represents the political aspect, the responsibility for order, law, and collectively binding decisions. But there appears to be no place for the question concerning the unity of state and society, which would be a super-system. At issue is the specific emphasis and thus also the problem of ideology. Do you emphasize the economy or the state? Is your position more in keeping with the Western or the German position? Depending on the choice one makes, one assumes an ideological position, precisely because it is not possible to thematize the unity of the distinction. All of this can be rehearsed with reference to the various distinctions that arose around the middle of the nineteenth century. One example is the distinction between the individual and the collective. Moreover, the distinction between the state and society was introduced into the constitutional debate only after Hegel, by Lorenz von Stein to be precise. The distinction between society and community is a similar case. It is perhaps sufficient to adduce these three distinctions to see what they have in common. In all of them it is apparent that the question concerning the unity of the distinction is no longer posed. For the same reason, one no longer searches for a kind of rationality that ought to exist on both sides of the distinction in accordance with the Old European view.

Towards the end of the nineteenth century, a more insistent return to the problem of rationality and the distinction "rational/irrational" was apparent. One distinguished between rational forces that express themselves, for instance, in the economical sphere, in the rationality of a nationally oriented politics of alliances, in colonial politics, and in many other areas, and irrational forces that could come to the fore in all sorts of ways. In Pareto, the distinction "rational/irrational" becomes sociology.[92] The distinction between reason and life has a somewhat longer tradition. But it is a rather peculiar story that the counter-concept of the concept "life" gets changed. In earlier times, one had distinguished between life and death, a distinction that is very plausible. Either one is alive, or one is dead. Of course, the fact that people die was not forgotten, but the counter-concept to life and, in consequence, the concept of life itself increasingly pointed in the direction of the mechanical and of rationality. The opposite concept of life in the emphatic sense of the philosophy of life [*Lebensphilosophie*] and also of Romanticism is not death but the mechanical, the machine-like, Newton's world. And the life that is located on the other side is not the law-like calculability of its process but the immediacy of being at one with the world. This thought of the immediacy of existence is prevalent all the way though Martin Heidegger, at least through *Being and Time*, in which the immediate and the mediated relation to the world play a role.[93] I cannot explain this in detail at this point. I have sketched all this in rather broad strokes. I intended merely to give you an impression of the general tendency to turn the problem of rationality into a sort of island, if you will, and to isolate it in a determined domain that in each case is covered by one functional system. Thus, the rational can be that which is economically rational – for instance, in the form of optimizing means–ends relations or devising strategies for dealing with scarcity. In another version, the rational is based on the correct application of scientific laws. If one applies science, one acts rationally, as exemplified in a model of science that dates from the beginning of the twentieth century. Today one would be much less likely to claim that every application of science is automatically rational. We have moved far away from such a view. However, the notion that scientific mistakes do not simply fail in their functioning but, in addition, are not rational was very widespread and contributed to the tendency towards applying the concept of rationality to individual functional systems and seeing society at large as an area that was not defined by this terminology.

The tendency towards typifying models of rationality is based especially on Max Weber's work. Of great importance in this context is his juxtaposition of value rationality [*Werterationalität*] and instrumental rationality [*Zweckrationalität*] or, in Jürgen Habermas's terms, strategic rationality and communicative rationality that is in search of mutual understanding.[94] In these cases, as well, one has the problem that the concept of rationality in some way would have to be the same on both sides of the distinction, since rationality is used to designate both sides. As far as I can see, neither Weber nor Habermas gives an answer to the question of what this common component is.

Nowadays, one tends to understand rationality as the rationality of action (regardless of whether this is understood strategically or as oriented in some other way by goals) and to formulate goals in terms of preferences. Depending upon one's specific preferences, one pursues the corresponding goals. The focus on costs that can be projected leads to the exclusion of everything that happens unexpectedly and could be a reason for regretting one's decision. Phrased in the current terminology, one might say that the entire area of risk is at first excluded from the discussion of rationality. Only afterwards is it reintroduced as a sort of experiment and with great difficulty via the figures of risk management and risk calculation. As a matter of principle, the concept of risk formulates a future that one cannot know. Therefore, it cannot rule out that one might later regret one's decisions, even if one calculated their risks. After all, when risk becomes a reality, the situation presents itself quite differently. The current way of thinking in action theory tends to view rationality as a calculable area of means and ends and to include this area in a world that, taken in its entirety, does not obey such rational calculus and instead reacts with surprises.

Speaking in Spencer Brown's terminology, we have here, too, a "marked space," a calculable rationality, in which it is possible to calculate probabilities and improbabilities and which thereby also approaches all that which cannot be calculated. Nonetheless, this space or rationality is not able to calculate a large array of factors on the far side of the distinction. Risk can never be brought under the form of costs in such a manner that, regardless of what happens, the decision would have been correct all along, precisely because the eventual success covers the costs. You could try to conceive of this problem of risk with the help of such examples as technological risks or other ecological risks. You will see that such risk calculation does not work. There is always a non-rational zone outside the marked space. That is to say, we are faced, in this case as well, with the broken continuum of rationality.

The central question is whether it is possible to get beyond this issue. I would like to try briefly to sketch one attempt to do so. This attempt is being conducted under the name "system rationality." Its other, related purpose is to reintegrate the problem of complexity. After all, this problem does not stop once the tradition of discontinuing "rationality" takes hold. Rationality refers only to the system, not the world. This is a point that has been criticized. Habermas takes this view when he says that this is all merely system rationality and that the system is not all there is. But of course this would also be true for communicative rationality. After one has reached an understanding, there are still things that are left over, things about which and people with whom one has not yet reached an understanding. And the conditions change more swiftly than the readiness to find new understandings. This area on the far side of the relevant distinction plays a role in every model. It seems to me that systems theory in a certain way is better equipped to deal with it than the theories of action rationality or communicative rationality. In those cases, the other area is not even called a "life-world." In fact, I have no idea how Habermas could successfully prescribe such a name.

I would like to speak of "system rationality" to the degree that aspects of the environment can be accounted for in the system. You may recall that the system concept is defined with the help of the difference between system and environment as well as operational closure. This means that a system is defined by means of its indifference in regard to the environment. In light of this definition, system rationality means that one takes this back or that one denies the indifference of the system (the fact that whatever happens in the environment does not happen to us), and instead strengthens the irritability, sensitivity, or resonance (or whatever term may be used) of the system. This is a paradoxical and, if you will, utopian move. It means that one excludes the environment only to include it again. If we think of this maneuver in terms of the premise of constant sums, it would actually be a senseless to and fro without effect. But if one includes complexity in one's considerations as a variable of increase – which, by the way, is the reason for my bringing together the discussion of rationality with the discussion of complexity – then it is possible to conceive that a system whose rationality and complexity have been tested operates and organizes things differently than simpler systems that have not gone through the same evolution or planning stage. In other words, one may come to believe that among the patterns of complexity there are some that are more suitable than others for the processing of environmental irritations in the system. You may actually recall that such patterns of complexity are always patterns of selection.

If one looks at our question in this way, one finds many areas in which such a view can be made plausible in sociological terms. For instance, how or by what can politics be irritated economically? Only by the non-fulfillment of its plans? One does not even know *why* these plans have not been executed, only *that* they have not been executed. Does this mean that one must simply put a wager on them, or decrease the said wager, or perhaps something else? Or is there perhaps a sensitivity for highly aggregated economic data about such things as unemployment, inflation, the exchange rate [*Außenwert*] of a country's currency – things to which one can react with political means and for which one can choose and stress a number of different political options? Of course, one does not know exactly where these data are coming from, but the economic think tanks are considered reliable. A democratic opposition in these matters is not imaginable under the economic conditions of state planning, but only under the conditions of an unrestrained sensitivity to the economic indicators of the public weal and its opposite. Under such conditions, one can actually say that one judges a situation as threatening or as transitory, and one can suggest Keynesian remedies, or one may state that the market will help itself, as long as one is patient and waits. Thus, the political options are more varied than in the case of state planning. And, thus, democracy in our sense of the word is possible. At the same time, the probability of an economic disaster that thoroughly affects politics is lower. But only if all of this is correct! I have formulated all of this merely in terms of a model in order to show that there are solutions that react better to complex environmental states that they did not create and which therefore do not just register the effects of their own operations. They do not proceed in the sense of "what we intended did not work out and cannot be done or, alternatively, can be done." Instead, these modes of problem-solving develop a kind of sensorium for problems that are independent of them. With regard to the economy, this would mean an increase in political rationality as system rationality. In other words, it would mean that the political system would be increasingly able to recognize and handle more environmental states.

Similar questions can be posed in the case of the legal system. Is it possible for the legal system to bring about social change by juridical means? Can social change be imported into the legal process by means of such general legal entities as, for example, property, contract, constitutional law, and constitutionally guaranteed rights? Or is the legal system rigid, because the articles of the law are textually fixed and the legal system can therefore register only what is in accordance with the law as opposed to what is not in accordance with it? Or does the manner in which legal concepts are formulated, legal entities are created, and legal proceedings are structured lend itself to making additional information legally relevant even though the texts are preset? For instance, the means at our disposal to test subjective states of affairs are much more refined than they were in the early modern period or the Middle Ages. In earlier times, it would have been impossible to think of volition involved in a contract as legally relevant, because it would have been impossible to determine volition or motivation. But today's standardization of legal proceedings makes us confident that we can do this, regardless of how well it is done in the end.

If we place these considerations in the context of a theory of society, we may perhaps say that the differentiation of functional systems has the function of increasing chances for rationality, irritability, sensitivity, and resonance in the functional systems. It makes it possible for the ability to be disturbed to increase and at the same time provides counter-measures or procedural concepts, but only at the level of society in its totality. This, it seems to me, is one of the reasons why ecological problems do have an effect at the level of functional systems. We ask the questions of what kind of scientific research we need, what we ought to do economically, what can be achieved politically, and what kind of legal forms are suitable or not suitable for our society. Yet, at the same time, we cannot conceive of an agency that covers society in its entirety and balances it in relation to the ecological problems that it has caused. For, in that case, we presumably would have to do without the form of system rationality that I have outlined, which is to say, without trying to achieve higher complexity as far as reintroducing the environment into the system is concerned. Once again, we are dealing here with a re-entry figure or a paradox that we unfold by assuming that complexity is variable and that there are forms that function better than others from an evolutionary viewpoint and perhaps can even be designed or planned better, if you will.

With these remarks I would like to conclude this section on general systems theory. I would like merely to add two additional comments that are meant to encourage a skeptical assessment, as it were, of what we have achieved so far.

Well, for one thing, one always hears the complaint that all of this is terribly abstract. I tried to give examples. But, at the same time, I also did not want to deny the abstractness of my subject matter. The real question, however, is what kind of problem the abstractness of systems theory actually poses. Criticisms are voiced as complaints about or also as attacks on the fact that I allegedly cannot give empirical proof for my claims or, alternatively, that it is logically illegitimate to handle paradoxes in the way I have suggested. The best way of formulating these criticisms can be found, to my mind, in a Latin expression that cannot be translated at all, or only with great difficulty. The term is "*supervacuus*," or "*supervacaneus*" in the old Latin of the Republic, which is even worse. If you consult a dictionary, you will find that it is translated as "superfluous." The theory is superfluous! But what is really meant by "*vacuus*" is something empty. However, one cannot say "more than empty" or "*über*-empty" or "over-empty." How could one express something like that? Let us stick with "*supervacuus*." We can then ask whether general systems theory aims at a semantics that offers little information but leaves open the question as to whether it is possible to use its concepts operationally, or in a theory-tactical (if you will) or theory-technical manner. What needs to be demonstrated is how it is possible (and how it is not possible) to connect something different to such concepts as "operational closure," "autopoiesis," "self-organization," "difference theoretical approach," and "paradox." It is a matter of finding out whether it is not possible at this level to make decisions clear. "If you start in this way and from this starting point, you will subsequently no longer be able to do just anything." Thus, I tried just a moment ago to show that the concept of complexity becomes untenable if, on the one hand, one holds fast to elements and relations and, on the other, one works with the concept of relation.

It is not necessary to answer such questions right on the spot. The genuine achievement of such theories, it seems to me, lies first of all in the possibility of inserting probes into the established conceptual language and to see whether it still works or has to be changed. Only when a sufficiently complex theoretical edifice has been built will it be possible to see what its outcome is and whether it can serve certain fields of research better than before.

Finally, here is my last point. If one takes the concept of an autonomous or autopoietic system seriously, the system would actually have to include its own negation. A system is not perfectly autonomous or self-contained as long as it does not include its own negation. This leads to the question of whether this theory has a place where it can negate itself. In order to give an answer to this question, I have to rely on my experiences with my personal "card catalogue."[95] Some of you know that there is a gadget that contains several thousand notecards on which I always write down everything that I find interesting or of possible use. This gadget is pretty big and is, by now, approximately forty years old. In this catalogue, there is one notecard that says that all other notecards are wrong. In short, the argument that negates all other notecards is thus written down on a notecard. But, when I open the catalogue, this notecard disappears, or it is given a different number and looks for a new place. You can imagine that I cannot search for this one card among the other 50,000 or 60,000 – particularly since this card has the ability to jump from one position to another like the joker in a card game. For this reason, I cannot explain to you in this lecture why everything is wrong. Instead I must leave this to you as an assignment over the holidays. I hope that you will return after the New Year with the argument that I cannot find in my catalogue.

III

Time

Ladies and gentlemen, let me begin by wishing you a happy New Year. I hope that during these turbulent times you have been able to reserve a private island for yourselves that helps to decouple you at least partially from world events without excluding all possibility of participation.[1]

Now, after the unit on systems theory, I will begin a new unit. I will stick to the outline for this lecture course, but perhaps I should state beforehand the purpose of it all and what determined the choice of topics. I would like to try to apply formulations taken from general systems theory to topics that are relevant in different ways to sociology and the social sciences. Often they are introduced without being defined, as if one always already knew what is meant, for instance, by "meaning," "action," "time," "communication," or "expectation." My impression is that conceptual suggestions can be derived from changes in the landscape of systems theory. Moreover, I believe that we could see it as our task to figure out how concepts in everyday parlance and also in scientific language are changed and made more precise, or even have to be abandoned, if one uses a systems theoretical approach. In addition, a familiar and well-known conceptual apparatus is offered to you for reflection, even though one cannot ever be entirely certain that the results will actually be useful and help our concrete investigations along.

I think that this kind of approach can be demonstrated best in regard to the topic of time. For it is here, it seems to me, that the most radical torpedoing, as it were, of regular ships takes place. And this happens precisely by means of the concept of the observer, which is to say, not so much with the most characteristic systems theoretical means. If you read the literature about time, you will find that it is generally agreed that time is always a system-relative concept. I myself played around with the distinction "world time/system time," but my results did not amount to much more than the distinction between world and system.[2] If on the following pages we speak of the observation of time relations, or of the observer, or of the one who makes distinctions (I have already explained these concepts), it is possible to project this onto a system. The first question, then, is always who is the observer or which system is being spoken about. Are we talking about a specific person or an organization? Or are we talking about a student who thinks at first that he has a lot of time, before he notices that his time is running out? Or are we perhaps talking about a woman who is about to give birth? In every case, we must include the system reference when we ask who is observing.

However, the analyses I would like to present are all situated at a more radical level. After all, it is not of much use to say, "This is the time of the university," "This is the time of person X," and "This is the time of modern society." First of all, one would have to know what exactly is designated by the term "time," and only then can one examine whether connections can be established with structural problems of modern society, the individual who has come under pressure in terms of his biography, or in terms of a complex organization – say, the fashion industry.

If we use the observer as our basis, we must begin by reminding ourselves that observation has to do with a double perspective. On the one hand, observing is an operation. It happens concretely, and the reality that is observed is guaranteed first of all by the fact that the observer is able to observe. Whether an object is described correctly is indeed a question. But how the observer is put into the position of observing at a particular moment is another question. The discussion concerning constructivism and realism focuses increasingly on the issue of operation. Arguments are made not unlike the ones I have just adduced. If someone processes observations, he must have an opportunity to do so; the world must allow it; the ecology must be right; he must be alive; his head must function at least to the degree that he can draw distinctions; and so on. Thus, one is dealing, on the one hand, with this operational approach and, on the other, with the assumption that observing amounts to handling distinctions. In the first place, we must ask questions about when observation happens, who is doing it, and what else is involved when we say that time is something that has to be observed. In the second place, we must ask what exactly these distinctions are.

Before analyzing these two aspects further, I would like to point out a fundamental change in our semantic disposition. This change is linked to the fact that we base our views on the observer, and that we therefore understand the questions of who observes and what distinctions are being used in a radical sense and take them very seriously. After all, if I interpret our tradition correctly, the general mode of thinking has always been of a different kind. What I would like to call a distinction or an operation has generally been seen as a division of the world. This has had consequences especially in the area of time and, of course, also as far as our categories and concept formation are concerned. Presumably, you start with the assumption that time "is" something. After all, you say that "this 'is' already past." There is an extensive philosophical discussion of the question as to what the "is" in "it is" actually means. The "is" and "being" indicate that there is something about which one is talking, and the natural way of dealing with it is by creating divisions. As far as time is concerned, the division into past, present, and future may well be dominant. If you try to describe time, you will probably refer to this division. Time, then, is represented as a line on which something moves.

This manner of describing time in terms of a division and a movement across the division led to difficulties that in philosophical debate are usually demonstrated with the help of quotations from Augustine. In pretty much every study of time, one finds the quotation in which Augustine states that he knew what time was before he began to think about it, and that it became increasingly less clear the longer he thought about it.[3] But apparently the confusion did not make the idea of the division disappear. In the *Confessions,* we find remarks stating that time comes from the unknown, the dark, *ex occulto,* and disappears into the dark.[4] But it is "there" for as long as that illuminated path exists along which one can see when Rome was sacked, when Christ was born, and so on, and thereby can fix points in time. All of this culminates in the enigmatic character of the concept of movement.[5] What is a movement? Why do we need the concept of movement whenever we want to talk about time? Apparently this need is linked to the image of a dimension or section of a line, through or on which something, but not everything, moves with a certain velocity through time. An alternative image is the river of time that flows right through us. Now, river or flow, movement, and process are categories that presuppose that an ontological disposition or description of the world in the dimension of time is available. The world "is" divided up, and something is moving in the world.

But what happens if we replace this metaphysics of divisions with the question of who distinguishes something or who is the observer? This is positively the last question that can still be asked. For, if one wants to observe the observer, one must already have an observer who observes the observer. One cannot get beyond this. In this language, the *"meta ta physika"* is the observer. And this is one reason why I hope that, through this perspective, I will arrive at sociological questions which will lead into the field of discussion that is traditionally under the philosophers' care. The observer can be society at large.

Let me, then, try to make clear, once again, from this perspective the difference between operation and distinction. If one takes as one's basis the observer who makes temporal distinctions, the first question is when exactly this happens. This question is always posed by a different observer, perhaps even an observer who would like to observe himself and asks himself why, for instance, he has to present a lecture right at this moment and not earlier or later, or why he might not do this faster or slower than he is currently doing it. The starting point is generally that time is localized as a reality in an action or an operation that takes place at some point in time. The question is how the observer of the observer intends to describe this "at some point in time." That is to say, an observer must be determined first of all: an observer whom one intends to observe, so as to find out how and under which perspective he divides time. It seems to me that such an inquiry has a radical consequence that can be stated as follows. Everything that happens happens simultaneously. The operator, the observer of time, observes when he observes and does not do so when he does not do so. Everything that happens happens in the moment when he reflects on the future or the past, on velocity or acceleration, on the present, on urgency, and, in fact, on anything else. It all happens neither before nor after this moment.

At least this would be a way to make clear the relativizing and keying of the idea of time to an observer as opposed to the notion that time is present in different temporal modalities and with indices for the future, past, and present. A counter-perspective to this view must state that everything happens simultaneously. This counter-perspective contains a demand or an invitation to experiment in one's mind and to see what one gets to see, if one has clearly established in one's mind the fact that everything that happens happens simultaneously. Everything that happens now happens now. It does not happen earlier and it does not happen later. There are very few explicit treatments of this problem. At some point, I held a lecture about it in Vienna because I knew that Helga Nowotny would be in the audience. She had just published a theory of the extension of the present with the title *Eigenzeit*.[6] An expanded version of my lecture is published in volume 5 of *Soziologische Aufklärung*.[7] According to Nowotny, the present expands more and more. How one can arrive at this idea did not become clear to me, either in her text or in the discussion after my lecture. My anti-thesis stated, "No, we are shrinking." We do what we do, and already it has gone and can no longer be changed. We cannot do it over, and we also have to take into account a future in which we cannot yet act, or work, or make plans and prepare for things. And nobody else can do these things either.

In the sociological literature, particularly in Alfred Schütz's early book *Der sinnhafte Aufbau der sozialen Welt*, one can find the thesis that all human beings age simultaneously.[8] I believe that he speaks of "growing older together."[9] Although it contradicts the visual evidence, nobody can age faster than others. We live in lockstep, independent of our actual physical wellbeing or the density, concreteness, variedness, or boringness of our lives. Nobody, now, is able to be present in our future and tell us to watch out since this or that is going to happen to us. Of course, there are those hard-to-explain attempts to see the future, and naturally nobody can stay in the past. This is especially tragic today. Looking at the generation of '68, for instance, one cannot get rid of the feeling that these people would have liked to stay in "their" past. When they make public appearances today, they deal with a past that for them has not passed. When they meet, they congregate like the old war-horses who want to hear the sound of the trumpets once more. But, of course, it is not possible to live today in a time that has passed. If one lives in conscious awareness of one's environment, looks beyond one's own time, and sees objective connections, ideas, recollections, and political memories, it also becomes clear that one cannot possibly pretend that one is still in the same situation. This point is equally important for the discussion of tradition and traditionalism. One can no longer live as if one were living in times past. One can, however, make an ideological commitment to the past. Thus, Joseph Marie Comte de Maistre and other authors of the nineteenth century cultivated tradition as ideology. That is something different. But in each case this deployment of tradition, too, must be done in the present. One of the more important points for our purposes is that you gain clarity by the fact that everything that happens happens simultaneously, and that, for this very reason, no one has an advantage or a disadvantage.

A second point, to which I shall return when I speak about organization, is the uncontrollability of the simultaneous. If something is simultaneous, we cannot reach it operationally. In keeping with the customary ideas about causality that presuppose a time difference between cause and effect, we cannot affect, change, or reorganize it. In addition, we cannot react to our environment insofar as its reality is simultaneous with ours. All this opens perspectives concerning problems of synchronization, which always requires us to venture out into that which can no longer be changed as well as into that which is still invisible, indeterminate, and yet to come. As a result, this point raises questions that refer back to notions of control, steering, and causality as such. Here I see a connection between our present concern and the thesis of operational closure, as well as the thesis of cognitive constructivism, which states that the system deals only with its own recursions but cannot operationally handle the simultaneously existing environment.

I have spoken earlier about this, in relation to operational closure. Now, we see this point again from the perspective of time, as it were. We cannot change what happens simultaneously. We can only diminish or enlarge to a certain degree the temporal extensions of simultaneity. We can speak more slowly and expand our mode of talking a bit, so that we can respond to the reaction that our speech elicits within the same speech situation. We can slow down certain things and observe what happens. And then we can resize the temporal slightly differently. However, the possibilities of playing with the present and of prolonging what has been called the "specious present" (that is, the visually extended present) are rather limited and are linked to the *modus operandi* of a system. This means one thing for communication and another for perception. If an experienced soldier perceives an imminent danger or hears the bombs fall, he knows how much time is left to drop to the ground.[10] In such moments, the present has a certain perception-like expandability. But this changes nothing in principle. It merely shows that a small expansion of the respective present is built into this conception of time as a variable.

This should suffice for the moment on the issue of the operational approach. The second question of at least equal importance concerns, then, the distinctions with which those people work who thematize or perceive time – which is to say: What are the distinctions by means of which they observe time? Here, too, we encounter the distance of systems theory from the ontological approach to a theory of time. The latter approach would have to claim that time is something that exists and that theories of time represent their object either correctly or incorrectly. According to this, it ought to be possible to treat time as if it were something given. In consequence, speaking about time would be a question of cognition and of the discussion of the truth or falsity of time concepts and representations. In contrast, from the viewpoint of the observer, questions of how and with the help of what distinctions time is thematized must remain open. Based just on the assumption of simultaneity, such questions are not necessarily predetermined. If I say that everything that happens happens simultaneously, I am not yet saying much about time. Simultaneity is a concept that requires its opposite, non-simultaneity, but does not say anything about it. Time comes alive, and it becomes possible to describe or indicate time only when one includes a distinction. Merely claiming simultaneity is not saying much besides the one statement that all time distinctions must be made by someone at some particular point in time.

For instance, one result of this claim is that the future and the past always occur simultaneously. That is very strange. One could talk about this at greater length. But what is decisive is that the distinction *qua distinction* or *qua unity* is a distinction that was made at some point, and in which both of its sides are posited simultaneously. It would make no sense to speak of the past if there were no future. But perhaps the theory of distinction itself forces us to indicate from which side we start, which is to say, to indicate whether we are interested in the past or in the future. You may recall that we must always indicate to which side of the distinction we are referring. To the degree that distinguishing between the past and the future does not make a difference, time itself disappears. Both sides of the distinction of time, as is the case with all distinctions, have simultaneous actuality. Yet, at the same time, this distinction, too, is constructed asymmetrically, so that at any given time only one and not the other side can be used. This is how the operation "observation" is defined.

One possibility for approaching sociology as well as general issues of historical semantics by means of this perspective becomes apparent if one poses the question as to which distinctions play a role in each particular case. The respective distinctions cannot be arbitrary. Nothing is ever arbitrary. If one claims that the choice of a distinction is arbitrary, one clearly has not reflected on this sufficiently and not worked out a follow-up question either. From the viewpoint of this concept, the distinction of time, it would have to be possible to see what kind of system the observer is. It would also have to be possible to see what structural burdens, conditions of its own autopoiesis, and operational types of perception, communication, and perhaps even life, it carries with it and has to maintain. On this basis, one then could see what kind of distinctions play a role.

The first step, however, consists in forming an idea as to which distinctions have played a role. You will find quite a bit in the literature on this topic. One discussion that was largely worked through has pretty much been given up. It concerned the questions as to whether time is thought of as linear or cyclical and whether there is a linear as opposed to a cyclical time-consciousness. One had this idea that there were cultures whose time-consciousness had a primarily linear and others whose time-consciousness had a primarily cyclical orientation. To show this, it is always possible to cite selectively specific texts from ancient literature. Yet, as a matter of fact, it is rather unimaginable that a culture would limit its entire temporal orientation exclusively to one or the other type. It has been claimed that the Hebrews thought in primarily linear terms, and the Egyptians as well. As the Nile flows through the land, so time was seen as a line that leads somewhere. However, in Egyptian mythology, the rhythm of the year or of the days naturally played a role, as did the rising and setting of the sun and the return of the seasons. Repetition played a big role in Egyptian rituals, which were performed, among other things, to make sure that the course of the sun and everything that is connected to it would indeed be repeated. Thus, there were linear as well as cyclical ideas of time. And it was probably not any different in ancient Greece. I cannot get my mind around the thought that the Greeks had the idea that the Persian Wars had to be renewed from time to time and that the battles of Salamis and Marathon had to be fought again. True, to the degree that the Greeks recalled their own history and gave rise to a rudimentary consciousness of progress in their literature concerning the cosmos of divinities and Greek history, it is apparent that they were not very well able to imagine that all of this takes place on one side of a cycle and repeats itself. I believe that today the issue of "cyclical versus linear" can no longer be seriously discussed. The type of criticism that I sketched a moment ago is widespread in the literature. However, there is also a sort of routine repetition of the conception that pits a cyclical against a linear temporal orientation, precisely in the form in which it was picked up from earlier authors.

Another issue concerns the distinction between "moving" and "unmoved."[11] It appears that this distinction had a decisive influence on European history, especially with regard to the difference between a divine reality or mode of observation that was located on one side of the distinction and a human reality that was located on the other side. We are accustomed to think of time in terms of movement and to imagine that there is something stable, like the bank of a river, without which we could not perceive time or movement. At the same time as movement, there must be something that does not move and in relation to which time moves. But this is a culturally, historically, and quite possibly socially conditioned way of seeing the problem. Today, it is by no means the case that all cultures to which we still have access worked primarily with the schema "moving/not moving." Jan Assmann, the Heidelberg Egyptologist, has published beautifully conceived studies on the Egyptian time-consciousness. In them, he interprets two different conceptions of time that are handed down in the form of entirely different vocabularies, as if they had nothing to do with each other. He calls the first of them "resultativeness," which is to say that one imagines time as originating somewhere and being present as a result, as being that which it is. To the second he designates the term "virtuality" and refers here to time as possibility.[12] This could be read in terms of the difference between the past and the future. I am not sure whether such a translation would overburden the available material. It would be necessary in any case to make a linguistic decision. Which term ought one to use? Would one prefer to thematize the time dimension more in relation to the events that led to the current state of affairs and had as their result such outcomes, for instance, as a city having been built or a king having died? Or would one prefer to think rather of time in terms of chance, possibility, the insecurity of what is yet to come, and what is yet to be done? If it were possible to immerse oneself in the material, and if one still had the chance to interview those people, one would of course very much like to know how the two conceptions are connected. Is it possible to couple "resultativeness" and "virtuality" in such a way that one can see that the result limits the possibilities? Or is it the other way around? Do we have certain possibilities because we have developed technology, have writing at our disposal, and have received more freedom from a new generation of gods? I cannot answer such questions. But they do impose themselves if one really looks at the distinction more closely. Are "resultativeness" and "virtuality" different aspects of the world that have nothing to do with each other? Or are there also conceptions of the unity of time? To the degree that I have followed Assmann's work, it seems to me that the development towards a consciousness of the unity of time and also towards a symbolism that could serve to unite different situations, such as life and death or sunrise and sunset, is a very gradual achievement. Essentially, this was accomplished in a narrative fashion. But it did not lead to a conceptual and theoretical penetration of the unity of the different elements. However, I am speaking here about something in which I have no expertise. My aim is to draw attention to the fact that the occidental, as opposed to the Egyptian, tradition works with specific distinctions that should not be taken as self-explanatory, as if they were concomitant with time-consciousness as such or constituted an essential element of all conceptions of time.

The distinguishing feature of the occidental tradition of the "moving/not moving" distinction is that it provides a possibility to conceive of the unity of this distinction – namely, in God himself, the unmoved mover, in the Aristotelian sense. God is the authority who, unmoved himself, is responsible for the totality of everything that does or does not move, observes it, and externalizes it out of himself (or whatever formulation you prefer). At a level above the distinction between what is moving and what remains unmoved, there is unity. This can be worked out in detail in models of emanation or in the form of a cosmology. In the case of emanation, the unity of the unmoved gives rise to a dualism of moving and unmoved. The unity itself is unmoved, but it draws the distinction between moving and unmoved, not unlike the "I" in Fichte, which gives rise to the difference between the "I" and the "Not-I." One can see here that it is possible to go beyond mere distinction, or the merely qualitative differences of temporal aspects, and ask in a mythological, and subsequently also philosophical, manner how all of this was originally. What is the beginning, and how does a difference come about? What are the consequences of all this for our situation today? Do we have to consider "time" as something specifically human? Is God beyond all times? Does God see all of the past and the future simultaneously? On the basis of our claims concerning simultaneity that we made a few moments ago, one would have to say that, for God, all of time is simultaneous, and that his own presence lasts as long as time, as such, is going to last. Such claims can indeed be found in theology.

If we follow up on this with an analysis in the style of the sociology of science, one could ask what kind of society describes time in this way. One could also pose the question of what is put on the side of the unmoved or unmovable and what on the side of that which moves. In the tradition that is in part Aristotelian and in part Platonic, essences are among the constants, and history, for instance, belongs to the realm of that which moves. This also means that history ought not to be taken too seriously because it is a state of affairs that is always disturbed anew and perfection cannot really be achieved in it. In the sixteenth century, a lengthy debate about poetry and history took place. In it, it was said that poetry, although it consists entirely of untruths, gets to the essence of things. In contrast, history constantly disturbs and irritates itself, which leads to occurrences that were not pre-programmed in nature or the essence of things. One may surmise that a sort of compromise between an interest in stability and an interest in the possibility of change is at work here. It is possible to transform this view into sociological analyses. For example, there is the theory of nobility. According to this theory, a nobleman is historically defined by the old wealth of his family and a corresponding "virtue," and his status is marked already at birth. As the legal scholars of the Middle Ages used to say, his status is not affected and cannot be changed by morality. There were discussions as to whether the noble status could be lost due to infamy – that is to say, through having acted in such a way that one's reputation was damaged beyond repair. But the legal examination of such infamy was so complicated that for practical reasons one more or less abandoned it. Noble status was therefore seen as a constant that was given at the moment of birth. Time was reintroduced only via the detour of politically defined ennobling processes. However, this discussion did not deal with concepts such as "the future" and "the past." Instead, it distinguished between "constant" and "variable." The question was to what degree everyday behavior introduced variability into the world of nobility. For instance, a nobleman was not permitted to carry on a trade. So, what does he do if, come October, he has to sell his harvest? Does he simply lose his nobility for three weeks and then regain it afterwards? This is indeed a difficult question. These remarks, however, are intended merely to indicate that a culture produces problems on the basis of a neutral background distinction between "moving" and "not moving," "variable" and "invariant." With the help of such problems, a culture attempts to render its own reality comprehensible to itself. In the process, it always has to consider both sides of the distinction, as the example of nobility shows.

As far as the transition to modernity is concerned, it seems important to me that the difference between past and future plays an increasing role. In a discussion that appears somewhat anachronistic to us, it was claimed that there are people whose language did not include temporal concepts and therefore could express neither the future nor the past. Even in discussions of our own Indo-European languages, it is debated whether our preterit, our aorist, our imperfect, our future, and our future perfect were originally temporal modes. This is a terrain in which one can search a lot and find little, it seems to me. After all, it is very difficult to transport oneself back to the moment when these languages took shape. Why, for instance, did the Greek aorist, which designates a past activity and not a past state, like the perfect, disappear in Latin but not in Greek? Was it kept because the Greeks included an "s" in its form and this "s" was very hard to ignore acoustically in their language? Or were there other reasons? I will not enter into this debate. There have been studies, some of them also in ethnography, in which it was assumed that time-consciousness depends entirely on language. For instance, the Hopis allegedly did not know time. But it seems to me that one must always check how such cultures expressed temporal relations, which they naturally knew by different means. To this purpose, they may use conditional forms or single out typical occurrences. They may say, "I'll be back *to milk the cows.*" This would be something we could actually say as well, provided we actually have something to milk. It is entirely possible to mark certain points in time by referring to typical occurrences of which everyone knows when they take place. Such conditional forms, then, are forms that express time.

At the basis of this lies, presumably, the deepest, most elementary distinction between "before" and "after." Time can really be perceived only if one can distinguish between before and after. At least this is the basic agreement in the current discussion. The distinction between before and after is thought to be the elementary distinction that makes it possible that time can be related to the "now," the present moment. This relation is based on the possibility of asking what is before and what is after as seen from the perspective of the "now" or of this very hour. However, it is possible to shift the moment of this "now" so that one is able to state what came before and what came after in the context of reconstructing an event. We may think, for instance, of the reconstruction in court of an accident or a crime. This distinction between before and after can be handled, even if one abstracts to a large degree from notions of movement. It is possible to pin down earlier states even if one does not know what kind of movement, process, or causality brought about the "after." On the basis of the time distinction, the distinction between "before" and "after," it is possible to pull apart states that cannot be mentally projected on top of each other because this would lead to contradictions already at the neurophysiological level. I cannot be here and, at the same time, make a phone call in my room. The different states can be pulled apart as a series of temporally differentiated situations. This can be done, it seems to me, independently of whether one is capable of conceiving the causal connections at work or determining the processes that link the entire situation. If we did not have the distinction of "before/after" at our disposal, causality or a corresponding process could not even be perceived as that which connects. However, if the distinction of before and after is taken in this elementary sense, it is important for the moment to keep the distinction between the future and the past at a certain distance from it. There is a wealth of descriptions of situations in everyday language and also in literary terms that are based on before-and-after relations, and in which the past and the future do not appear prominently in one's time-consciousness.

Whether and how I can keep these two things conceptually apart from each other is not entirely clear to me. For one thing, Husserl's concept of the "horizon" allows us to conceive of a "before" and to assign another "before" to this "before," and so forth. In such a case, I can never reach the end, but I can continue in a specific direction and presuppose that everything that will come within reach of the next step can be determined in turn. Only the horizon has, as the metaphor tells us, a sort of infinitude. It moves. The future, then, would also be a temporal horizon that can be filled by a sequence of "afters." However, it does not consist of a sum total of events but of the "and-so-forth" of the movement. In Husserl's terms, we are dealing here with an intentional act of aiming at future determinations. Thus, we can handle this concept of the "horizon." The real question, however, is on what grounds a culture may have to describe time in terms of the future/past difference and thereby switch from the before/after perspective to a more global one, within which there is always a past and a future as seen from any specific present. This happens in all cultures as soon as the future is no longer understood merely in terms of individual occurrences. But, in modern society, this distinction becomes dominant for obvious reasons. This happens all the more when society increasingly assumes that the future will be different than the past. The invariable features, the constants that are present throughout, decrease until one eventually no longer considers anything as "stable future" [*zukunftssta-bil*]. The only question concerns the length of time it takes for something to change. In fact, we do not even assume that the human being is "stable future." Man will kill either himself or his entire species, or with the help of genetic technology he will create beings that are genetically similar to humans but possess superior qualities, and then he will disappear in the course of competing with his own products. In a way, everything is conceivable. The only remaining question is how much human time we still have ahead of us. Since we are talking about the future, it is also entirely possible that all of this will not happen. Regardless, the possibility of working with something stable, with impossibilities and necessities, and with other invariables has been decreasing significantly. This is true even for longer phases within an individual lifetime, as Hans Blumenberg has shown in his beautiful and very long-winded analysis.[13] In one of these longer phases, we observe numerous changes, which leads us to extrapolate that, at some point in time, everything will be different.

To the degree that this assumption imposes itself, we are practically obliged to describe society and more generally time relations, including those in the life of the individual, by means of the difference between the future and the past. The distinction between "moving" and "not moving" is now merely a question concerning the length of the periods of time under consideration. In the short run, many things appear as stable. But in the long run, they are no longer stable. Many modern structures have been switched to this mode. Thus, the notion of a human life no longer depends on birth and descent. It has switched to one's career and a consciousness of one's biography. Autobiographies as well as the biographies of others are no longer written from the perspective of how unusual these people were. The focus is not on what Alexander conquered and how, in individual situations, he proved himself time and again as Alexander. Instead, biographies are nowadays written from the viewpoint of decisions for a specific option that now has become the past, from which one must begin. In other words, they are historicized biographies. That would be one example. And the French Revolution was another marker. Even in France – with its king, magnificent Versailles, and the absolutist state in its most perfect form – it took merely some small upheavals for everything to collapse. The entire universe of ideas was replaced. Contemporaries who took note of this immediately realized the consequences this had for time-consciousness. In Novalis, I once came upon the sentence "We have left behind the time of stable forms." If the French Revolution was possible, then everything is possible, at least in the social sphere.

As far as the mode of observation is concerned, this means that the present is contracted into a mere point that posits the future and the past as different. The present is the point of difference between the future and the past. In Novalis, one can find formulations stating that "the present is the differential of the functions of the future and the past."[14] Whatever he may have had in mind, under these conditions the present is no longer a span of time, no matter how short, between the past and the future that would prevent them from crashing into each other. Nor is it the point of contact with God, for whom everything is present, whereas we humans have the chance of linking our present with God's present only during the brief span that is our life before our death. This notion, too, disappears. Instead a sort of pressure to make a decision appears, a switching point: "Now we have the latitude, now we all are simultaneously in the position to do something different." Yet, as soon as something has become the past, it is *there*. As soon as, say, these nuclear power plants have been built, they stand there, and it would be toilsome, expensive, and perhaps even impossible to get rid of them again. The past present was a present that in the opinion of many made the wrong decisions concerning these issues during a time when these decisions still could be made. Now we can no longer decide. We find ourselves in a different present, and the situation in which we make these decisions is different from the past one. The present is understood as a switching point that can easily be lost sight of. One can miss doing something or do something that one later comes to regret. However, the only possibility one has of acting freely is in the present. In the future we cannot act yet, and in the past we cannot act any longer.

It is astonishing that one can find only little that is written about the present. There is a discernible reflective weakness when it comes to the question concerning the actual meaning of the temporal mode of the present. As those of you who study philosophy will know, Jacques Derrida has formulated the thesis that the old ontological metaphysics was built around the notion of *"presence."*[15] The forms that are being used, the distinctions that are drawn, Husserl's intentional operations of expression, perhaps even communication, all presuppose that there is something towards which or into which one forms or formulates something, or attempts to influence it with one's intentions. In this sense, the present is understood as a quality of being that is indeterminate or, as it were, becomes frayed in relation to duration. For Derrida, this metaphysics is past. In light of his difference-consciousness, which comes relatively close to the theory of distinction, we would have to posit difference as primary. The present, then, would be the other, always unknown side of

our operations. Derrida speaks of *"ichnos"* (Greek for "trace"). This means
that we can do something *now*, but presence in the old sense is the absence
of that which we can see with our own eyes. This is linked to the idea
that all difference is essentially the operation of deferral or difference. We
cannot keep any difference stable but are constantly forced to change our
reference by thematizing an object and then another object, or a distinction and then another distinction. Derrida brings out this point in his pun
"différence/différance."

In short, there are relatively advanced theories of the present. However,
they are intended as interventions in the context of the history of
philosophy, and they come to their end in a critique of ontological metaphysics rather than making the transition into contemporary sociology
– for instance, the sociology of risk, responsibility, and different temporal perspectives. It would be possible to devise an attractive research
program to investigate the possible link between our contemporary
unrest and stress phenomena (whether in individual careers, in society,
or in regard to ecology and technology) and the fact that we have so little
time to do anything at all. The future is not yet and the past is no longer at
our disposal. Therefore, we already put pressure on ourselves merely in
the way in which we thematize time. That is not to say that we are making
a mistake. It means merely that, if we see our society under the aspect of
time, we can only grasp it as described.

A final point on the topic of time concerns the question of synchroniz-
ing phenomena. If we grant that we are hard pressed in the present, since
we have to act but have only little leeway and time to do so, it might seem
a reasonable assumption that we ought to stick with planning and to consider that we ought to plan ourselves, as it were, as a past that could be
put to good use in the future. We always have to keep in mind a multiplicity of time relations. We need to distinguish the present "present" from
future "presents" that are still indeterminate but for which our current
"now" will be the past. Time is reflectively mirrored in itself, precisely as
the mentality of planning and not so much as the mere historical perspective (which is quite familiar). Already in the eighteenth century, historians had come to the conclusion that the national history is our past but
had a very different meaning during the present of the Germanic tribes.
In retrospect, the present is a present with a different past and a different
future than the ones that we have today. It is said, for good reason, therefore, that the *zeitgeist* constructs its own time and its own history. One
may write national histories or world histories or histories of ideas. But
all of them are written from the standpoint of a particular time. Therefore,
one's calculations must be mindful of the fact that the described historical
times are seen not though the lens of their own present but through the
lenses of different presents. As described, this insight is part of general
culture. It is also acknowledged by historians, even if they do not formulate it in such a complicated way and with the help of terms that express a

double modality ("past present," "future present," and "present future") and even a triple modality ("future presents of the present future").[16]

If one keeps an eye on these double and triple modalities, one very quickly reaches the limit of what can be mastered by means of planning – or, more precisely, organizational planning, which is actually at issue here. If one formulates exactly and asks an organizational type of person which past for which future present is of importance to him, he will, first of all, be confused, because he is not accustomed to thinking in these terms. However, at the factual level, this is exactly how a huge planning project works. Think, for example, of the planning of oil wells in the North Sea. Complex technological, economical, action-related, financial, and other planning must be united as an enchainment of events.[17] The present in which something has to be finished is the consequence of when it must be finished so that something else can take place. Throughout, what matters is reflection on what will be a particular future's past that can no longer be changed. As a consequence of these problems of planning, there are also possibilities of disturbing plans and using time gaps and time problems in planning in order to have some sort of effect. But all this is familiar from the sociology of organization.

Think of the organizational problems in the domain of fashion. In this case, one is first of all dealing with a problem that has no persistence in time. The fashion of this summer is no longer the fashion of last summer. Nor is it the fashion of next summer. And for winter the same is true. Now, the fabrics and garments that are being produced must match the seat-covers in the cars. For this reason, it is important that, first of all, decisions are made concerning the range of colors. This happens about two years ahead of time. As soon as the range of colors has been decided on, one may move on and begin with the planning of designs. Then there are the big trade shows where the retailers do their shopping. The fashion that we experience as unstable in the moment when we purchase it is a fashion that is, in a certain sense, exactly planned in relation to its temporal rhythm. This is linked to the financial power of the involved companies, the size of the production facilities, the speed of the fabric printers, and many other aspects. Over the last five to ten years, the following arrangements have become standard. At the big trade shows, the designers and fabric dealers show their fabrics and try to get the retailers to purchase them and have evening robes made of them. Usually, big, well-funded companies are also at these shows. They copy fashion products. Of course, they do not create exact copies. Otherwise they would be caught. Instead, they create slight variations that do not provide sufficient reasons for legal complaints. These well-funded companies immediately send the patterns electronically to Hong Kong and have their wares ready in the department stores when the ladies come to buy, for five or six or ten thousand dollars a piece, evening gowns that they will wear only once. Yet then the ladies go to Target and see that ready-made clothes with the same patterns are already on offer. The group of people who can afford to spend five or ten thousand dollars for a gown that they will wear only once is getting smaller. One reason may be that they do not buy in Germany anyway, but in Paris – for tax reasons. The French in turn have to buy in Germany so that the French revenue office will not begin an inquiry into the source of all that money. These are the relevant considerations. And then there is also the question of whether the jeans culture has not, as it were, become naturalized, so that the type of gown I described will no longer be worn in the future. Finally, there is the possibility on the part of the big companies of using the technique of copying and of mass producing the successful designs in order to ruin smaller companies (after all, they know who bought the designs and who has the intention of manufacturing the corresponding garments). Moreover, there is supplementary technology. One must deal increasingly with production errors and failures. In such cases, one can offer the new patterns only belatedly. But they get produced right away. Someone who bought the wrong things or whose delivery has been held up or cancelled, or who did not receive the right information indicating that his decisions were unwise, nowadays still can catch up and finalize his purchases at a point in time when it is, by all accounts, really too late.

These are developments that took place over the course of a few years, and which indicate how one calculates with time. We are not dealing here with the time that sociologists describe when they describe fashion phenomena as unstable. Instead, we are dealing with a strange mixture of deadlines and appointments, of "no longer possible" and "still possible," and of the different perspectives of financial soundness, the clientele, and the modalities of financing. The famous fashion designers do not finance their operations with their own money but with the help of credit suppliers. They can easily be wiped out financially. Time is extremely important in this arrangement. To see that, we do not need to make our calculations on the basis of the somewhat highfalutin terminology of future pasts, and so on. The time perspective enters the business and marketing planning under specific aspects. For you this is nothing new. We read in the papers that the Japanese change their car models more often than we do, and that this is seen as a skill. Of course, one could have a different opinion on this. In this case, temporal gains, speed, and change are seen as marketing strategies.

In addition there is a second aspect. We need to reflect on the increasing shaping of one future or another with the help of time spans and deadlines, which has the consequence that certain things can be done only up to a specific point in time and not any later. In this process, entire arrangements of priorities and values are lost or at least strongly modified. For instance, if a young scientist knows that he has to finish his doctorate before he reaches a certain age in order to make sure that he will find a position that would not be offered to him if he were older, then this fact may well influence his choice of a dissertation topic. And if we have to begin with our lectures at a specific point in time, it is impossible to do something meaningful during the half hour before, since this time does not suffice to embark on a long-term project. Time aspects thus enter into the objective priorities or value preferences. The entire discussion of values is thus subject to generalities at either end. However, under everyday conditions, entirely different factors are decisive, among them the question of how much time I have and when I cannot yet or can no longer do certain things.

As a final point on this issue, I would like to stress that it is necessary to distinguish temporal considerations at the level of an organization as well as at the level of individual careers from the social dimensions of time. If we formulate a theory of time and in the process observe how other people observe time, we need to distinguish whom exactly we are observing. Are we observing persons or social systems? This is the point with which I started this lecture. It is necessary, then, to distinguish, first, the perspective of society; second, the perspective of an organization; and, third, perhaps also the individual life perspective, precisely in order to see how these perspectives may coincide or to perceive on what causes certain mutual conditions may depend. I have said a few things about the area of organization that can now be presupposed. One can already recognize the specificity and the limitations that result from time planning in organizations. Yet, organizations are the only mechanism by means of which, for instance, fundamental technological changes or thoroughgoing reactions to ecological problems can be implemented. After all, it is not of much use to formulate an ethical canon that is then distributed in all mailboxes. One must always think in terms of an organization that can provide the time planning for the desired goal. This, however, leads to many limitations regardless of how important the desired goal may be. In consequence, it becomes extremely difficult for an external observer to have a good idea of what can actually be done technologically, economically, and in organizational terms.

I recall a discussion in Linz (Austria) concerning the Voest Alpine company, which owns coke- and steel-producing industries. The company was attacked for its environmental pollution. There was pressure from the city of Linz as well as from Vienna. They demanded that the company find ways of reducing its emissions. But, at the moment when the time plan was being devised, according to which the emissions had to be cut by half by a certain year, nobody knew how much this would cost. It was impossible to figure out the expense. In addition, the company was already operating in the red. As far as the technological challenges were concerned, it was not known how they could be solved. It was clear that above the sinter plant one had to attach boards, along which the fumes would rise, and which would be chemically prepared so as to bind the sulfur. But it was not known how these boards could be cleaned, whether chemically or perhaps mechanically merely by shaking them, or how long these boards would last, depending on the mode of cleaning. And there were no scientists that could be consulted. They simply do not know such things. One could not hire some graduate in chemistry or physics and pay him for consulting the relevant literature; there was nothing to be found in books. Now, large companies have lots of contacts. In Pittsburgh, there were people working on similar problems. But, in Linz, a division of labor had been implemented, so that one group worked on one set of experiments and another group on another. Yet the question concerning the durability of the boards, the question of what would happen with the production during the time when the boards would be replaced, and so on and so forth – the answers to all these questions were entirely unclear. In consequence, the costs exploded, and it was impossible to adhere to the agreed-upon timeline. Naturally, there was much commotion. But the more closely one looks at things from the company's perspective, the more one is tempted to place those who voice complaints in the position of those about whom they complain, and then to ask them how they would do things if they had to do them. During this period, when not only the technology and the finances but also the organizational possibilities were uncertain, the coke was no longer transported on open wagons. Instead it was covered and the transportation was automated. These processes freed the air of fumes. In addition, they led to mass layoffs of workers who had hitherto done the work with shovels. However, the question was whether it was actually possible to get rid of the workers or not. This question, in turn, was related to the financial plan, since the intention was to save part of the costs by layoffs, although this option is never popular. In the end, the question that imposed itself was where and when a political explosion would happen.

Behind such temporal questions that must be posed whenever we are forced to change something very quickly and fundamentally in technology or in ecological policy, we must also have regard to this kind of organizational problem of implementation. I do not want to claim that there is not a certain range of better and worse solutions, but there are very different time perspectives in play. There is the time perspective that is dictated by ecological reality; then there is the time perspective that is customary in a rationally governed organization; and, finally, there is the time perspective of a politician, who would like to have an effect during the temporal constraints of his term of office, to which such other constraints as, for instance, a scandal may be added. (I merely remind you of Salzgitter.)[18] How much time is there to react to a scandal? In all of this, so many different issues intersect that one gains the impression that the time dimension is a decisive aspect at all these levels, at the level of organization as much as at the level of society, and perhaps even more at the level of the ecological context of social reality.

In fact, I have not even mentioned yet that all people who cannot rely on family achievements or privileges face their own synchronization problems. These problems occur when those people who cannot rely on a status that was conferred to them at birth or on an inheritance of stocks that will be passed on to them with absolute certainty, and who therefore have to make something of their lives while no longer having standardized temporal targets at their disposal. In earlier periods, those were still in place. One had to earn one's baccalaureate by a certain time. Graduate studies took exactly this amount of time. Perhaps one was allowed to add another year (but not more). One could marry only after one had found a job. But the job came only after one had graduated. Such temporal patterns are quickly disappearing. In many areas, time has become more elastic. But, as a consequence, it also provides less connective security. One no longer knows very well the right time for marrying or when one should have children. One does not know how long one can count on working in one's field of expertise. One does not even know whether the professional training one has chosen will continue to be in demand and for how long. There are only few social norms that regulate these areas. One cannot simply look at how the neighbors' children do this or that, or how people in our circle of friends handle a problem. There are always a wide variety of solutions. I suspect that precisely this situation also sharpens our time-consciousness and therefore our consciousness of contingency. One always faces the question of what one is going to miss if one does what one finds important. And one also faces the question of whether it will be possible at a later point in time to make up for it. Thus, one has, on the one hand, more possibilities to choose from that ever before but, on the other hand, one is also faced with the question of how the future present will appear from the present future.

For these reasons, I began with these reflections on time. As a matter of fact, they constitute only one aspect of the topic that I would like to discuss in my next lecture – namely, the topic of meaning [*Sinn*]. Time is a dimension of meaning. In my next lecture, I will try to speak about the problem of meaning. Once again, I will address this problem from the perspective of the distinction with which we observe meaning. Therefore, I will return briefly to "time" when I get to the point where time becomes relevant to the theory of meaningful experience and action.

IV

Meaning

Tenth Lecture

I thought that it might be helpful to use the transition between the section on time and the section on meaning to return once again to the observer. In other words, I want to remind you that the standpoint from which my reflections on meaning are made is also linked to the question of who observes by using meaning. This is particularly difficult in the case of meaning, because we simply cannot imagine that something is observed without the implication of meaning. For this reason, let me try once again to use the example of time in order to make clear what is meant when one poses the question of the observer or, to put it differently, the question of the distinction with which the observed state of affairs is articulated. To this purpose, I have consulted two texts, Hegel's remarks on time and Aristotle's lectures on physics. I will begin by reading to you the paragraph that introduces the section on time in Hegel's *Encyclopedia of the Philosophical Sciences*. I am speaking of §258, in case you would like to read it for yourselves and attempt to understand it, which would probably be quite difficult, presumably even for Hegel himself. I need to read this slowly, so that it becomes clear: "Time, as the negative unity of self-externality, is similarly an out-and-out abstract, ideal being. It is that being which, inasmuch as it *is*, is *not*, and inasmuch as it is *not*, is. . . ."[1] That is enough. For I would like only to ask the question of why the problem is tackled with the schema of being and not-being. Why does Hegel use the distinction of being and not-being in order to speak of time? From the first sentence on, he runs into the problem that time apparently is something that is and, at the same time, something that is not, which is to say, something that is no longer or something that is not yet. He is heading for a paradox, and this is apparently what he wants. But it is less clear why he wants this. And the text does not tell us.

But there is a tradition for this sort of thing. If you look at Aristotle's physics lectures, specifically at book IV, chapter 14, you will see that he also begins with being and not-being and with formulations that presuppose that both being and not-being exist.[2] What is in all this the meaning of this "is"? Is it something that is not? Or is it something that is? In Aristotle there is a further interesting turn when he speaks about the "now," in which the not-being of the past and the not-being of the future, as it were, become identical and two not-beings are promoted, if you will, to the status of a being. How so? How is it that one asks about being and not-being when it is already known beforehand what time is – namely, something that is not yet or no longer, and thus something that is to be divided up in terms of before and after, past and future? What kind of knowledge does one have of time already before one begins to apply a distinction? Moreover, I noticed with interest when I re-read this text by Aristotle that the "*nu*," the now, is nominalized. He speaks of "*to de nu*," which is to say, of *the now*. The French translation renders it as "*le maintenant*," and my German text has "*der Jetztpunkt*." But when I say "now" now, then I say "now" now, and you know what I mean when I say "now" now, namely, precisely the moment when I say it. It is a sort of adverb or indexical expression, something that one can understand only if one is there when it is uttered. This reference to the situation when something is said is removed by changing it into a noun. Now, we have "the now," which apparently possesses a quality that can exist and actually exists continuously, and has existed and will exist at all times. If one reads this text as a sociologist, one may ask why an adverb that is common in the context of everyday language use has been changed into a noun in this case. In oral speech, the term is understandable in the situation. In the written text it becomes something of a peculiarity. In consequence, we all of a sudden tend to see behind the distinction, behind the treatment of the "now," the difference between speaking and writing. Furthermore, we see that, on account of the artificiality of the talk about time and the use of the ontological schema of "being/not-being" (and in Aristotle, there is, in addition, the schema of the whole and the part), the now apparently becomes a part of time, although it is two not-beings that are combined to form a now. The fact that one is able to say that the now is a part of time, and that time is the whole that is divided into a series of nows or points in time, seems to be, in terms of our schema, an effect of writing. But, in formulating the issue in this manner, one relies on a distinction that does not agree with the semantics that is used by the culture of writing to articulate itself.

I will not give answers to these questions right now. I would merely like to point out that everything that follows from all this can be traced back to the primary distinction. For instance, the concept of movement connects to these issues. Apparently, it is a concept that combines being and not-being. But this is not sufficient for a definition of time. After all, time does not move in the sense that something, as it were, passes by us, and at some point one had time and then time ran out, and, finally, time has had enough of it all, and there is no more time left. Aristotle sees this. The structure that is needed to work out a theory of time depends on a distinction. The question is, however: Who draws this distinction, who is the observer? And immediately the next question is: Who poses this question? It is the characteristic structure of the concept of autopoiesis and of the things that I will be saying about meaning that allows us to pose this question and to attempt to answer it with the help of the concepts of recursiveness and implication, and also the concept of meaning.

This was my transitional section that was merely intended to remind us of the observer, and to then let him disappear. Now, I will attend to the concept of meaning.

Perhaps it is best to take the everyday understanding of "meaning" as our point of departure. It seems that, in everyday contexts, meaning is understood as something that we can lose or that is missing or simply not there. We are permanently suffering from loss of meaning. When the question of meaning arises, one invokes, for example, religion to give us the meaning that we lack. However, this is rather strange if we look at the history of religion. Religion was the interpretation of the world, and the world had been created by God *in exactly this way*. In the historical temporality of sacred history, the world was as it was, and this was no answer to the question of how we could find meaning. It is remarkable that nowadays we understand religion in terms of its meaning function and thus presuppose that we, as observers, can distinguish between what is "meaningful" and what is "not meaningful." But are we really capable of this? Furthermore, is the distinction between "meaningful" and "not meaningful" really meaningful? And, if so, for whom?

If we present these difficulties to philosophy, the discipline that claims to be in charge of such questions, then we receive what is still, I believe, the prevalent answer – namely, that meaning is related to the subject. Thus, if one feels compelled and able to pose the question "For whom does something have meaning?," one has in mind a subject, not in the formal sense of the term, but in the sense of an individual that lives, reflects on itself, and operates with meaning as a form of orientation *tout court*, or at least of a satisfactory orientation. Husserl, for instance, makes the claim in [*The Crisis of the European Sciences and*] *Transcendental Phenomenology*, especially in the part that deals with the critique of science and technology, that experience [*Erleben*] takes place in productions of consciousness that create meaning.[3] And my colleague Grathoff would probably make the same demand.[4] This, however, presupposes first of all that intersubjectivity is a problem that can be solved. After all, if every subject produces, constitutes, and evaluates meaning all by himself – regardless of whether this meaning actually makes sense or not – one ends up with the problem of what happens between the subjects and whether there is a sphere of "intersubjectivity," as it is called, that has its own meaning. But for what subject would it have that meaning?

I believe that this difficulty brings us to a turning point, or at least to a point where we can gain clarity about the fact that we must apply the category of meaning to two different system types (this is my way of putting it). We have psychic systems – consciousness systems that have meaningful experiences – and we have social systems – communication systems that reproduce meaning by using it in communication. This does not say anything about the questions as to what exactly meaning is, how we would like to define meaning, and how we understand the term. At first, we merely witness a difficulty that results from having lost the subject, or, to put it differently, having lost an ontological authority to which we can refer the constitution of meaning. This would be the authority in charge of the constitution of meaning, the authority we would consider to be responsible for meaning. One might even have to know this "subject" personally in order to know what meaning is for him. Perhaps meaning is a sort of background beingness; perhaps it is no more than some rules for constituting meaning that would be valid *a priori* for all empirical subjects. But, if you make the theoretical move of drawing a sharp distinction between consciousness and communication (I will have more to say on this in a later part of my lecture course), then the concept of meaning is, in a manner of speaking, deracinated, since we would no longer have any addressee for it, no observer whom we could observe, but merely two distinct things – namely, on the one hand, consciousness and, on the other, social communication. The question, then, is whether we can find a concept or an order within which the entity we call "meaning" does not depend on shifting the burden by referring to a subject or another carrier of meaning. The point is not to shift the burden onto some agency that constitutes meaning but to find an order within which it is possible to formulate a sufficiently formal concept of meaning.

My next attempt to formulate a concept of meaning without a specific system reference, and thus without a specific ontological reference, relies on putting the distinction of medium and form to use. But, first, I must say a few things about this distinction, because its relation to systems theory is not without problems and because I would like to exploit this fact in order to speak about meaning in the sense of a relation between medium and form. In this discussion, I would like to avoid, for the time being, any assumption as to what kind of system is operating so as to constitute meaning, experience meaning, discover meaning, reproduce meaning, and so forth. The advantage of this distinction between form and meaning is that one is not automatically returned to a carrier of meaning. Instead, one can begin to think about meaning in entirely abstract terms and work on the specific terminology that helps us gain clarity about the relation between medium and form. I ended up on this track when I encountered a distinction that was made by Fritz Heider in an essay that was published in 1926. In the following years, this essay disappeared almost entirely, but it was republished in 1959 in an abbreviated version in English and subsequently rediscovered by Karl Weick.[5] In one way or another, every-thing derives from the Austrians, or so it would seem!

Heider focuses first of all on the media of perception. He is a psy-chologist. His question is: How is it possible that we can identify and hear certain sounds or noises and see certain things (this is why the essay is called "Thing and Medium") and see that something has specific con-tours, that it begins somewhere and ends somewhere else and has a spe-cific shape or form? The idea of "medium" is that there is an area of loose couplings of abundant elements, such as particles in the air or physical carriers of light. "Light" is not a physical concept. Rather it is the concept that names the medium in which we can see something. Without light, we see nothing. (It will take little time to test this.) That is to say, there is apparently a difference between the invisible medium and a visible "form" (as I would like to call it) or shape. If we also saw the light itself and thus would be constantly bombarded by light reflexes, the contours of things would be unrecognizable for us. In borderline cases we still would be able to interpret data, since we are creatures of habit. I wonder, however, whether you have ever had the experience of driving at night on a wet road. Suddenly, you see nothing but a flickering light or combina-tion of lights, and you are not at all sure whether you are still on the road, and whether perhaps another car is travelling in your direction or not. To the degree that shapes are reduced to mere light, even if this light still has a form – think of lamps and such – perception becomes difficult. The same is true, even more so, with hearing. If the air itself produced sounds all the time, it would become difficult to perceive language or other articulated and already identified sounds.

From this follows the possibility of working with a distinction that in the contemporary literature is generally designated with the terms "loose coupling" and "tight coupling." In systems theory, the use of this distinc-tion has, at least in part, taken a direction that I would like to ignore for the time being – namely, the direction that is associated with the claims both that systems that are capable of being alive and are stable have to be loosely coupled,[6] and that not everything must depend on everything else and interdependence must be interrupted, etc. In our, as it were, pre-systematic distinction of medium and form, it is said that, first of all, elements abound that do not have the status of elements due to specific couplings. These elements nonetheless provide the material for couplings to emerge. Heider was thinking of the media of perception. But it is also possible to think of language as a vocabulary and a set of sentences. This is one of the reasons why I make the switch from "medium and thing" to "medium and form." It thus becomes possible to include language.

There is a wealth of words, and there are certain combinatory rules. One can create sentences. The sentences are forms in the medium of lan-guage. The words, in turn, are forms in the medium of possible noises or possible optical designs. We have light and air as the media of perception in which one can form words either orally or in writing. The words, in turn, are a medium that allows us to form sentences and make meaningful statements. What is at stake in all these cases is the opening up of a domain of loose coupling for combinatory possibilities. It is at this level that in the process of the regular operation of all kinds of systems – conscious systems as well as communicative systems – the possibility of creating forms arises. In fact, the underlying domain of loose coupling itself presupposes forms at the basal level of the elements.

In all of this, some additional considerations that I can sketch only briefly here are important. One issue to consider is that the medium is always reproduced only by means of creating forms. If one never formed any sentences, one would eventually forget the words. Language cannot maintain itself merely as a lexicon. Moreover, the lexicon itself can only be invented when writing is available. In addition, a lexicon has a specific purpose. Language as such, however, is speaking, writing, and reading. It reproduces the possibility of creating forms, and its own condition of possibility is that it is used. This is the first of my additional considerations.

A second consideration concerns the fact that the medium is more stable than the creation of forms. A sound fades away, and an object may disappear. Nevertheless, with the help of a medium, we hear or see something else in their place. This leads to certain problems in terms of the classical conception of stability, for stability precisely does not lie in the forms. What is stable is loosely coupled and has no form. In classical language it is called "matter" or "indeterminacy." Everything that gains stability is valid only for a certain time and thus becomes unstable, precarious, and temporary. One formulates a certain sentence, and it fades away. It will never be used again, nor is it written down to be activated again on some other occasion after we are done with what we need to do in the meantime. The whole thing is a striking mixture of the durability of the possible, on the one hand, and the temporary creation of forms that leads to the reproduction of the possibilities, on the other. This is not a simple conception of "stable" and "unstable" or "durable" and "transitory." Rather, what we have here is a loose coupling of mixed components that are bound in tight forms, but only temporarily, for a longer or shorter amount of time, depending on how the respective systems operate. Moreover, these components are always bound selectively. In consequence, the possibilities of a medium can never be captured in *one* form. If we try to do this, then we arrive at the form "the medium of language," and we pronounce the words "the medium of language" or write them down in a different medium. This allows us to define what the elements of this medium are that make possible loose couplings. In our case, they are words. Apart from this, every medium is always re-created anew for the specific use to which it is put in temporary forms that often change rapidly.

Since all of this is part of a sociological explication, I would like to mention briefly that one can also reconstruct Talcott Parsons's symbolically generalized media of communication and media of interaction in this manner.[7] It is possible to understand money as a medium that can be crystallized in payments. One can pay only at a set price. If you go to your bank and hand in a blank check with the instruction that you want to give, pay, or donate something, the bank will not act on it. It is the same when you want to say something but you do not know what you want to say. It is the same with power, when one has it but does not use it to give orders but instead just says: "Here I am. I will tell you later what you have to do." There is this entire sequence of media of perception, media of communication, language, and the media that are function specific in a more narrow sense, such as money or power, and it is this sequence that is of interest in sociology and the theory of society. Time and again, we encounter new media for limited areas of application, and these media in a certain sense always decouple their elements again in order to make them available for new combinatory possibilities.

After having briefly outlined evaluation and application possibilities with the help of these conceptual resources, I would like to return now to the concept of meaning. I would like to pose the question of whether it is conceivable that meaning is not something substantial or phenomenal – that is, some qualitative unity – but a determined mode of difference between medium and form. I am not entirely sure whether these concepts can successfully be made to fit. But, for the moment, I imagine that meaning is indeed something like a continuous request to create specific forms. These forms characteristically are created in the medium of meaning, but they do not represent meaning as a category in general – except perhaps in the word "meaning" itself. One can hear this word when it is spoken and one can read it if it has been written down. Yet, the word "meaning" is not the only thing that has meaning. It merely occurs here and there in sentences.

If one wants to distinguish the medium of meaning from the forms of meaning, it must be possible to reflect and pass judgment on what the medium-like side of meaning actually is. Perhaps it helps to adopt the term "medial substrate" in this case. After all, if the respective medium always amounts to the possibility of creating forms in a medium, we are in need of a threefold terminology. First, we have the substrate, the elements that are loosely coupled and can be tightly coupled; however, in the latter case, one must always proceed selectively. In the second place, we have the forms, and, in the third place, the interaction in relation to which the entire apparatus of medium and form has meaning only when it is being used. If one decided to work with the conceptual crutch "medial substrate," one might say that every experience of meaning always happens in two parts and assumes the form of a distinction. If one prefers to express this state of affairs in Spencer Brown's terminology, one may say that, on the inner side [of the distinction], one always has a kind of form at one's disposal with which one can work. Something specific has been seen. Thus, I see that the meaning of *this* apparatus[8] can be actualized if we turn the screws and put in some microscope slide. In every other respect, it is merely a nuisance. One might take offence and simply destroy it. Meaning in its specific configurations, its specific shapes, and its specific forms is merely the inner side of the medium. There is always also the outer side of all other possibilities of use. And, in the case of perceptible objects, we have an outer side that indicates where they end. To this outer side belong the "and-so-forth" of space as well as the relative persistence of things, according to which one nevertheless would not assume that in 300 years' time they will still be found in the same spot.

As you can see, I am jumping back and forth between entirely different theoretical resources, and what I have just offered is merely *one* approach. My reflection can be described a bit more clearly with the help of Husserl's phenomenological analyses. Husserl published these analyses himself – unlike many of his writings, which were published only posthumously. You find good investigations of these topics in the *Ideas I* of 1913 and later in *Experience and Judgment*.[9] The basic thought, always conceived as relative to the subject, is that the subject or consciousness works intentionally, which is to say, in the form of acts. The actualization of the intentional activity of consciousness is directed to something specific. One identifies, among other things, objects, human beings, or symbols, but always within a horizon, as Husserl calls it, of references to other possibilities. One never ends up in an ontological trap in such a way that one thinks of something and is so taken by it that one is no longer able to detach oneself and always thinks merely of "this." One does not always think of "living room" or, to give a most relevant example, "systems theory" and can no longer think of anything else but "systems theoretical things." On the contrary, if one is involved in this mode of thinking, one always has the thought as to why exactly all this is in fact "theory" or what exactly is named by the term "system." That is to say, everything, whether the symbolism or the things, refers to other possibilities within a horizon of possible determinations, as Husserl puts it, or the determinability of a particular style. One never ends up in an unmarked space in Spencer Brown's sense or in an entirely indefinable situation from which one can never extricate oneself. One always works on the inner side of the distinctions and always with other possibilities that are close at hand. Thus we know, when we exit this building today, we will have to take certain paths in order to leave the university, get to our cars, and start the engines. We have the necessary keys in our pockets. There are always clusters of meaning creations [*Sinnbildungen*].

Meaning, however, is not merely this reference to other possibilities, but also the localization of such references in everything that we concretely imagine as an object of our actuality or our actual experience. Similarly, when we switch from consciousness to communication, everything that can be said, all information, has a corresponding range of selection. What did I expect, and what is actually happening? What surprises me in relation to all that which would also be possible? Every item that is operationally actualized lives and has meaning merely insofar as it is placed within a horizon of different possibilities.

If one operates at the level of phenomenological descriptions, one has the possibility of asking whether a particular experience is different for somebody else. If everybody affirms that this is not the case and that it is the same for everybody, then one has good reason to state that it is so. From a methodological perspective, we are dealing with a description that imagines something and subsequently can be tested in respect to the peculiarities of its subjective or subject-centered processing of meaning. I believe that this is a strong methodological argument for the fact that one introduces items of evidence first and sees whether anyone doubts them. If someone has doubts and good arguments for these doubts, one must assess what needs to be corrected in one's own theoretical edifice to take this other view into account. But as long as no one doubts and no one comes and says that he continuously experiences meaning that does not provide him with a point of departure for carrying on, there is no reason for correction. Even if someone said something like this, he would be contradicted by the mere fact that he says it in a specific situation. One would have to clarify what is meant by a "reference" [*Verweisung*], how one handles "reference," and how one recognizes that one is handling "reference." At the level of mere phenomenology, it seems to me, this argument is quite strong. For me, this mode of gathering evidence was, if I may state this in such biographical terms, the actual point and almost the only point that I derived from reading Husserl: if this is so, then I must carry on with it in the future.

This, however, does not mean that we have already found the best form of distinction. The terminology of "intention" and "act" (Husserl also speaks of "expression" and a series of other terms that need not be introduced here) does not yet offer the form that is most favorable in terms of theory. I think that the distinction of medium and form provides one possibility of showing that meaning always requires an "appresentation" (again, I am using one of Husserl's terms) or concomitant making-present of other possibilities in a concrete act. The real and the possible are thus not separate spheres. One would again be dealing with an ontology, if one arranged things in such a manner that one placed the possible here and the real over there, and stated that the real is not possible and the possible not real. This is certainly not the way to go. Instead the space of potentialities, the totality of references, and the horizon-like quality of all meaning form an enlivening or meaning-producing moment in everything that is specific, in every identity, in everything that is communicatively enunciated as information, and also in everything to which one can attend consciously and which one can thematize. It is not a matter of regionally arranging different spheres of being that exist side by side. Rather, what is at stake is a mutual interpenetration [*Ineinander*] of the actual and the potential, to use the terminology that I currently prefer. If one insisted on a definition, one might say that meaning is the medium that works with the difference between the actual and the potential. This difference is to be taken in the sense that the unity of the difference always also plays along, which is to say that everything one can actually see also contains perspectives of possibilities, and that, vice versa, one cannot thematize, conceive, or communicatively use possibilities if this is not done as something actual. One has to be capable of talking or thinking about possibilities, be it in the manner of a modal logic or in some other way. But, if this is not made into something actual, it is not a possibility either. Then it is simply not "there," it does not exist, or it is not an "operation," if we want to revert to this manner of speaking. I hope that you are not confused by my constant combining of these different theories! It is one part of my attempt to bring back together what has been developed intellectually as separate ideas – always under the perspective of what is and what is not useful for us *as sociologists*.

The next point concerns the thesis that the medium of meaning is apparently inevitably and universally valid. This means, in the first place, that we also have to use it when we use negations. In other words, meaning is a non-negative category. After all, if we say that something makes no sense [*keinen Sinn*], this statement itself makes a claim to meaning [*Sinn*]. By the way, this argument has a certain philosophical tradition: "If I think that I cannot think, I have at least to think this and thus refute myself." This is the figure of an operational self-refutation or, to use Apel's terminology, a performative (self-)contradiction.[10]

This is my first point. We cannot get outside the medium. As soon as we operate consciously or communicatively, we are always already forced to use the medium of meaning. At this level, it is our language that confuses us, since it suggests that we could say that something is not meaningful [*nicht sinnvoll*]. I will return to this. It might be useful to draw yet another distinction between "meaningful" [*sinnhaft*], or "related to meaning" [*sinnbezogen*] in a general sense, and the idea, which can be negated, that something is or is not meaningful. I believe that we ought to state in the first place that all negations require a sort of world presence that, for its part, has the form of meaning and thus constitutes a form. The reason for this is that negations do not operate within an undefined frame of reference. Rather, as determinate negations, they always refer to something determinate. And, vice versa, every determination implies the negation of other possible determinations. If one states that something is not the case or says that something does not make sense [*macht keinen Sinn*] in a particular situation, one has a determinate intention – one would like to exclude something determinate and thus would like to process meaning. This is the reason why we cannot conceive of, and situate ourselves in, a

world in which there are no meaning-processing systems. Perhaps I ought
to formulate this more carefully. Of course we can conceive of a world in
which all human beings and all computers have been destroyed and only
rocks and perhaps insects, desert conditions, and remainders of radia-
tion exist. We can imagine a world in which no meaning is operationally
produced or reproduced any longer. But we can arrive at this conception
only in terms of meaning. We depend on imagining what could be left
over as the remainder of nature, and we think of all that used to be and
has been destroyed. Also, we cannot really imagine the world relation
[*Weltverhältnis*] of stones, or what a stone feels and perceives, or how
"stony" it is. This is an imaginary conception that we can construct but
not realize. We are capable of negation and we can say that the world is
not at a stone's disposal in a meaningful way. But this statement makes
sense for us only because we can contrast it with all that has meaning for
human beings and with the function that meaning has in the human space
of orientation.

It gets difficult when one considers animals. Whether the category of
meaning can be applied to animals is an issue that we have discussed on
occasion and which I consider to be irresolvable. The reason for this is
that, when we observe animals, we observe them always in a meaningful world and therefore have difficulty imagining the world from the
viewpoint of a bat, a chaffinch, or a cow and to contemplate how such
animals order the space they see outside themselves, the perceptual
environment that they are undoubtedly able to recognize. In fact much
speaks in favor of seeing this process as related to meaningful transitions
or proto-meaning, especially if one takes note of the fluidity and elegance
with which animals move from one situation to the next. One has the
impression that it is apparently not just some sporadic or *ad hoc* affair. We
tend to imagine that the animals perceive space as meaningful, as a relation between what came before to what will come after. But I do not know
whether we can know this, precisely because we rely on the support of
meaning at all times. This, however, is a special problem that points us to
the form of universality and inevitability of the medium of meaning for
specific systems, namely, consciousness and communication systems. It is
a trait of this universality that its own negation is built into the medium
and that it still is meaningful to imagine that the medium of meaning may
not be available for other points of departure and other kinds of systems.
This is yet another statement that is at our disposal only as a meaningful
statement.

I believe that this may be enough for the moment on the topic of which
distinction is actualized via meaning – namely, the distinction between
actuality and potentiality – and on the question concerning the system reference, according to which there are meaning-constituting systems whose
modes of operation inevitably include the use of meaning.

I now move on to a brief transitory passage. From this starting point, it is possible to look back on a discussion that took place in the sixties and early seventies, when the world was still divided according to the older model of spirit and nature, that which is meaningful and that which is mechanical, interaction and technology, and when, in correspondence with these divisions, different methodical conceptions were endorsed. For the natural sciences and technology, there were specific knowledge mechanisms that were tied to methods from the natural sciences, to natural laws, and to causalities that were understood as fixed. For the domain of meaning, in turn, there were, for instance, hermeneutic methods. If we experience the world as meaningful – something which we do not have to do, according to this description – then we experience it as a "text," and meaning has something to do with "interpretation," which is to say, with a meaning that one produces oneself on the occasion of a text. The text does not have to be a book. It is possible to conceive of the world as a text and state that hermeneuticians interpret the world. From your sociological studies, you are familiar with this as one specific method.

What I find noteworthy in this discussion is the parallel position of the concept of meaning, on one side of the division, and of complexity, on the other. For technicians and theorists of planning, complexity was the decisive problem back then. Planning runs up against complexity. The agent in charge of planning stands outside of what he plans and does not have the "requisite variety"[11] – that is, the possibility to assume as many states as the entity that is being subjected to planning or as the external world. He must reduce complexity. That is the formula. He must attempt to find elegant solutions for much more difficult problems. He must simplify, and he must abstract, turn things into technical problems, build models, and attempt to control systems by means of such models.

In the part of our lecture course that dealt with complexity, however, we already noted, as you may recall, that complexity amounts to selective pressure. If one describes complexity as a multiplicity of elements that cannot be connected with every other element, then it is clear that selective pressure is included in complexity. Every pattern of actualized complexity is selective. For instance, one may speak only with one's superiors and one's subordinates, but not with one's peers. Certain things belong there and certain other things belong here. A machine whose parts, screws, wheels, and rods are combined differently no longer works. One has to put it together exactly as set out in the instructions. There is no other way, even though there may well be other possibilities. Complexity is always a relation of selectivity under specific criteria.

If you now juxtapose this with the analysis of meaning, you will see that meaning also amounts to selective pressure. We have an excess of reference and we need to know what to do with it. That is to say, we must know what to do next after having excluded other possibilities. We may have a car, but we still have to decide where we want to go in it. We have linguistic competence, but we still have to decide what we are going to say.

I would like to consider whether the controversy between the management of complexity, on the one hand, and meaningful interpretation, hermeneutics, and directedness towards texts, on the other, is perhaps a controversy that is possible only because both sides have the same problem which they merely formulate in different ways: namely, the problem of selective pressure. I speak very consciously of "pressure." Without selection, it is not possible to reproduce what is actual, to get anything done, or to get it going operationally. However, selection is in need of criteria. In the domain of technology as much as in the domain of hermeneutics, one may disagree about the criteria. For these reasons, it would be possible to summarize this discussion as follows. Meaning is a very potent technology to deal with complexity. This does not add much by way of information. One still does not know how one ought to deal with meaning. However, certain possibilities of managing meaning or of limiting the possibilities of dealing with meaning may become understandable if one pays attention to the actualization of selective pressure. One does this and not that. One experiences something as information, which is to say, as selected from other possibilities, or one performs an action that is, once again, selected from other possibilities. This actualization of selective pressure and of the search for decisions or criteria (for something suitable/not suitable, for convenience, for the possibility of consensus, or whatever name you may prefer) is forced upon us by the quandary in which we find ourselves when we have meaningful experiences. We are in the very quandary when we imagine ourselves under pressure from complexity, which is to say, when we ask ourselves how one particle fits in with another. This is the same problem. At a different level, we can still ask to what degree it is possible to use technology that more or less autonomously takes care of these questions of combination and selection for us. Nowadays, one would, of course, think of computers in this context.

Let me repeat. The formula stating that meaning is a potent form of the reduction of complexity, and thus a potent solution for the problem of selection that is forced upon us, does not give us very much information yet. But the reason that has led me to add these considerations is the idea that, from this viewpoint, it may be possible to resolve the old discussion of "technology versus hermeneutics." Moreover, one may also ask the question why something like the medium of meaning came about in the process of evolution. That is to say, one may ask why it turned out to be advantageous to establish this difference between actuality and potentiality as a structural law or articulatory medium of certain systems and thereby force them to make selections continuously or, to put it differently, to adapt temporarily to temporary situations all the time. If we use evolutionary theory as our frame of reference, why does this have evolutionary advantages in a world that has in any case become extremely complex through evolution?

It is possible to have theories about this and to conceive of the evolutionary advantages of such developments as consciousness or communication. But all this does not change the fact that we are stating our arguments *always* in the medium of meaning. Nevertheless, formulas such as "complexity," "selectivity," "reduction of complexity," and "evolution" are parts of theories within a landscape of science that has come into being only recently, and which can be situated precisely, can be put into a specific context in the meaningful world, and can be understood only if one actually does precisely that. Yet, this also means that the attempt to present meaning as a functionally equivalent "technology of power" – that is, as something extremely effective that is in a certain sense superior to everything produced by less well-equipped animals or plants – is still just a theory. As such, it represents a standpoint that must autologically claim for itself and apply to itself that which it analyzes. We therefore arrive at the conclusion that the insight that this medium provides us with evolutionary advantages must itself be formulated within this same medium. We cannot escape. Now, one might say that this is an argument *pro domo*: since we are subject to meaning, we even justify this fact in terms of evolutionary theory!

I now move on to the next part that deals with a question we have hitherto postponed: namely, whether more can be said regarding the content of the domain of meaning and the medium of meaning. After all, hitherto we have spoken only of meaning as such. Without any rational justification, I began at some point to distinguish between the objective, temporal, and social meaning dimensions.[12] To this day, I still cannot provide a rational justification for this distinction. In the meantime, the distinction has reappeared in many places, as if ordering the meaning dimension in terms of "objective," "temporal," and "social" were a product of theory that can be repeated in routine-like fashion without even trying to give an explanation for this order. I must admit that I am unable to give such an explanation myself. The concept of meaning does not itself unfold into these dimensions. Rather, it is posited phenomenologically in this way. When asked to give a justification, I tend to respond by requesting that he who asks for a justification should try to suggest yet another dimension in relation to meaning. Then I think through whether the suggestion works or not. On occasion, "space" has been suggested. But this does not work very well, since space cannot be separated from the object dimension. For the time being, just accept my model. Who knows, you may yet find alternative categories or additional dimensions.

There is another aspect that is more important than this particular justification for the reflections that follow. It has to do with the phenomenon that a specific distinction is massively forced upon us. One could rephrase this by saying that a certain state of affairs, which is at first just given as it is, is subsequently duplicated and applied to something else. If one accepts Husserl's terminology (and, in one specific area, explicit claims are actually made by Husserl), one could conceive of the issue under consideration in terms of double horizons. At stake is not the horizon in the sense of a spatial metaphor, according to which one can always go on and the horizon constantly shifts, and at some point one gets tired and stops without having reached the horizon. Rather, we are dealing here with two horizons in such a way that every dimension is constituted through a distinction and thereby is itself distinguished from the other dimensions. Every dimension has its own characteristic double horizon and thereby is distinguished from the other dimensions.

To begin with, I would like to represent this in formal terms. Subsequently, I will address the question as to whether the difference is itself historical, which is to say, whether it has developed. First of all, one can say that the time dimension – we spoke of this in the previous lecture (and I can therefore keep this brief) – is marked by the difference between the future and the past. This means that there are these two horizons. We can always go back further into the past in our imagination until it has no more meaning for us to try to imagine what happened before the Big Bang. And one can always go further into the future. With every step one loses some of the precision and determinability of that which one tries to imagine. But in principle it is always possible to go on, until our present and thus our own system tells us that it is of no operational use to go on. We have the future and the past. Moreover, one has the possibility (this was also said in the previous lecture) to duplicate horizons by imagining that there will be "presents" in the future, for which the current present will be the past and the presents that will be yet to come will be the future. The entire game is played doubly. One has the difference of future and past as related to the present, and one has future and past differences of different temporally localized presents that have in each case their own temporal horizons. It is apparent that this mode of looking at things is historical. If we look at the history of ideas and historical semantics, we see that it was by no means always self-evident and that this particular mode of reflection has only been ours since the eighteenth century, although we can be quite sure that it must already have played a role in terms of practical orientation earlier.

I think that, in the object dimension, these double horizons can be described with the distinction between inside and outside. This does not mean that the inside/outside difference always refers to systems. One must not see systems just in the object dimension. This analysis could be conducted even without any reference to systems theory. In fact, in Husserl one can find the notion that everything which one identifies has an inner and an outer horizon. One can, as it were, move from one thing to another, to other modes of usage, and to another who might use it. But one can also reflectively move into a thing, perform a penetrating analysis, reflect on the parts of which it consists, and all this, once again, *ad lib*. Theoretically, one could split up a thing into atoms or even sub-atomic worlds. As seen in terms of the object dimension (and not the time dimension), one has developmental possibilities in two directions if one wants to identify something. One may analyze the object and continue until one no longer has any interest in continuing. Alternatively, one can classify the object with respect to other objects, localize it in space, or ascribe to it other external relations and follow the corresponding references.

Finally, the social dimension appears to pose the same problem. One encounters sociality when one refrains from taking oneself as the only observer and instead takes others into consideration as observers of the observing. Then one does not stand, as it were, frontally and flatly in relation to the world, but one sees that others also observe what one is observing oneself. This builds on the object dimension at least insofar as one does not have to thematize the others as identifiable through self-analysis, which is to say, as something that is elsewhere. The notion that the others are not just objects, not just bodies that come closer or move farther away and that are or are not threatening to me, but instead are observers that see what I do – this notion of sociality split off from the object dimension at some historical point. On the basis of this social dimension, there emerges a double horizon, as well as what we later shall analyze as double contingency.[13] "I consider what I must do, so that you will do what I would like you to do for me." The reason for this historical separation has to do with the fact that the social dimension is not attached to the qualities, whether dangerous or beneficial, of objects, nor can it be arrived at by means of the decomposition or analysis of the other. I do not get very far if I try to find out with increasing precision what is going on in the mind of the other. If I have the other, as it were, on my couch and I sit in the armchair and reflect on what is going on in him and continue to do so, on and on, I will arrive at a situation in which I will be observed myself, and the one who is, as it were, being treated, will slowly find out what he has to do in order to shorten or prolong the treatment or affect me in other ways.

My thesis is that the three dimensions of meaning have a parallel structure. They build on the doubling of horizons that leads in each case to just two horizons. The question as to why this is so returns us once again to the concept of distinction or the concept of the observer. If we are historically socialized in such a way that we can draw distinctions, we learn apparently to differentiate our observation schemata according to time, sociality, and objective details. In all three instances, reflexivity occurs. In the time dimension, we find futures and pasts also in the past. In the object dimension, we find parts in the interior, for which the remainder of the interior is their environment, or we find objects in the environment, for which the original object is environment. One can deal with this more elegantly in terms of systems theory than object theory. But I would like to insist on the fact that, as a theme of a description, this entire configuration is not tied to systems theory. Rather, in this case, too, the structure repeats itself. Everything that can be identified can be elaborated inwardly or outwardly, and this repeats itself inside as well as outside, so that one also finds something inside that once again can be elaborated inwardly and outwardly and something outside that can once again be elaborated inwardly and outwardly. We encounter the same situation in the social structure. Here, the following reflection is possible if one takes one's departure from ego and alter ego. I begin with myself and then reflect on the fact that the other is also an "I" for whom I am another "I." In other words, I am doubly in myself, as ego and as alter ego. If this becomes beneficial, or if one has the time and interest for this reflection, one then may consider what happens if this becomes known, which is to say, if everyone reflects on the fact that he is both ego and alter ego. Can one even deal with this situation, and, if so, with what kind of actions? Or are there some stopping rules within the operational constraints of systems that indicate that something like this ought not to be done any longer or ought to be viewed merely as a theoretical possibility within the horizon of sociality?

If these dimensions with their analogies and resemblances are distinguished in this way, one may ask the question as to whether it is a historical phenomenon that these dimensions can be separated. The question then would really be whether we can understand older societies if we proceed from the distinction between the dimensions. Alternatively, must there have been simpler modes of perception, simpler types of cognition, and simpler types of experience for which it was neither clear nor in need of clarification whether a certain object of experience or topic of communication was dealt with in terms of temporality or sociality (that is, in terms of consensus and dissent, and so forth) or objective peculiarities? If one projected these considerations back onto older societies, this would lead to extraordinarily difficult analyses, because we would have to get out of the habit of thinking in the differentiated fashion to which we are accustomed today. As I mentioned before, when preparing these lectures, I re-read the introduction to Aristotle's lectures on physics. In the process I noticed him doing something that I always do myself – namely, weaving an "at the same time" into his texts, "*hama*" in Greek. If you look it up in the dictionary, you will find that it has a spatial as well as a temporal meaning. "*Hama*" is "together" and "at the same time." In the context of Aristotle's text, the word can be interpreted in temporal terms. However, it is not uninteresting to imagine that "at the same time" always also designates a "together." One might say that, for Aristotle, who still had a natural or quasi-natural sensitiveness, things that were far away were also temporally distant. Even in Augustine one still finds the formulation that I quoted earlier and in which he maintains that time emerges from the dark and vanishes again into the dark and apparently forms a subterranean timeless muddle into which everything returns.

This means that one may pose the question of how time-consciousness develops. One may equally well pose the questions of how the social dimension separates itself from the object dimension and what this might mean for the temporal relations. In what way and to what degree does it become habitual that human beings are not just seen as bodies but also have opinions that one has to know and which one can influence? What is the role, say, of religion in all this? What is the role of the institution of confession? Confession appears to have been an instrument with which one convinced people that they have beliefs and opinions or suggested to them that they have to give their inner approval to what they do. At the very least, they had to take it as a real nuisance that they acted as badly as they did in spite of knowing that they were sinful and not able to act differently. At what point in time, then, does the social relevance of one's behavior become internalized? When does the demand for motives arise that can be represented and for which one must take responsibility? Is this self-evident? It is self-evident to us that we are always able to think in this way so that we can even pose the question of Caesar's motives and we can impute motives according to our own understanding as to what made Neanderthals go hunting. It is, however, an entirely different question as to whether the social order is really regulated through the orientation by motives, the criticism of motives, or the suspicion of motives.

On the basis of this reflection, one arrives at an immense project that is, of course, not realizable. It would amount to thinking over the relation between the differentiation of the meaning dimension and the social development, as well as reflecting on the socio-structural reasons that might have favored and initiated a more pronounced separation of the dimensions. If one keeps this latter issue in mind, one finds sporadic hints, for instance, in the Middle Ages that point to the separation of economic time from religious time, the time of the day, the daily rituals, the feasts, and the yearly rhythm. There was a time when, in winter, the hours were longer during the night and shorter during the day. Imagine the consequences for the organization of labor if the night as well as the day lasted six hours, but in winter the hours lasted longer during the night than during the day, and the opposite were true in summer! In relation to paid labor, questions of time become relevant in terms of the organization of labor. If one receives money for one's work, one wants to earn the same amount every hour. One does not want to have to work sometimes for a longer and sometimes for a shorter time for the same payment, merely because the hours are shorter or longer. This leads very quickly to detailed questions. A similar issue is of relevance for an American project dedicated to medieval drama. At least, I would like to include this issue in my discussion of this project. It concerns the historical relevance of a type of theater that is performed on public squares and in which there exists no clear separation of stage and audience. In this type of theater, the stories or plots are usually well known. Often they are taken from history and many of them are heroic tales. The bodily movements of the actors are also known. It is possible, then, to recognize what the bodies that one sees can and cannot see in space. This may even include complex stories of deception, for instance, in Shakespeare (*Hamlet*). The viewer sees that the characters do not know something that he already knows, or that some of the characters on stage know something that the others do not know and on this basis attempt their deceptions. The entire dramaturgy depends on the processing of deceptions, including the feigning of motives and social relations. In Racine, this leads very clearly all the way to the dissolution of a guaranteed social order. In fact, one could write a history of the theater from the perspective of the differentiation of a particular social dimension in relation to the professional and bodily behavior in well-known stories.

With this I have arrived at the end of my lecture. But if you allow me to continue for a few minutes, and if the tape is still running, I can perhaps add one more point that is part of my conclusion. This point concerns the question (and this means we are returning to our initial question) as to whether it does not make sense, after all, to distinguish between "meaningful" and "not meaningful."

Let me remind you once again of the features of the meaningful. They are: non-negativity; universality; the necessity of use [*Gebrauchszwang*], which is to say, the necessity of connecting [*Zwang zum Anschluss*], as it were, to the medium of meaning; inner-worldliness; and, finally, the fact that the system that constitutes meaning has meaning itself, for when this system executes reflections it does so, once again, in the medium of meaning. These are the theoretical principles that guide the use of the concept of meaning. Yet, if this is the case, what is meant exactly if one would like to formulate a narrower concept of the "meaningful"? What kind of meaning is meaningful? In this context, I find one of Alois Hahn's considerations eminently important. He published it in a rather haphazard way in the context of his research on confessions, admissions, self-descriptions, autobiographies, and such. He claims that the category "meaningful" can be used when integration through self-description is concerned.[14] One may divide this further into subjective, personal, consciousness-related self-descriptions, on the one hand, and social self-descriptions, on the other. In order to do so, a discussion of the category of self-description would be required. In any case, the meaning of this entire pursuit is that no system that uses meaning can become entirely transparent to itself. It is impossible for us to subsume under one formula the result of a long chain of operations, the structures that we have, and the possibilities of differentiation that we possess. Instead, we are able to imagine who we are. We can describe what the meaning of a university is. In the process, we may very quickly have the experience that much of what happens at a university is meaningless and, in this sense, is not suitable for the self-description of the university.

In this pursuit, we arrive at the idea that the complaint about meaninglessness – and this is undoubtedly one of the major complaints in our society – increases in tandem with the self-description requirements [*Selbstbeschreibungsanforderungen*]. The more we are held accountable, the more pressure to legitimate ourselves we experience, the more we are forced to state what the meaning of our own life, an institution, or a part of an organization is – the more all of this happens, the more the difference of "meaningful/meaningless" is imposed on us. The development of language appears to suggest that meaning can actually be negated and is in many instances merely deficient. Our analysis also reaches and actually pushes us beyond this perspective, for systems theory allows us to see that there is a connection between the need for meaning and even the consigning of this need to religion, on the one hand, and the increasing pressure of individualization, on the other. This pressure is being exerted not only on individuals, but also on organizations that nowadays are looking rather blatantly for a corporate identity and a corporate culture, and even on functional systems. For instance, one may wonder why politics has to offer formulas that explain what it is good for, why it is needed and why such and such an amount of taxes has to be collected. I wanted to mention all of this only briefly and thereby come to the end of my section on meaning. In my next lecture, I will deal in more detail with something that has hitherto merely been assumed: namely, the distinction between psychic and social systems.

V

Psychic and Social Systems

---

1 Problems of "Action Theory"

Eleventh Lecture

In today's lecture, I will begin with a section on psychic and social systems. I thought that it might be useful first of all to refer explicitly to the topic that is not directly addressed under this heading, but of course provides the background for our discussion – namely, the relation between the individual and society. This, in any case, is the classical formula, the name of a problem that reaches much further back than the history of sociology. It began probably in the eighteenth century and became the central topic of an ideological or idea-political debate in the nineteenth century. In all of this, the separation of individual and society resulted from the abandonment of the unity of nature that had been postulated in the European tradition through the concept of nature, the concept of human nature, and the order of living beings that divided them into the species of animals, humans, and angels. We are dealing here with a period during which this orientation towards nature ceases or at least weakens. Instead the attempt was made to take society into account and no longer assign to human beings their natural place in villages, cities, nations, and their respective times. Instead a more individualistic notion of the human was developed. This also related to the new meaning that was given to the word "individual" at this time. In the earlier tradition, the term had been understood literally, which is to say as something indivisible. Naturally, there were many individuals, many indivisible units of being. In the eighteenth century, the use of the word "individual," in the sense that is familiar to you, was restricted to human beings only. Perhaps this use was linked to the decline of proficiency in Latin, or let us just say that people no longer thought in Latin and therefore no longer reflected on the peculiarity of calling human beings "individuals" and treating them as if they were indivisible. At this point, the word as detached from its roots, as it were, could be used for all sorts of purposes and was applied exclusively to human beings.

I believe that, from this point of departure, two possible paths can be taken if one wants to account for a more prominent individualism or a stronger individuality of the human person in the sense of uniqueness and personal character. One of these paths has been dominant; the other is yet to be discovered. The first tradition relies on the concept of the subject. The human being is seen as its own subject and as the subject of the whole world. The other tradition, marked by a much less obvious path, relies on the concept of population that follows in the steps of the old ordering of species. Now, a "population" is said to consist of individual specimens and does not simply pass on characteristic and essential species traits throughout history. Instead, it is receptive to demographic and revolutionary developments. Evolution sorts out the individuals in a population. This transition from a history of the species to the evolution of a population begins in the eighteenth century. It is one further way in which the conceptual frame is recalibrated in terms of recognizing the individuality of single specimens. It is important to recognize that biology, demographics, and the theory of evolution proceed along this path and thus exemplify one way of giving a better account of the individuality of each individual. But one ought not to lose sight of more comprehensive viewpoints that are also in evidence in these developments.

Regardless, the dominant tradition is the tradition of the subject. Among other things, it dominates because it attracts the attention of philosophers, which is to say, it takes root in philosophy. If one examines this tradition from a greater distance and without thinking of oneself as a subject, one notices that there are two topics that elicit complaints and which are, paradoxically, at variance with each other. The first one is the complaint about alienation. Society does not install the subject in its own essential being. The subject is no longer what a human being ought to be by nature. It is no longer the norm that the subject is oriented to human perfection. Instead, society has the effect of alienating the subject. This complaint is immediately followed by a demand for emancipation. This, too, is a recalibration of an old conception. In earlier times, "emancipation" meant the release from domestic authority and thus, from a legal viewpoint, the establishment of legal independence. However, by the eighteenth century, human beings were legally independent. A general theory of legal competency and a general theory of citizenship were in place. For us today this is normal. But, with this development, another concept, another word becomes available for a different usage. "Emancipation" becomes a demand on society that usually is associated with a decrease in domination. In a sense, the theory oscillates between alienation, on the one hand, and emancipation, on the other, and attempts to integrate both in the idea that society ought to make possible man's "self-realization," as it is called today.

In a way, then, there is simultaneously too much and too little connection with society. Sociology, which begins at the end of the nineteenth century, inherits this theme. Each of the classic sociological accounts offers an answer to the question of how it conceives of the relation between society and the individual. This is so with Émile Durkheim, Max Weber, Georg Simmel, and any other sociologist of the period. At the same time, and parallel to this sociological debate, there is also a philosophical, even metaphysical discussion that begins with Kant. This discussion can be assessed best if one keeps in mind that it concerns a reanthropologization of philosophical concepts. The subject is defined abstractly through self-reference and consciousness. However, in the wake of Kant, a reanthropologization takes hold, in the sense that now, when one speaks of the subject, one thinks of concrete human beings with bodies, a specific habitus of consciousness, a personality, and so forth. One has in mind empirical specimens as materializations of the subject in material reality, if you will. In fact, the same happens once again at a later stage. Just consider how the discussion that was linked to the names of Husserl and Heidegger was conducted in Germany. It had clearly anti-humanistic or at least anti-anthropological tendencies. Thus, in §10 of Heidegger's *Being and Time*, you will find an explicit rejection of anthropology as a fundamental theory of metaphysics.[1] But all of this gets lost when the theory is imported into France. Since World War II, the French talk about Husserl and Heidegger as if they had provided theories of man. However, they are cautious and use the formulation of a "*réalité humaine*," or human reality, as if they did not really mean the individual specimens that run around. But here, too, there is the tendency to think of the orientation towards man as being indispensable for philosophy. They do not even construct a philosophical theory first that would be based in conceptual categories (or in something else) and then examine whether man can be classified in a certain way. Instead, the need for an orientation towards man is apparently a very powerful force, on which we, as sociologists, can now reflect.

Sociology has its own specific difficulties with this issue. On the one hand, since we also have biology and psychology, sociology cannot assume that everything that happens to and in man ought to be a matter for sociology. On the other hand, sociology nonetheless feels the indispensability of a humanistic or anthropological orientation. I believe that one can say quite emphatically that only systems theory provides a possible model. Only when the conceptual apparatus that I outlined has been mastered, can one properly locate the problem of assigning a place to human beings in a theory, which in our case is a theory of society. I will return to this point in a moment and deal with it in greater detail. For the time being, I would only like to show that sociological solutions have been located in a border zone between the individual and society. One has attempted to find concepts that are, however, neither fish nor fowl. These concepts want to have it both ways. I believe that this is one of the reasons why sociologists in general rely strongly on the concept of action. After all, it is difficult to speak about action if one attempts to abstract entirely from the human being and introduce into the theory actions that exist as entirely detached from humans. I think that, where "communication" is concerned, everything is different. I will give a more detailed justification for this claim. "Action" first of all refers to an individual human being and not to a process that links different human beings. The concept of action almost inevitably suggests that human beings are behind it all or, to use a different formulation (you may prefer other alternatives), that human beings are the cause, carriers, and subjects of actions.

I think that, in the final analysis, all other concepts that form part of this context concerning the connection between the individual and society can be traced back to the concept of action. This is especially true for the concept of the "role." The role is often seen, especially by Parsons (among others), as a concept that is explicitly intended to connect the individual and society. The role has a format that is made to fit the individual human being. The university is not a role, but the professor and the student are role designations, according to which only one of them is the professor. *Two* cannot be *one* professor, although it is of course possible, under certain circumstances, that two people share one job. The concept of the role fits individual human beings but has, at the same time, a more abstract format. After all, a role may be executed by different people in more or less the same form. Furthermore, there are modes of orientation that can completely abstract from the person that occupies the role. For instance, think of a bus conductor. If he knows his job and possesses no incidental qualities that attract unfavorable attention, it will do. The concept of the role that is normally defined through the expectation of behavior or action, and which identifies and fixates bundled expectations, also belongs to the problem area of how man and society, the individual and society, can simultaneously be included in a theory.

If one intends to proceed from the concept of action, it is worthwhile taking a closer look and to ask oneself what might be meant by "action." To put it differently, what is meant when people talk about action? You recall that I always develop concepts from the standpoint of the observer who has to decide what distinction he wants to use to define action, if "action" is supposed to mean something specific. He also has to decide what falls by the wayside and is excluded when a theory of action is constructed. Already such questions that aim at more conceptual precision and more conceptual effort lead us into considerable difficulties. If one browses through the literature, one notices that there are different connective aims, different intentions in perceiving something as a non-action. As far as the difference between "action" and "behavior" in American English is concerned, "behavior" is understood as something of which animals as well as humans are capable and which for human beings occurs in a way that is quite similar to animals. Perhaps, in humans, a more sophisticated coordinating brain mechanism or perhaps higher complexity is involved. "Behavior" is a concept that comes with empirical intentions and in a certain way excludes the subject. Parsons always insisted on this distinction in the American context. He always saw his work as leading the revolt against behaviorism and attempting to refute behaviorists who think that they can engage with guinea-pigs and American students at the same level, and who see no essential difference between them, except perhaps in the way that they respond to inputs and outputs. This controversy was dominant in America in the thirties. While it lasted, the interest in Parsons's work was taken to be of a European, non-empirical, almost philosophical, and voluntaristic kind. After all, this was how the theory of action presented itself. This is one of the front lines that one can find in the literature.

In recent times, there has been an insistence upon the rationality of the disposition to act. You can find the sources of this view in Max Weber. Max Weber thought that, in order to explain actions, one must proceed from the distinction between means and ends. This is to say that the actor has both to understand himself and be able to be understood, were one to ask him the objectives of his actions. Thus the problem of rationality has been inserted into the concept [of action]. In consequence, it is difficult to determine what has been excluded and how or in what manner it has been excluded. Is action that is not oriented towards means and ends no longer action but merely behavior? Is rationality the decisive component in determining the meaning of this concept or its decisive reference?

In rational choice theory, the problem has developed in such a way that it is not usually even addressed anymore. One simply assumes that it is possible to develop substantial social theories if one refers to rational action, which is to say, if one analyzes the choices someone makes when he expects certain benefits, seen from a particular perspective. Of course, it needs to be acknowledged that some deviations from the theoretically calculated results are only normal. This was one of the reasons why Weber relied more on "ideal types" than on a complete description of reality.

Besides this issue of a rational core as the characteristic feature of the concept of action, I have two further difficulties with this concept. Perhaps they could be called "the problem with the external limitation" and the "problem with the internal limitation of action," respectively. As far as the external limitation is concerned, it is not clear to me which consequences are part of the action and which are not. Where exactly does the chain of consequences break off, so that one can actually say that up to this point everything is action and beyond it everything is effect and no longer belongs to the action itself? For instance, is it my action when you hear what I say? Does this take place simply inside your head, or are the acoustics, the air movement, and the movements of my mouth still part of my action? Where do the consequences begin and where does the chain of consequences that are still considered as part of my action end? Once one begins with adding on consequences and ascribing responsibility, one tends to include as many consequences as possible. In contrast, if one would like to respect the liberty of action of other actors and of the environment, one would have to limit the notion of action to the immediate intention that gives it shape and, as it were, that causes a body to do something – but nothing more. This line of demarcation is far from obvious. I do not know the relevant literature well enough to say that this problem is not addressed anywhere, but it is generally the case that people assume that everybody knows what is meant when they speak of "action." I have some difficulties with this. All of this concerns the external limit and thus the question of the degree to which action fades into the environment.

The internal limit has to do with the question of motivation. Normally one talks of action only if one can find a motivation, or (to use a more narrow formulation that is not absolutely necessary) only if the intention of the actor can be fixed and thus the action can be attributed to an intention. For this reason, there is a tendency to formulate "action" in terms of a theory of attribution. That is to say, the occurrence of action is assumed if someone – be it the actor himself or another – ascribes the action to an autonomous decision on the part of the actor if one intends to hold the actor responsible for his action, or if one suspects that there are understandable motives that can explain why the actor acts in precisely this and no other way. In sum, the occurrence of action is assumed whenever we have an explanatory schema at our disposal that in a certain sense reaches its end within the inner being of the actor and allows us to read into or attribute motives and intentions to it. However, this strategy has its own difficulties. In this case, one must ask the question of what these motives consist. Are they truly psychological causes? Or are they merely possible "accounts," as they are called in some phenomenological literature? If I am asked why I did something, I can say something that seems convincing to me. Under normal circumstances, one is prepared to answer such questions, while in some instances the question is completely ridiculous; one had not expected it at all and therefore cannot even refuse to answer it. For instance, if I walk into a shop to buy something and am asked why I am buying this item, I can respond by saying that I want to have it. End of story! That *is* the explanation!

At this point, one may want to return to the distinction between action and behavior and ask oneself whether an attribution of motives has been a given all along. Was it the case for Neanderthals or ancient Greeks or for peoples at the time of mass migrations? Does one always have motives ready? Or is it possible to claim that the necessity of having motives corresponds to cultural development? Does the need for an explanation of actions or the need to identify actions as such through internal attribution become relevant merely to the extent that there emerges a wider range of possibilities for action? Society becomes more complex. One has the choice of doing this *or* that. One is constantly confronted with situations of choice. For this reason, the need for motives arises, and only then does a concept of action develop that relies on dispositions, intentions, motives, and internal states. We ought not to impose this view onto the theory of the Greeks that was rooted, as it were, in natural right and natural ethics. Nevertheless, it needs to be said that it is not really possible for us to understand how the Greeks got along if they completely disregarded the reasons that led someone to act in a certain way.

In short, the question of motive-related action can be meaningful if one wants to conceptualize the development of an understanding of actions that is keyed to individuals as an evolutionary or cultural development. But, even if this is a meaningful question, it does not, it seems to me, solve our problem. To be sure, I do think that this question is meaningful. Similarly, I have no intention of eliminating the concept of action on the grounds that this concept is no longer meaningful. But our real problem is how an individual can be connected to society, if we take the concept of the individual seriously in biological and psychological terms and also keep in mind all that we have learned about it. In light of this question, one has the impression that the theory of action functions as a sort of glue between the individual and society. Action is something that is meaningful on both sides of the divide. Strictly speaking, it cannot be dissected into an individual and a social part. It cannot be cut up.

In this context, there are at least two further points on which we need to comment. The first concerns the controversy "action theory versus systems theory." This is one of those current discussions that, I believe, poses the problem in the wrong way. After all, systems theory in its sociological tradition has always understood itself as a theory of action or a theory of action systems. I remind you of Parsons, and I remind you of my presentation of Parsons's theory with the help of the formula "action is system." As seen from this perspective, it would appear difficult to start an argument between action theory and systems theory. In fact, people who think in the terms of this controversy tend to skip Parsons. They see his theoretical enterprise as a failure and instead prefer to return to Max Weber. But this move does not answer our question concerning the contours or limits of the concept of action. Nor does it answer our question as to how a system can emerge from actions if every action in this sense is biologically and psychically rooted in the individual human being.

In the second place, there is the objection on the part of sociological empiricism. Both its method and the theories that are used to interpret the data rely on the concept of action. One poses questions about dispositions and all sorts of things, but each question and each answer are already actions. The idea that an acting subject is the empirical material that one can grasp in the usual mode of research is widespread among all the sociologists who work empirically. In a remark that is frequently quoted, Renate Mayntz once stated that, if systems theory does not take action into account, it is like the fat lady without a stomach. In truth, it is even worse! For this lady has no upper body either. She has no body at all, and the entire body is not even part of the social system. In this case, Renate Mayntz will certainly ask what one can actually talk about if one disregards that people act. The point, however, is not that one ought to disregard all this. Rather, the concept [of action] is to be liberated from functioning as the glue or the hinge between individual psychic and biological systems, on the one hand, and social systems, on the other. However, this makes sense only if we already know approximately what problems await us if we do this, and what kind of theory remains possible under these circumstances.

Looking at the development of systems theory, I believe that it is well prepared for this challenge. In the first place, systems theory has adopted concepts of self-reference. Recursiveness and other traits that used to be the privilege of the subject are now features of systems, including communication systems. Thus, there are different versions of self-reference. Yet, there is also a certain similarity that connects an entire area of systems that could be called self-referential. In the second place, there is the shared medium of meaning. It was the topic of the preceding lecture that one accepts that psychic systems as well as social systems, operations of consciousness as well as communicative operations, work with an equivalent medium. That is not to say that they execute the same operations. Both consciousness and communication, however, work with this peculiar medium that deals with the excess of possibilities, the need for selection, setting the sights on something determinate, and the necessity of excluding everything else. Now, finally, we have the thesis that a system is not a particular object but the difference between the system and the environment, which means that the body and conscious occurrences actually belong to the environment of a system if one states that they belong to the environment of a [social or communication] system. This is not a judgment on what is considered important or unimportant. It is merely a judgment on the question of how the system and the environment can continuously be coordinated with each other.

Placing man in the environment does not imply a negative or devaluing moment, as is often assumed. On the contrary, the position in the environment may perhaps be even more pleasant, especially if one keeps in mind our usually quite critical view of society. I myself would certainly feel better in the environment of society than in society where [if such a position were really possible for man] other people would think my thoughts and other biological or chemical reactions would move my body in completely different ways to what I intended. That is to say, the difference between system and environment also offers the possibility of conceiving of a radical individualism in the environment of the system in a manner that would not be available if one considered man as a part of society and thus subscribed to the humanistic idea that turns man either into an element or even the end of society itself. If we imagine that society is moving towards a humane goal or that it ought to create humane living conditions, I have the feeling that this belief is simply wrong and that to believe it is entirely unrealistic. It is possible to conceive of political ideas and goals and to initiate all sorts of critical communications – but always *in* society only. The results of such efforts up to this point in time do not exactly oblige us to be very optimistic when it comes to the question whether society makes an acceptable human life possible. But, at the very least, one ought to keep this option open in theory.

2 Two Modes of Operation of Autopoiesis

These are the outlines of the theoretical decision according to which man in the sense of a biologically and psychologically individualized being belongs not to the social system but to the environment of the social system. This decision can be encouraged or confirmed by a precise analysis of the operations that reproduce a system. What is it that a consciousness does? What really happens in a cell or an organism, in a nervous system, a hormonal system, an immune system? How does a consciousness handle attention? How does a communication transmit options? How does it posit premises that subsequently are either taken into consideration or negated? And so on and so forth. If one has an operation-based systems theory and, with its help, takes time into consideration, one has to define the type of operation very carefully. One has to state that a system type like the social system can be produced only through one kind of operation and not through a mixture of all sorts of physical, chemical, biological, psychological, and other phenomena. One system, one operation, time, and so on: if you reflect on this theoretical constellation, you are compelled to accept a complete separation of psychic and social systems and, *a fortiori*, the complete separation of living, psychic, and social systems. One has the choice either of giving up the operation-based system concept or of accepting that man and the social system, human beings, individuals, and society are separate systems that cannot possibly overlap in any way.

This does not exclude the possibility of imagining that an observer, whoever he may be, can nevertheless define operations that simultaneously occur in the psychic and the social realms as a unity. It is at this point where the argument becomes difficult because it leads to a strange conclusion. In the first place, an observer is always free to make identifications as he sees fit and plausible. We are not excluding the possibility that someone may say that he hears somebody speak and that there is somebody who speaks and tells something to someone else. To say, "He's pretty far away. I can barely hear what is being said and cannot understand it. I must move closer. I with my body must move closer and listen to him if I want to understand him," amounts to an act that is at the same time psychic, physical, and social. For such an observer it is totally nonsensical to separate the psychic, bodily, and social realms completely. It is therefore up to an observer to identify how all this can be arranged in such a way that it appears purposive or how the world that he observes is best ordered. You see, to a certain degree I now revoke everything that I have said hitherto and claim the opposite under the impression of this ominous observer. For now the question is "Who is the observer?" In the theory game, one could put the ball back into the court of the observer and simply tell oneself that there are, on the one hand, theories that prefer to conduct their observations as if the psychic and the social were the same and, on the other hand, alternative theories that reject this standpoint and consider it meaningful to keep these things separate. Performing this somersault, this circular motion, we notice that we ourselves recur in our own theory. We see ourselves as one of many observers, an observer who is theoretically obsessed by the idea that everything has to be separated and who can adduce good arguments for this in his theory. At the same time, he can also construct the view that there are other theories that do things differently in this reality, which he observes and in which he himself is a player as a theoretician with specific preferences. This leads to the question as to whether we are moving within the realm of science and are able to decide this issue on scientific grounds, or whether there are deep-seated prejudices or plausible common beliefs that exert an influence on science and may motivate us to observe either according to the terms set by the theory of action or otherwise without such a great conceptual expenditure as this.

I hope that I have made clear that the science of sociology describes itself when it uses the category of the observer. Whenever it is said that a mode of identification or a way to form a unity is the business of an observer, the next question is "Who is the observer?" Accordingly, the entire terrain must be reconstituted in keeping with this mode of second-order observation.

But now let us return to our somewhat simpler way of looking at things. I would like to go through this argument once again from the perspective of emergence. "Emergence" is a word that occurs in many sciences and in some of them has a methodological meaning. We are concerned with the emergence of social systems. In sociology, one may, for instance, have in mind Durkheim's version. Durkheim states that social facts can only be explained through other social facts.[2] This is a methodology that constitutes a sociology that is limited to social contexts and does not include, say, physical or psychological determinants. It is a mode of separating sociology from psychology and perhaps also biology. This is one form in which the argument concerning emergence appeared. A second form concerned the issue of reductionism. Is it possible to reduce social states to psychological ones? Is it possible to explain everything that is perceived socially by conducting psychological investigations of all the people involved? If this is indeed possible in terms of psychology, it is perhaps also possible in terms of neurophysiology, and, if that works, it may also be possible in terms of cell chemistry. Finally, everything has to be traced back to the uncanny, inner world of atoms. But, here, one encounters indeterminacy, as the physicists say, and has to start from scratch. Alternatively, one may try to return to a type of holism. This is the movement that can still be observed today.

This entire discussion of emergent phenomena deals with shifting the explanatory emphases from one level to another. I think that this theory does not yet ask, let alone answer, the question that I would like to pose: namely, how and by what characteristics an emergent level or system distinguishes itself. What is the characteristic trait that distinguishes an emergent order from the state that can be conceived without it or, to put it differently, from its material and energetic basis? What criterion makes emergence possible? It is a stroke of luck, it seems to me, that the *Kölner Zeitschrift für Soziologie und Sozialpsychologie* has just published an essay about the autopoiesis of social systems. The author is Wil Martens. This essay deals precisely with our problem and relates it, in essence, to the concepts of autopoiesis and communication.[3] I will return to the theory of communication. For the time being, I would only like to add that I have introduced a three-component theory that has, incidentally, its own tradition in linguistics and that can also be found in ancient philosophy.[4] According to this model, there is a difference between information (What are we talking about? What is being communicated in contradistinction to all the other facts of the world?), utterance, and understanding. Someone must have understood, otherwise no communication takes place. (We leave aside the question of what he does in reaction to this.) Whether he agrees or not is his own business. He may start a new communication about this. This tripartite distinction is defined in Wil Martens's essay as the psychological and even bodily foundation of communication. According to this theory, communication is something that is negotiated in one's mind [*Kopf*]. First of all, I must reflect on what I am going to say and what I will not mention, on what I can present as news, what I can assume to be unknown, and what I can make known. That is my mind's work. Moreover, I have to utter something, which means that I have to be physically present at least in some location. My brain must have sufficient blood circulation, and my muscles must be strong enough to keep me upright, and so on and so forth. Similarly, understanding also has a psychic and a bodily reality. I must not be unconscious or overwhelmed by pain. In addition, I have to be able to concentrate (especially during difficult lectures). Thus, understanding, too, is a physical and psychic achievement of a more or less exacting kind.

Now we have these three things. My thesis is that sociality comes about only in the fusion or synthesis of these three components. In other words, the social comes about whenever information, utterance, and understanding are produced as a unity that has feedback effects on the participating psychic systems. The psychic systems must behave in a specific way for this to succeed. The unity and the emergence of the social, however, is only the synthesis itself, whereas one may and even has to continue to describe the elements in strictly psychological or biological terms. We cannot do without this basis. What we have here, then, is clearly a theory of the emergence of a new order on the basis of a combinatory gathering of elements in new units. I hope that you will be taken in by this! After all, it is very plausible at first sight. Then, however, one begins to ask questions. Just read Wil Martens's essay! I received on offprint and I also received a letter. I can read the letter and the offprint, but, in doing so, I ask myself what elements of the author are in the text, or what exactly is being communicated. Certainly it is not, for instance, the blood circulation in his brain at the moment when he wrote the essay. In the text published in the *Kölner Zeitschrift*, there is no blood. The editors would reject an essay that came in as a flood of blood. Nor is it a conscious state. I do not know what exactly the author was thinking about. I imagine that the blood circulation in his brain was sufficient, that he had enough strength to sit upright in front of his computer, that he was interested in participating in science and drawing attention to himself, and that a certain case fascinated him sufficiently to conclude that others should also know about it. These are constructions (later I will talk about "interpenetrations") that are suggested by our communication but which are not present in the communication itself.

For this reason, we now face the following questions. What claims are made in the text? Does the text not contradict its own claims? Does the text import blood and thoughts into communication, or does it not? Since I routinely pay attention to paradoxes and am fascinated by them, I notice a paradox in this case, too. The text makes a claim that it refutes through its own operations. There is no blood coming out of it and no thought either. There are really only letters and what a trained reader can make out of these letters, words, sentences, and so forth. This is communication. Thinking in realistic and operational terms, I cannot see more than that. Martens's essay can be enjoyed only from the perspective of a history of theory. One will find it interesting only because it constitutes one more attempt to combine the individual and society and give each its due. The individuals contribute moments such as information, utterance, and understanding. But these are mere fragments, and the individuals would not even have thought of them if there were no social synthesis. So, if there is such a social synthesis, individuals have to adjust to the possibilities of communication and to change their internal states accordingly.

When one has received this message, one may proceed as follows. One may say to oneself that everything is alright in principle. It would be possible to describe a communication entirely at the level of psychological or physical facts. In fact, nothing would be missing – except for autopoiesis itself. What does communication as communication try to maintain? How is it possible that it continues on and on? How is it possible that communication reproduces itself on the basis of its own resources – that is, on the basis of communication – without including psychic and physical operations? I believe that the theory supports no other conclusion than to say that this happens through complete exclusion, the exclusion of all psychic and physical reproductions, facts, states, and events.

In a lecture here at the University of Bielefeld, Maturana claimed that it is possible to describe a living cell completely in chemical terms.[5] Everything that can be found in a cell can be represented in the form of descriptions of the chemical structure of the corresponding molecules, and this would describe the state of the cell – but not its autopoiesis. Autopoiesis is a principle that can be realized only in living cells and only as life. It is possible to depict this principle in chemical descriptions, but not to explain it according to its own reproductive autonomy. If we assume that the theory is correct, this has consequences for the question of emergence. It would seem to indicate that emergence – the emergence of life, in this case – is possible only through a complete decoupling from all energetic, material, biological, and psychological conditions that are the causes of system formation at a different level. We are dealing here with a complete self-enclosure or decoupling or exclusion of all effects that transcend these distinctions and which, if they actually did happen, could only be destructive. If you were really able to include states of consciousness in communication, this would create extraordinary difficulties and would very likely be destructive. Imagine a doctor who visits you in your hospital bed and asks how you are doing. It would be rather embarrassing to find out what this doctor is really thinking! One would not be able to answer. Communication would fall apart if one even knew approximately what the doctor was thinking when he asked how one was doing. Take another famous example, Tristram Shandy's autobiography.[6] Tristram Shandy attempts to write down every moment of his life, including the moment of writing down these moments. He never gets to the latter task, however, because, already in the case of the first few weeks of his life, his description does not proceed as swiftly as his life runs on. In this case, we are not even talking about the linking of communication with consciousness with communication with consciousness. We are merely looking at the attempt to give a communicative account of the realities of a biological or psychological existence. Communication could not do the job, even if it were limited to its own devices and used them to the fullest. Communication is much too slow. Every attempt to get the job done would be destructive. The demonstration of this fact is the meaning of the gigantic novel *Tristram Shandy*. This is true even when the attempt is made merely within communication, which is to say, in the novel itself. In fact, one cannot imagine any alternative way of doing it. I believe that the same argument can be repeated at all other levels. It is well known that the inner electricity of atoms is affected when these atoms are linked together in molecules. We are not dealing with, as it were, little balls with a thick skin that are glued together to form molecules. Rather, these entities change their inner state (whatever this means in micro-physical terms) in the process of communicating with other atoms and establishing a chemical bond to form a molecule. All this notwithstanding, luckily none of their nuclear energy gets mixed up with the chemical level. This is to say that you do not have the possibility of unleashing nuclear energy by means of chemical reactions. That is an entirely different level. Only in this way is a lasting world, based on chemistry, possible – a world that may enable the emergence of life, consciousness, society, and similar phenomena. Well, that is enough on the notion of emergence!

Now, I would like to add one more remark, and in the next lecture I will talk about the concepts of structural coupling, language, and other concepts that link consciousness with the social system. We have time right now to talk about one of these concepts – namely, the concept of interpenetration. I want to address this concept also for another reason. It is the central concept in Wil Martens's essay, whereas the concept of emergence is only touched on.

If one adheres to the theory of the operational separation of systems, one cannot speak of overlaps. As always, it is possible to introduce the observer, who is in a position to synthesize multiplicity and unite the dissimilar. If the observer does this, *he* does it, but from an operational point of view the systems are separate. The activity of the observer depends on functioning physically, chemically, biologically, psychologically, sociologically, and in other ways. This frees up the concept of interpenetration. In fact, Parsons used it, as I reminded you in one of my lectures, in order to couple different partial systems, which is to say, in order to explain how culture enters into the social system or stands in a relationship of interpenetration with the social system, and further to explain how social systems affect individuals through socialization and how individuals domesticate their own organisms through learning processes. Parsons used the concept of interpenetration to indicate the areas of overlap between these different systems and to state that something cultural has to enter into the social system. In terms of theory architecture, this was not conceived of from the operational viewpoint. On the contrary, Parsons thinks that these systems contribute to the emergence of action, which is to say that they are not operational on their own. If they get differentiated, this happens once again only at the levels of action and of the formation of systems, and these levels in turn must fulfill all the requirements of system formation. The concept that would have to tell us what elements contribute to another system, or in what way culture is part of the social system, could never really be coordinated with the fourfold division of Parsons's boxes. After all, to this purpose it would be necessary to

internalize, as it were, several systems relations, and these must be shown
to be internal sub-systems. Only then would the system be fully differentiated by relations of the interpenetrative type. For several reasons this
proved impossible. Therefore, it remained unclear how different systems
could overlap, intersect, and be congruent with each other.

In a conversation, Parsons once referred to a sociologist called Loomis,
who used to work on models of intersecting systems and developed a
conceptual apparatus according to which there could be contexts in which
different systems produced effects as if they were one united system.[7] I
do not think, however, that Parsons made use of this point in any of his
publications. The entire claim was presented very much in the systems
theoretical jargon of the fifties and early sixties. I have a really hard time
getting my mind around all of this. In fact, I also have the problem as to
whether the concept of interpenetration ought to be dropped altogether
or whether another use can be found for it. From a terminological viewpoint, my own suggestion is not all that felicitous either, and I am not
entirely happy with having reused this concept while charging it with
a different meaning. However, there is indeed a phenomenon that must
be considered – namely, the way in which systems react to complexities
created by their environment.

If we recall the image of blood circulation and communication, we may
ask how the fact that humans are sufficiently stable and reproductive to
participate in communication is accounted for in communication. Is it
not the case that, whenever I talk with you or present a lecture, I always
presuppose that your consciousness is awake? Do I not at least presuppose that the blood flow in your brain is sufficient for you to control your
body to such a degree that you can sit there upright, albeit with the help
of all sorts of supports? Does communication not always presuppose that
the environment guarantees some very complex preconditions of communication? Whatever is excluded and does not participate operationally
is nevertheless treated as if it were present. The delimitation of the system
vis-à-vis everything psychological or biological is included in the system
as a presupposition or precondition of its functioning. These are theoretical figures of thought that reappear occasionally in philosophy. In Jacques
Derrida, for instance, one can find the idea that there is a non-present
element that leaves traces [*Spuren*] (*traces* in French, *íchnos* in Greek).
Then, these traces are erased. None of it is made visible. In communication, one constantly discusses whether the blood flow in the head is sufficient. Traces are erased and the erasing of the traces is made visible again.
If one has doubts, one can talk about them. It is this "if" coming from afar,
this possibility of talking about things, which presupposes that, whatever
"it" is, it is always already there. The "absent," in Derrida's manner of
speaking, is present, although it is actually not present. There is clearly a
paradox in this formulation.

Applying this to the entire domain of system theory – a maneuver that probably would be unacceptable for Derrida – one may claim that interpenetration amounts to something like taking into account what is absent. Whatever is excluded is treated as present simply by the fact that it is excluded. Thus, one presupposes that the world (whatever that something is about which one cannot speak) makes speaking, writing, printing, and communicating electronically possible. Without this presupposition, the operation could not begin. Moreover, it could not gain any contours. It could not use its own selectiveness to do this or that, if there were nothing else that, though not taken into account at the moment, is the condition of possibility of the operation itself. Perhaps it is problematic to call this state of affairs "interpenetration." Yet it fits thematically. If, however, we do not want to accept this concept, we will have to invent another name. Regardless of all the misunderstandings my decision may bring with it, I have adopted this concept because, in sociology, similar states of affairs have been referred to as "interpenetration." Besides, the problem of potential misunderstandings typically arises in the case of a theory that is increasingly tied up by the constraints resulting from its selection of concepts and which barely tolerates its own jargon any longer. Is it better to reformulate all these insights with the help of artificial terms or to use one's own choice of concepts to indicate that there are connections with issues that hitherto have been discussed under those very headings? I do not have a clear policy in these matters. Quite often, however, I prefer continuity in terminology, precisely in order to indicate discontinuity *within and by means of* the chosen terminology. Enough for today.

Twelfth Lecture

Already in the last lecture, we were dealing with the consequences of certain theoretical decisions, and now we will have to deal with them once again. You witnessed how I opened a big gulf between psychic and social systems, in stark opposition to what appears plausible from our everyday experiences of human beings who meet up in order to talk to each other. These experiences force the theory to provide, as it were, some compensation. After all, it has to be recognized and said that there are causalities at work in both directions between psychic and social systems. For this reason, we first of all draw a conceptual distinction between operational closure and causal openness. It is only operational closure that constitutes an object or system that is capable of causal sensitivity. Without such closure, it would not exist as a self-referential system. An entirely different systems theory would be needed. But that is not all. We must avoid a reunification of system and environment or of psychic and social systems. We have to make the theory and the concept of autopoiesis compatible. One of the great provocations of this term is that it forces us to rethink all of our concepts that are intended to harmonize with the concept of autopoiesis. I will return to this point repeatedly. This also means that one cannot move directly from autopoiesis to empirical applications.

If one considers the relation between system and environment from this theoretical viewpoint, two concepts would seem to suggest suitable forms for this system–environment association. (Perhaps two is enough. In any case, at the moment, I cannot offer more than these two.) The first one is the concept of interpenetration. Of this I already spoke in my last lecture. Right now, I will recapitulate this only briefly, so that you can see the connection with the second concept, the concept of structural coupling. I am not entirely sure whether it is actually necessary to distinguish these two concepts in the long run. They have different theoretical origins and a different history, but they are rather similar. However, it seems useful for the time being to keep things separate. In the case of interpenetration, it is important to stress that one ought not to think of it in terms of a mixing together, an overlap, or the entering of one system into another. One might suspect the last simply because of the name of the concept. I have already talked about the fact that terminology is a problem. Interpenetration means that the active operation of a system depends on complex achievements and conditions that must be guaranteed in the environment, although these conditions cannot operationally participate in the system. In other words, the environmental conditions cannot be included in the system or become their own independent operations.

It is obvious that this applies in the case of a possible participation of consciousness in communication. Communication functions only if a consciousness is present, which is to say, if there is somebody who pays attention to the process of communication. This is not always noted in the communication. At times, one might say, "Pay attention!" or something similar, or one gives certain signals that are meant to motivate the other to be attentive. Naturally, however, one cannot introduce every sentence with "Pay attention!" The thematization of interpenetration indicates an alarm and a state of exception and thus does not enter into the regularities of communicative situations. Moreover, communicative signals cannot bring about attention in the sense that one consciousness *qua* consciousness can be addressed by another. But there is the possibility of registering interpenetration and of addressing it in each case of system operations – when, for instance, a disturbance occurs or something special happens. However, in this case as well, the operation cannot ever leap into another system.

The same is true in reverse if one looks at this state of affairs from the side of the psychic system. Whenever we decide to talk, we presuppose that language can be understood. When we think about what sentence we would like to utter, we are not at all concerned with the complicated processes that are involved, the complicated grammatical structures, the meaning of the words, and the impossibility of defining most of them. We presuppose the functioning of the social order. We can reflect on it in individual cases, when someone does not understand a word, or when we find out that somebody does not understand a certain language. For instance, one is dealing with a foreigner and addresses him in one's own language, and then one notices that he does not understand. Then one may try in English and, if that does not work, in French. At some point, one may even give up entirely. In one's consciousness, one has certain possibilities stored in order to deal with difficulties in understanding. Yet, here again, it is true that in our thoughts we can never actualize everything that is necessary for language to work. Thus, consciousness becomes the recipient of complex environmental conditions without being able or wanting in order to decipher them and bring about or change their details. The same is true, the other way around, for communication. This is how I have, on occasion, formulated the problem in question.[8] And this is what I mean by "interpenetration."

As already mentioned, the concept of structural coupling is closely related. It is, however, formulated more from the perspective of an external observer who is observing two systems simultaneously and asks himself: "How are they connected? How is it possible at all that a system functions in an environment in spite of being autopoietic, which is to say, in spite of reproducing itself through its own operations? It has to do this. The alternative is that it has to cease to operate and thus to exist." For Maturana, who coined the concept (I briefly told this story in the general part of my previous lecture), "structural coupling" meant that the structural development of a system depends on structural couplings insofar as it cannot produce structures other than environmentally compatible ones, regardless of the fact that the environment does not intervene in a deterministic way. This concept is "orthogonal," in Maturana's sense, to the autopoiesis of the system.

It is relatively easy to find examples for it in biology. Birds, for instance, develop only if there is air. If there were no air, birds would have a hard time developing wings. They would have no idea of wings! Evolution would never even come up with the idea of producing such complicated apparatus if it is not possible to fly with them. This is the case, even though the cell chemistry and autopoiesis of the reproduction of life are not adversely affected by flying and are, in fact, compatible with it. They cannot do the flying themselves, however, and they cannot continuously reproduce on the side the conditions of flying – that is, air. Autopoiesis is one thing, structural coupling is another. The evolutionary trend is that autopoietic systems either do not exist at all, which is to say that they do not develop a sequence of operations that possesses connectivity, or else they exist in this form of compatibility with the environment. In the latter case, adaptation is not an operational directive. Systems can behave in a highly non-adaptive way or develop entirely new structures. Wings, for instance, are not air-like phenomena but something completely different. This difference of adequacy in relation to a certain environment is made possible through the combination of structural coupling, autopoiesis, and autopoietic evolution.

Taking this idea of Maturana as my point of departure, I would like to emphasize one factor in particular. I am not sure whether this is stated in the same way by Maturana, but it seems to me that we have to stress the selectiveness of structural coupling more strongly at least in the case of meaning systems – that is, consciousness or communication systems. To speak in terms of Spencer Brown's concept of form, which I have already introduced, structural coupling is also a form that includes something and excludes something else. In general, this methodology or theoretical position tends to pose the question of what is *not* meant or excluded in each case, and then the question is posed of how we can afford excluding or ignoring something or, in turn, what the advantage of such exclusion may be for us.

In the case of structural coupling between social and psychic systems, one thesis – quite possibly the decisive one – has it that social systems are coupled only with consciousness and nothing else. In other words, it claims that communication can be completely independent from everything that happens in the world: how atoms and molecules were formed, how winds blow and how storms whip up the sea, and also how letters actually look or how sounds are turned into words. All of this is said to play no role at all. Only what is mediated by consciousness plays a role. Naturally, the consciousness in question is capable of perception. It is necessary to stress time and again that communication is incapable of perception. It functions in darkness and silence, if you will. One has to have consciousness in order to transform the external world into consciousness via perception. Only then can a consciousness decide to spend kinetic energy in order to write or speak. Communication itself can neither speak nor see and feel. It does not have perceptive abilities. I am not sure whether everybody who speaks about communication is clear on this issue. If one does not get this point, then the purpose of the separation between psychic and social systems does not become clear. What remains unclear in particular is the theoretical decision to see consciousness very much from the viewpoint of its perceptive achievements and not to consider thinking as its main achievement. Thinking derails much too easily for one to base the existence or autopoiesis of consciousness on it. Perception, however, is an extraordinarily demanding and complex arrangement of simultaneous processing that depends on the brain.

If we think of this structure with its sharp division between social and psychic systems, the effect is that the classical concept of consciousness is changed. There is no point in denying that consciousness is able to think. There is also no point in denying that it possesses imagination, even fancy, and that, in a sense, it is able to simulate perception. But, even in the process of thinking, one is hard pressed to turn off the perception or even the simulated perception of words as acoustical and optical phenomena. Try thinking a thought without letting the impression that you see writing or hear sounds enter into it. Thinking is a special achievement that does not simply arise all by itself when one runs open-eyed through the world. Thinking must be learned in a certain way. Yet the fact that thinking depends on perception is presumably true all the way into the details of thought formation. All of you can try to find this out for yourselves by conducting your own experiments.

We thus are left with a structure in which communication can be influenced only by consciousness, not by sound phenomena or the visual signs of writing. It took me a long time to get this straight in my mind! In the beginning, I had always assumed that there was a direct structural coupling between communication and physical phenomena such as sound. But I believe that it is more consistent (you may want to think this through experimentally for yourselves) to state that physics has no direct influence on communication, except of course a destructive one. Everything that is communicated must pass the filter of consciousness in the environment of the system of communication. In this sense, communication depends completely on consciousness and at the same time excludes it completely. In itself, consciousness is never a communication.

I do not know whether you will manage quickly to handle this perplexing theoretical structure. But I believe that this structure is the inevitable result of conceiving of self-referential, autopoietic systems in terms of their temporal operation and not just as a network or a relational structure. If one asks the question as to what operation produces what kind of system and system boundaries, the options available within the theoretical structure dwindle. In the final analysis, one arrives at the question of whether it is not necessary to come to some conclusions in regard to the connection between consciousness and communication by bringing concepts such as "structural coupling" to bear.

If one considers the possible gains of such a maneuver, one will be able to recognize the advantages of this form of structural coupling. After all, it is completely unthinkable that communication would have to consider everything that happens physically, chemically, or biologically within all the participants of a communication. Something similar applies in the case of the topics about which one communicates. It is completely unthinkable that all presuppositions that must be guaranteed in the environment for communication to function could be included in a communication as message or information. It would be unthinkable that the freedom and speed of changing topics, and the free fancy that can be elements of a communication, could come about if all this would have to be guaranteed. This is to say, that they would have to be included in the operations, as simultaneously physical, chemical, biological, and even operational-psychological in the full sense of the term. Communication is able to have such fanciful freedom only by controlling it through its own conditions, such as possibilities of understanding and the acceptance or rejection of a message, and by viewing all this as an emergent level. We are dealing here with the exclusion of almost everything that exists in the world. The compensation for this exclusion is the total dependence of communication on consciousness, which in turn depends completely on one's brain, and the brain requires that the organism be alive. At best, it survives the death of the organism by a few seconds. Even if the organism is revived, the brain may already be gone. This sequential structure is possible only on the basis of structural coupling. The structure consists of a series of structural couplings that is characterized by their orthogonality – namely, their total dependence on one another in combination with total operational autonomy.

This is the theory I would like to present. If you formulate this major point merely in terms of the simultaneity of total dependence and total independence, you end up with a paradox, and, as always when one formulates a paradox, it makes sense only if one knows how one is going to get out of it. The conceptual distinction between autopoiesis and structural coupling offers a way of turning the difference between system and environment (in the sense of a totality of unity and difference as artificially stated in the formula of simultaneous total dependence and total independence) into a form that can be handled scientifically.

I insist on repeatedly going through the ideas concerning the architecture of my theory, because one of the intentions of this lecture course is to make clear the particular rigor and methodology of theory constructions that also have a disciplinary effect. One loses one's freedom when one begins with certain concepts. This is not the same as aiming at empirical verification. In other words, I am also, of course, talking about facts, such as the fact that communications cannot be perceived. At this point someone may intervene and say, "Yes, they can!" and show me how to do it. In all likelihood, we are thinking of different concepts and will have to talk about that. The suggested method is not one that completely abstracts from reality. It controls itself by comparing itself to that which is claimed as reality. Yet this control specifically does not take place by way of an empirical verification of stated hypotheses. The trend in epistemology, and also in sociology, is moving increasingly in the direction of constructivism. It is for this reason that we must pay attention to, and recognize, an increasing number of methodological problems and additional constraints and limitations on questions concerning the construction of theories.

This was a digression that was meant to explain, among other things, why I consider it useful to strengthen the concept of structural coupling considerably. In fact, we should make it much stronger than I did in *Social Systems*, since at the time of writing my book it was not so clear to me. I would even suggest this concept as in essence a replacement for the concept of the subject. If one attributes communication or action, or any other operations, to a specific carrier, and if one states that someone has to be there for action to take place and then asks the question who this might be and offers the subject, which one has kept in reserve to this purpose, as an answer, then one overburdens the attribution capacity of a certain theoretical edifice. After all, one then has to say, "True, it is always *a human being* who acts." But who communicates? Here, it gets already more difficult. Are we dealing with two human beings or only with one? I will return to this in the section on communication. In short, one always ascribes communication to an identity that has to be groomed accordingly and that must possess the necessary capacities and be appreciated for them. In fact, this identity must be stressed emphatically as long as there is no replacement in sight: "We will not let the subject be taken away! We cannot do without the individual in our theory!" The most radical replacement on offer consists of thinking in terms of a difference instead of a unity and to refer to the paradox of simultaneous total dependence and total independence. Communication happens only via consciousness and with the help of consciousness but never operationally as consciousness.

Taking this formulation as one's point of departure, one eventually arrives at the concept of structural coupling and can link the inclusion/exclusion effect to the concept or phenomenon of structural coupling. On this basis, one can show (and by this I really mean show empirically) that communication is responsive to consciousness and only to consciousness. It is for this reason that the irritability of communication can actually be increased through occurrences in consciousness. This would be completely unthinkable if communication also had to react in a meaningful way to physical phenomena or chemical changes. The environment can have only negative effects. I have only to pour ink over my manuscript and the text will be gone. It is quite unlikely that a splotch of ink or a fire could add anything meaningful to my manuscript. Moreover, if a fire started and I still finished writing down a sentence, I would not, in all likelihood, be able to extinguish the fire. If I described the situation, this would not prevent the paper from burning. Yet, in spite of the negative effect of the environment, autopoiesis has been shaped and selected in such a way by evolution to ensure that this occurrence is rare and, if it comes to pass, that it does not stop evolution. From time to time, some books burn or something becomes illegible, a book may fall apart, and there are losses involved. Nevertheless, libraries grow bigger, and one obtains the books one desires. Thinking continues in the psyche with the help of books, and science continues as well. In this sense, autopoiesis is strong and capable of survival, and this is the only reason why it occurs. The actual point is that the inclusion/exclusion dichotomy, this form with the two sides, the included and the excluded, leads to a relief, a high degree of indifference, and subsequently to an increase in sensitivity on the inside. In communication it is difficult to ignore something that occurs to a consciousness if that something is given expression. If communication is responsive to consciousness – which is not automatically the case simply because of the fact of consciousness – it is almost inevitable for communication to engage with this phenomenon and to keep the consciousnesses concerned going.

These rather formal reflections on structural coupling between psychic and social systems do not make any claims regarding the origin of structural coupling. The concept of structural coupling is abstract and can also be applied to the relation between consciousness and the brain or between neurophysiological systems and the organism. What is special in our case? What is the mechanism of structural coupling between psychic and social systems, between consciousness and communication? I am tempted to answer: "Language!" Language is the answer to a theoretical problem that is posed very precisely. Language is obviously double-sided. It can be used psychically as well as communicatively, and it does not prevent the two modes of operation – namely, the dispositions of attentiveness and communication – from running separately and staying separate.

Seen from the psychic standpoint, language is an attractor of attention. Language fascinates. This is easily tested. It is relatively easy to distinguish the sounds of language from other noises, even if one does not understand the language in question. Whenever you hear noises of a certain continuous frequency with distinct sequences, you assume that you are dealing with language. Perhaps it is music. But there are not many other options, even if you do not understand the sounds. Other noises, such as passing cars or the humming of an elevator, would never lead you to listen attentively and try to understand what is being said or what is meant. Moreover, language distracts and attracts attention to such a degree that it is almost impossible to do something else when speaking occurs. There is only one strange phenomenon that compares to language and about which I have no clear theory but which belongs in this context. There is only one other sound that is equally irritating, equally fascinating, and equally imposing: the ringing of a telephone. It is almost impossible not to pick it up. Even if one is determined not to pick up the phone, eventually one will do so anyway – provided the caller is patient enough. But why? Because language is behind it all? I do not know. The ringing of a telephone may well be distinctive enough to stand on its own feet.

I would almost say that the phenomenon of language, like very few other noises, functions as a fascinating object and also as something that prevents us from paying attention to other things as long as speaking occurs. You may well write down the text that I am presenting at this very moment. However, if you try to write a novella, you will have a hard time, since I will always interfere with my speaking. In such a case, it would be better for you to leave. They say that, in Vienna, writers write in the cafés and are apparently not distracted by other people talking. I have a hard time imagining that. Perhaps it is a special talent, or these cafés have a special atmosphere that allows writers and journalists to write their articles and other people to talk at the same time, and it does not matter. Usually, language demands attention and attracts it, especially via the distinctness of perception and not so much via its meaning. It is quite possible that one cannot help paying attention to silly gossip or something that one has already heard a hundred times before. In any case, one is distracted, although one would like to concentrate on something else. This is the cause of the difficulties one encounters if one wants to read or work during a train journey. Even in coaches with open-plan seating people talk so loudly these days that I always have to change seats in order to find a place where it is possible to read in peace.

This is one side. Language fascinates and thereby guarantees the presence, the continuous accompaniment, of consciousness. In return, it seems to me that language is indispensable for the conveying and fixing of meaning in communication. If we want to communicate without language, this may be possible by relying on standardized gestures. We can make certain gestures that are clear-cut as far as their meaning is concerned – for instance, shaking one's head or something along these lines. Beyond this small field of possible non-linguistic communication, there are a number of perceptible signals. One may frown or raise an eyebrow. One may shrug one's shoulders or make a very slight movement that signals to the other that he should watch out or change the topic or something else, but it is difficult to convey such gestures in communication. If somebody asks, it is always possible to deny that one had a particular meaning in mind. If it is not fixed in language, a meaningful message is not easy to convey. As you will see instantly, this is a bad way of expressing things, since I am about to reject the metaphor of conveying. However, the fixing of meaning that allows for repeated reference to it in the course of a communication is indispensable. In any case, it is hard to imagine that the autopoiesis of communication would have come about merely by means of non-linguistic bodily postures and such. Language, it seems to me, is indispensable for the stability of the recursive processing of meaning in communication. Now you see that, compared with what I had to say when I began with psychic systems, if I intend to come to terms with the communication system, I will need a different form of argumentation.

The cumulative effect of these reflections is that one may well assume that communication systems and consciousness systems develop in a co-evolutionary way, in the precise sense that the development of language differentiates consciousness from that domain that we may ascribe, say, to animals. In particular, it differentiates consciousness from the complex perceptual achievements of many animals. We then have consciousness in the sense of an orientation towards meaning, on the one hand, and ongoing communication, on the other. Thus, there is no reason to fear that one might get into a situation in which no one can understand anyone else any longer and communication simply ceases. Communication is autopoietically stable enough to prevail, regardless of what happens, be it a stock market crash, a war, or anything else. One can always still talk about it and comment on it once again. Even if a large part of the population disappeared, the rest would still talk and complain about what had happened. Like life itself, communication is a very robust invention of evolution that, *qua* autopoiesis, has a highly elastic form.

I believe that this continuity of meaning-dependent systems and the persistence of their reproduction came about as an evolution by means of language. This does not mean that I claim that consciousness or communication can be reduced to language use. It is an open question whether communication can emerge only through language. In any case, once it has emerged, there are also non-linguistic possibilities of expression, the so-called indirect communication. Much research exists on this topic. However, indirect communication arises only after a system of communication has been established – a system that would not have emerged without language and which makes switching back to language possible at any point. In the same vein, one could say of consciousness that its achievements are and remain perceptual achievements, as in the case of the animals. One does not need words to understand and process perception. There are numerous controversies regarding these topics. The question concerning the dependence on words, even in the case of color perception, is one of Maturana's research areas.[9] Regardless of the position one takes, it would not be correct to state that we can only see what we can formulate in words.

From this viewpoint, I would now like to comment briefly on the relation of the conception of language as structural coupling (including the claim that this is the task or function of language) to familiar theories of language. First of all, this claim would mean that language is not a system. *Language is not a system.* Ever since the foundation of linguistics as an independent discipline, which was essentially Ferdinand de Saussure's achievement shortly after the turn of the century, it has been generally assumed, in keeping with Saussure, that language is a system. In fact, modern linguistics is Saussurean linguistics through and through. Hardly ever has there been a case in which one single author or lecture series (it was not then even a book) determined an entire discipline to the same degree as happened in this instance.[10] Now, the assumption that language is a system was made for all sorts of different reasons. However, the system concept in question is generally not put into a relation with the system's operation. Rather, this system concept has, as I would say, a simpler shape. This system conception brings structures, grammar, and differences into conceptual relations with each other without making clear what the operation of the system is. Saussure distinguishes between *"parole"* and *"langue,"* between spoken words and language itself. But what remain unclear from an empirical perspective are the basal operations themselves, unless one refers to communication. However, this decision would in turn force us to distinguish more sharply between the psychic and social aspects than is customary in linguistics.

This is the first point: language is not a system. The second point is: language has no mode of operation of its own. There is no linguistic operation that is not communication or thinking in language. The reason for this has to do with the depth at which the concept of operation is situated and also with the precision of the question concerning empirical references, as well as the question as to what is to be excluded by means of this concept. That language in and of itself is not yet communication is due to the fact that communication always requires more than one speaker. There must always be someone who hears what is said and is able to understand it. The concept of communication (on which I will have more to say shortly) attempts to yoke these two aspects together. In contrast, the word "*parole*," and more generally words as such, aims at something that tends to pay attention only to the action or speech act.

For this reason, I would like to adduce a third point that makes the difference clear. If one refers to the paradigm of structural coupling, then language use is no action, no deed, no "act." For language always also requires understanding for its continuation. The difference between a theory of communication, as I envision it, and a speech-act theory or a theory of communicative action has to do with the question of whether or not one includes understanding in the unity of communication. If one has a concept of communication that is based on action, one takes the mere conveying of a message (precisely what I am doing at the moment) for communication and one does not include understanding. This necessitates corrective theoretical measures. If the actor or conveyor of the message acts rationally, he is said to conform to presuppositions of understanding [*Verstehensvoraussetzungen*]. He will not say something that, as he knows, cannot be understood. Furthermore, if he notices that he is not being understood, he will not continue speaking for long. However, all this would seem to imply that, in the beginning, the recipient is excluded from the speech act or the communication. He is reintroduced into the theory merely as a disciplining element. The recipient and also understanding are not included in the intention of communication. They are merely an expected effect. This leads to the question of who expects this effect. Naturally, one has to take recourse to the subject once again. One controls oneself by way of anticipation, regardless of whether one talks in a comprehensible or an incomprehensible way.

If I reflect on what distinguishes my concept of communication from Habermas's theory of communicative action,[11] I arrive at the following. One has a choice. One can – and this is the first option – understand language as action, exclude the understanding recipient from the unity of the action, and integrate the necessary disciplinary elements and rational calculus or, as Habermas has it, normative requirements in the action. The action then is faced with the pressure of reflection, the conditions of rationality, and normative ideas precisely because the understanding recipient is an alter ego and must be taken into consideration in one way or another. The other option is to build a theory in which understanding is already a part of the "unit act" of communication, which is to say, of the elementary unit of the system. In seems to me that, in this second case, one is not faced with the necessity of distinguishing different types of speech acts or communicative actions. For instance, one does not have to draw a distinction, as Habermas does, between strategic action and action that is communicative in the proper sense, namely, oriented towards consensus and understanding. Instead, one has a comprehensive concept of communication at one's disposal. Granted, such a comparison of theories can provide only very limited results, if it is meaningful at all. However, it makes clear that it is necessary to make decisions and that the decisive question always concerns the proper point where a decision must be made. Is one dealing with an ideological question in this context? Or did one simply read different things and therefore consider different things as important? Habermas relies on speech-act theory. However, there is no straightforward agreement between him and Searle, the author of speech-act theory.[12] In any case, the real question concerns how one constructs the concept of communication, and this in turn concerns the underlying theory of language. In a correspondence I had with Habermas, he accused me of not having taken sufficient account of the achievements of linguistics in my systems theory. This is indeed correct. Notice that a particular theory option and a specific conceptual apparatus serve as the points of departure for linguists. I do not use them and, therefore, have to translate all their findings painstakingly. In the process, a lot of things turn out to be trivial and other issues vanish altogether. The normative connection between actors, for instance, cannot be introduced via the concept of communication but has to be reintroduced in a different way.

These were just a few remarks to clarify theoretical differences and front lines in the field of theory. If one conceives of language as a mechanism of structural coupling between heterogeneous and completely different systems, then language is no system and it has no mode of operation of its own. The operation modes at work are either communication or the conscious repeat performance of linguistic meaning. Language is not action, in spite of the attributions that are made in regard to speech acts. One attributes the conveying of a message to someone and knows whom one has to ask if one did not understand it. One knows whom one can hold responsible and whom one might want to contradict. In other words, one knows who can be held accountable. That much is clear. However, all of this is merely a secondary phenomenon that is part of the autopoiesis of communication. It is not the primary, basal, elementary unit of communication. Thus, we have to leave behind three familiar aspects of the theory of language: system, operation, and action.

There is, however, another element that one might adopt if it is redefined accordingly. This is again a tactical consideration in regard to theory. The element in question is the idea – among the oldest conceptions in this context – of language as sign use. A language is the use of signs. This conception reaches far back into ancient times, at least as far as Stoic theory. In this theory, the distinction between word and thing, *verbum* and *res*, was worked out first. Language is taken to be a depiction of things in consciousness and thus the possibility of speaking internally about things with the help of the correct names and designations. In Plato and, of course, in the older religious tradition, knowing the correct names of things had still been an important trait of wise men. I recall that I read in Plato that it requires a certain purity. One has to be pure to know the correct names. Naturally, making the names of things known was an act in the course of creation that put man in his place, to begin with, and enabled him to engage the world independently and from a distance. Man was outside. Moreover, he was either cunning or rational, or both, and enacted his distance from things by manipulating signs.

In this sense, the doctrine of the sign has always been a part of the theory of language. If I understand all of this correctly, this changed with Saussure and certainly with the arrival of modern semiotics or semiology. (The latter is the term coined by the French, who nowadays also use the term "semiotics.") In semiotics the mode of thought is actually more complicated. Here, the sign and the signified are both taken as internal to language. One would not have any words if it were not possible to express meaning with them. Yet, what is meant is not the external thing. Ever since Saussure, the tendency towards a constructivist theory of language has increased. This theory distinguishes between the signifier (*signifiant*) and the signified (*signifié*) and understands this difference as the condition of the operation of language and also of the fact that language is able to create its own differences without being restricted by reality. One may create as many words as one wants for apples. One may distinguish apples according to varieties. One may create words for winds, for the weather, and for houses. In the field of the law, one may create concepts for different forms of grievance, all of which receive their own name and can be distinguished from one another, if necessary. It is possible to supplement, extend, and refine them by differentiating the appropriate signs and without in any way duplicating or multiplying the corresponding reality. Just by coining a new word for a particular variety of apples, we do not yet have the apples. It is more likely that the instigation to coin a new word is caused by the discovery that there are apples that taste different from all other apples or which ripen at a different time.

This constructivist turn in the theory of language has the effect that we now have a more complicated structure of distinctions and must ask ourselves, "What is designated by a sign?" A sign designates that which it means in the context of the use of a particular language. In the case of the apples, it designates the meaning of "apples," but it does not have recourse to the apples themselves. Alternatively, it may designate that which the speaking subject had in mind when he used the word. But, in

this case, the theory of the sign becomes ambiguous. The sign designates
the inner state of the speaker. When talking about certain things, it is only
natural to conclude that one has these things in mind. For this reason the
reference associated with the use of signs is ambiguous. This is one of
the problems I have with the theory of signs. However, I am really not at
home in this field and observe it rather from a distance, as a non-believer.
Therefore, you ought to take my remarks merely as an invitation to
examine this literature yourselves.

So much, then, for the sign's double reference to subject and object.
Another important point is well established in the literature, and it is
possible to reconstruct it with the help of an approach that is based on
the theory of distinction. Ever since Charles Sanders Peirce, an American
philosopher who nowadays is categorized mainly as a semiotician, it has
been clear that there is always a triadic structure involved. There is, first
of all, that which designates something else. Then there is that which is
designated. Whether one is thinking of an external thing, or the image
or meaning-content of the external object, is of no great consequence.
Finally, there is the "pragmatic" effect (this was the typical manner of
speaking around the turn of the last century) – namely, for whom and to
what purpose a sign is used to designate something. In keeping with the
philosophical taste of the period, this triadic structure was formulated in
"pragmatic" terms. It is for this very reason that we still encounter the
pragmatic component in today's semiotic literature and theory of language. The famous classification distinguishes between syntactics, which
is concerned with structure, semantics, which deals with designation, and
pragmatics. The last gives answers to the following questions. What is the
purpose of this? What is the intended effect? Who is eager to understand
this? To whom is this addressed?

This triadic structure can be reformulated, as you may recall, with the
help of reflections on distinctions, forms, and re-entry. One may conceive of the sign as the unity of the distinction between the signifier and
the signified. In French or English, this is easier to formulate. The word
Bezeichnendes is hard to pronounce. In German, there is always the tendency to say that the sign signifies something and thereby to reduce the
triadic structure of the sign to a dichotomy – namely, the sign and that
which it signifies. But, in keeping with the theory, it is more appropriate to use a triad of terms such as *"signifiant," "signifié,"* and *"signe,"* or
"signifier," "signified," and "sign." If one sticks with this terminological
distinction, the concept of the sign can be used as the signifier (and I say
"signifier" quite deliberately here) of a distinction. The sign is the unity of
the distinction between the signifier and the signified. At the same time,
the sign is itself *a sign*. The word "sign" is the sign for the unity of a distinction. Starting from this consideration, ideas for a second-order semiotics are being formulated at the present time. These attempts are quite
interesting, but they are still in the beginning stages. Moreover, they are

limited to semiotics and therefore cannot explore potential interdisciplinary contacts.[13] From this perspective, it would be necessary to compare second-order semiotics with second-order cybernetics or second-order observation. I observe observers and I designate signs. When I say, "I designate signs," I designate the distinction between signifier and signified that I use or that someone else uses. That is to say, I refer to a distinction and I also imply that the theory of the blind spot must be taken into consideration in this context. He who uses a sign cannot use the unity of signifier and signified as a unity. To this purpose, he would have to have a concept of the sign to designate the concept of the sign, which is to say that he would have to operate as a second-order observer.

One then can also introduce the figure of re-entry. (With this I will have arrived at the end of this rather abstract digression.) One can speak of the re-entry of a distinction into the distinguished and say that the old distinction between *verba* and *res*, words and things, is now copied into language as the distinction between signifier and signified. We are dealing here with a decoupling from the external world. Following Saussure, we render the system indifferent to changes in the world and use it only to produce differences and work with these differences within semiotics, within the doctrine of the sign, and thus within language. The original distinction with which the Old European theory had worked is no longer used except in the form of re-entry. That is to say, it operates exclusively within linguistic confines or within semiotics. One has to assume that this language is compatible with any kind of external world and reacts only to internal needs for additional or eliminated supplies of signs. The system monitors itself with regard to those words that no longer occur and are no longer needed, as well as those that are newly in demand. It monitors which references still play, and which ones no longer play, a role in language and, in fact, in communication, as I would claim, if I apply this model to social systems.

If all this is correct, then we are dealing with a development in semiotics that is parallel to the one we know from second-order cybernetics or the theory of observing systems. In all these cases, the theoretical issue concerns the transition to formulations that are premised on the re-entry of a distinction into the distinguished. If one begins with *verba* and *res* in the domain of words, the *verba* are signs in the sense of a distinction between the signifier and the signified.

I added these remarks only for the reason that there are tendencies in the theory of art, as well as in several other fields, to discuss a possible fusion of semiotics and systems theory. I really believe that one must go back to this level of abstraction in order to enable such a project to take off. Presumably, this would lead to a theory architecture that would effectively aim at the integration of the different theoretical elements, but always under the condition that said elements have to be reshaped accordingly. Whether this has beneficial consequences for sociology, I

cannot say yet. I suspect that many additional theoretical achievements
will be necessary to make the benefits tangible. As among the most important of these achievements, I propose exclusiveness or an exclusionary
effect in combination with an enhancement effect, a combination that I
perceive as connected to structural coupling and also to language.

This point becomes a topic of discussion at more concrete levels, as
can be seen if one follows the discussions that have been conducted in
the domain of ecology. These discussions took as their point of departure
the thesis that one can only talk about ecology, whereas it is difficult for
us as a society to change the ecological state of affairs directly, independently of the rhythms of communication, which is to say, the slowness and
system-specific differentiation of communication. The system depends
on communication. Naturally, it can experience disasters whose effects
are felt not via communication or via irritation, but in a more straightforward manner as the destruction of the system. As you may conclude
from this reflection, the system is extraordinarily sensitive to consciousness. If one assumes that all structural coupling is organized by means of
consciousness, then the perceptive capacity of consciousness is the actual
bottleneck. What does one see if one walks through a forest and is not a
forest ranger? Does one see the damage done to the trees or does one not
see it? If one sees the damage and identifies it as damage done to the trees,
is one going to talk about it or not? If this entire observation is conducted
by consciousness, and the needles fall from the trees, then the needles fall
from the trees, and that is it. And, if the exhaust fumes of cars smell bad,
then the exhaust fumes smell bad, and that is it. For a long time, it was
assumed that producing fumes that smell bad was one of the qualities
of cars, and many cars together produced more fumes that smelled bad.
That was a connection that was perceived as compact and which could
not be dissolved, or so it seemed. If perceptions change, this change may,
through social movements, introduce into the social systems some political pressure to make certain decisions. The social systems in turn have to
deal with these perceptions by means of communication. As one can see,
they have great difficulties in accomplishing this.

I adduce this example merely to illustrate that one arrives relatively
quickly at phenomena that are of general interest and also of special
sociological interest, if one adheres to the sequences of distinctions that I
have discussed.

I guess I will leave it at that. What I would like to do in the next two
lectures is to outline a somewhat more specialized reflection on the
operation that constitutes the social system – that is, on communication. In this context, I will first deal with the question of how we have
to shape and redefine the concept of communication so that it fits our
theory. The "fitting" of concepts is a theory technique that I would like
to stress in this context. It cannot be done at will and without any respect
for disciplinary habits and theory traditions. But, in this context, it is

important to be able to formulate the available options consciously. The design of our theory forces us to define the operation that produces a social system. Furthermore, it forces us to state that it can be only *one* *operation*. It cannot be some mixture of operations. For only one form of operation can produce one systems type. If life is defined through its biochemical circularity and consciousness through its focus on attention or its potential for attention, as I should perhaps say, the question arises as to whether it is possible to reconstruct our field, sociology, under the theoretical constraint that its basic element has to be an *operation* and, in fact, only *one* operation. If we proceed along these lines, the issue arises as to what operation fulfills these criteria. I think that communication is the only genuinely social operation that we ought to take into consideration. Only communication involves or implies (if I may formulate it in this way) a simultaneous presence of at least two consciousness systems for its emergence. Sociality is already built into the elementary level of this operation. It is not just an effect that may or may not take place, as is necessarily the case for the concept of action. Well, I will leave it at that. In my next lecture, I will speak about communication and see how far we will get when we examine its consequences for sociology.

VI

Communication as a Self-Observing Operation

Thirteenth Lecture

Ladies and gentlemen, we still have two two-hour lectures ahead of us. For these lectures, I would like to limit our field of reference, this time to social systems only. This does not mean that we are giving up on theory. However, there is a sort of funnel effect. After a short introduction, in which we examined how systems theory in sociology got bogged down, we moved on to a general discussion of new developments in systems theory over the last twenty or thirty years. The next part of our lecture course dealt with the comparison of psychic and social systems from the viewpoints of the concept of meaning and the concept of time. That is to say, within our horizon we were still dealing with two completely different systems types. Now, in the last part of this lecture series, I would like to focus our attention exclusively on social systems. In other words, what I will present constitutes a sort of transition to a lecture series that would have to be entitled "Social Systems." In this process, we will continue to be bound by the theory options that we have discussed and the theory decisions that we have made in previous lectures. This holds true especially for the central claim that is rarely emphasized to the same degree in the literature: namely, the claim that the system is produced entirely by its operation and that, in terms of observation, it is defined accordingly. Thus, we have an operation as the system producer. We have to calibrate our theory in such a way that it refers to this operation. This means that systems theory and communication theory have to be thought of in combination. After all, the operation in question is communication, as I have already said.

Thus, systems theory and the theory of communication enter into a closer connection. This means that we have to start by questioning our preconceptions of communication and that we have to investigate the conceptual apparatus that is deployed in the wide-ranging literature. After all, by now there are professorial positions for "communication science," and "communication" is discussed in a number of very different disciplines. It seems to me that, in this process, we will end up in a minority position. Generally, you will think of communication as a transmission process, and if you bother to check you will find this also in the literature. You take yourself to be the author or recipient of a communication and your partner or *alter ego* is in charge of the utterance, the message, the information, or whatever term you prefer in your formulation. First communication is here, and then it is there, and you participate in it actively or passively. Even in the cybernetic literature of the fifties this was an unquestioned presupposition. Much technical research aimed at calculating the susceptibility to disturbances and the transport capacity of such transmission processes.

In the meantime, criticisms of the transmission model have been voiced, albeit in a relatively concealed manner. Maturana, for instance, clearly does not want to conceive of communication or language use, as he calls it, as a transmission process. Instead, he understands it as super-coordination of the coordination of organisms.[1] There are further objections that, it seems to me, focus on two points. The first point is perhaps a little superficial. All along it has been acknowledged that, in communication, nothing is given away. He who communicates something does not lose the corresponding knowledge in his head. It is not the same as in an economic process. There, you no longer have the money after having made a payment, or you no longer possess the object whose ownership you have handed over. In the case of communication, we are instead dealing with a process that has apparently multiplying effects. At first, you are the only one to have it; then two or more know about it – perhaps a hundred or even millions, depending on which network we have in mind. Even if we stick with the metaphor of transmission, we are at the very least dealing with an unusual transmission process in which nothing is lost but everything is multiplied instead.

In many of Gregory Bateson's diverse writings, essays, and presentations you can find the idea that communication is a matter of producing redundancy, which is to say, of superfluous or overabundant knowledge. It is overabundant from the standpoint of one who wants to find out about it with the help of questions.[2] If A communicates something to B, C can ask either A or B about it. If something was on the television, you can ask pretty much everybody about it later on. An overabundance of knowledge is being produced. Knowledge multiplies itself, and the result is that the rate of forgetting or the de-actualization of this communicative content is accordingly very high. The knowledge of yesterday is no longer of interest today. The production of redundancy is one way of describing communication. However, it does not advance the actual understanding of the corresponding operation. With what kind of operation are we dealing here? How do we describe the operation that produces this effect of overabundance and its subsequent selective treatment – in short, overabundance and selection? Nothing has yet been said about all of this in Bateson's important critique of the transmission model.

Another type of criticism is less widespread but, I believe, weightier. At issue, in this case, is whether the transmission model presupposes, not only for an observer of a communication but also for a participant, that the inner states of all participants are known. That is to say, one would have to know what meaning a piece of knowledge has in A's head and what meaning it has in B's head. In order to find this out, one would have to know, in the first place (for this is the same thing), what is in those heads. After all, if the knowledge in B's head is entirely different from the knowledge in A's head, it would be difficult to speak of "communication." But how do you want to go about finding out what someone knows? And how could you know that a certain piece of information – say, which bus one has to take to get to the university – is the same in all heads? Some people like to take the bus, others do not. Some keep forgetting the correct connections, have to ask again, and are upset with themselves. Others do not have this problem. The more concrete is one's systems theoretical conception of systems in terms of their specific empirical states, the more difficult it becomes to assume that there is a sort of identity or at least similarity between them. To put it differently – namely, with reference to the observer – it is of course possible for an observer to say that it is all the same, exactly as we would treat the announcement that this lecture course is being relocated to another lecture hall, as if it had already been processed. We have communicated it, and what we know is that we have communicated it. I do not know what your feelings are if you have to find the new location or what difficulties it poses for your psychic equilibrium to understand this, in spite of the fact that it was said in our last lecture that the move will actually not take place. We recall communication. Why, then, should we not limit ourselves from the start exclusively to communication? All the more so because it would be extraordinarily difficult if communication depended on finding out the concrete empirical states of mind of subjects, individuals, and even entire social systems (for instance, trade unions) who participate in a communication. What internal state of the trade union is relevant in the moment when a contract is being signed? What purpose would be served by this knowledge? If one had to find all this out in the psychic as well as in the social domain, what painstaking efforts and what delays would this involve? If communication had to occupy itself constantly with its own presuppositions, would it all come to a dead end? Perhaps all this is not really necessary.

To these arguments a third one may be added (which will, however, turn out to be devoid of application when we move on to written communication). One may say that communication depends on the simultaneity of utterance and understanding. It does not happen that I say something and someone else understands it after some considerable delay. Because the acoustics and the sounds are present simultaneously, I hear myself

speaking at the moment I speak. The delay is minimal and is not registered psychically. Moreover, I assume that you, too, hear what I say
in the moment when I say it. The simultaneity of communication is an
essential moment at least of oral communication, which automatically
comes to mind first. This simultaneity indicates the unity of the operation.
Communication is simultaneous and happens in a space that is manageable and can be surveyed, or which is identified by the communication
itself. Whoever hears something, whoever sits in front of the television,
witnesses what is being said in the very moment when it is being said.
Thus, further reflection on the unity of communication is not needed.

Only when we ask whether utterances in texts that were written down
long ago are still communication (when we read, say, Aristotle or Homer,
of whom we do not even know whether he really existed) do we have a
problem. We do not know how we could assess the unity of communication that took place at such remote points in time. For a start, however,
the moment of guaranteeing the unity of communication by replacing the
analytic unity with a relation in time and space is an important moment
of communication that does not become clear in the transmission theory.

Of course, the critique of a theory or a model is successful only if one
is able to suggest a replacement. If the transmission model is not satisfactory, what model is preferable? The conception that I would like to
sketch briefly now is treated in more detail in my book *Social Systems*.[3] It
uses a division that has ancient roots and dates back at least to the Stoics.
In the more recent discussion, it was presented in Karl Bühler's *Theory
of Language*, which was published in the early 1930s.[4] This theory was
subsequently adopted by American theorists and somewhat softened in
the theory of speech acts. In each case, there is a tripartite division that
is, however, formulated slightly differently, but which emphasizes the
same aspects of communication. To give you a bit of terminology, let me
tell you that I speak of "information," which is the content of the communication, "utterance" [*Mitteilung*], and "understanding" [*Verstehen*].
The theoretical treatment of this triad varies. On the basis of speech-act
theory, one can isolate different acts, depending on whether the information or the expressive behavior of the sender or the reception of the
message is brought to the fore. There is a considerable amount of literature that uses "speech act" as its designation. Austin and Searle are points
of reference that come to mind.[5] In the meantime, speech-act theory has
become a comprehensive linguistic theory that on many issues exceeds
linguistics – for instance, in the discussion of "intentionality." In this
theory the impression is given that the triad can be split up into different
acts or types with specific emphases. Bühler had spoken only of language
functions, not of distinct acts. He pointed out that language effectively has
to offer possibilities for utterances, fix information, and make room for
pragmatic effects or effects of understanding.

If we limit our question to the problem of what a communication is and what its "unit act" is, which is to say, what the elementary unity of a system consists of, then we may use this distinction between information, utterance, and understanding – but only in the sense of components of a unity. This would imply the thesis that communication happens only if the unity of utterance, information, and understanding has been achieved. At first sight, however, this would appear to be an evolutionary improbability. If you recall our reflections on language, it should be clear that communication presupposes language, at least if communication is supposed to happen on a regular basis and not be limited to individual gestures that can be easily understood. This also means that this unity of its components – information, utterance, and understanding – cannot occur in isolation. Rather, they are always aspects of a unity that has been produced operationally, but not in the sense of its elements, atoms, or other isolated states that can be fitted together.

This point can be clarified if we examine the concept of information. In the process, we encounter issues that Maturana has worked out in order to criticize the usual (even in biology) theory of information, which is apparent in such expressions as "genetic information."[6] In this context, information is always part of a communication. It is something that functions as information only within the system and within its autopoiesis. Its function is to provide an occasion for, and be part of, finding the next operation. This is understood relatively easily if one reflects on the meaning of the term "information." In colloquial language, one sometimes speaks of "data" and sometimes of "information," as if they were the same thing. One has in mind something like little note cards, little pieces, or units that can be pushed back and forth. One receives "information" from somewhere and passes it on after one has added one's own piece and deformed or falsified it. In any case, information is seen as a sort of commodity that passes from hand to hand. Yet, if one looks at the definition of information more closely, one always ends up with a surprise or a choice from several possibilities.[7] If one utters a specific sentence, this sentence is chosen from the set of all sentences that could be uttered. This set is determined by what was said beforehand. Whenever one receives a message (for instance, when one reads in the sports news in the paper that someone won or lost in some competition or was so sick that he could not even participate), then one has to rely from the start on a certain context within which such occurrences are possible. True, one does not know ahead of time who will win at what time and who will lose. But a tennis player cannot claim victory in soccer. The horizons of selection for information are always defined in some fashion, and usually they are defined in quite narrow terms. Thus, one does not have to get a sense of the full range of possibilities before one is able to understand a message. We are always dealing with a two-step process. First there is the defined range of possibilities, and then there is the actual selection according to which *this* and nothing else is the case.

As I mentioned when I introduced the concept of meaning, one consequence of this is that "meaning" ought to be distinguished from "information." Information is always a sort of surprise in the process of selection. If it is repeated, the only information that is still there is that apparently someone considers it necessary to repeat it. If a military command is uttered, the soldier always has to repeat what he has been told. From this one can derive the information as to whether he has understood the command correctly or merely pretends to have understood it. In addition, one can derive the information as to whether he obeys the command or not – and anything else that may be information in this context. In every case, however, a new horizon of expectations has to be generated and the corresponding reduction has to be conducted anew.

This is a strong argument in support of the thesis that this kind of information processing can occur only *within a system*. After all, how could we make sure beforehand that the horizon of expectations, the number of possibilities, and thus the informational value or surprise value is the same inside and outside or in one system and another? If one is thinking of small commodities that can be traded back and forth, one could at least find some sort of explanation. Yet, as soon as one examines the structure of the concept of information more closely – namely, the dual structure of horizon of selection and actual choice – it becomes increasingly difficult to imagine how exactly such trade could be conducted. It becomes necessary to determine the horizon of information if one wants to observe and find out what constitutes "information" for a particular system. This is, of course, possible.

If one would like to observe, for instance, how the erstwhile socialist political-economic systems generated information about the economy, one has to take note of the fact that this happened with the help of production plans. So many tons of this or that product was supposed to be produced and it was supposed to be transported to this or that location. Then one saw that not enough had been produced, or the whole thing did not work for other reasons. The targets of one's own plan were thus understood as an apparatus for the collection of information. Information about economic rationality was not included in this apparatus. There was only the information that referred to the plan. Therefore it became necessary to observe the political system if you wanted to find out what information about the economy was circulating in politics. As we discussed once before, we have different modes of gathering information concerning the economy. But we also have the same problem, albeit in a different way. Thus if we orient ourselves towards unemployment numbers, the gross national product, or the foreign exchange value of our currency, then these are aggregated economic data. However, I would not assume that a large business would orient itself towards these data in this way. The framework that includes everything that registers on a company's balance sheet and therefore controls economic rationality to a large degree, on the one hand, and the framework of all the politically relevant information that is derived from the economy, on the other hand, are clearly distinct. It is always necessary to be aware of the context of selection that confers informational value to data, irritation, and news.

We now have to project these insights back onto our more abstract topic – namely, that information is one aspect of communication. If you would like to know what kind of information and what presuppositions and constraints of the horizon of selection that are determined beforehand are relevant, you have to observe the system in which these things effectively take place. If you are interested in another system, you have different information. This fits well with the thesis of operational closure and autopoiesis. It fits well with the claim that information is always a system-immanent process, an aspect of an operation that is internal to the system.

The same would be true for utterance as well (and here one would not need as many arguments). After all, without utterance neither information nor understanding can be generated. Therefore, someone has to create a coupling with information and must be observable in the process. I guess that I do not have to explain this in greater detail right now. Probably, nobody has yet been able to conceive of communication without utterance, as long as one concedes that the utterance in question may well be involuntary and that the construction of intentions may be necessary for certain purposes, but not in principle.

On to the third component: understanding. In this case it is equally apparent that only something that has been said can be understood. That is to say, understanding is not something that can be grasped as detached from communication. Of course, this can be changed if one subscribes to a hermeneutic conception of understanding and transcends the texts that are used for communication and instead treats the entire world as a problem for understanding or something along these lines.[8] Hermeneuticians tend to start with the concept of the text, which they subsequently expand beyond the domain of communicative uses. Accordingly, one ends up with a different conception of understanding. At least since Schleiermacher the hermeneutic conception has been closely coupled with understanding in the psychic sense. If one desires to understand why someone acts in the way he acts, it is not necessary to refer to or to rely on communication. One needs knowledge and must be able to trace back what one has observed – for instance, a certain behavior – to the internal horizon of the other, to that which he or she might have meant and as to why he or she sees these things in this and no other way.

The concept of understanding can be expanded in other scientific contexts. However, if we refer to understanding for the purposes of a theory of communication, what is meant is always a component without which communication could not be brought to conclusion and which contributes to the realization and actualization of communication. Here, as in the case of the concept of information, what is meant is not an external state – say, the psychic state of the one who understands – but a condition that guarantees that communication can continue. In other words, understanding and non-understanding must be distinguished. If someone does not understand what has been said – for instance, because he does not know the language – communication cannot continue or, at best, it reverts to a very elementary level. Perhaps one tries to communicate in another language,[9] but that does not work either. Then one tries it with gestures, and somehow one begins to understand that he does not understand. Under these circumstances, communication may actually continue for quite some time, if one succeeds in shifting it to another level. Typically, however, non-understanding is the occasion for going back and asking for clarification of what has been said within the process of communication. In other words, non-understanding is typically injected back into communication itself. If someone said something in too low a voice, and one therefore noticed only that he wanted to say something but did not understand what it was that he wanted to say, then one would go back and ask and the problem might be corrected.

Misunderstanding or non-understanding is included in this conception of understanding as long as it does not terminate autopoiesis. One can actually continue to communicate for quite some time on the basis of misunderstanding [*Missverstehen*]. It is not necessary that all misunderstandings [*Missverständnisse*] are untangled. Such a requirement would be a heavy burden for the process of communication. Sometimes it simply does not matter because the next act makes a choice. One recognizes that one has not properly understood what was being said and one may even be wrong about this, but it suffices, in any case, to assume that communication continues in this or that way. Conversely, the speaker notices that the hearer assigns another meaning to the spoken words, but he is not interested in constantly making corrections. He has not been born or socialized as a teacher. Rather, he thinks that it is alright and that the two of them will do fine even with these misunderstandings. Thus, the question of whether one ought to probe further and make corrections, whether the subsequent communication ought to be brought to a halt and directed to this problem, is actually a question that is decided in the system. No doubt an observer may recognize certain regularities in this respect, provided he is interested in them.

After having discussed these three components, the central question is How is the unity of the operation constituted? In other words, what turns communication into a unity? It is not enough that information, utterance, and understanding occur. In addition, something else has to happen and produce a synthesis. How does such an occurrence come about? We have taken for granted that our requirements for proper understanding are not particularly difficult. The communicating speaker does not have to disclose his inner state, and one does not really need to know from which horizon the information was selected. Granted all these pragmatic concessions, it is still not clear how the unity of communication is brought about. I would suggest that focusing on understanding is a good start [in order to tackle this problem]. This distinguishes our approach quite clearly from any theory of action. In constructing a theory formulated in terms of differences, which relies on the theory of distinction, and which has the observer as its point of departure, we notice that we are always dealing with a triad of elements. Why three elements? In most instances, we are dealing with two sides: good and bad, big and small, the universal and the particular, and so on, and like to exclude any possible third side. Now, however, we are suddenly dealing with a tripartite distinction. How are we to conceive of this? Perhaps one way is to assign to the third factor the task of seeing the other two as a duality, as a distinction, which it then unites. If you like models with different levels, you might say that this unification happens at a different level. We should not let this disturb us. We may simply be amazed, first of all, about the fact that the creation of unity is an order that emerges on the side. Of the three components, one is, as it were, in charge of treating the duality or distinction of information and utterance as a unity. We might say that this is a leap into unity for the purpose of continuation.

Perhaps you recall that I dealt with a similar problem when I spoke of the theory of signs or semiotics. There we have the signifier and the signified. What is the unity of this distinction? What is a sign? In this case, too, we have a triad that ever since Peirce has been discussed in the literature and pushed towards a pragmatic solution. What is noticeable from a point of view that is informed by theories of distinction, difference, and observation is that one component observes, as it were, the other two. In other words, it occupies the position of the observer in this model. If no distinction is made from the position of understanding between utterance and information, no communication can come about. It is only in the component "understanding" that communication generates the duality of information and utterance by which it is actually made into communication. Please excuse this complicated mode of expression, but it is important to be very precise on this point.

We are faced with the question of how unity is generated, and we cannot assign responsibility to an external factor that intervenes graciously and puts the components together. Rather, this must occur autopoietically in the mode of operation itself. The idea is that this happens in understanding. How explicitly it happens is another question. However, it always has to happen in such a way that communication is perceived only in those moments when one sees or notices that someone said something and one is capable of distinguishing the relevant "someone" from the "something." This also includes the possibility of someone talking about himself. He may say, "Tonight, I am really tired" or "I am not in the mood" or "I would like to do that." In such cases, he conveys information about himself, and we are sophisticated enough not simply to believe the pieces of information that someone conveys about himself. Rather, we immediately reflect on the reasons why the speaker may have such a desire. We may also ask ourselves why he is in his present state or why he describes himself as someone who is in the state of having such desires. Such sophistication on our part is limited merely by time and our own capacities. Whenever such fine points seem important to us, we prove capable of reacting with great subtlety, but usually, when that is not the case, we just do not do it.

My thesis is that the difference between understanding, on the one hand, and information and utterances, on the other, is fundamental. Otherwise we would experience only behavior. Behavior can also give us information about other people, but it is precisely not communication. Understanding effects the connection between information and utterance, for the most part by means of language. If someone expresses himself in language, it is obvious that he wants to convey what he utters. In such a case, the content is fixed by the language, and speaking makes clear that the speaker wants to convey it. Speaking does not just happen to a speaker. At least in my normal state, speaking does not simply happen to me. Rather, I want to convey something – namely, that which I have uttered. We need to add an amount of uncertainty here, for it is possible that what has been said is a lie. In fact, one can, when uttering something, indicate that, in reality, one meant to say something different than what one has actually said. Once again, we are getting involved with the subtleties of colloquial communication. Yet, all this does not change the fact that the synthesis is generated in understanding and that understanding includes itself in this process. Understanding understands that it understands, if you will. It understands that something can be done with this and that it is not simply an explanation of the world. Rather, what is at issue is the condition of participating in communication or, seen from the viewpoint of the communication system, the condition of continuing communication. If the result of a communication does not elicit our own reaction to a sufficient degree or does not allow us to follow the subsequent course of the communication, we simply tune out and exclude ourselves from the communication. In such a case, communication loses some of its capacity for including participants, and this fact becomes conscious in understanding. One pays attention, pricks up one's ears, thinks along in however weak or engaged a mode (depending on the specific context), and thus constantly creates the possibility of helping to continue the communication. This description sounds psychological. Yet, what is actually meant is always at the level of communication. That is to say, if communication is happening, it can be assumed that there was sufficient understanding, which always includes sufficient misunderstanding.

This is the reason why communication can also be described as a self-observing operation. You may recall how we abstracted the concept of observation. It is a matter of using a distinction in order to designate something. The distinction that is used in communication for the purpose of the self-observation of communication is the distinction between utterance and understanding. Without this built-in self-observation communication would not happen at all. This trait is in many ways not typical. After all, in this case we distinguish very clearly between operation and observation. Self-observation is not built into regular life processes, biochemical processes, or organic behavior in the same way. There are complicated feedback mechanisms that presuppose that different states can be distinguished. If you want to call that "observation," you subscribe to a different concept of observation. Under such conditions, it would be possible to conceive of a continuous self-observation on the part of, say, the immune system or the nervous system. The difference is clear, and in matters of communication it is inevitable. If we put forward our concepts in this way, we cannot help stating that operation and observation can be conducted only *uno actu* or as a union. The question would have to be, then, what is the purpose of all this, why is it the case, or what advantage does the system have if it operates using such operations?

The answers to these questions are linked to another question. What is achieved by a communication, what is its effect or its function? Once again, we are faced with a controversial situation. There is a conflict between normal understanding or the normal way of seeing things, on the one hand, and a widespread theory that assumes that the meaning of communication is the production of a consensus, on the other. According to this latter theory, communication is the attempt to persuade someone else. One tries to transport something, tries to carry over a piece of information that is in one's head into another head and then to take this very piece of information as the point of departure for a common orientation in the world or common action and the like. In this case, the function of communication is the production of consensus. However, since this fails more often than not or remains uncontrollable, one simply turns consensus into a norm and says that, although it does not really happen, it ought to happen. People ought to try to reach consensus. In Habermas's terminology, this and only this is called "communicative action." Although there are many ways of behaving communicatively, according to this account, *communicative action* is said always to be oriented towards consensus.[10]

If one instead takes the concept of autopoiesis as one's point of departure, one takes fright, precisely because one may have some doubts about what will happen once a consensus has been reached. Strictly speaking, communicative action would have to come to an end in that case. Helmut Schelsky asked Habermas once, "What comes after consensus?" Of course, for Habermas the world holds enough difficulties in reserve. We do not have to, and in fact cannot, imagine that we will ever arrive at a consensus among all people concerning all questions. The life-world as the posited underlying consensus contains such a number of discrepancies that we are hardly in danger of simply leaning back in our chairs and stating, with a satisfied smile, that now everything has been accomplished and communication is no longer necessary, since we all agree. Yet, if it is the case that those problems concerning the complexity and amount of discrepancies are indeed as massive and dramatic as indicated, one may ask what sense it makes to demand the opposite and integrate the search for consensus in the concept of communication in such a way that everything else is declared not to be communication at all. Why do we turn impossibility into a norm? To put it differently, who identifies the cases where we must adhere to this norm if it is not possible to adhere to it in every case?

These ideas are connected to discussions about "communicative action" and to the conception of the communicative actor as someone who can be brought under a norm, someone who fits the norm and who does or does not communicate with a view to understanding and consensus. This actor is himself responsible for bringing his action to a conclusion. He directs his own communicative action in accordance with a norm.

All of this changes when we occupy a different terrain and state that communication is an independent process within which utterances may be defined as action. However, this does not include the entirety of communication. At best it singles out addresses – that is, whom we have to consult if something is in doubt. The one who said it! Or it assigns responsibility – that is, who manipulated the information in such a way that we are taken in by it, only to notice later that it had all been wrong and something important had been ignored – for instance, that risks had been underestimated (or in whatever way one would express such states of affairs nowadays)? Communication is a process that is detached from action, a process that attributes, assigns, and constructs actions but is not an action itself. Under these circumstances, one may as well drop the idea that action can be brought to a conclusion and that one has normative control over whether something is strategic or instrumental, whether someone was abused or whether his treatment was ethically correct, and whether or not an action is guided by the categorical imperative.

In lieu of this idea, I would propose the following theory, just to make the difference abundantly clear. In my theory, the act of communication, the unity of a communicative event, or a communicative operation ends in understanding. Such a theory leaves entirely open what is going to happen next, and, in particular, it leaves open whether one says "yes" or "no" to what has been understood. After all, what is the purpose of the "no" in language? What is being produced by communication is not consensus in the normal or ideal case and regrettable deviation or failure in other, exceptional cases. Rather, what is being produced is a bifurcation. Once the process has arrived at the point of understanding, it can either adopt or reject what has been understood as the premise of further communication. First of all, communication is open with respect to "yes" and "no," provided one sees it in entirely abstract terms and without further embellishments such as truth and the like. It would be terrible if communication itself was already weighted against the "no's" and seduced us to take mere communication as true, although such truth is invented after the fact as a rhetorical device or a technique of persuasion only. I will come back to this. The option of "yes" or "no" is open. This means that the result of an uttered information – either "yes" or "no" – continues to contribute to further communication as its premise.

James G. March and Herbert A. Simon's book on organization, written in 1958, is a classic in decision-making oriented organizational theory. In it, one finds one page or one and a half pages on "uncertainty absorption." In these pages, it is shown that information is processed, results are communicated, and the successors, the next generation of participants in a particular communication, are guided only by results and no longer by the evidence from which conclusions were drawn.[11] Now, this insight refers to organizations. The possibility of generalizing it has not really been discovered yet. It seems to me, however, that this is a thought of great reach, and it may in fact help us out at this point. "Uncertainty absorption" means that, in the normal course of events, we do not have the possibility of starting from scratch every time and that we cannot ask the speaker every time why he said what he said and not something else, or what his horizon of selection was, and so on. We cannot, time and again, burrow into what is already past. We would run out of time. But we can say "yes" or "no." We do not need investigations into why something came about, why some piece of information became a text or was spoken audibly, why a certain issue is on the agenda right now, how a fact is described, and so on. Perhaps we no longer have to bother about such things and can say instead that we do not believe something or, within reason, ask for additional explanations. To some extent, the process of communication is in a hurry. It depends on sequencing. It cannot continuously get entangled with itself. Thus the "yes/no" option is an entirely abstract operation that functions as a shortcut and subsequently determines the next steps. One may continue at the level of the "no" and head for conflict, or one may accept an utterance at face value as the basis for further communication.

Incidentally, there is a very nice definition of "authority" that I once offered to Habermas as a replacement for his understanding of "domination" [*Herrschaft*]. It is Carl Joachim Friedrich's and can be found in the first volume of Nomos, a book series published in the US. It defines authority as the "capacity for reason elaboration" – that is, the ability to give reasons – which, however, already has tangible effects merely as a capacity.[12] If one always asks what reasons one has and then finds further reasons for these justifications, one finally arrives at the impossibility of a permanent recourse to the past. Authority, then, functions as an absorption of uncertainty, as a sort of simplification that makes it possible to continue with communication on the basis of the assumption that someone can actually give reasons why he selects a certain topic rather than another. If Habermas can manage at all without domination and thus without the potential for coercion, one may ask whether, practically speaking, he can really do without authority. I believe that this notional complex of authority and the absorption of uncertainty, of simplification and the reduction of complexity ought to be included in an absolutely fundamental position within the theory of communication. It serves as the precondition of continued autopoiesis and the precondition of connecting operations. The option between "yes" and "no" is part of this as well. It has a control function in relation to continued communication. However, it does not require that the fundamentals – specifically the process of uncertainty absorption – are recapitulated, replayed, or expanded on a regular basis.

There are two different inducements for the replay of communication: misunderstanding, on the one hand, and rejection, on the other. A speaker who feels misunderstood can react to misunderstandings with clarifications. He can bring the process to a halt, as it were, and say, "I see that this did not get across as I meant it: I really wanted to say the following." In the second case, he reacts to a "no" and asks, "Why do you reject this?" Alternatively, he may anticipate the "no" in his utterance and from the outset give arguments that would overcome the possible "no" that he fears and considers probable. All of these options are mere modifications of the fundamental bifurcation. According to my thesis, we need to recognize that there is a connection between autopoiesis and thus the openness of continuing on and the non-linearity of connection, according to which communication does not just proceed along a certain course but always has two different possibilities. This binary simplification compensates for the inscrutable complexity of the actual process.

If this is how things are, one cannot help questioning whether there will not be an equal distribution of instances of "yes" and "no." Why are there more instances of "yes" than of "no"? Is this in fact really the case? How is this binary option controlled? These points can be worked out from different angles. One possibility is to claim that communication begins logically, if you will, with understanding and not with the utterance. The speaker who makes an utterance always already anticipates whether it will be understood and whether it will be taken as pleasant or unpleasant, acceptable or unacceptable. In this way, the condition of understanding is always already circularly anticipated in the utterance. The participants are sufficiently socialized and the communication process itself is sufficiently transparent to make it possible to estimate whether one's communication will be successful or not. I believe that these preconditions are elementary preconditions of communication. Without them, it would in fact be entirely unlikely to generate understandings that do not constantly lead to rejection. After all, one must always assume that different heads are involved and that the process of communication is always selective because it deals with information. Furthermore, it always indicates a selection of other possibilities that are also represented in it because it deals with meaning. How could all this continue to stand the test if this kind of anticipating self-control were not built into communication?

Most certainly, this self-control is connected to the elementary situation of communicative interaction. If communication takes place among present participants, one notices relatively quickly whether it meets with approval. Many people are impervious to such approval, but they, too, take note when they are not well received and can guess merely from the facial expressions of those present whether all is well or not. The interactions, the simultaneity, and the perception that accompany communication provide a certain control over what is being said and make sure that it is acceptable, or that it can be recognized if someone is looking for conflict. Of course, it is possible at the level of interaction to base communication entirely on conflict. I think that this, too, can be understood, and therefore functions as communication. Whether it is also pleasant and what the consequences may be are different questions. We are, however, at the level of the process of communication, and in this context a "no" or a conflict is entirely understandable. If something is not understood, it ends in any event, whether it is pleasant or unpleasant, whether it operates by means of a "yes" or a "no."

This standard situation is interrupted – here I have to anticipate the concluding part of this lecture – when we come to written communication. Written communication as such is an odd thing. As already mentioned, I will return to this shortly. For my current purposes, it suffices to know that writing has existed for several thousand years and that it became customary to use writing for communicative purposes, which was not the case in the beginning when it was used only for recording purposes. In the case of writing, the situation is such that the writer is alone. You will notice this in any situation when you are in company and suddenly begin to write. As you continue to write, the others are sitting there, waiting for you to come around and be communicatively available again. Writing isolates as much as reading. One can only be alone with one's own text. The others play no role in this. Whether one can afford this in an interactive situation is another question. Sometimes it is permitted – for instance, in the present situation. Right now, you are of course allowed to write! But sometimes it is difficult. However, the possibility that is truly interesting is, of course, the possibility of producing a text when no one else is present, no one objects, no one offers corrections, and no one intervenes. Then, later, you have a reader for whom the same is true, a reader who thinks his own thoughts, is capable of reading in the normal sense, and discovers contradictions, implausibilities, and the like.

There are highly interesting novels that are based on love letters. In them, seduction is depicted through letters.[13] The lady receives a letter that indicates a certain interest. She is indignant and does not answer. Then a second letter arrives. The writer would like to know whether the first letter actually arrived, and she writes back, "Yes, it did arrive, and now please end this correspondence." And then the next letter arrives, stating, "Many thanks for your response." She keeps everything in a casket and keeps reading the letters time and again. Or, at the very least, she counts on being able to do so, and at some point she will be in the situation when she has to say "yes" or "no." In the French epistolary novels, either situation is fatal. If she says "yes," she will end up unhappy, because her lover does not offer the fidelity that he promised. If she says "no," she will also end up unhappy because she will constantly have to come to terms with her missed opportunity. All this relies on writing. Seduction through writing is the actual topic. That it is possible to seduce someone through one's nice looks and the pleasantries that are exchanged between people who are pleasant is a different matter. That was always presupposed. But how seduction works through writing is an interesting question. In the seduction through writing, the "yes/no" acquires yet another pitch.

From the standpoint of cultural history, one may perhaps say that writing did not provide merely a stimulus for expressing oneself more clearly (a point to which I will return). It also provided the impulse to develop countermeasures in order to bypass the new likelihood of a "no." After all, why would I accept a written text as usable information? Such countermeasures were, for instance, the verse form in poetry, rhythm, or, as Plato would say, rhapsodic organization. One is swayed by the rhythm, much as in oral communication, does not worry about anything else, and in the end will accept everything that is said. Or perhaps the counter-impulse relies on a more elaborate rhetoric that emerged during the same period, shortly after the alphabet was established. On the basis of earlier texts, language in such cases is often stylized as persuasion. That is to say, it is burdened with motives, expressions, and other such embellishments in the hope that in this manner one may elicit more instances of "yes" than of "no." This is true even for something like a court summation or, in other cases, when one has to expect resistance and opposing interests. The tradition of rhetoric played an enormous role in European history, as you may know. It served as an educational program, a sort of training in eloquence for the nobility, which then was not obliged to enforce its interests simply by force of arms, but could do so also by force of words. The central issues were whether the orator had to have knowledge, whether he was allowed to work with deception, and whether he would be successful merely because of his superior knowledge. See especially Cicero, Quintilian, and their successors on these issues.

This, however, is only one strand of the general reaction to writing, and it belongs to the domain of orality. As soon as there is writing and the likelihood of a "no" increases as a consequence, orality has to regroup. Other, new possibilities can be found in the domain that I have designated as "symbolically generalized media of communication." Here, we are dealing with symbols that condition what can be said for motivational purposes. Thereby a new equilibrium between conditioning and motivation is built into communication. Conditioning means that the ruler must be able to threaten, to keep violence at his disposal, and to display this credibly. In this way, he will be able to generate the motives of compliance and uneasy obedience that he desires but which do not come about all by themselves. Then there is money as another medium that is being used to receive something that one would not get otherwise. There is also truth as the possibility of gaining acceptance for new knowledge – not the knowledge that everyone already has, but new, and even improbable, knowledge. To this purpose, one must have proofs or arguments at one's disposal in order to demonstrate a state of affairs. This means that the discourse on truth is itself conditioned with the purpose of overcoming a "no" that seems highly likely at the outset whenever innovations or deviations from familiar modes of understanding are concerned. This was the case, for instance, in the classical period of ancient Greece when religiously oriented medicine was supplemented by empirical, scientific medicine.

My point is that these parallels between pre-circuit controls that are always necessary and the amplification of mere chance to the point of positive resonance can be grasped with the help of a single theoretical conception – namely, the theory of bifurcation, the theory of the equal distribution of "yes" and "no." Moreover, this theory also contains the idea that communication happens even if it has not yet been decided what its use is, whether it is going to be used positively or negatively, and whether or not it is going to be needed as the basis for subsequent communication. Finally, this theory also accounts for the fact that all of this is repeated in every communicative act. As soon as a new communication is added, the bifurcation is there again, and one can, once more, say "yes" or "no." I imagine that this situation was a sort of cultural-revolution program in the sense that one had to endeavor constantly to make unlikely a rejection which at first sight is highly likely. At this juncture, the structure of our theory has recourse to historical research on the question of why, among other things, politics emerges or an economy evolves that subsequently operates with minted money.

This was a first reflection on the reaction to the "yes/no" bifurcation. At this point I would like to adduce another question merely *as a question*. It is, however, a question that, it seems to me, is worth considering in our contemporary situation. Is it not possible to achieve a reflected agreement on the basis of a "no"? Are there no possibilities in politics or, for instance, in a marriage of letting the other keep his convictions and not converting him? Are there no such possibilities for making no attempt to get the other to utter an honest "yes," but which nevertheless achieve a form of agreement that neutralizes the tolerance of this "no" for the time being, as it were, and is valid until revoked? The "no" remains present as a probability. Yet, one agrees to do things in one way and then in some other way. Sometimes you are right and sometimes I am right. Thus, we may increase the uncertainty concerning what is right to such a degree that, henceforth, decisions can be made only pragmatically. This does not really matter, as long as the respective positions can be revoked. It seems to me that such figures of thought have emerged lately in research on risk.

Recently, Alois Hahn gave a talk in Bielefeld, in which he reported once again on his research on marriage and especially couples that had been married for only a short time. Using a circular technique of questioning, these couples were asked, "What do you think your husband (or wife) thinks about this question, and do you think that this is the same as what you think?"[14] The result of this survey was that there is a high degree of discrepancy in combination with functioning agreements. Apparently, these young couples found ways to forget or ignore what they think their partner actually thinks. At this level, they no longer reconcile their respective individual stances. Instead they simply make such concrete statements as, "Well, today we are going to the movies" or "This has to be paid first and then that," or whatever may be of importance in a marriage.

In St Gall, Switzerland, a research project on risk dialogues is under-way. The idea is to assemble together industry, insurance companies, pol-itics, grassroots movements, and other people who might have an interest in protest. Here, too, the issue is whether it is possible to bring about a mode of politics or communication in which everyone accepts that the others think differently.[15] Mutual understanding is constructed like a prognosis. One does not see the future, but one can see the point where it must be changed. One then makes clear what the presuppositions of this claim are. Under certain conditions a certain "scenario" (or whatever term you prefer) makes sense. Then, you agree on the next few steps, which allows you later to recall the basis of your transaction, especially if, in the meantime, it has been "cancelled," to cite a legal term.

It could indeed be the case, then, that our present cultural program, as one may call it, consisting of rhetoric, persuasive techniques, argumenta-tion, domination, money, and even love (as a phenomenon of communi-cation), has reached the limits of this technique and that we have to learn the hard way how to work with modes of understanding that are not conceived as depending on the actual opinions. This is very much like in the period when religious tolerance was learned in a very painful manner.

Now, I would like to add a few words on orality and literacy, and that will be the end of today's lecture. I suspect that you always think of two people when you talk about communication. At least, this is my standard experience. The first person says something. The other listens attentively and then says something in turn, to which the first person listens atten-tively. This is what is meant by "oral communication." As far as I under-stand the history of the term "communication," this situation has always been the primary focus. The idea that Aristotle actually communicates with me is limited to the writing desk and could not simply be part of colloquial language. The same is true with respect to early modernity. I recall passages in Galilei, in which he expresses his amazement that, via the printing press (that was *the* issue in his day), we can communicate with people in India or with people who died long ago and even with people who have not yet been born. This amazement can be explained by the fact that the standard against which it is measured is oral communication. How is it possible to speak with someone who has not yet been born? How can I hear what Dante said? For this reason, we have to pose the question of how we can arrive at a conception of communication that covers these phenomena. Alternatively, we may ask ourselves whether we prefer to regard such phenomena as *para-communication* – that is, not as true communication. I do not know whether Habermas is able to include literacy or the written word in his theory of communication. Can he truly assume that the wealth of available texts is being read? And who reads what? Communication according to Habermas would have to guarantee, in a sense, that everyone has at least read the same texts. But this goal is not even achieved in a seminar course, let alone in the world at large! The entirety of written communication actually bypasses such model reflections.

Yet, what exactly is achieved by written communication? What is achieved is the transcendence of temporal and spatial limits. As long as a text is physically stable, does not fall apart, and is not destroyed, one can in principle communicate with remote places. Of course, nowadays this is also possible by phone. Even in that case, however, it is once again increasingly turned into writing – for instance, by using the fax machine – because the people who are called may not be available at the dialed number. They may not be there, and a fax can be sent quickly. The written word thus bridges vast spatial distances and, of course, temporal distances as well. Just think of the printing press and its consequences. The question is, then, whether, in this case, we are not losing the unity of communication. You may recall that I defined that unity from the perspective of understanding and the anticipation of understanding. The person who makes an utterance has to endeavor to be understood. If he simply fiddles around in the landscape of everything that is linguistically possible, communication will come to an end rather soon. Yet, if we are dealing with centuries or a transmission into contingent and unknown horizons of reception, where does this leave the anticipation of understanding, the anticipation of the horizon of reception, and the anticipation of the conditions of meaning that are necessary for communication to continue? In terms of time as well as space, one communicates at random and into the unknown, as it were.

There are a number of possibilities for imagining what happens in this situation. In one of them we notice that the modes of communication are becoming increasingly specialized. Science, for instance, works in such a

way. One knows precisely what one has read [on the topic] and one imagines the recipients of one's own products as if they had read all of this as
well and therefore have been prepared accordingly. One does not simply
go about scattering references indiscriminately across the disciplines.
This is true in other contexts as well. Consider the economy. Individual
companies have their markets, and their sales representatives are unable
to operate in other markets. The preconditions of communication are
extremely specialized. This is one of the difficulties that one encounters if
one tries to convert the entire economy, say, by switching from a military
industry to a consumer products industry. In such a case, you simply will
not know with whom you are going to communicate. It is impossible to
estimate, among other things, under what conditions your goods will
arrive, whether you can count on the recipients' willingness to pay, and
what criteria will determine product choices. For you, this would be an
impenetrable territory.

To a degree, such open questions can be addressed and corrected
by specialization. But of even greater importance is the requirement
that texts ought to be understandable all by themselves. There is a lot
of research dedicated to the question of how writing and subsequently
the printing press have affected the grammatical structure and syntactic
order of texts. It has become clear that sentences must be understandable
on their own or in the context of the sentences that precede or follow
them. They do not depend on situational references. Of course, there are
books for specialists. This fact belongs to the first set of correctives that
I have outlined. But even these books ought not to be interspersed with
"indexical expressions"[16] (as these terms are called). I already gave an
example for this when I introduced Aristotle's conception of time. He still
used words such as "simultaneously" or "the now," which is "*to nu*" in its
nominalized form and as such occurs in the text. One really has to reflect
on what exactly a "now" is. But if you simply say, "Now it is a quarter to
six," everyone knows what is meant. Such types of situational reference
have to be dropped. The text must be constructed in an entirely different
way. It is a typical phenomenon that occurs in school and also in con-
versations with relatively uneducated people that situational references
are used, and speakers do not notice that the other with whom they are
speaking has no clue what they are saying. This characteristic language
of the lower classes, this non-writing culture, can be introduced into
sentences if one throws in words such as "now" or "a moment ago" or
"this stuff." One would not know what "stuff" is meant. Moreover, such a
manner of speaking also indicates that the speaker has not been socialized
through writing. Dealing with Swiss mountain peasants, I noticed that
they even leave out verbs and nouns in their Swiss dialect, if these terms
are self-evident. If one manages to understand the remainder acoustically,
one is dealing with very incomplete sentences that seem, however, to be
sufficient for communication among the peasants. Next, one notices how

the culture of writing also enters into this colloquial language via school education. Many of the older peasants barely attended school, since they had to work on the alpine pastures in the summer. Education brings home the point that one also has to be understandable to people whom one does not know, and that one can use the same kind of language also for people who live far away or in future times. On these issues, there is a relatively voluminous literature. Medieval texts that derive from the oral tradition still show that familiarity with the story was presupposed. The audience has heard it a hundred times before. Think of the *chansons de geste*, such as *The Song of Roland*.[17] The entire literary achievement consists of embellishing a well-known story with intricate details. One adds something, and the story expands in a certain direction. This mode of production makes it abundantly clear that the producers do not count on the dissemination of their texts by means of the printing press. Moreover, one recognizes that the structure of written communication is quite different and that it took centuries for this structure to become standard.

A final, wide open question to which I have no answer is whether we can still count on communication if seriality is abandoned – namely, when one has at one's disposal computer systems that make it possible to search for something on a case-by-case basis, which then can be recombined. In this computer world, it is not the case that one sentence follows another. Instead there is a piece of information, followed by a spectrum of references to other information that comes with it. One simply sits there, creates one's own pathway, and calls onto the screen whatever one deems necessary to this purpose, without being able to distinguish between information and utterance. One has been returned to the position of first-order observer. One presses a few keys. A text to be read pops up, and then one has to do something with it. Perhaps one simply feeds it back into the machine. In the case of such modern hypertext systems, the recycled text may not be signed with a proper name. As a consequence, a host of suggestions develop that include, by way of selection, an enormous mechanism of concealed uncertainty absorption and an equally enormous mechanism of uncertainty production. Who exactly is now communicating with whom? Is our concept of communication still suitable in this situation? Or have we arrived at a threshold where it is already becoming apparent that important modes of information-processing in our society can no longer be classified as communication? Or do we have to redesign this concept? And, if so, how?

I will end this part of my text with the remark that all of this depends, of course, on society. Whether such computer systems or writing or the printing press come into existence or not and what concept of communication we consequently need in order to grasp what is going on – all of this is temporally and historically determined. It depends on what society offers us.

VII

Double Contingency, Structure, Conflict

Ladies and gentlemen, we have come to the last lecture of this course. I would like to try to reinterpret a few sociological concepts or, to put it differently, to gain access to rather typical sociological topics from a different perspective. In this context, I am also interested in relating the conceptual angle of our theoretical labor to the classical controversies for or against systems theory in the sixties. This should show us what changes occur in discussions conducted in terms of ideology critique or the politics of ideas when one formulates higher standards of conceptual precision.

The first issue concerns "double contingency." This term refers to a topic that I have discussed in *Social Systems*. If you consult my book you will find that my current presentation of the topic follows approximately the same outline.[1] Historically speaking, one ought to know that the reformulation of an old question lies hidden behind the strange expression "double contingency." This old question is simply "How is social order possible?" But this question is actually not all that old, since it employs a Kantian technique of questioning. For it asks not just "What is the case?" but also "How is this possible?" How is it possible at all that there should be such things as cognition, aesthetic judgment, or, in our case, social order? In addition to the Kantian triad of cognition, rational praxis, and aesthetic judgment, we now also have the question "How is social order possible?"

In the tradition before Kant, this question was answered with reference to assumptions concerning human nature. In fact, to be more precise, the reference was to the social nature of man or, as the older tradition put it, man's "political" nature. That is to say, human nature was conceived of as depending on communal or city life. Man depends on living with others. This has consequences. Such communal life does not just happen in some unspecified way. It is possible only on the basis of a social regulation that is either formulated in political-ethical terms or is allegedly decreed by God. In the sixteenth and seventeenth centuries, after the religious wars, a massive shift took place. Man was seen in more skeptical terms as far as his desire for battle and bloodlust was concerned. The idea of a social contract seemed to be necessary. This did not last for more than a hundred years, but apparently human beings are totally overwhelmed by their desire to harm and kill each other and by the future prospect that it will always be this way. As a consequence they agree on a contract in the present and submit to a sovereign who can do everything necessary or everything that he considers necessary (just think of the pope). A contractual constitution of social order is deemed possible. This assumption led to many logical problems and complicated discussions. From the eighteenth century onwards, one reverted to the position that the establishment of an order was effected by violence. One actor overwhelms all others. Over time, a modicum of reason helps to civilize this structure of domination somewhat.

The concept of double contingency attempts to recover this problem at a different conceptual level. Parsons spoke of a "Hobbesian problem of social order"[2] and thereby made a direct reference to Hobbes. However, he could not use the contract as his starting point, because he saw (as did everyone after him) that a contract already presupposes an established order, the consequence of which is that contracts have to be kept. Thus, the contract itself stands in need of a social explanation. Initiated by Durkheim, the tendency to claim that the social order is valid ahead of all contracts applies to Parsons as well. Of course, a family already exists before there is family law, religion before there are any ecclesiastical regulations or dogmatics, and so forth. However, this insight merely pushes the question of how social order is possible one step back. One still has to find an answer to the question of how it is possible that, under the conditions of evolutionary drift, a social order emerges with the capacity to become increasingly complicated and construct regulations that come with an increasing number of prerequisites. As far as I can see, the concept of double contingency was invented in the context of interdisciplinary plans for a new department of social relations at Harvard University. That is to say, it came about in the context of attempts to unite different disciplines such as cultural anthropology, psychology, sociology, political science, and whatever else was available within a common theoretical framework. It is quite obvious that the term "double contingency" was intended to bypass the perspective of value as well as the structure of expectation at an even deeper level. That is to say, it was intended as an explanation of how common values and the symbolic encoding of social behavior come about, and how cultural anthropologists, psychologists, and sociologists are able to isolate specific aspects and work on them according to different methods.

It would seem that Robert Sears invented this concept. However, it became famous through the "General Statement" that was published in the volume *Toward a General Theory of Action*, edited by Talcott Parsons and Edward A. Shils.[3] Parsons reverted to this general statement repeatedly, but without working the concept of double contingency into his theory in the appropriate place. The reasons for this must have been that this concept provided a suitable explanation for the emergence only of social systems but not of general action systems. The concept disappeared for some time, and then it suddenly reappeared again. It did not have the meaning or conceptual position, however, that one might have expected were one to assume that it actually could provide an explanation for the possibility of social order. In this phase of theory development, contingency was understood as dependence, very much along the lines of the English expression "contingent on." The idea of dependence expressed in this term has a theological tradition that can no longer be gleaned from the use of the word. The concept, taken purely in the terms of modal theory, that something is possible in another way as well, and is thus neither necessary nor impossible but something in between, was reformulated in theological terms as dependence on God, who could have constructed the world differently. Both of these semantic components of "contingency" can be found in the English-language tradition. On the one hand, there is "contingency" in the sense of "being dependent on" or, as one says colloquially, "contingent on." On the other hand, there is "contingency" in the sense of the possibility that things could be different, which is to say, as the negation of impossibility as well as necessity. Earlier, I spoke briefly about this.

In this first attempt at basing social theory on double contingency, the model includes an *ego* and an *alter* that oppose one another. Each of them can be an individual or a group and has its own needs and effective abilities. The former depends on the successful performance of the latter, and the latter on those of the former. Each one is able to perform the required service or to refuse it. Under such circumstances, the question arises of how a course of action can be found in which expectations and the corresponding achievements can be established as complementary and not simply be pulled apart as separate elements.

Later, this model was also applied to conflicts. For instance, there was the model case of a battleship and a merchant vessel that are heading towards the same island. The island lies between them, and the combat vessel would like to catch the merchant ship. If the latter decides to circumvent the island on the northern route, then the battleship has to do the same thing. But if the battleship steers north, then it is prudent for the merchant vessel to go the other way. Right now, they are positioned on either side of the island, and the Parsonian claim is that they have a "shared symbolic system" or world orientation in common. However, it is apparently not working when conflict is involved, except if one wants to claim that what the two opponents have in common is a positive/

negative disposition vis-à-vis the same value – that is to say, in our model, getting through or being caught.

This reformulation of the model in terms of a theory of conflict indicates that we need a more abstract solution than the one along the lines of a common value orientation that was suggested by Parsons in keeping with Durkheimian sociology. If you recall the section of this lecture course that dealt with Parsons, we might say that his suggestion depends on the distinction he drew between culture and social systems and the fact that he positioned culture in a hierarchically higher position. That is to say, Parsons proceeds from the assumption that social systems are not possible without a cultural regulation or without the common recognition of values and norms. The latter two terms are not very clearly distinguished. For Parsons, even language belongs to values and norms. Language is understood as a sort of normative code that determines what kind of speaking is possible if one wants to be understood, and what kind of speaking is invalid. In this model, language, culture, values, and norms are tied very closely together. They have the function of regulating double contingency for the sub-system at the next level below – namely, the social system.

One can just accept this, particularly since even an empirical investigation may turn up hardly any societies in which there is not at least a minimal consensus in evidence concerning values or common normative principles of law, morality, and language. Nevertheless, there is no clear road from this insight to a regulation of the problem of double contingency that would be useful under everyday conditions. After all, if one already has common values, one may actually fight more fiercely under certain circumstances. For instance, let us look at our large socialist and Christian-democratic parties, who claim to be capable of governing, and then let us look at the lists of their proclaimed values. We will find barely any differences between them. At most, we may notice a difference in the order of priority. One side puts security first followed by freedom. The other side turns this on its head. In any case, there cannot be more than three values, to ensure that car drivers will still be able to read them on posters – provided that they always keep to the speed limit. The values are the same. Yet, the parties are in conflict over every issue. The question is, then, how one can move from a program of values to an interactional and operationally manageable regulation of situations of double contingency. As soon as one gives an answer to this question, it becomes apparent that the emergence of common values or of common uncontested positions happens in all likelihood only as a second step. In the beginning, one does not even know yet what values one actually has. But, after solving the problem of double contingency operationally for some time – that is, after forming complementary expectations and enacting suitable actions and action sequences – one may perhaps find oneself capable of formulating the consensus that has, as it were, revealed itself during the course of the process.

On the basis of this reflection, I asked myself whether pure temporality and temporal asymmetry may be the crucial point. One actor acts first and thereby marks a date that imposes on the other the alternative of saying "yes" or "no," of accepting or rejecting what is on offer. You may recall my commentaries on the concept of communication. The other cannot simply do whatever he wants or act on a whim. He has to comply with the situation that has already been established. "Yes/no" may be sufficient to manage the situation, but he cannot just do something entirely different. If I am correct, then a specific temporality or temporal structure replaces the idea of a value consensus as the premise or answer to the question of how social order is possible. Social order comes about when someone sets the agenda, begins with an activity, makes a suggestion, or presents himself and thereby forces everyone else to react. They have either to show an interest in this agenda or ignore it. They can also initiate processes of clarification, but always in light of what is already given or posited. Thus, the asymmetry that is so obvious in this model is not first of all a hierarchical but a temporal one. In other words, it is not the case that there is a higher level of values which is more or less intact and which serves as the motivator. Moreover, it is not the case, as it is in the objective hierarchical model, that these values can be modified in detail depending on the way in which one communicates or feuds with one another. Rather, one is dealing here, first and foremost, with a temporal order. How does it happen that, in situations of double contingency, a sequence occurs that functions like a funnel and puts the system on a course that leads either to conflict (I will return to this topic) or to cooperation and the determination of certain positions that will serve as common points of departure and as elements of a common history in the future? It is this shift that I have in mind when suggesting that we move away from the Durkheim–Parsons paradigm towards a theory that pays more attention to the question of how operations emerge that are connective or have the ability to create systems, and thus the ability to draw distinctions in order to distinguish systems from that which does not belong to them.

All this is based on a model that starts off with self-reference and circularity, since double contingency is circular: "If you do what I want, I will do what you want!" But who is responsible for breaking this circle? Who creates asymmetries? The answer is: time and he who acts first. The quickest actor calls the shots. He will thereby not necessarily get all the others to follow his lead, but he will define the issues, the topics, and the positions that are going to be at stake in every "yes" or "no." In a certain sense, he determines the tone or the type of system that can emerge in consequence.

The form of the model may give rise to the idea that double contingency comes first, and then systems develop. Social contract theories have often been read in the same way and criticized for the same reason – as if they had claimed that, in the beginning, there were savages, all of whom carried arms and were eager to kill others in their sleep. Only in retrospect, after some time, did they begin to recognize that this was not as pleasant as their natural endowment had seemed to suggest. Thus one arrived at a contract. It would seem that one could say the same about our present theory. First, there is the problem of double contingency, and then someone has the idea of saying what ought to happen, what is the case, and in which direction one ought to move. Of course, this view is illusory in both cases. No one was ever able to tie down historically the state of nature in Thomas Hobbes's sense of the term, although it may be possible to distinguish less clearly ordered societies from more civilized ones. The issue of double contingency is also not a problem of a before-and-after model. Rather, the question is to be posed in such a way that, whenever one problematizes social order and, in fact, continues to do so and dissolves all presuppositions in the process, one finally arrives at the question of how one handles double contingency. It is possible to examine every social situation and ask how it happens that it does not result in a circle such as would lead to total inactivity, because no one knows what expectations he is supposed to develop to allow the other to develop expectations that he appreciates and is willing to fulfill.

This model models the reconstruction of the conditions of possibility for social order and is not intended as a historical model. The same is true for the Kantian problem of how cognition, rational action, or aesthetic judgment is possible. In that case, one would not say either that, in the beginning, human beings had to make do without all that, until some day a transcendental, epiphanic realization occurred, and they became rational. Rather, in this case as well, the question is where one is led if one pushes the dissolution of pre-understood or pre-understandable, familiar, and accepted premises to the extreme. This type of questioning is closely tied to the transition to modern society. In this situation, for instance, the hierarchical order of society was no longer accepted and it was no longer assumed that some people were better than others from and by birth. However, when a hierarchy collapses, one has to face the question of how social order is possible. As soon as the modern territorial state is no longer secured by a stratified structure or by religion, but only by itself, one arrives at the question of how social order is possible. An analysis that is schooled in the sociology of knowledge makes clear that this entire mode of posing questions has been invented to master certain situations of uncertainty and transition, and to offer concepts that can be applied to them. Perhaps it is no coincidence at all that the theory of double contingency emerged in a society that did not dare to have recourse to specific natural constants, absolutes, or *a prioris* in the social order but already practiced what today we would call "postmodernism." That is to say, this society accepted no situation in which it was not possible to pose the question of why someone was using exactly *this* figure of thought. It must be possible in every situation to ask how someone substantiates his reasons [*seine Gründe begründet*]. No one can rely on having access to a position that meets with everyone's acceptance.

This also means that the concept of double contingency brings with it the rejection of all metaphors of the "source"; the rejection of every return to an origin; and the claim that this model is compatible with an evolutionary theory that is neither able nor willing to furnish particulars with respect to its origin. In a manner of speaking, evolution engenders itself. I have not had the opportunity to discuss the theory of evolution in this lecture course. The basic idea is that, in some way, a split between variation and selection occurs, and this process stimulates the emergence and change of structures. Evolution stimulates itself to produce order. References to the primeval soup or the primordial condition of the emergence of life, language, and social order cannot explain their occurrence. However, if we look at the concept of double contingency as an idea that problematizes functional analyses, or as the invention of a problem of reference for the said analyses, then we can recognize the parallel with the theory of evolution and other attempts to decouple the description of social development from questions of how everything originated and what the primary historical causes were. Of course, one can reintroduce these questions time and again, but one will never arrive at the origin. Thus, one may ask what reasons there were for the special development of Europe, as compared to China, in the late Middle Ages, and one may point to such factors as geographic differences and the like. Yet, such an answer always already presupposes a prior history and thereby conceives of society as already in existence and ordered. The only question that remains with regard to our example is why the technically much more advanced, much richer, much more populous, and much better ordered Chinese society did not make the transition to modernity.

I think that this is enough, for the time being, on double contingency. You see that one has to invest quite a bit of work in this concept in order to make the concept itself compatible with our theory in the first place and not simply let it run along the sidelines as a relatively disconnected piece of conceptual thinking. In my view, the latter outcome was the fate of double contingency in Parsons's theory. The effort to make this concept compatible with our theory also allows us, in the second place, to import it into other familiar contexts, such as the theory of evolution or the Kantian technique of questioning.

My next example is the concept of structure. If you reflect for a moment on the thoughts that you had when I mentioned "the concept of structure," you will in all likelihood conclude that a minimal notion of persistence and permanence came to mind. This is due in part to the tradition that usually designates systems and other states of affairs with the help of the concept of relation. There are elements and there are relations, and the latter are, in a sense, constant across time. Of course, they may change. However, one speaks of a relation only if one is dealing not with a one-time event, but rather with a typical connection between A and B. In the tradition, relations typically show a certain ontological deficit. After all, the *relata*, or the elements (the souls, etc.), come first, and then there are relations between them, which are therefore, in a sense, secondary.

On the one hand, there is this connection between concepts of structure and relation and thus a moment of constancy. On the other hand, another cognitive or analytic moment is added on, as it were, in structuralism, especially by Lévi-Strauss and other French thinkers from the period of the fifties and sixties, but also by Parsons.[4] Among other things, structures are conditions of cognition, regardless of who is the subject of this cognition, whether a particular science or a participant in social relations, social networks, social groups, and social systems. It is necessary to recognize what it is all about and one's ability to identify the type of something. One must be able to know where one is. Is it a university or a pub, a bus or some other location? If everything could be connected with everything else, if the structural patterns did not contain some clear promises in regard to cognition and orientation, then, according to this view, one would not really be dealing with functioning structures. If one actually enacted a suggestion that was made by William Blake and transposed the ale-house to the church in order to improve the singing,[5] certain ways of orienting oneself would become rather doubtful. One has to pull structures apart and disentangle them [*auseinander ziehen*] in order to know how one must behave in different contexts. All of this comprises, it seems to me, the terms of reference that nowadays constitute a specific theory paradigm under the heading of structuralism – namely, relationality, the relative permanence of relations, and totality as the condition of cognition.

Within this discussion, some progress, in the form of additional developments, has occurred. I would like to address two of these developments. The first concerns the coordination of structure and expectation. This issue pertains specifically to psychic and social systems and thus not to the general concept of structure as such. The emergence of this concept (here, I repeat a point to which I have alluded already) was connected to the idea that there is an input/output model. Accordingly, one conceived of a living system as an entity that depends on resources in the environment, has a certain effectiveness in regard to the environment or excretes its waste, and, between input and output, runs processes that do not have a point-by-point correspondence with the environment. Apparently, there is a structure within the system that is not a mere depiction of environmental differences but includes generalizations instead. For instance, we want to buy fruit but we do not know yet what kind of fruit. We look at what is being offered. Some fruit is going bad and some is too expensive. Other types of fruit may contain no vitamins or are not produced organically, as one prefers today. In other words, one has criteria that create a distance from what is seen concretely and thereby make it possible that motives for buying or not buying something can be formulated. Roughly put, in the thirties, this internal order of processing, which is decoupled from the distinctions that affect the psychic system via perception, was described in terms of the concept of expectation. This conception of complementary expectation also entered Parsons's theory.

The problem with this conception of expectation has to do with a certain privileging of the future. Expectations refer not to the past but to the future. From a formal perspective, the resulting difficulty (of which we have spoken repeatedly in my seminars) has to do with understanding why the concept of structure is being related to the future. Presumably because one is dealing with systems whose past is over anyway or is made invariant in the form of facts or memories, so that elasticity or the achievement of comprehensive generalizations is needed only for stipulating future behavior. This is an important point that ought to be kept in mind. If structures are coupled with expectations, the perspective of the future will receive preferential treatment in the entire theory. If you recall Parsons's fourfold paradigm, it will become apparent that this was exactly the case in his arrangement. There was the instrumental aspect, which was oriented towards the future, and the consummatory aspect, which concerned the effectiveness of satisfying certain needs, and which was oriented towards the present. The system itself was already its own past (or whatever else you want to call it). All this is connected to the concept of expectation. Abstracting from this concept of expectation, however, is not so easy. It is most worthwhile to think about how this might be accomplished. Maybe someone will come up with a good idea! I for my part have to say that I have not found a satisfactory solution.

Moreover, this topic has to be decoupled from the issue of the so-called subjectivity of structures that are defined merely by expectations. This is an objection that was voiced repeatedly in our discussion with Johannes Berger.[6] From the viewpoint of a pattern of expectations that still relies on Marx, structure would have to be something objective and not subjective. The relations of production, and so on, are pure objectivity. Whether someone shapes them into a part of his own expectations or not is entirely independent of this objectivity. Whether one even sees and perceives the relations of production and evaluates them in the same way that Marx or another theoretician would is a secondary question. The purpose of this developmental history of the concept of expectation was precisely to release systems from their determination by the environment. In this context, "subjective" merely means "relative to the system," and it is inevitable for a type of systems theory that radicalizes this viewpoint. There is no order that is not created by a system, either as its own internal order or as the ordering of its environment, and thus is constructed as being relative to the system. That is to say, I find the bias towards the future problematic, although I do not know how to revise it. By contrast, I consider system relativity as essential for a systems theoretical approach.

This was the one important development in structuralism or the formation of the concept of structure. The second development rests on a marginal but important comment that Parsons made in an essay from the early sixties and also, repeatedly, in his lectures.[7] Quite possibly, this comment can also be found in other places that I cannot recall at the moment. It concerns a distinction. Parsons claims that two different distinctions have to be distinguished. On the one hand, there is the distinction between structure and process and, on the other, the distinction between stability and change. Systems have a structure, and systems have processes at their disposal. This implies that it is possible to distinguish between the structures of processes and the processes of structures. In a very long-term perspective, it would then be possible to see structural change as a process – for instance, an evolutionary process. Without making the suggested distinction, however, one would not arrive at this claim, according to Parsons, since the claim depends on the possibility of abstractly distinguishing between structure and process. This distinction is directed against the criticism that structuralism cannot speak about change and related phenomena. Parsons claims that structuralism can definitely do that. According to him, one has only to decouple the distinction between structure and process from the question of whether one is actually speaking about structures or about processes as the object of procedural changes or of structures, respectively.

The distinction between stability and change – or the problem of change – is a different matter. It does not make sense to construct the concept of structure in such a way that it insists on something unchangeable. That is to say, stability without change of structure is the object of a different distinction that is orthogonal to the first distinction between structure and process. It is possible to reflect on and investigate whether and for how long unchanged structures are used. In contrast, it is also possible to investigate structural change or the change of structures. In such cases, it is possible that one is dealing with relatively short-term changes. For instance, we may think of the dynamics of the development of computers or of specific international financial instruments. We may also have in mind the thematic structures of public opinion. Relying on this second distinction, one can investigate fast and slow processes of structural change. However, whether a specific structural change is a moment in a larger process is a question that belongs in the context of our first distinction. It is possible to discern the change of a particular structure – say, changes in a constitution – without being able to identify a corresponding process that effected this structural change by means of a series of individual sequences. One perceives the change in relation to a "before" and "after" but not necessarily in relation to an overarching process.

In the situation of the late fifties and the early sixties, it was important for Parsons to soften such criticism of structuralism as inherently conservative by offering increased precision in his apparatus of distinctions. For him, it is still a question whether structures change, and, if so, in which contexts and by which means this change is brought about. Of course, in this connection it is also important to distinguish between structures and processes. Structuralism cannot be accused of being a theory that is anti-procedural or that ignores processes altogether. All this has more to do with a change in sociology. In this discipline, as in ethnology, anthropology, cultural anthropology, and other fields, a sort of fashion was prevalent that insisted on the necessity of replacing structuralist tendencies that ignored time by procedural tendencies, as if the latter were better and more correct than the former. At the end of the twenties, themes that were related to process had been very much in fashion, especially in connection with Whitehead's philosophy[8] and other philosophical developments. In a similar vein, there were conferences dedicated to the topic of "process." Social change also was a prominent issue. Structures were somewhat neglected, but in the fifties this changed. The purpose of this distinction between distinctions [*Unterscheidungsunterscheidung*] is to make clear that one does not have a choice. What is at issue is always the way in which the distinction between structure and process is handled and how one distinguishes between continuity and discontinuity, stability and change, and, furthermore, that these two orthogonal distinctions are not confused.

One can already see that the discussion is quite complicated, even if we limit ourselves to the points that have been made in print in essays or books. A simple categorization that follows the schema of "in the service of society/against society" or "conservative/critical" is no longer possible. But what I have in mind is yet another substantial shift of the ground on which the discussion unfolds. This shift is to be achieved with the help of the concept of a strictly operational systems theory – that is to say, with the help of the conception that I have worked out in the first part of this lecture series. You recall that, according to this conception, systems always consist of operations and continue to exist as long as they are able to actualize new operations. Systems exist only in the present of their real operation, which is to say, only when communication takes place or, in the case of psychic systems, only when attention is activated.

In our thematic context this means that structures, too, are real only when they are being used. We no longer have at our disposal a higher level which, like a world of ideas or an ontological invariant, has a stability all of its own, existing above the actual occurrences, as it were. Operation is itself the only reality. The central question is, then, how one operation connects to another, and here we encounter the function of structures. How does an operation find the next suitable operation? Or how does it generate itself, starting from a given point of departure? This is especially relevant since, in this case, the one thing has already passed and is no longer real, whereas the other – namely, the future – is not yet real. The reality of a structure, then, is not its durability as an existential mode. Rather, the reality of a structure lies in its being cited and thus

being used. Structures exist only when they are used. The first consequence of this insight is that systems theory is removed from the division
between structures and processes. There are no structures *and* separate
processes. Rather, systems are generated through the type of operation by
means of which they realize themselves. Whatever shows up is needed,
is reused or not used at all as structure in the process, and depends on
the operations that are called up or retrieved in the respective system.
Under these theoretical premises, one has a clearer picture of the unity of
the system as related to the corresponding operation, which in our case
is communication. Moreover, one does not have the same difficulties that
one would have if one conceived of the system as a compound of two
types of components – namely, events and processes, on the one hand,
and structures, on the other.

One may say, then, that structures are the representation of the recursive interconnectedness of operations that is used in the system. An operation draws on past occurrences and anticipates future ones. In a specific
situation, one reflects on what has happened and what presently would
make a good fit with these occurrences. One has a selective memory in
such a situation and corresponding ideas about what one would like to
achieve or what the purpose of one's actions is supposed to be.

This means that we have to deal with the question of how recursions
– whether it be as recourse to the past or anticipation of the future – are
handled as the constitutive elements of the identity of a single operation.
How do a sentence, a command, a request, an assertion, or a statement
come about in specific situations if not through a pre-orientation towards
what has taken place before and what can be connected to it afterwards?
Structures would then be the general representation of the continuous
activation of recursive orientations in a system. That is to say, structures
themselves would be something that is fluid from moment to moment
and which serves merely to furnish the continuation, processing, and
continued operation of the system with information and directions.

A number of different consequences result from this. One of them is
the issue of how the same structure can be deployed repeatedly. Do we
reinvent our past and our future in each case, or do we have something
like memory at our disposal so that we can use the same structures time
and again for operational purposes? Taking this problem as our point of
departure, it is easy to imagine the terror that must have struck society
when writing was invented and suddenly everything that had been
thought continued to be available and readable and thus could not vanish
anymore. Writing is a sort of limitation of a system's chances for forgetting. In contrast, a normal memory is as good at remembering as it is at
forgetting. If we could not forget, oh God, what confusion we would have
to face in every situation! From an operational perspective, therefore, the
question arises as to whether society can relinquish the ability to forget
and what that would mean in the context of writing. The situation has

become even more dramatic with the arrival of the computer. The computer stores everything and has the problem of not being able to forget. Is it necessary, then, to create an authority that erases what has not been called up for three weeks? How does one get rid again of the computer's memory? In certain systems, this problem is handled splendidly – especially in the monetary system. When I accept a payment, I do not have to ask where the money came from or who gave the money to the person who gave it to me. Likewise, I can spend the money without providing information about the way in which I earned it. Even stolen money moves smoothly from my hand! From a legal viewpoint, this constitutes a problem. Stolen goods can still be traced. Someone who sells stolen items has to answer for this. But stolen money cannot be traced. In this precise sense, money has no memory, and that is a good thing, too! Otherwise, every single operation would require an enormous research effort in order to find out where the money came from and where the person who paid me, the last one in the chain, received the money. There is a parallel situation with regard to the system of land registration. In English law, there is no land register. For this reason, it is sometimes necessary to go back a few centuries to make sure that the alleged owner who is interested in selling the land really owns it.[9]

How is it possible to get rid again of memory? Although I am not very familiar with computers and their technology, I can imagine that, the more information we store in computers, the more likely it is that this question could become a problem of dramatic proportions.

One of the advantages of an operation-related concept of structure is, as it were, the equal validation of recollection and forgetting, depending on operational necessities. This equal validation, however, is disturbed by certain cultural inventions such as writing and, of course, the printing press. You probably have encountered this problem when writing a scholarly paper. You may have the suspicion that, in a certain scholarly book, there is something that you need to include in your argument. Yet, you could be reading and searching for an infinite amount of time, and you would still never be certain that you have used everything that has been stored in the memory of your scientific discipline. Naturally, there are possibilities for shirking responsibility. Science has developed forms of dealing with the impossibility of truly applying its memory. For instance, knowledge may be outdated. It is no longer worthwhile citing old theories. When, on some occasion, I cited Habermas and an author from the seventeenth century as evidence for the same thesis, this was noted as pronounced brazenness. One ought to forget the seventeenth century. That was another time!

One must, however, face the actual problem. Only then is it possible to recognize the strains to which new inventions expose complex organizations. Of course, these inventions have their uses. Otherwise they would not have come about in the first place.

A second problem ought to be distinguished from this first one. It would be good to know in more detail how recursiveness develops. How is it possible to extract something from memory, take something from the past as relevant, and aim at a sort of future without activating the past situation in its entirety and without knowing the future situation? Is it not necessary for some process of selection to intervene? Is it not necessary that we already have established identities in order to be able to identify what we need from the past – for instance, whom we cite in science and to what purpose – without taking into account the complete works of this particular writer? Or, to give another example, what can be presupposed in an everyday situation if one asks someone to take a letter to the post office? Can "post office" be presupposed as familiar? And what about "letter"? And, if so, why is that? Does it depend on what is written down in the letter or when the post office is open or whether the letter is properly stamped? And, and, and! Relying on the concept of meaning, one could very easily drift into a sequence of endless references and expansions. However, the highly selective extraction of invariants, of moments of meaning that are sufficient for the concrete purpose and operation of connecting the past with the future, succeeds in some way.

Adopting a formulation that for Spencer Brown has an entirely different purpose, I call this "condensation."[10] In a certain sense, meaning contexts are condensed through their repetition. That is to say, they are reduced to forms that can be marked and designated while omitting almost everything that was plausible in the situations of their invention and earlier uses. Now, in Spencer Brown one finds the interesting thought that there is a second operation, namely, confirmation.[11] (Once again, this operation has a different purpose, but it informs the following thoughts. For this reason, I have to mention it.) When we use something again, it has to fit into the changed situation. For instance, we take a letter to the post office, or, rather, we ask someone else to take the letter to the post office for us. This is feasible even if we do not know the person to whom we entrust the letter very well and, in fact, do not know whether the letter will simply vanish into that person's pocket to be discovered only months later. (The French sometimes speak of "*poste restante.*")[12] We have, then, a situation in which something or someone has to stand the test from case to case in vastly different situations.

Can such condensation and confirmation be reduced to one concept? Or is the production of structure, of identities, and of reusability a two-step process of specifying and generalizing, of reducing and expanding, for which there can be no unified formula? That is the question. For the time being, until I am able to think of a unified formula, which would of course be a welcome simplification, I tend to work under the assumption that there is a complex tension between condensation and confirmation. One can then imagine that structures become somewhat indefinable through the sequence of their repeated uses. One has the feeling that the purpose for which something can be used is not really clear or defined distinctly. One cannot simply hand it over to someone else with the simple instruction "This is how it is done!" In other words, if the experience of use is brought into the form of an instruction, one reduces it to words that are used by the instructed person as well as to the assumption of a rigid identity for which the actual context is completely irrelevant.

The enormous importance of the appeal to experience can be appreciated only if one recognizes that this type of instruction does not work. In social relations, we always have a need to rely on our own experience without being able to give an account of our decision that one thing can be done whereas something else cannot be done. Thus, we have no means of persuasion at hand that would make it possible to convince the one whom we beat over the head with our experience that it is in fact correct. Such a situation is characteristic of the relation between different generations. When I was a novice in a governmental department, I was always amazed by the old hands operating with their experience in a most self-evident manner.[13] I recall my first public presentation before a parliamentary committee. I had prepared thoroughly and managed to say everything that I had prepared beforehand. Afterwards a minister who happened to be present by accident approached me. He patted me on the shoulder and said, "You still have quite a bit to learn. You prepared for *Don Carlos*, but here they perform *Charley's Aunt*."[14] And for this, he continued, one has to develop an instinct. Between generations, the problem is often that someone likes to refer to experience and to take it as the basis of authority, but without giving understandable reasons and arguments, without being Habermasian, as it were. Such justification cannot be asked of the speaker. After all, there is authority in the statement itself, and, in some way, one accepts this. I think that this can be formulated well with the help of the concept of structure if one recognizes that structures are always composed of mixed demands. There is, on the one hand, the issue of specification and generalization, freedom from context, and the extraction of identities. On the other, there is the question of fitting into, and dependence on, a context as well as affirmation in a context by means of repeated use.

Finally, I would like to address the context of observation briefly. I would like to remind you that I have claimed that, in structuralism, especially in Lévi-Strauss's work, structure is always also an instrument of cognition. If one wants to know in what situation and what system one is acting, then one inquires about the structure. This can be easily integrated in my operational theory, especially if I conceive of observation as another operation. That is to say, I recognize that nothing can force us to claim that there is something constant behind the fluid realities of the everyday and all the actions or operations, and that this constant element has to be recognized in order for real understanding to happen. *We* say that the observer himself constructs a structure. In the very moment when he observes, he takes certain things, distinctions, and identities as decisive for the identification of an object. One option, then, is to see the observer as the system that operates. If the issue concerns how to find out what past experience is relevant in what way for what kind of future, the system is observing itself in the very moment when it operates, regardless of how reduced the means of this self-observation may be. The system itself recognizes its structures in its operation and in its commitment to certain preset meanings that can be reused. But one might as well say, and this is the second option, that one is dealing with an external observer who identifies systems from the perspective of structures that cannot be observed by the system itself or which, under normal circumstances, cannot be activated, because a much too complicated mechanism would be required to provide answers to all sorts of questions.

If we rely on the operation of observing with the help of structures, we encounter the phenomenon that I briefly outlined in the section on observation and second-order observation. Our conception is completely observer-related. However, what makes this much less damaging than might appear is the statement that the observed system also observes. An observer of a system that generates and develops its own structures does not understand the system if he does not know how the system itself conducts its observations. He may well see other structures behind this, and he may postulate and recognize latent structures. Yet, the latency has to refer to the mode of observing structures on the part of the system, which in turn is itself being observed. Thus, the cognitive aspect – namely, the observer relativity of the concept of structure – is not lost, but it becomes more complicated to the degree that one has to decide who exactly is this observer who constructs structures. In addition, it becomes more complicated to the degree that one recognizes that, without the construction of structures, there would be no transition from one operation to the next.

My final topic is conflict. I have chosen this topic because here, once again, an ideological controversy, a theory controversy dating back to the fifties and sixties, is of interest. Back then, Ralf Dahrendorf distinguished himself with his attack on Parsons.[15] Others followed who read an overestimation of consensus and an underrating of conflict into Parsons's theory. It is quite possible that there was textual evidence for such a reading. However, the real problem is whether it is at all possible to conceive of any theories that opt exclusively for one or the other side at the level of consensus versus conflict or cooperation versus competition, which latter juxtaposition is an old theme going back to the Chicago School of the twenties. In other words, is it at all possible to have a theory that commits our society essentially to being a society of conflict, that is a class society, or that stresses, in the opposite case, that consensus is the *sine qua non* of a society and that nothing can come about without consensus on at least some things? Quite obviously, both of these versions are correct. If you recall our reflections on the concept of communication, in which the point was that every communication engenders a bifurcation between "yes" and "no" as soon as one has understood it, then you will recognize that, in the operations themselves, conflict and consensus are constantly reproduced as a duality and as alternatives. This means, however, that we always weigh down a theory with one-sidedness whenever we prescribe that it has to describe society primarily in terms only of consensus or of conflict.

On this issue, we have, once again, adaptive phenomena that occur in the development of theory. Any somewhat elaborate theory has to take into account the problem that consensus and conflict, cooperation and competition, always occur in tandem. One possibility of evaluating theories results from examining how this problem has been solved. For Max Weber, the problem is essentially addressed in terms of value relations, which is to say, a plurality of values, and the idea that there are different modes of ordering life, such as religion, love, the economy, or politics. Each of these modes posits an *a priori* value that offers it orientation. Conflict between individuals arises when one has to decide whether, say, reasons of state are more important than love. As a consequence, kings may not be allowed to marry in accord with their love but have to take into account dynastic viewpoints, issues concerning succession, and the like.[16]

This point was picked up by Robert Merton when he proposed that structures in social systems, especially in societies, have to absorb value contradictions.[17] There are latent structures that have the effect of "anomies," as Merton puts it. (I would speak of paradoxes and antinomies.) For instance, a society is based on the expectation that everyone can make money, rise to the top, and become president – everyone, but not everyone at the same time. This expectation is, however, entirely unrealistic and therefore is constantly disappointed when it is offered as a lifestyle or in terms of encouragement and motives. The question that arises, then, is how a society handles a paradigm or structure that proclaims values only to disappoint them all the time. This question is an attempt to formulate conflict and structural contradictions in such a way that sociological investigations can be connected to it. Merton provided important reflections on this issue. He came to the conclusion that apparently there are different possibilities of reacting to this state of affairs, and the choice of one of these possibilities is itself in need of sociological explanation.

This is only one example to show that the conflict–consensus dichotomy did not simply remain in place as a crude alternative. Rather, there have been attempts to integrate it in sociological theories. In this case, too, I think that all of this is pretty much all right and there is nothing that would have to be revoked. Yet, we can certainly go one step further if we apply the systems theory that I have outlined. The key statement for this purpose is my claim that conflicts themselves are systems. Conflicts are systems because one creates a situation that limits the bandwidth of variation concerning the other, if one treats him as an opponent and acts in a correspondingly aggressive, defensive, or protective way in his presence. He can no longer proceed at will. Of course he can (if he really can) walk away, shrug his shoulders, and say that all this is of no interest to him. In typical social situations, however, when one does not have the option of leaving, the notion that there is in fact a conflict, or even a mere insistent "no" as an answer to repeated interpretive offers, is a motive that produces a system, which is to say, a motive that organizes connectivity. For instance, it may lead to the creation of coalitions, to the search for resources, and to the idea that everything that is to the other's disadvantage is to my advantage. A friend/enemy relation is formed, which is an extreme simplification of the real situation. This, too, is an old topic. As far as I can tell, Cicero was the first among the Romans to pose the question whether the enemies of my friends are also to be taken as my enemies, or whether I can keep my friend and, at the same time, stay friends with his enemies as well. He also asks whether conflicts in the structure of an aristocratic society that is based on family ties and patron–client relationships are defined in such a segmental manner that it is impossible to invite to one's house someone who is an enemy of one's own friend.[18] Here, the organizing power of conflicts can be seen in social coalitions as well as in their themes. If someone contradicts a particular point I have made, I generalize his opposition and suspect that he will also contradict me on other issues. From this viewpoint, moral perspectives serve to generalize conflicts. After all, if someone has shown himself to be ignominious, he is so in every respect and not just the one that I happened to notice. Whenever I argue morally, I have the tendency to generalize conflicts! The formula is that conflicts are an excellent principle of system formation, and that systems theory can deal as well with conflict as with cooperation. It is absurd to claim that conflicts are neglected in systems theory. In fact, conflicts are highly integrated systems.

This also leads to a new conception of integration. Usually, when speaking of integration, sociologists imagine a well-oiled machine, something pleasant and harmonious. If everyone is well integrated, the future and cooperation will be secure, one will get along, and there will be peace. But what exactly is integration? If we define this concept, too, in more formal terms and say that integration is the limitation of the degrees of freedom that components have, then it is obvious that conflict has a strong integrative effect. Components are integrated to the degree that the options, states, and qualities that a system can have are reduced. Similarly, an opponent or enemy has considerably fewer moves or behavioral options at his disposal in a conflict. He has to be cautious and needs to consider how he is going to sharpen his own weapons and dull those of his enemy, how he is going to protect himself, how he can prevent an attack, and how he has to conduct his attack. To begin with, his options are fewer. They increase when he looks for new topics, new weapons, new friends and allies in order to control the conflict situation and achieve final victory. A theory of conflict must also be a theory of too much integration in a social system and of the tendency to regain additional options and introduce them into the conflict. This tendency is a sort of cancer. There is rampant growth in the system because it is too integrated. If one has the time to work this out in detail, which I cannot do here, since I have already reached the temporal limits of this lecture, one arrives at a theory of conflict that is, in my view, highly relevant and which is constructed with systems theoretical means. The subsequent analyses would have to deal with the question of how conflicts arise and how the problem of negation or rejection in communication is prevented from immediately turning into conflict. After all, every "no" immediately suggests the question "Why do you say this?" Yet one is piqued when one is even asked about one's reasons for rejecting something and becomes more agitated. The tendency of letting a "no" mushroom into a conflict system is very strong. The question is, then, how this can be prevented under normal circumstances. Why does no conflict arise when I walk out of a shop without having purchased something?

This is one option for a theory of conflict. It concerns the issue of how we order our social system so that the probability of conflict does not become too great. On this topic, there are good investigations of archaic societies that are extremely averse to conflict. I am not referring to the late archaic but to the early tribal societies and societies that are constructed on the basis of specific home or family regulations. In them the paterfamilias is in charge of solving conflicts directly with his counterpart. Such societies always have the problem of quarrelsome wives who compensate for the conflicts which the men prefer not to get into but which, for a number of reasons, they cannot ignore entirely.[19] This is also an important theme in old myths. I assume that the idea that women are quarrelsome is derived from this situation as a sort of anthropological wisdom and actually concerns the difficulty of men's conflict management. In any case, this is merely a speculative suggestion, but its investigation would be most worthwhile. There is some research on extended families in the Balkans, where husband and wife sleep in a large room where others also sleep. They are allowed to whisper under the covers, but the wife is not allowed to look for help from or to make public bad news about the others who are sleeping nearby.[20]

The control of conflict concerns the social structure. Usually, this is viewed as if the destructive effects of conflicts were primarily at issue – the possibility of destroying bodies and things, of burning down houses and ravaging entire regions, and even of eradicating humankind. However, in these explanations, an intermediary step is usually missing – namely, the question of how it was possible at all that things could get to such a point – that is to say, how a conflict can become so dynamic that it no longer manages to rein itself in. To address this question, one needs systems theory. At least, it can be used in recognizing that conflicts are over-integrated and therefore in need of receiving new fuel. It is for this reason that they are expansive, sprawling, and dangerous – even if we disregard what they will eventually do to humans and other resources in their environment.

Another idea that belongs in this context is that it is possible to conceive of the law as an institution for the domestication of conflicts. (In *Social Systems*, I spoke of immune systems.)[21] That is to say, the law really encourages conflicts. If one is the owner of an object, and someone else comes along and wants it, one can say "no." This rejection must be accepted. If needed, a court of law will confirm that. That is to say, the possibility of saying "no" is strengthened by the legal structure, and usually this suffices to nip a potential conflict in the bud. In the reverse case, when conflicts do happen, the law can lead to a peaceful decision. My little book on *Legitimation through Processes* has the purpose of demonstrating how conflicts are being absorbed. This happens when someone participates in a lawsuit and thereby is led to contribute to legal regulation, to present his viewpoint, and to accept the legal process as such, although he does not know yet how his lawsuit will end. When the suit comes to an end, he is already part of the system and has accepted beforehand that he will accept the decision.[22] By then, he has already isolated himself as a participant. This way of looking at things agrees with the view that conceives of conflict absorption as one of society's problematic tasks, and it also recognizes the necessity of relieving politics of conflicts or downplaying conflicts by appointing mediation commissions and the like. Another way of achieving the same goal is the habit of quarreling constantly, only to reconcile afterwards.

I have to break this off here. Perhaps one last point is in order. This problem of conflicts is closely connected to conceptual resources that have newly entered the discussion – namely, the distinction between *tight coupling* and *loose coupling*. If social processes are tightly coupled, conflicts spread. If they are loosely coupled, it is easier to isolate conflicts. If families are integrated in a political order and have great economic importance, then family conflicts can have very far-reaching consequences. This is familiar from studies on family enterprises – that is, medium-size businesses, in which father and son no longer get along. It is, for instance, well known what consequences this can have for the workers and for the town in which such a business is the main employer. The thesis that stability, contrary to what the old type of systems theory had assumed, is based precisely on the interruption of connections, on loose coupling, and on the non-proliferation of effects is in turn compatible with the thesis of the omnipresence of conflicts and possibilities for conflict, and of society's dependence on the most diverse possibilities of holding such conflicts in check.

I hope that these examples have shown a little bit how it becomes possible from this perspective to dissolve some controversies in sociology at the conceptual level and at the same time arrive at theories and hypotheses that can be converted into empirical research. The intention of this lecture course, however, was not so much to produce a whole bunch of empirically testable hypotheses and leave it to the busy bees of the discipline to verify all of them and to repeat the verification to make sure that it stands the test. Rather, my intention was to give you an idea of the importance of the architecture of a theory and of questions pertaining to the design of a theory – that is, of decisions that can be made at this level and which may well have their own evidence and argumentational resources. By "introduction" I do not mean so much what is easily understood or has been popularized or is suitable for beginners. At least, that is not what I had in mind when I chose the title for this lecture series. I have attempted to introduce conceptual tools. I did not just summarize things that can be read in books, only to abstain from saying anything further about them. Whenever possible, I tried instead to introduce the relevant concepts in the context of their use and in relation to their meaning. I thought that it ought to be possible to follow this lecture course, regardless of its unusually abstract quality, merely on the basis of the explanations that were produced in the course of the lectures themselves. I hope that I have succeeded fairly well in this. In any case, the idea that there is a particular methodology or, as I would like to say, a particular carefulness when it comes to dealing with conceptual and theoretical questions seems important to me. This idea is also relevant with regard to a theory of society, which is the task we are given but which we have hitherto not been able to accomplish. Moreover, I would also like to stress that the doctrine of method is not limited to dealing with the erosion of empirical data but is also capable of making transparent decisions and their consequences in the area of theoretical dispositions.

True, from the outside such theories may give the impression that one has either to enter into them wholeheartedly or stay outside, which would be the prudent option, since it is assumed that one might no longer find the exit once one has entered. Moreover, there is apparently also no emergency lever that would make sure that the whole thing can be made to collapse from the inside. I have often heard these resounding reservations especially with regard to systems theory. It has been said that systems theory gives the impression of a fortress that has been erected for the purpose of self-defense and may quite possibly have been moderately successful on that count. The truth in all of this has to do with the fact that thoroughly constructed theories do not have one super-norm that one can simply negate in order to undermine the entire theory. Fully constructed theories are complicated formations. In a sense, they are works of art. It is difficult to get involved with them and still know how one will relativize all that again or how one will be able to detach oneself when the time comes. This is an experience that many a theorist has with Hegel. These

Hegelians are so familiar with the modes of argumentation and the forms of development of his theory that they know them by heart. They can speak like Hegel. But they have no language left but the dialectical one. The countermeasure I have in mind is to make the theory decisions as transparent as possible. To do this, it is necessary to single out the following questions at every juncture. What are the different options? What is connected to the decision in favor of *this* concept as opposed to another one? Where is there an exit point? Where does one have the freedom to choose something else in order to see what else needs to be changed if one revises a certain decision?

The purpose of today's lecture was, among other things, to illustrate these principles with the help of material that was taken from sociology. In other words, I showed that, when one calls a conflict "highly integrated," one has to have a clearer conception of integration than the one that is common in the sociological literature. This has the effect that other people will have to refine their concept of integration if they want to keep up. I meant to contribute not to an exclusionary effect but rather to awareness concerning construction and decision-making in matters of theory. I also had in mind a comparison of theories: on the one hand, a comparison with other theory traditions in the discipline of sociology and the larger field of the social sciences and, on the other hand, and perhaps primarily, a comparison with the Old European mode of thinking, the mode of thinking that is characteristic of this ontological-metaphysical tradition and its specific humanism. In this tradition, humanism is nothing but ontology applied to the human being, if I may say so. Yet, when we speak of the human being in our context, we are faced with the opacity of a self-organizing individual in its absolute singularity and empirical incomparability. We no longer think of an abstract entity named "man" that could somehow be included in the normative structure of society. Furthermore, the purpose of this entire conceptual labor is to address the following question: Are we able to re-enact this break with the European tradition and decide that such a break is indeed needed and that we are willing to take responsibility for it, in spite of already being able to see where such arguments will lead us? This is what I tried to convey at least a little bit in this lecture course. I thank you for your perseverance.

Notes

System – Autopoiesis – Form

1 Niklas Luhmann, *Social Systems*, trans. John Bednarz, Jr., with Dirk Baecker (Stanford, CA: Stanford University Press, 1995), p. xlix.
2 See Eva Knodt, "Foreword," ibid., pp. ix–xxxvi, esp. pp. xx–xxiv.
3 Luhmann, *Social Systems*, p. 4.
4 Ibid., p. 1.
5 Niklas Luhmann, *Love as Passion: The Codification of Intimacy*, trans. Jeremy Gaines and Doris L. Jones (Cambridge: Polity, 1986). The German original appeared in 1982, two years before *Social Systems*.
6 An excellent attempt at such integration – including a number of open questions – can be found in Frank Becker and Elke Reinhardt-Becker, *Systemtheorie: Eine Einführung für die Geschichts- und Kulturwissenschaft* (Frankfurt: Campus, 2001), pp. 136–45.
7 Niklas Luhmann, *Die Gesellschaft der Gesellschaft*, 2 vols. (Frankfurt am Main: Suhrkamp, 1997), vol. 1, p. 11.
8 Kenneth D. Bailey, "The autopoiesis of social systems: assessing Luhmann's theory of self-reference," *Systems Research and Behavioral Science* 14 (1997), pp. 83–100, here p. 84.
9 See Becker and Reinhardt-Becker, *Systemtheorie*, which contains a concise biography on pp. 161f. See also Walter Reese-Schäfer, *Luhmann zur Einführung* (Hamburg: Junius, 1992), pp. 205f.
10 Talcott Parsons, *The Social System* (New York: Free Press, 1951), p. 20.
11 Ibid., pp. 5f.
12 Ibid., p. 18.
13 Ibid.
14 Luhmann, *Social Systems*, p. 162.
15 Ibid., p. 139.
16 Humberto R. Maturana and Francisco J. Varela, "Autopoiesis," in *Autopoiesis and Cognition: The Realization of the Living* (Dordrecht: Reidel, 1980), pp. 59–134.
17 Ibid., p. 94.
18 Ibid.

19 Humberto R. Maturana and Francisco J. Varela, *The Tree of Knowledge: The Biological Roots of Human Understanding* (rev. edn, Boston: Shambhala, 1992), pp. 87f.

20 Ibid., p. 180.

21 It should be said that Maturana and Varela disagree on the question whether social systems are autopoietic (and thus, in their terms, biological) systems. For Maturana, whose views on the matter are prevalent in *Autopoiesis and Cognition*, a social system is "a composite system" that emerges as a result of the coupling between autopoietic systems – that is, of human individuals. The emerging system of "coupled human beings" is not necessarily autopoietic itself ("Autopoiesis," p. 118).

22 Ibid.

23 On the notion of "superorganisms," see Melanie Mitchell, *Complexity: A Guided Tour* (Oxford: Oxford University Press, 2009), pp. 3–6.

24 John R. Searle, *The Mystery of Consciousness* (New York: New York Review of Books, 1997), pp. 212f.

25 Maturana and Varela, *The Tree of Knowledge*, p. 199.

26 In fact, as the concluding eponymous chapter of *The Tree of Knowledge* shows, Maturana and Varela recognize that their own investigation *as a scientific enterprise* happens at the level of social communication and involves the resources of consciousness. In systems theoretical terms, it may prove considerably easier to provide a description of the social while bracketing its "biologic roots" than to conduct biological research into the roots of human understanding that simultaneously seeks to reflect on its own social status as science.

27 Luhmann, *Social Systems*, p. 219.

28 In social systems, *communication* takes place in the medium of meaning, or *Sinn*; in psychic systems, the *processes of consciousness* happen in the medium of meaning.

29 See Luhmann, *Die Gesellschaft der Gesellschaft*, vol. 1, p. 45.

30 Spencer Brown's *Laws of Form* was first published in Britain by George Allen & Unwin in 1969. Luhmann refers to the American edition, which contains an important preface written in 1972; see George Spencer Brown, *Laws of Form* (New York: Julian Press, 1972). A paperback version of this edition was published in 1973 by Bantam, New York. All references to Spencer Brown are keyed to this edition.

31 Luhmann, *Social Systems*, p. 499 n. 5.

32 Spencer Brown, *Laws of Form*, p. v.

33 One can thus distinguish between "summative" and "constitutive characteristics," as suggested by Ludwig von Bertalanffy, "Some system concepts in elementary mathematical consideration," in *General System Theory: Foundations, Development, Applications* (New York: George Braziller, 1969), pp. 54–88. However, both of them are premised on whole-and-parts relations – that is, on the idea that systems are complexes of different elements. Although von Bertalanffy recognizes that constitutive characteristics cannot be explained in terms of the characteristics of isolated parts, he insists that these new, emergent characteristics can be explained if we know "the total of parts contained

in a system and the relations between them" (p. 55). Newer findings in complexity theory do not support this reductionist claim. See Mitchell, *Complexity*, passim.
34 Luhmann, *Social Systems*, p. lii.

I Sociology and Systems Theory

1 *Translator's note*: Luhmann uses the German term "*Sinn*," which covers the semantic range of both "sense" and "meaning." I have generally chosen "meaning" for reasons of consistency. However, it should be kept in mind that Luhmann's "*Sinnsysteme*" are as much "sense systems" as they are "meaning systems."

2 In his essay "Wie ist soziale Ordnung möglich?" [How is social order possible?], in Luhmann, *Gesellschaftsstruktur und Semantik: Studien zur Wissenssoziologie der modernen Gesellschaft* (Frankfurt am Main: Suhrkamp, 1981), vol. 2, pp. 195–285, here p. 260, Luhmann quotes the sentence "Action is system" – without putting it in quotation marks – from Talcott Parsons's essay "The position of identity in the general theory of action," in Chad Gordon and Kenneth J. Gergen (eds), *The Self in Social Interaction* (New York: Wiley, 1968), vol. 1, pp. 11–23, here p. 14.

3 From Talcott Parsons, "A paradigm of the human condition," in Parsons, *Action Theory and the Human Condition* (New York: Free Press, 1978), pp. 352–433, here p. 361. The other three fields are left empty, since Luhmann merely mentions their function but does not discuss their substance. Parsons calls them the "telic system" (L), the "physico-chemical system" (A), and the "human organic system" (G).

4 *Translator's note*: The German text (p. 30) has "*interne Präferenzen*" here. I suspect a transcription error, since the subsequent "*externen Referenzen*" would seem to require "*interne Referenzen*."

5 Added by Dirk Baecker, the editor of the German edition.

6 *Translator's note*: Cf. Talcott Parsons, "On the concept of political power," *Proceedings of the American Philosophical Society* 107 (1963), pp. 232–62.

7 See Parsons, "A paradigm of the human condition," especially pp. 362ff. and 374ff.

8 On this, see the German edition of Talcott Parsons, *Zur Theorie der sozialen Interaktionsmedien*, ed. and introd. Stefan Jensen (Opladen: Westdeutscher Verlag, 1980).

9 See, e.g., Talcott Parsons, "Social systems," *Social Systems and the Evolution of Action Theory* (New York: Free Press, 1977), pp. 177–203.

II General Systems Theory

1 Today this association is called the International Society for the Systems Sciences (ISSS); see www.isss.org.

2 See János Kornai, *Anti-Equilibrium: On Economic Systems Theory and the Task of Research* (Amsterdam: North-Holland, 1971).

3 *Translator's note*: The published version of Luhmann's lecture course has

"entropy" here. The context makes it clear, however, that he meant to say "negentropy" or "the absence of entropy."

4 David Easton, *The Political System: An Inquiry into the State of Political Science* (New York: Knopf, 1953).

5 See Niklas Luhmann, *Das Recht der Gesellschaft* (Frankfurt am Main: Suhrkamp, 1993), p. 42 n. 10, where Jay A. Sigler, "A cybernetic model of the judicial system," *Temple Law Quarterly* 41 (1968), pp. 398–428, and additional literature is mentioned.

6 Namely, in Niklas Luhmann, *Zweckbegriff und Systemrationalität: Über die Funktion von Zwecken in sozialen Systemen* (2nd edn, Frankfurt am Main: Suhrkamp, 1977), pp. 101ff.

7 *Translator's note*: Luhmann has in mind the German Federal Constitutional Court. The American equivalent would be the Supreme Court.

8 See especially W. Ross Ashby, *Introduction to Cybernetics* (London: Routledge & Kegan Paul, 1964).

9 To give just one example, see Arturo Rosenblueth, Norbert Wiener, and Julian Bigelow, "Behavior, purpose, and teleology," *Philosophy of Science* 10 (1943), pp. 18–24.

10 See, e.g., Magoroh Maruyama, "The second cybernetics: deviation-amplifying mutual causal processes," *American Scientist* 51 (1963), pp. 164–79 and 250A–56A.

11 *Translator's note*: Here, and in most other contexts, Luhmann's notion of science corresponds to the German *Wissenschaft*. In other words, it is not limited to natural science but also includes the social sciences and the humanities, which in German are called *Geisteswissenschaften*.

12 See Heinz von Foerster, *Observing Systems* (Seaside, CA: Intersystems, 1981), and, for a discussion of the work conducted at the Biological Computer Laboratory, Heinz von Foerster (ed.), *Cybernetics of Cybernetics: The Control of Control and the Communication of Communication* (Minneapolis: Future Systems, 1995). The entire paragraph in brackets was added by Dirk Baecker, the editor of the German edition of the present book.

13 See Gotthard Günther, *Beiträge zur Grundlegung einer operationsfähigen Dialektik*, 3 vols (Hamburg: Meiner, 1976, 1979, and 1980).

14 See the collection of essays that was of the highest importance for Luhmann, Humberto R. Maturana, *Erkennen: Die Organisation und Verkörperung von Wirklichkeit: Ausgewählte Arbeiten zur biologischen Epistemologie*, trans. Wolfram Karl Köck (Braunschweig: Vieweg, 1982). See also, more recently, Humberto R. Maturana, *Biologie der Realität*, trans. Wolfram Karl Köck (Frankfurt am Main: Suhrkamp, 2000).

15 See George Spencer Brown, *Laws of Form* (London: Allen & Unwin, 1969).

16 Heinz von Foerster, "Laws of form," *Whole Earth Catalogue* (spring 1969), p. 14.

17 Reproduced from *Organization* 13(1) (© Sage publications Ltd, 2006), by permission of Sage Publications Ltd.

18 Ferdinand de Saussure's *Cours de linguistique générale* was originally published by Charles Bally and Albert Sechehaye. For the critical edition, see Ferdinand de Saussure, *Cours de linguistique générale*, ed. Tullio de Mauro (Paris: Payot, 1972).

19 Gabriel Tarde, *Les Lois de l'imitation: étude sociologique* (2nd enlarged edn, Paris: Alcan, 1895).
20 See especially René Girard, *Violence and the Sacred*, trans. Patrick Gregory (Baltimore: Johns Hopkins University Press, 1977).
21 Gregory Bateson, *Steps to an Ecology of Mind* (Chicago: University of Chicago Press, 1972).
22 See, for instance, Vincent Descombes, *Modern French Philosophy* (Cambridge: Cambridge University Press, 1980).
23 Louis H. Kauffman, "Self-reference and recursive forms," *Journal of Social and Biological Structure* 10 (1987), pp. 53–72.
24 For more on this issue, see Niklas Luhmann, "Die Unterscheidung Gottes," in Luhmann, *Soziologische Aufklärung*, 4: *Beiträge zur funktionalen Differenzierung der Gesellschaft* (Opladen: Westdeutscher Verlag, 1987), pp. 236–53.
25 See also the criticism voiced by Paul Cull and William Frank, "Flaws of form," *International Journal of General Systems* 5 (1979), pp. 201–10.
26 See, for instance, Charles S. Peirce, "Pragmatism in retrospect: a last formulation," in *Philosophical Writings of Peirce*, ed. Justus Buchler (New York: Dover, 1955), pp. 269–89.
27 *Translator's note*: Cf. Humberto Maturana, "Autopoiesis," in Milan Zeleny (ed.), *Autopoiesis: A Theory of Living Organizations* (New York: North-Holland, 1981), pp. 21–32.
28 For a more detailed treatment, see Niklas Luhmann, *Social Systems*, trans. John Bednarz, Jr., with Dirk Baecker (Stanford, CA: Stanford University Press, 1995), ch. 4, pp. 137–75.
29 See Jakob von Uexküll, *Theoretische Biologie* (2nd rev. edn, Berlin: Springer, 1928); also Jakob von Uexküll, *A Foray into the Worlds of Animals and Humans; with A Theory of Meaning*, trans. Joseph D. O'Neil (Minneapolis: University of Minnesota Press, 2010); the original German edition of *Streifzüge durch die Umwelten von Tieren und Menschen* was published in 1934, also by Springer.
30 George H. Mead, *Mind, Self and Society from the Standpoint of a Social Behaviorist* (Chicago: University of Chicago Press, 1934).
31 See Edmund Husserl, *Ideen zu einer reinen Phänomenologie und phänomenologischen Philosophie*, vol. 1: *Allgemeine Einführung in die Phänomenologie* [=*Husserliana*, vol. 3], ed. Walter Biemel (The Hague: Martinus Nijhoff, 1950).
32 Alfred Schütz, *The Phenomenology of the Social World*, trans. George Walsh and Frederick Lehnert (Evanston, IL: Northwestern University Press, 1967).
33 *Translator's note*: A more extensive treatment can be found in Niklas Luhmann, *Die Gesellschaft der Gesellschaft*, 2 vols. (Frankfurt am Main: Suhrkamp, 1997), vol. 1, pp. 44–59.
34 Thus Lars Löfgren, "Unfoldment of self-reference in logic and computer science," in Finn V. Jensen, Brian H. Mayoh, and Karen K. Møller (eds), *Proceedings from 5th Scandinavian Logic Symposium, Aalborg, 17–19 January 1979* (Aalborg: Institut for Elektroniske Systemer, 1979), pp. 205–29.
35 See Niklas Luhmann, *Ecological Communication*, trans. John Bednarz, Jr. (Cambridge: Polity, 1989).
36 See *Geschichtliche Grundbegriffe: Historisches Lexikon zur politisch-sozialen Sprache*

in Deutschland, ed. Otto Brunner, Werner Conze, and Reinhart Koselleck (Stuttgart: Klett-Cotta, 1972–97).

37 Karl Mannheim, *Structures of Thinking*, trans. Jeremy J. Shapiro and Shierry Weber Nicholson, ed. David Kettler, Volker Meja, and Nico Stehr (London: Routledge & Kegan Paul, 1982).

38 Particularly following Fritz Heider, "Social perception and phenomenal causality," *Psychological Review* 51 (1944), pp. 358–74.

39 Thus Charles Perrow, *Normal Accidents: Living with High-Risk Technologies* (New York: Basic Books, 1984) and Niklas Luhmann, *Risk: A Sociological Theory*, trans. Rhodes Barrett (New York: de Gruyter, 1993).

40 Heinz von Foerster, *Wissen und Gewissen: Versuch einer Brücke* (Frankfurt am Main: Suhrkamp, 1993), pp. 244ff.

41 Luhmann, *Ecological Communication*.

42 See, for instance, Heinz von Foerster, "Was ist Gedächtnis, daß es Rückschau und Vorschau ermöglicht?" in *Wissen und Gewissen: Versuch einer Brücke*, pp. 299–336.

43 See Johannes Berger, "Autopoiesis: Wie 'systemisch' ist die Theorie sozialer Systeme?" in Hans Haverkamp and Michael Schmid (eds), *Sinn, Kommunikation und soziale Differenzierung: Beiträge zu Luhmanns Theorie sozialer Systeme* (Frankfurt am Main: Suhrkamp, 1987), pp. 129–52.

44 See Noam Chomsky, *Aspects of the Theory of Syntax* (Cambridge, MA: MIT Press, 1969).

45 *Translator's note*: The multi-volume *Duden* is the decisive authority on German orthography and grammar.

46 See Maturana, *Erkennen*, and also Huberto R. Maturana and Francisco J. Varela, *Autopoiesis and Cognition: The Realization of the Living* (Dordrecht: Reidel, 1980).

47 The definition in question can be found in Humberto Maturana, "Autopoiesis."

48 *Translator's note*: The term "normal" should be taken in the sense that Thomas Kuhn gives it when he speaks of "normal science" in his classic study *The Structure of Scientific Revolutions* (Chicago: University of Chicago Press, 1962).

49 Gunther Teubner, *Recht als autopoietisches System* (Frankfurt am Main: Suhrkamp, 1989), pp. 38ff. Also see the printed discussion in Gunther Teubner and Alberto Febbraio (eds), *State, Law, and Economy as Autopoietic Systems: Regulation and Autonomy in a New Perspective* (Milan: A. Guiffrè, 1992).

50 See Werner Kirsch and Dodo zu Knyphausen, "Unternehmungen als 'autopoietische' Systeme?" in Wolfgang H. Staehle and Jörg Sydow (eds), *Managementforschung I* (Berlin: de Gruyter, 1991), pp. 75–101.

51 See Heinz von Foerster, "Über selbstorganisierende Systeme und ihre Umwelten," in *Wissen und Gewissen: Versuch einer Brücke*, pp. 211–32.

52 See the works by Maturana mentioned above.

53 See, e.g., Heinz von Foerster, "Über das Konstruieren von Wirklichkeiten," in *Wissen und Gewissen: Versuch einer Brücke*, pp. 25–49.

54 On this concept of information, see Claude E. Shannon and Warren Weaver, *The Mathematical Theory of Communication* (Urbana: University of Illinois Press, 1963).

55 Bateson, *Steps to an Ecology of Mind*, e.g., p. 272.

56 See also Heinz von Foerster, "Bemerkungen zu einer Epistemologie des Lebendigen," in *Wissen und Gewissen: Versuch einer Brücke*, pp. 116–33.

57 *Translator's note:* Luhmann is concerned here with the different "reception" of a text in a psychic system and in a social system.

58 Paul Watzlawick, Janet Beavin Bavelas, and Don D. Jackson, *Pragmatics of Human Communication: A Study of Interactional Patterns, Pathologies, and Paradoxes* (New York: W. W. Norton, 1967), p. 51.

59 E.g., in Maturana, *Erkennen*, p. 34. "Everything that is said is said by an observer. Through his utterances an observer speaks to another observer, whom he could be himself. Everything that characterizes one observer also characterizes the other."

60 See John von Neumann, *The Computer and the Brain* (New Haven, CT: Yale University Press, 1958).

61 See James Keys [a.k.a. George Spencer Brown], *Only Two Can Play This Game* (Cambridge: Cat Books, 1971).

62 See, e.g., von Foerster, "Über das Konstruieren von Wirklichkeiten."

63 Ranulph Glanville, "The same is different," in Milan Zeleny (ed.), *Autopoiesis: A theory of Living Organization* (Amsterdam: North-Holland, 1981), pp. 252–62.

64 For instance, in Humberto R. Maturana, *Biologie der Realität* (Frankfurt am Main: Suhrkamp, 2000), pp. 93ff.

65 Presumably, Luhmann has in mind his discussions with pedagogues that have been documented in a series of volumes. See Niklas Luhmann and Karl Eberhard Schorr (eds), *Zwischen Technologie und Selbstreferenz: Fragen an die Pädagogik* (Frankfurt am Main: Suhrkamp, 1982), *Zwischen Intransparenz und Verstehen: Fragen an die Pädagogik* (Frankfurt am Main: Suhrkamp, 1986), *Zwischen Anfang und Ende: Fragen an die Pädagogik* (Frankfurt am Main: Suhrkamp, 1990), *Zwischen Absicht und Person: Fragen an die Pädagogik* (Frankfurt am Main: Suhrkamp, 1992), *Zwischen System und Umwelt: Fragen an die Pädagogik* (Frankfurt am Main: Suhrkamp, 1996), and Dieter Lenzen and Niklas Luhmann (eds), *Bildung und Weiterbildung im Erziehungssystem: Lebenslauf und Humanontogenese as Medium und Form* (Frankfurt am Main: Suhrkamp, 1997). On the discussion with the theologians, see Michael Welker (ed.), *Theologie und funktionale Systemtheorie: Luhmanns Religionssoziologie in theologischer Diskussion* (Frankfurt am Main: Suhrkamp, 1985).

66 Edmund Husserl, *Cartesian Meditations*, trans. D. Cairns (The Hague: Martinus Nijhoff, 1977).

67 Philippe Ariès, *L'Enfant et la vie familiale sous l'ancien régime* (Paris: Plon, 1960).

68 Maria Helena Vieira da Silva (1908–1992) was a Portuguese painter.

69 Heinz von Foerster, *Observing Systems* (Seaside, CA: Intersystems, 1981).

70 Talcott Parsons and Gerald M. Platt, *The American University* (Cambridge, MA: Harvard University Press, 1973).

71 See Spencer Brown, *Laws of Form*, p. 105.

72 August Wilhelm Schlegel, "Die Kunstlehre," in *Kritische Schriften und Briefe*, vol. 2 (Stuttgart: Kohlhammer, 1963), p. 49.

73 See Robert K. Merton, "The self-fulfilling prophecy," in *Social Theory and Social Structure* (rev. and enlarged edn, New York: Free Press, 1968), pp. 475–90.

74 Heinz von Foerster, "Principles of self-organization – in a socio-managerial

context," in Hans Ulrich and Gilbert J. B. Probst (eds), *Self-Organization and Management of Social Systems: Insights, Promises, Doubts, and Questions* (Berlin: Springer, 1984), pp. 2–24; also available in German in von Foerster, *Wissen und Gewissen*, pp. 233–68.

75 *Translator's note:* The German term is *"Komplexitätsgefälle."* In this passage, *"-gefälle"* is put in italics in order to stress that the term itself implies that the level of complexity is lower in the system than outside of it.

76 W. Ross Ashby, "Requisite variety and its implications for the control of complex systems," *Cybernetica* 1 (1958), pp. 83–99. See also W. Ross Ashby, *An Introduction to Cybernetics* (London: Routledge & Kegan Paul, 1964).

77 Jerome Bruner, Jacqueline J. Goodnow, and George A. Austin, *A Study of Thinking* (New York: Wiley, 1956).

78 See Kenneth Burke, *A Grammar of Motives* [1945] (Berkeley: University of California Press, 1969), pp. 59–124.

79 See, e.g., W. Ross Ashby, "The set theory of mechanism and homeostasis," in *Mechanisms of Intelligence: Ross Ashby's Writings on Cybernetics*, ed. Roger Conant (Seaside, CA: Intersystems, 1981), pp. 21–49, here p. 48.

80 See Robert B. Glassman, "Persistence and loose coupling in living systems," *Behavioral Science* 18 (1973), pp. 83–93, and, following this lead, Karl E. Weick, "Educational organizations as loosely coupled systems," *Administrative Science Quarterly* 21 (1976), pp. 1–19.

81 See, again, Charles Perrow, *Normal Accidents: Living with High-Risk Technologies*, and Niklas Luhmann, *Risk: A Sociological Theory.*

82 See Herbert A. Simon, *Models of Bounded Rationality*, 2 vols. (Cambridge, MA: MIT Press, 1982).

83 For all this and the subsequent passages, see Niklas Luhmann, "Komplexität," in Erwin Grochla (ed.), *Handwörterbuch der Organisation* (2nd edn, Stuttgart: Poeschel, 1980), cols 1064–70.

84 See, e.g., Alex Bavelas, "Communication patterns in task-oriented groups," in Dorwin Cartwright and Alvin Zander (eds), *Group Dynamics, Research, and Theory* (Evanston, IL: Row, Peterson, 1953), pp. 493–506, and Alex Bavelas, "Communication patterns in problem-solving groups," in Heinz von Foerster (ed.), *Cybernetics* (New York: Josiah Macy Jr. Foundation, 1952).

85 See Niklas Luhmann, "Temporalisierung von Komplexität: Zur Semantik neuzeitlicher Zeitbegriffe," in *Gesellschaftsstruktur und Semantik: Studien zur Wissenssoziologie der modernen Gesellschaft*, vol. 1 (Frankfurt am Main: Suhrkamp, 1980), pp. 235–300.

86 See Donald M. MacKay, "On the logical indeterminacy of a free choice," *Mind* 69 (1960), pp. 32–40.

87 Gotthard Günther, "Cybernetic ontology and transjunctional operations," in *Beiträge zur Grundlegung einer operationsfähigen Dialektik*, vol. 1 (Hamburg: Meiner, 1976), pp. 249–328, here pp. 318f.

88 See, e.g., Robert Rosen, "Complexity as a system property," *International Journal of General Systems* 3 (1977), pp. 227–32.

89 Max Weber, *Economy and Society: An Outline of Interpretive Sociology*, ed. Guenther Roth and Claus Wittich, trans. Ephraim Fischoff (Berkeley: University of California Press, 1978), esp. chs 1 and 2.

90 Stephen E. Toulmin, *Cosmopolis: The Hidden Agenda of Modernity* (New York: Free Press, 1990), and *Return to Reason* (Cambridge, MA: Harvard University Press, 2001).

91 See Stephen Holmes, "Differenzierung und Arbeitsteilung im Denken des Liberalismus," in Niklas Luhmann (ed.), *Soziale Differenzierung: Zur Geschichte einer Idee* (Opladen: Westdeutscher Verlag, 1985), pp. 9–41, and *Benjamin Constant and the Making of Modern Liberalism* (New Haven, CT: Yale University Press, 1984).

92 See Vilfredo Pareto, *The Mind and Society: A Treatise on General Sociology*, 4 vols., ed. Arthur Livingston, trans. Andrew Bongiorno and Arthur Livingston (New York: Harcourt, Brace, 1942).

93 Martin Heidegger, *Being and Time: A Translation of Sein und Zeit*, trans. Joan Stambaugh [1927] (Albany: State University of New York Press, 1996).

94 Jürgen Habermas, *The Theory of Communicative Action*, trans. Thomas McCarthy, 2 vols (Cambridge: Polity, 1984, 1987).

95 *Translator's note*: Luhmann is referring to his famous *Zettelkasten*, which contained notecards on all his readings and allegedly was organized according to a most intricate system of cross-references. A free program (version 3.1.8 as of March 14, 2012) that simulates Luhmann's *Zettelkasten* is available at http://zettelkasten.danielluedecke.de.

III Time

1 This is an allusion to the collapse of the Soviet Union (the Union of Independent Soviet Republics was founded in December 1991) and the dissolution of Yugoslavia (Europe recognized Croatia and Slovenia as independent states in January 1992).

2 See, e.g., Niklas Luhmann, "Weltzeit und Systemgeschichte: Über Beziehungen zwischen Zeithorizonten und sozialen Strukturen gesellschaftlicher Systeme," in *Soziologische Aufklärung*, 2: *Aufsätze zur Theorie der Gesellschaft* (Opladen: Westdeutscher Verlag, 1975), pp. 103–33.

3 Augustine, *Confessions* XI 14, 17.

4 Ibid., XI 17, 22.

5 Ibid., XI 23, 29 – 24, 31.

6 Helga Nowotny, *Time: Modern and Postmodern Experience*, trans. Neville Plaice (Cambridge: Polity, 1994).

7 Niklas Luhmann, "Gleichzeitigkeit und Synchronisation," in *Soziologische Aufklärung*, 5: *Konstruktivistische Perspektiven* (Opladen: Westdeutscher Verlag, 1990), pp. 95–130. Luhmann held the original lecture on November 9, 1989, at the University of Vienna.

8 *Translator's note*: Translated literally, the title of Schütz's first book reads *The Meaningful Construction of the Social World*. In fact, it was published in English as *The Phenomenology of the Social World*, trans. George Walsh and Frederick Lehnert (Evanston, IL: Northwestern University Press, 1967).

9 See Alfred Schütz, *Der sinnhafte Aufbau der sozialen Welt: Eine Einleitung in die verstehende Soziologie* (Frankfurt am Main: Suhrkamp, 1974 [orig. Vienna: Springer, 1932]), p. 144; *The Phenomenology of the Social World*, trans. George

Walsh and Frederick Lehnert (Evanston, IL: Northwestern University Press, 1967), p. 103, where Schütz speaks of simultaneity as the "phenomenon of growing older together" [*Phänomen des Zusammenalterns*].

10 And there is no need to drop oneself into a puddle, as Luhmann pointed out in a conversation with Alexander Kluge. See "Vorsicht vor zu raschem Verstehen," *News & Stories* of July 4, 1994, on the private German TV station SAT 1.

11 *Translator's note*: In German, the distinction is between "*bewegt*" and "*unbewegt*." The latter means "immovable," "motionless," "not moving," but also "unmoved" in the sense of Aristotle's "unmoved mover," to which Luhmann refers in the course of his discussion. Depending on the immediate context, I have chosen "not moving" or "unmoved" to translate "*unbewegt*." The reader is advised to keep the Aristotelian connotation in mind in either case.

12 See Jan Assmann, "Das Doppelgesicht der Zeit im altägyptischen Denken," in Anton Peisl and Armin Mohler (eds), *Die Zeit* (Munich: Oldenbourg, 1983), pp. 189–223, and also Assmann, *Stein und Zeit: Mensch und Gesellschaft im Alten Ägypten* (2nd edn, Munich: Fink, 1995), pp. 32–58.

13 See Hans Blumenberg, *Lebenszeit und Weltzeit* (Frankfurt am Main: Suhrkamp, 1986).

14 See Novalis [= Friedrich von Hardenberg], "Das allgemeine Brouillon" (no. 1132) in Novalis, *Werke, Tagebücher und Briefe Friedrich von Hardenbergs*, 3 vols., ed. Hans-Joachim Mähl and Richard Samuel (Munich: Hanser, 1978), vol. 2, p. 717.

15 See Jacques Derrida, *Margins of Philosophy*, trans. Alan Bass (Brighton: Harvester Press, 1982).

16 Compare Reinhart Koselleck, *Futures Past: On the Semantics of Historical Time*, trans. Keith Tribe (New York: Columbia University Press, 2004).

17 It is possible that Luhmann is thinking of the studies collected in Arthur L. Stinchcombe and Carol A. Heimer, *Organization Theory and Project Management: Administering Uncertainty in Norwegian Offshore Oil* (Oslo: Norwegian University Press, 1985).

18 Here, Luhman is presumably alluding to the fierce quarrel over the construction of a final repository for radioactive waste in the former Konrad Mine in Salzgitter, Lower Saxony.

IV Meaning

1 Georg Wilhelm Friedrich Hegel, *Enzyklopädie der philosophischen Wissenschaften im Grundrisse* [1830], ed. Friedrich Nicolin and Otto Pöggeler (7th edn, Hamburg: Meiner, 1975), p. 209. The translation is by A. V. Miller.

2 Luhmann refers to the German edition of Aristotle, specifically to "Physik: Vorlesungen über Natur," in *Philosophische Schriften*, vol. 6 (Hamburg: Meiner, 1995).

3 See Edmund Husserl, *The Crisis of the European Sciences and Transcendental Phenomenology*, trans. David Carr (Evanston, IL: Northwestern University Press, 1970).

4 The reference is to Luhmann's colleague Richard Grathoff at the University

of Bielefeld. Compare his book *Milieu und Lebenswelt* (Frankfurt am Main: Suhrkamp, 1989).

5 See Fritz Heider, "Ding und Medium," *Symposion: Philosophische Zeitschrift für Forschung und Aussprache* 1 (1926), pp. 109–57; Eng. trans. as "Thing and medium," in *On Perception, Event Structure, and Psychological Environment: Selected Papers* (New York: International University Press, 1959), pp. 1–34. Karl E. Weick, *The Social Psychology of Organizing* (Reading, MA: Addison-Wesley, 1969).

6 See, e.g., Herbert A. Simon, "The architecture of complexity," *Proceedings of the American Philosophical Society* 106 (1962), pp. 467–82. Robert B. Glassman, "Persistence and loose coupling in living systems," *Behavioral Science* 18 (1973), pp. 83–98.

7 See Talcott Parsons, *Zur Theorie der sozialen Interaktionsmedien*, ed. Stefan Jensen (Opladen: Westdeutscher Verlag, 1980) [this collection includes previously published articles from various sources translated from the English].

8 Presumably, Luhmann pointed at an apparatus that stood in the lecture hall and which was used by chemists.

9 See Edmund Husserl, *Ideen zu einer reinen Phänomenologie und phänomenologischen Philosophie: Erstes Buch: Allgemeine Einführung in die Phänomenologie* [= *Husserliana*, vol. 3], ed. Walter Biemel (The Hague: Martinus Nijhoff, 1950). Edmund Husserl, *Erfahrung und Urteil: Untersuchungen zur Genealogie der Logik*, ed. Ludwig Landgrebe (Hamburg: Meiner, 1972).

10 See, e.g., Karl-Otto Apel, "Auseinandersetzungen," in *Erprobung des transzendentalpragmatischen Ansatzes* (Frankfurt am Main: Suhrkamp, 1998), pp. 33ff. and 81ff.

11 W. Ross Ashby, "Requisite variety and its implications for the control of complex systems," *Cybernetica* 1 (1958), pp. 83–99.

12 Niklas Luhmann, "Sinn als Grundbegriff der Soziologie," in Jürgen Habermas and Niklas Luhmann, *Theorie der Gesellschaft oder Sozialtechnologie: Was leistet die Systemforschung?* (Frankfurt am Main: Suhrkamp, 1971), pp. 25–100, here pp. 48ff. See also Luhmann, *Social Systems*, trans. John Bednarz, Jr., with Dirk Baecker (Stanford, CA: Stanford University Press, 1995), pp. 74ff.

13 See chapter VII below.

14 See Alois Hahn, "Identität und Selbstthematisierung," in Alois Hahn and Volker Kapp (eds), *Selbstthematisierung und Selbstzeugnis: Bekenntnis und Geständnis* (Frankfurt am Main: Suhrkamp, 1987), pp. 9–24.

V Psychic and Social Systems

1 See Martin Heidegger, *Being and Time* [1927] (Albany: State University of New York Press, 1996), pp. 42–7.

2 Émile Durkheim, *The Rules of Sociological Method and Selected Texts on Sociology and its Method*, ed. and intro. Steven Lukes, trans. W. D. Halls (New York: Free Press, 1982).

3 Wil Martens, "Die Autopoiesis sozialer Systeme," *Kölner Zeitschrift für Soziologie und Sozialpsychologie* 43 (1991), pp. 625–46. See also Niklas Luhmann, "Wer kennt Wil Martens? Eine Anmerkung zum Problem der Emergenz

sozialer Systeme," *Kölner Zeitschrift für Soziologie und Sozialpsychologie* 44 (1992), pp. 139–42.

4 On this claim, see Niklas Luhmann, *Social Systems*, trans. John Bednarz, Jr., with Dirk Baecker (Stanford, CA: Stanford University Press, 1995), esp. ch. 4.

5 Humberto R. Maturana was Luhmann's guest at the University of Bielefeld during the winter semester 1986–7.

6 See Laurence Sterne, *The Life and Opinions of Tristram Shandy, Gentleman*, which appeared in nine volumes from 1760 to 1769.

7 Presumably, Luhmann's reference is to Charles P. Loomis and his book *Social Systems: Essays on their Persistence and Change* (Princeton, NJ: Van Nostrand, 1960).

8 See, e.g., Niklas Luhmann, *Social Systems*, ch. 6, esp. pp. 213–18.

9 See Humberto R. Maturana, G. Uribe, and S. G. Frenk, "Eine biologische Theorie der relativistischen Farbcodierung in der Primatenretina" in Maturana, *Erkennen: Die Organisation und Verkörperung von Wirklichkeit* (Braunschweig: Vieweg, 1982), pp. 88–137.

10 Ferdinand de Saussure's *Cours de linguistique générale* was originally published by Charles Bally and Albert Sechehaye. For the critical edition, see Saussure, *Cours de linguistique générale*, ed. Tullio de Mauro (Paris: Payot, 1972).

11 Jürgen Habermas, *The Theory of Communicative Action*, trans. Thomas McCarthy, 2 vols (Cambridge: Polity, 1984, 1987).

12 John R. Searle, *Speech Acts: An Essay in the Philosophy of Language* (Cambridge: Cambridge University Press, 1970).

13 See Dean MacCannell and Juliet Flower MacCannell, *The Time of the Sign: A Semiotic Interpretation of Modern Culture* (Bloomington: Indiana University Press, 1982).

VI Communication as a Self-Observing Operation

1 See Humberto R. Maturana, *Biologie der Realität* (Frankfurt am Main: Suhrkamp, 2000), pp. 121ff. and pp. 361ff.

2 See, for instance, Gregory Bateson, *Steps to an Ecology of Mind* (Chicago: University of Chicago Press, 1972), esp. pp. 411–31.

3 See Niklas Luhmann, *Social Systems*, trans. John Bednarz, Jr., with Dirk Baecker (Stanford, CA: Stanford University Press, 1995), ch. 4.

4 Karl Bühler, *Theory of Language: The Representational Function of Language* [1934], trans. Donald Fraser Goodwin and Achim Eschbach (Phildelphia: John Benjamins, 2011).

5 John L. Austin, *How to Do Things with Words*, ed. J. O. Urmson and Marina Sbisà (2nd edn, Cambridge, MA: Harvard University Press, 1975); John R. Searle, *Speech Acts: An Essay in the Philosophy of Language* (Cambridge: Cambridge University Press, 1970).

6 See Humberto R. Maturana, "Information – Mißverständnisse ohne Ende," *Delfin* 7 (1986), pp. 24–7.

7 Compare the definition given by Claude E. Shannon and Warren Weaver, *The Mathematical Theory of Communication* (Urbana: University of Illinois Press, 1963), p. 31.

8 See, for instance, Hans-Georg Gadamer, *Truth and Method*, trans. J. Weinsheimer and D. G. Marshall (2nd rev. edn, New York: Crossroad, 1989).

9 *Translator's note*: The German original of Luhmann's lecture course has "in English" here.

10 See Jürgen Habermas, *The Theory of Communicative Action*, trans. Thomas McCarthy, 2 vols (Cambridge: Polity, 1984, 1987).

11 See James G. March and Herbert A. Simon, *Organizations* (New York: Wiley, 1958), p. 165: "Uncertainty absorption takes place when inferences are drawn from a body of evidence and the inferences, instead of the evidence itself, are then communicated."

12 See Carl Joachim Friedrich, "Authority, reason, and discretion," in Carl Joachim Friedrich (ed.), *Authority* [= Nomos I] (Cambridge, MA: Harvard University Press, 1958).

13 See, for instance, a novel such as Charles Jaulnay, *L'Enfer burlesque, le mariage de Belphégor et les épitaphes de M. de Molière* [1677] (Geneva: Slatkine, 1969).

14 Compare Alois Hahn, "Konsensfiktionen in Kleingruppen: Dargestellt am Beispiel von jungen Ehen," in Friedhelm Neidhardt (ed.), *Gruppensoziologie: Perspektiven und Materialien* (Opladen: Westdeutscher Verlag, 1983), pp. 210–32 [special issue 25 of *Kölner Zeitschrift für Soziologie und Sozialpsychologie*].

15 See Roswita Königswieser, Matthias Haller, Peter Maas, and Heinz Jarmai (eds), *Risiko-Dialog: Zukunft ohne Harmonieformel* (Cologne: Deutscher Industrieverlag, 1996).

16 *Translator's note:* The term "indexical expressions" is in English in the original. Luhmann refers to the discussion of "indexicals" (cf. Gottlob Frege, Saul Kripke) or "shifters" (cf. Otto Jespersen, Roman Jakobson) in the philosophy of language and in linguistics. These terms designate expressions whose reference shifts depending on the context. Examples include the first-person pronoun as well as such temporal and spatial adverbs as "now" and "here."

17 *The Song of Roland* (or *La Chanson de Roland*) is the oldest of the so-called *chansons de geste* or French medieval songs that celebrated legendary heroic deeds.

VII Double Contingency, Structure, Conflict

1 See Niklas Luhmann, *Social Systems*, trans. John Bednarz, Jr., with Dirk Baecker (Stanford, CA: Stanford University Press, 1995), ch. 3.

2 Talcott Parsons, *The Structure of Social Action: A Study in Social Theory with Special Reference to a Group of Recent European Writers* (New York: Free Press, 1937), p. 89.

3 See Talcott Parsons, Edward A. Shils, Gordon W. Allport, Clyde Kluckhohn, Henry A. Murray, Robert R. Sears, Richard C. Sheldon, Samuel A. Stouffer, and Edward C. Tolman, "Some fundamental categories of the theory of action: a general statement," in Talcott Parsons and Edward A. Shils (eds), *Toward a General Theory of Action* (Cambridge, MA: Harvard University Press, 1951) pp. 3–29, here p. 16.

4 See, e.g., Claude Lévi-Strauss, "Social structure," in *Structural Anthropology I*, trans. Claire Jacobson and Brooke Grundfest Schoepf (New York: Basic Books, 1963), pp. 277–323.

5 See Blake's poem "The little vagabond," from the *Songs of Experience* (1794).

6 See Johannes Berger, "Autopoiesis: Wie 'systemisch' ist die Theorie sozialer Systeme?" in Hans Haverkamp and Michael Schmid (eds), *Sinn, Kommunikation und soziale Differenzierung: Beiträge zu Luhmanns Theorie sozialer Systeme* (Frankfurt am Main: Suhrkamp, 1987), pp. 129–52.

7 See Talcott Parsons, "Some considerations on the theory of social change," in *Rural Sociology* 26 (1961), pp. 219–39.

8 See especially Alfred North Whitehead, *Process and Reality: An Essay in Cosmology* [1929] (New York: Free Press, 1979).

9 *Translator's note:* As Michael King informs me, this is factually incorrect. All land transactions after 1925 have had to be registered at the Land Registry, so there is now only a tiny proportion of properties where the need to establish ownership by reference to old deeds applies. Obviously, Luhmann's larger argument is not affected by this error.

10 See George Spencer Brown, *Laws of Form* (London: Allen & Unwin, 1969), p. 5.

11 Ibid., p. 10.

12 *Translator's note*: Of course, Luhmann is joking. Generally speaking (although there are differences from country to country), "poste restante" is a service where a particular post office holds the mail until the recipient calls for it.

13 This is an allusion to Luhmann's employment as an aide in the ministry of education and cultural affairs in Lower Saxony.

14 *Translator's note*: The references are to Friedrich Schiller's tragedy *Don Carlos* (on which Verdi later based his eponymous opera) and the cross-dressing theatre comedy of 1892 by Brandon Thomas, *Charley's Aunt*, which was later filmed more than once.

15 See, for instance, Ralf Dahrendorf, *Class and Class Conflict in Industrial Society*, trans., rev., and expanded by the author (Stanford, CA: Stanford University Press, 1959).

16 See, for instance, Max Weber, "Die 'Objektivität' sozialwissenschaftlicher Erkenntnis," in *Soziologie, universalgeschichtliche Analysen, Politik* (5th rev. edn, Stuttgart: Kröner, 1973), pp. 186–262.

17 Robert Merton, *Social Theory and Social Structure* [1949] (2nd rev. edn, New York: Free Press, 1968).

18 Marcus Tullius Cicero, *De amicitia*, ed. H. E. Gould and J. L. Whiteley (Wauconda, IL: Bolchazy-Carducci, 2004).

19 On this issue, consult the bibliographical references in Niklas Luhmann, *Die Gesellschaft der Gesellschaft* (Frankfurt am Main: Suhrkamp, 1997), vol. 1, pp. 466f.

20 Asen Abalikai, "Quarrels in a Balkan village," *American Anthropologist* 67 (1965), pp. 1456–69.

21 See *Social Systems*, ch. 9, esp. pp. 369–76.

22 Niklas Luhmann, *Legitimation durch Verfahren* (2nd edn, Frankfurt am Main: Suhrkamp, 1989).

Suggested Further Readings

Lecture 1 Sociology and Systems Theory

1   (1976) "A general theory of organized social systems," in *European Contributions to Organized Theory*, ed. G. Hofstede and S. Kassem. Assen: Van Gorcum, pp. 96–113.
2   (1983) "Insistence on systems theory: perspectives from Germany – an essay," *Social Forces* 61(4): 987–98.
3   (1984) "The self-description of society: crisis, fashion and sociological theory," *International Journal of Comparative Sociology* 25: 59–92.
4   (1986) "The theory of social systems and its epistemology: reply to Danilo Zolo's critical comments," *Philosophy of the Social Sciences* 16: 112–31.
5   (1987) "Modern systems theory and the theory of society," in *Modern German Sociology*, ed. V. Meja, D. Misgeld, and N. Stehr. New York: Columbia University Press, pp. 173–86.
6   (1989) *Ecological Communication*. Chicago: University of Chicago Press, chapter 1, "Sociological abstinence."
7   (1993) "At the end of critical sociology," *Faultline: Interdisciplinary Approaches to German Studies* 2: 61–71.
8   (1995) "The two sociologies and the theory of society," *Thesis Eleven* 43: 28–47.
9   (1995) *Social Systems*. Stanford, CA: Stanford University Press, chapter 1, "System and function."
10 (2006) "From *The Society of Society*," in Hans-Georg Moeller, *Luhmann Explained: From Souls to Systems*. Chicago: Open Court, pp. 229–39.

Lecture 2 Talcott Parsons

1   (1976) "Generalised media and the problem of contingency," in *Explorations in General Theory in Social Sciences: Essays in Honour of Talcott Parsons*, ed. J. Loubser, A. Effrat, and V. Lidz. New York: Free Press, pp. 507–32.
2   (1982) *The Differentiation of Society*. New York: Columbia University Press, chapter 3, "Talcott Parsons: the future of a theory."

Lecture 3 General Systems Theory: The Theory of Open Systems

1 (1982) *The Differentiation of Society.* New York: Columbia University Press, chapter 2, "Ends, domination, and system."
2 (1988) "Closure and openness: on the reality in the world of law," in *Autopoietic Law: A New Approach to Law and Society,* ed. G. Teubner. Berlin and New York: W. de Gruyter, pp. 335–48.
3 (1997) "Limits of steering," *Theory, Culture and Society* 14: 41–57.

Lecture 4 System as Difference

1 (1977) "Differentiation of society," *Canadian Journal of Sociology* 2(2): 29–54.
2 (1982) *The Differentiation of Society.* New York: Columbia University Press.
3 (1989) *Ecological Communication.* Chicago: University of Chicago Press, chapter 16, "Functional differentiation."
4 (1990) "The paradox of system differentiation and the evolution of society," in *Differentiation Theory and Social Change: Comparative and Historical Perspectives,* ed. J. Alexander and P. Colomy. New York: Columbia University Press, pp. 409–40.
5 (1999) "The paradox of form," in *Problems of Form,* ed. D. Baecker. Stanford, CA: Stanford University Press, pp. 15–26.
6 (1999) "Sign as form," in *Problems of Form,* ed. D. Baecker. Stanford, CA: Stanford University Press, pp. 46–63.
7 (2000) *The Reality of the Mass Media.* Cambridge: Polity, chapter 1, "Differentiation as a doubling of reality."

Lecture 5 Operational Closure

1 (1988) "Closure and openness: on the reality in the world of law," in *Autopoietic Law: A New Approach to Law and Society,* ed. G. Teubner. Berlin and New York: W. de Gruyter, pp. 335–48.
2 (1990) *Essays on Self-Reference.* New York: Columbia University Press, chapter 1, "The autopoiesis of social systems."
3 (1992) "Operational closure and structural coupling: the differentiation of the legal system," *Cardozo Law Review* 13: 1419–41.

Lecture 6 Structural Coupling

1 (1992) "Operational closure and structural coupling: the differentiation of the legal system," *Cardozo Law Review* 13: 1419–41.
2 (1995) *Social Systems.* Stanford, CA: Stanford University Press, chapter 1, "System and function"; chapter 6, "Interpenetration."

Lecture 7 Observing

1 (1988) "Observing and describing complexity," in *Complexities of the Human Environment: A Cultural and Technological Perspective,* ed. K. Vak. Vienna: Europa Verlag, pp. 251–5.

2 (1989) *Ecological Communication.* Chicago: University of Chicago Press, chapter 5, "The observation of observation."

3 (1993) *Risk: A Sociological Theory.* New York: W. de Gruyter, chapter 12, "Second-order observation."

4 (1995) "The paradox of observing systems," *Cultural Critique* 31: 37–55; also as chapter 3 in (2002) *Theories of Distinction.* Stanford, CA: Stanford University Press.

5 (2000) *Art as a Social System.* Stanford, CA: Stanford University Press, chapter 2, "Observation of the first and second order."

Lecture 8 Complexity

1 (1978) "Temporalization of complexity," in *Sociocybernetics*, ed. F. Geyer and J. van der Zouwen. Leiden, Boston, and London: Martinus Nijhoff, pp. 95–111.

2 (1985) "Complexity and meaning," in *The Science and Praxis of Complexity.* Tokyo: United Nations University Press, pp. 99–104.

3 (1989) *Ecological Communication.* Chicago: University of Chicago Press, chapter 3, "Complexity and evolution."

4 (1990) *Essays on Self-Reference.* New York: Columbia University Press, chapter 3, "Complexity and meaning."

5 (1992) "Societal complexity," in *Concise Encyclopedia of Participation and Co-Management*, ed. G. Szell. Berlin: W. de Gruyter, pp. 793–806.

6 (1993) *Risk: A Sociological Theory.* New York: W. de Gruyter, chapter 3, "Time binding: material and social aspects."

Lecture 9 Time

1 (1978) "Temporalization of complexity," in *Sociocybernetics*, ed. F. Geyer and J. van der Zouwen. Leiden, Boston, and London: Martinus Nijhoff, pp. 95–111.

2 (1982) *The Differentiation of Society.* New York: Columbia University Press, chapter 12, "The future cannot begin"; chapter 13, "World-time and system history."

3 (1995) *Social Systems.* Stanford, CA: Stanford University Press, chapter 1, "System and function"; chapter 8, "Structure and time."

4 (1998) *Observations on Modernity.* Stanford, CA: Stanford University Press, chapter 4, "Describing the future."

Lecture 10 Meaning

1 (1985) "Complexity and meaning," in *The Science and Praxis of Complexity.* Tokyo: United Nations University Press, pp. 99–104.

2 (1990) *Essays on Self-Reference.* New York: Columbia University Press, chapter 2, "Meaning as sociology's basic concept"; chapter 3, "Complexity and meaning"; chapter 8, "Society, meaning and religion."

3 (1995) *Social Systems.* Stanford, CA: Stanford University Press, chapter 1, "System and function"; chapter 2, "Meaning."

Lecture 11 Problems of "Action Theory"

1 (1995) *Social Systems*. Stanford, CA: Stanford University Press, chapter 4, "Communication and action."

Lecture 12 Two Modes of Operation of Autopoiesis

1 (1986) "The autopoiesis of social systems," in *Sociocybernetic Paradoxes*, ed. F. Geyer and J. van der Zouwen. London: Sage, pp. 171–92.
2 (2000) *Art as a Social System*. Stanford, CA: Stanford University Press, chapter 1, "Perception and communication: the reproduction of forms."

Lecture 13 Communication as a Self-Observing Operation

1 (1989) *Ecological Communication*. Chicago: University of Chicago Press, chapter 6, "Communication as a social operation"; and *passim*.
2 (1995) *Social Systems*. Stanford, CA: Stanford University Press, chapter 4, "Communication and action."
3 (1996) "On the scientific context of the concept of communication," *Social Science Information* 35: 257–67.
4 (2002) *Theories of Distinction*. Stanford, CA: Stanford University Press, chapter 7, "What is communication?"; chapter 8, "How can the mind participate in communication?"

Lecture 14 Double Contingency, Structure, Conflict

1 (1995) *Social Systems*. Stanford, CA: Stanford University Press, chapter 3, "Double contingency."
2 (1996) "The sociology of the moral and ethics," *International Sociology* 11: 27–36.
3 (1996) "Complexity, structural contingencies and value conflicts," in *Detraditionalization: Critical Reflections on Authority and Identity*, ed. P. Heelas, S. Lash, and P. Morris. Oxford, and Cambridge, MA: Blackwell, pp. 59–71.

Index